Self-Care, Translation Professionalization, and the Translator's Ethical Agency

This book draws on an interdisciplinary approach to investigate the impact of codes of ethics as prescribed in translator organizations, proposing alternative ethical pathways grounded in self-care ethics to enhance translators' symbolic recognition and ethical agency.

The volume seeks to provide a counterpoint to existing views in translation studies research on ethics by building on work in sociology and philosophical genealogy, particularly Foucault's notion of *Epimeleia Heautou*, to establish a framework of self-care ethics. Featuring analyses of various codes of ethics across different professional associations, the book offers a critical examination of the potential impact of codified ethics on translator autonomy and symbolic status and in turn, their broader social and planetary responsibilities within their roles as translators beyond the translation community. In setting out an alternative charter of ethics which promotes a culture of the self within larger institutions and critical pedagogy within translator education programs, the volume charts new directions in emergent debates on ethics in translation practice.

This book will appeal to scholars in translation and interpreting studies, particularly those interested in ethics and sociological and philosophical approaches within the discipline.

Abderrahman Boukhaffa is a practicing translator. He received his PhD in Translation Studies in 2021 from the School of Translation and Interpretation at the University of Ottawa, Canada.

Routledge Advances in Translation and Interpreting Studies

Collaborative Poetry Translation
Processes, Priorities and Relationships in the PoetTrio Method
W.N. Herbert, Francis Jones and Fiona Sampson

The Japanese Shakespeare
Language and Context in the Translations of Tsubouchi Shōyō
Daniel Gallimore

Audio Description and Interpreting Studies
Interdisciplinary Crossroads
Edited by Cheng Zhan and Riccardo Moratto

Gendered Technology in Translation and Interpreting
Centering Rights in the Development of Language Technology
Edited by Esther Monzó-Nebot and Vicenta Tasa-Fuster

Emerging Englishes
China English in Academic Writing
Alex Baratta, Rui He and Paul Smith

A Bergsonian Approach to Translation and Time
Toward Spiritual Translation Studies
Salah Basalamah

Self-Care, Translation Professionalization, and the Translator's Ethical Agency
Ethics of *Epimeleia Heautou*
Abderrahman Boukhaffa

For more information about this series, please visit: www.routledge.com/Routledge-Advances-in-Translation-and-Interpreting-Studies/book-series/RTS

Self-Care, Translation Professionalization, and the Translator's Ethical Agency
Ethics of *Epimeleia Heautou*

Abderrahman Boukhaffa

Routledge
Taylor & Francis Group

NEW YORK AND LONDON

First published 2025
by Routledge
605 Third Avenue, New York, NY 10158

and by Routledge
4 Park Square, Milton Park, Abingdon, Oxon, OX14 4RN

Routledge is an imprint of the Taylor & Francis Group, an informa business

© 2025 Abderrahman Boukhaffa

The right of Abderrahman Boukhaffa to be identified as author of this work has been asserted in accordance with sections 77 and 78 of the Copyright, Designs and Patents Act 1988.

All rights reserved. No part of this book may be reprinted or reproduced or utilised in any form or by any electronic, mechanical, or other means, now known or hereafter invented, including photocopying and recording, or in any information storage or retrieval system, without permission in writing from the publishers.

Trademark notice: Product or corporate names may be trademarks or registered trademarks, and are used only for identification and explanation without intent to infringe.

ISBN: 978-1-032-71354-0 (hbk)
ISBN: 978-1-032-71357-1 (pbk)
ISBN: 978-1-032-71355-7 (ebk)

DOI: 10.4324/9781032713557

Typeset in Sabon
by Newgen Publishing UK

To Massine, Adam, and Jamila

Contents

Acknowledgements   *ix*
Abbreviations and Acronyms   *x*

Introduction   1

PART I
Professionalization, Translation Ethics, and *Translation* in Codified Ethics   **21**

1 Translation Professionalization and the Sociology of Professions   23

2 Translation Ethics in Contemporary Translation Theory   37

3 The Concept of *Translation* in Codified Ethics   60

PART II
The Translator's *Capital* in Codified Ethics   **77**

4 Basic Tenets of Bourdieu's Reflexive Sociology   79

5 The Translator's Forms of Capital in Codified Ethics   88

6 The Translator's Capital Conversions   118

PART III
The Translator's Morality in Codified Ethics — 161

7 Bauman's Postmodern Morality: Beyond Rational Codification of Ethics — 163

8 The Translator's *Moral Self* in Codified Ethics — 172

9 Postmodern Ethics: From Institutionally Restrained Morality of Codes of Ethics to Aporetic Social Responsibility — 201

PART IV
Alternative Ethics — 221

10 Foucault's *Epimeleia Heautou* (Self-Care) — 223

11 Alternative Ethics in Institutions — 232

12 Transformative Learning Theory for Adult Education in the Service of Ethics of Self-Care — 243

Conclusions: Challenges and Project Ethicality — 272

References — 276
Appendices — 296
Index — 299

Acknowledgements

This work would not have been possible without the support of many people.

I would like to express my profound gratitude to Luise von Flotow, Malcolm Williams, Helene Buzelin, Marc Charron, Moira Inghilleri and Kamal El Alami for their constructive feedback that helped guide this work.

Many thanks to Clara Foz, Elizabeth Marshman and Salah Basalamah, whose insights have helped me shape some parts of this project.

I would like to express my gratitude to my friends and colleagues at the School of Translation and Interpretation at the University of Ottawa. Their constructive comments and discussions made me a better person intellectually and socially. Special thanks to Alexandra Yazeva, Shaily Zolfaghari and Daniel Josephy.

Finally, many thanks to my wife, Jamila, for her unconditional support and patience, and to my children, Massine and Adam, as well as my extended family for their continuous support.

Abbreviations and Acronyms

AI	Artificial Intelligence
ATA	American Translators Association
ATIO	Association of Translators and Interpreters of Ontario
ATPP	Asociación de Traductores Profesionales del Perú [Peruvian Association of Professional Translators].
AUSIT	Australian Institute of Interpreters and Translators
BoPC	Board of Professional Conduct
CAT	Computer-Assisted Translation
CBC	Canadian Broadcasting Corporation
CRAL	Regional Center Latin America
CTTIC	Canadian Translators, Terminologists and Interpreters Council
EU	European Union
FIT	Fédération Internationale des Traducteurs [International Federation of Translators]
IAFET	International Association for Egyptian Translators
ID	Identification
ITAINDIA	Indian Translators Association
MEMRI	Middle East Media Research Institute
MENA	Middle East and North Africa
MT	Machine Translation
NAATI	National Accreditation Authority for Translators and Interpreters
NATO	North Atlantic Treaty Organization
NZSTI	New Zealand Society of Translators and Interpreters
OTTIAQ	Ordre des traducteurs, terminologues et interprètes agréés du Québec [Québec Certified Translators, Terminologists and Interpreters Association]
RID	Registry of Interpreter of the Deaf
SATI	South African Translators' Institute

SFT	Société française des traducteurs [French Society of Translators]
ST	Source Text
TL	Target Language
TM	Translation Memory
TS	Translation Studies
TT	Target Text
TTR	Traduction, Terminologie, Rédaction
UN	United Nations
UNESCO	United Nations Educational, Scientific and Cultural Organization
WIPO	World Intellectual Property Organization

Introduction

0.1 Translator/Translation Ethics: An Age-old Debate

In 1987, the communication theorist, philosopher and psychologist, Paul Watzlawick[1], opens a speech at the Evangelical mission of the Stuttgart Hospital with a French anecdote. The story he tells his audience is about a French couple who desperately wanted to have a baby, but in vain. As time passed by, and the couple finally lost all hope to become parents; to their astonishment, the woman got pregnant. A baby boy was born nine months later. They were so thrilled that they wanted to give him a name that reflected their bliss. Hence, they decided to name him 'Formidable' [Great][2]. Unfortunately, as the boy grew up, he remained small and weak. His whole life was an awful journey in which he suffered from harmful jokes due to the contrast between his name and his shape. When he was dying, he asked his wife not to put his name on his gravestone. After his death, his wife – having had a happy life with the man – wrote: "here lies a man who has been faithful to his wife all through his life." Everyone who passed by his grave since then and read the note would say: "tiens, c'est formidable!" [Oh, this is great!]

The story is about "when the solution is the problem." It demonstrates that apparent good/ethical intentions or decisions (such as the wife's decision not to write her husband's name on his gravestone but to write a phrase praising him, instead) are ambivalent, in the sense that their positive outcome is never certain, guaranteed, or stable. What is seemingly a good/ethical solution may create other problems that may even be more complex than the initial problem.

In the long history of translation, translators and translation critics/theorists have always debated about the right way to translate and the solution(s) to translation problems – which can often be seen as ethical problems or dilemmas. The age-old debate about literal vs. free translation has, at least partly, been a debate about ethics. The implicit questions

DOI: 10.4324/9781032713557-1

2 *Introduction*

triggered by translation have always been: is it ethical to translate literally or freely? How can the text be represented? How close to the source text (ST) does a translation need to be? How can the divine spirit of a text be transmitted? Etcetera. In Europe, whether translation should be understood and practised as a word-for-word or a sense-for-sense rendering of a ST into a target language is as old a debate as recorded intercultural communication history. At least since Cicero, the issue has not ceased to be at the heart of all discussions about communication between cultures over time and space. But this debate has rarely touched upon deeper ethical matters that lie beyond immediate textual content and the alleged sacred nature of some texts. Besides, it has often overlooked the complex nature of translation and the difficulty of adopting one approach or the other independently of socio-political and cultural contexts in which the translation occurs and with no regard for the uniqueness of each translational/ethical event.

The dichotomous debate that often implies the wholesale embracing of one side of the dichotomy and the rejection of its opposite has developed in recent Translation Studies (TS) literature into other binarisms that are not less problematic, at least from an ethical perspective. These involve, to name a few, foreignization vs. domestication, source vs. target, adequacy vs. acceptability, original vs. copy, formal vs. dynamic equivalence, overt vs. covert translation, semantic vs. communicative translation. The least one can say about these binary labels is that they can themselves be problems, exactly like the lady's solution in regard to her husband's gravestone, in Watzlawick's story. The multifacetedness and complexity of *translation*[3] make it impossible to always derive the (ethical) choices that translation encounters require from the same overarching (ethical) principle. Moreover, there exist many other forms that may be called 'translations' (in other times and cultures) that do not correspond to either of the options proposed in the binary Eurocentric sets above (see Lefevere 1990, Trivedi 2006, Tymoczko 2007, Raihani 2024). That is why we probably have to live with the ambivalent nature of translation and its ethics as unwrapped dilemmas and inherent, never-ending problems.

With postpositivist thinking reaching TS, newer understandings of *translation* and translation ethics that value ethics of multiplicity and difference, and challenge the discussed binarism, started to emerge. These new propositions about translation/ethics differ in their premises, but they all refute cultural hegemony, obliteration of multiplicity and effacement of difference as well as patriarchal discourse and underlying atrocities in colonial contexts in which translation has been embedded in the very name of some binary concepts, such as original vs. copy, formal vs. dynamic equivalence (see Venuti 1995, 1998,2010/1993; Berman 1984,1999/1985; Baker 2006a; Tymoczko 2007; Flotow 1997, 2007; Simon 1996 and

Rafael 1993/1988; Cheyfitz 1991, Niranjana 1992; Jacquemond 1992, respectively). In parallel with these views – largely inspired by the post-structuralist thought – another area of scholarship has tried to respond to the growth of the modern 'professional'[4] translation industry and its ethical demands in the globalized world of communication, commerce and technology. The trigger for this scholarship of pragmatism, functionalism and efficiency was *Skopos* theory in the 1980s, which proposed that translation as a purposeful activity is determined primarily by the target text (TT) function and audience. Followers of this trend (who are not necessarily followers of *Skopos* theory), however, have once again paid little attention to the macro socio-ideological variables that are involved in 'professional' translation and its ethics (e.g., Nord 2005/1988, 1991, 1997; Pym 2012; Chesterman 2016/1997, 2001, 2019, 2021). They have generally underestimated or ignored the power dynamics pertinent to the institutional formation of the translation occupation (with very few exceptions, such as Pym et al. (2013), which I return to later on). In parallel with these academic insights, more translators started to gather in, or join, regional/national general associations, specialized associations, and even global networks, with the goal of regularizing the translation occupation and codifying its 'professional'/ethical conduct. I will explore how and which of the divergent TS views may have found resonance in translators' codes of ethics and conduct, later in this book.

0.2 Codification of Ethics and TS Response

The growing attempts to professionalize translation as a modern system, with professional associations as its governing institution, has culminated in the creation of standardized codes of ethics by many associations around the world in the late twentieth century and the beginning of the twenty-first century (Drugan 2011, Lambert 2023) – in parallel with the skyrocketing demand for all sorts of pragmatic translation. The purported aim of ethics codification is to reduce uncertainty and doubt in the relationship between translators and other agents. In these codes[5], associations adopt *a priori* principles/rules, the purpose of which is to unify the responses to the (ethical) concerns of the different agents/people and make them more predictable. Precise solutions are proposed to respond to the complex ethical issues of translation in a way that purportedly ensures the ethical/'professional' rights of all agents. These solutions may, however, be themselves problematic as they may, in many cases, ignore the complexity, the particularity and the ambivalence of ethical matters.

Ethics codification is seen as an important pillar of 'professionalization,' but it is not the only element in this process. The prior and primary component of the 'professionalization' process is the establishment of a representative body (i.e., an association) of practitioners that self-governs the practice, and establishes and ensures compliance with these codes of ethics. Most large translator associations we know today were created starting from the second half of the twentieth century (Pym 2014). Besides these two crucial milestones, the translation occupation started to claim a theoretical base as a practice that draws on a systematic knowledge specific to the field, with the institutionalization of translation programs and TS in higher educational institutions. This was followed with an international 'recognition' of the important role of translation/translators from the UNESCO, which adopted the 'Recommendation on the Legal Protection of Translators and Translations and the Practical Means to improve the Status of Translators' during its nineteenth General Conference session in Nairobi, Kenya on November 22, 1976. From the perspective of the traits approach in the sociology of professions, all these events can be seen as an accumulation of some of the main attributes of 'professionalization.'

The establishment of translator organizations[6] – a milestone in this process of 'professionalization' – visibly aims to determine the boundaries of the translation occupation. The institutional bodies representing practitioners seek to monopolize the occupation through interest group politics, in a sort of exclusionary 'social closure,' to use the Weberian concept (Weber 1978/1922). They supposedly construct their own internal communication, eliminate the intruders/parasites, and sanction those who breach codes of ethics and/or practice. They purportedly determine the definition of *translation* and its laws of practice, as well as the relational aspects of the occupation. Most large associations highlight, to varying degrees, some of what is known as 'traits of professionalism,' such as the possession of theoretical knowledge, educational qualifications, certification, experience, closure, autonomy and public protection, and establish and implement a code of ethics. They also stress their functions that range between the protection of the public, the defence of the translators' interests and the promotion of the profession – with some differences in emphasis depending on the nature of each organization (i.e., whether it is an order, a voluntary association, a union or a federation of associations). All these associations supposedly engage in communication and lobbying efforts vis-à-vis political powers, academic institutions, publishing industry and client/employer representatives to gain the due symbolic, economic, institutional and legal rights, and to promote the 'profession.'

Seeking support and more influence nationally and internationally, national associations gather in, or join, international bodies of translation/translators. For this purpose, the Fédération Internationale des Traducteurs [International Federation of Translators] (FIT) was established in 1953 in France. This international body lobbied the UNESCO for the adoption of the Nairobi Recommendation in 1976 – which is still considered by some as one of the main reference documents that highlight the value of translation/translators. All these efforts, nevertheless, may not potentially affect the status of the individual translators/interpreters in positive ways unless these associations are able and willing to further support the translators/interpreters' interests and impose their terms on the other agents, as we learn from the sociology of professions (which I discuss shortly).

Despite all the recent developments in the process of translation 'professionalization' and the (emerging) issues associated with the translator's code of ethics and conduct – which are part of that process – not many TS publications about ethics have thoroughly examined these documents in their wider context of professionalization and its intricate dynamics. Some TS scholars who have passingly addressed the translators' codes refute them for being too abstract, for restraining the translator's personal responsibility or for being unrepresentative of the actual and wide variety of ethical dilemmas translators face in their everyday practices (see, for instance, Baker 2018/1992, Koskinen 2000a, 2020, Davis 2001, Baker and Maier 2011b and Pym 2012; as well as Angelelli 2004, Baixauli-Olmos 2013 and Inghilleri 2008, 2012 regarding interpreters' codes of ethics[7]). One of the strongest objections to these codes comes from Kaisa Koskinen (2000a, 2020), who contends that codes of ethics are mainly designed to oblige the translator to adhere to the principle of 'faithfulness' in translation and refrain from making autonomous choices in the complex translational encounters. "To start making choices would lead to infidelity. The ethical code could thus be seen to consist, in short, of the requirement to refrain from choosing" (2000a, 13). Koskinen and Pokorn (2021, 4), in a similar vein, argue that "codes of conduct depict an ideal world, but the moral dilemmas are born of a messy and complex life." Baker (2018/1992, 307–308), likewise, calls on translators to use their critical judgment to make ethical choices, instead of "fall[ing] back uncritically on abstract codes drawn up by their employers or the associations that represent them." Rosario Martín Ruano (2017) remains among the rare scholars who clearly question codes of ethics for being one of the sites of a depreciatory discourse about *translation*. Although she does not dismiss them altogether, she contends that codes of ethics could be one of the sites where transformation of the understanding of *translation* and its complexity could begin (ibid., 32) in order "to enhance recognition by institutions and stakeholders" (ibid., 31). However, as the author rightly argues, "recognition is not only dependent on being understood by others; it also requires self-recognition" (ibid., 34).

Most of the few TS researchers who have studied translators' codes of ethics more thoroughly also question them for being incomplete, limited, restraining to translators, inflexible or difficult to apply to all situations. Andrew Chesterman (2001, 2016/1997, 2019), for instance, argues that current codes of ethics are incomplete and inflexible to cater to all ethical situations and text types. As an alternative, he proposes the "universal Hieronymic Oath" (2001, 153, italics added) – which is not radically different from the existing codes of ethics – as Lee and Yun (2020) also observe, even though it is centred on virtues. Kruger and Crots (2014), for their part, raise the issue of codified ethics being limited to the immediate 'professional' context. Julie McDonough Dolmaya (2011), similarly, argues that these documents "often do not address many of the issues translators are encountering as part of their practice" (ibid., 45), and their guidelines "sometimes conflict and are often not very clear" (ibid.). Not so differently, Joanna Drugan (2011) observes the lack of shared values and interpretation of the meaning of codes' articles among translators. Drugan and Megone (2011), likewise, underline that codes of ethics are not understood by translators "in a way that can inform practice" and are, therefore, of "very limited value" (2011, 187).

Quite differently, Hyang Lee and Seong Woo Yun (2020) question codes of ethics for responding mainly to the clients' expectations while ignoring the social roles of translators. Following on the discussions of Chesterman (2001), Baker (2006a, 2008), Inghilleri (2008) and Rafael (2012), the authors argue that translator codes of ethics should include community-based principles and virtues. They contend that the telos of symmetrical communication should govern such codes. Rosemary Arrojo (2013), for her part, argues that codes of ethics of contemporary translator organizations are based on the old view of *translation* as 'fidelity,' and their ethics as synonymous with impartiality and accuracy (2013, 2). A different code of ethics should recognize the transformative and partial nature of translation, Arrojo argues. Understanding ethics from this perspective, "it would actually be unethical and irresponsible for translators to insist on hiding behind claims of neutrality or to wash their hands of the responsibilities involved in the highly complex and influential work they do" (ibid., 4).

Conversely, Uldis Ozolins (2014), head/coordinator of the joint working team of Monash University and the Australian Institute of Interpreters and Translators (AUSIT) that revised the AUSIT code of ethics in 2012, does not question the 'conduit' orientation of the code and its "aversion to advocacy or cultural brokering" (2014, 355), nor does she raise any issues related to this model. Concerned mainly with 'practicality,' she observes that several translator associations' codes make "no reference to actual practice" (Ozolins 2014, 351). On the other hand, Lluís Baixauli-Olmos (2021), in a publication where he provides an overview of the evolution of codes of ethics in the field, argues that all reviewed codes, explicitly or implicitly, suggest that their tenets are not to be applied rigidly and that translators have the responsibility of applying them judiciously (2021, 310–311).

One of the most comprehensive studies about translation (codes of) ethics in recent years comes from Joseph Lambert (2018, 2023). Lambert laments the reductive understanding of *translation* advanced by codes of ethics, and rather insists on the subjective and non-neutral nature of translation and its ethics. "At the heart of enquiry in both areas, we are dealing with human beings who have their own personal interest, beliefs, and needs to consider, and this problematizes images of translation as simply a linguistic transfer activity" (2023, 76). Lambert criticizes codes of ethics for providing a false image to the client about what translation consists of (Lambert 2018). He even questions their ethicality as they mainly serve promotional agendas by representing translation as a neutral and impartial meaning transfer. Lambert claims that this image/representation is appealing to clients and "can benefit translators, too" (Lambert 2023, 128). He (Lambert 2023) also highlights the codes' limited coverage of the ethical issues translators actually encounter, the difficulty to enforce their regulations by associations, the conflicting and unrealistic nature of their guidelines, as well as the problems related to interpreting and applying their principles. He, therefore, calls for establishing codes of ethics that show translation as a multifaceted, subjective and "inherently-imperfect activity" (Lambert 2018, 284). Interestingly, Lambert (2021) raises the economic factor, social responsibility and power relations that come into play when considering ethics (Lambert 2021, 2023). In *Translation Ethics* (2023), he even goes a little further when he introduces what he calls "enlightened egoism," highlighting the translator's personal needs, including mental well-being and economic interests. Drawing on Hubscher-Davidson (2021), he contends that ethical stress that results from discrepancies between one's values and the expected behaviour, in addition to other occupation-related stressors (including the economic stressor, low status and technology competition), can cause psychological discomfort, and mental health issues (see Hubscher-Davidson 2021).

Most scholars cited in this review generally criticize translator codes of ethics for their difficulty of application, incompleteness to cater to actual practice, lack of awareness-raising among outsiders about the nature of the translator's work, or non-reflection of the nature of *translation*. Distinctively, Lluís Baixauli-Olmos (2021) argues that most codes of ethics insist on the non-rigidity of their principles/rules – like 'faithfulness' – and allow translators a margin of manoeuvres to use their judgment and apply those rules judiciously. A more critical perspective, however, would take issue with the fact that the associations' codes of ethics may (inadvertently) reinforce a devaluing discourse about translation/translators that does not reflect the complexity and importance of their work, as Arrojo argues (2013), or with the fact that translator associations may apply disciplinary measures in case of a 'misinterpretation' of a code rule – as

Baixauli-Olmos himself had previously acknowledged (2017, 261, 263). The autonomous and judicious use of the deontological codes is risky, as it is not clear what constitutes a breach of a code of ethics and what does not.

Interestingly, some publications raise the question of moral unaccountability when such codes of ethics are applied unreflectively (see Arrojo 2013, Koskinen 2000a, Baker 2018). More importantly, some of the cited scholars allude to the issue of power asymmetries in codes of ethics between the interlocutors in the translation encounter – as their predetermined rules/principles may be a restraining force to the translator's choice or agency (Koskinen 2000a, Arrojo 2013, Martín Ruano 2017, Lambert 2023, Lee and Yun 2020, Baker 2018 and Koskinen and Pokorn 2021). These scholars' critical remarks, while important, remain somewhat summative; they hardly examine the positioning of translators and the roles assigned to them in any specific clauses of codes of ethics. They, likewise, do not thoroughly contextualize these documents to establish a link to their driving conceptual or meta-narratives, nor do they investigate the symbolic or economic implications of the discourse of any specific codes on translators. Martín Ruano remains one of the rare scholars who have the merit of briefly but clearly referring to the issue of translators' recognition as reflected in codes of ethics. However, similarly to the other scholars, her writing falls short of making a clear connection between the lack of the translator agency reinforced in their own documents and the underlying social or institutional roots of the *status quo*. For instance, she does not situate the codes in their wider social context of 'professionalization' and how this modern process may impact on their discourse orientation.

I argue that the problems underlying these documents may be deeper and have yet to be examined thoroughly in TS. These codes of ethics did not emerge in a vacuum; they are influenced not only by some assumptions about *translation* but also by some social narratives and intellectual traditions, as well as practices in other occupations and institutions. While codes of ethics of some fields/occupations have been conceptually examined to unveil the place of the individual's ethical self and status[8], TS has yet to dig deeper by drawing on other disciplines to have a more in-depth understanding of the underlying foundations of translator codes of ethics and their ideological and social implications, as well as the profound problems they embody that may, in fact, be *ethical*. Some of this orientation can already be discerned in studies centred on interpreters' (codes of) ethics in Inghilleri's publications (2008, 2012), which draw on sociological and philosophical insights, as I explain in Chapter 2. Baixauli-Olmos (2017) is another study that draws on Bourdieu's notion of capital and claims that interpreters' codes of ethics have professionalizing power.

Also, recently, Wen Ren (2020) has drawn on Bourdieu's sociology to study some of the principles of codes of ethics in China's modern history and how these principles are interpreted differently depending on the interpreter's symbolic power in different historic eras. I will return to the discussion of some issues/strengths in the latter studies in the section devoted to Translation 'Professionalization' in TS and Power Dynamics in Chapter 1 shortly.

0.3 Approach and Aims of the Book

As mentioned earlier, a code of ethics can be seen as one of the important elements in the process of professionalization, in addition to the creation of governing bodies that establish them, as well the other traits of 'professionalism.' But as we learn from the sociology of professions, professionalization is not a smooth or ideal process. It is rather embedded in power asymmetries (see Johnson 2016/1972). One of the agents involved in an occupation always imposes their terms and conditions on the others. Hence the ineluctable and compelling question: how is this sought-after professionalization impacting the translator's status vis-à-vis the other agents involved in the translation circle and how are these power dynamics reinforced or not in their internal discourse?

- Is this process putting them in an imposing position?
- Are 'professional' associations defending translators' interests effectively?
- Are they producing a (new) discourse and practices (in their defining documents) that are empowering to translators?
- Are they *redefining translation* as a complex concept/endeavour that requires esoteric and complex knowledge?
- Are they showing the critical importance of translation to the other agents and the public?
- Or, are they simply reproducing/reinforcing the same old hegemonic discourse that represents translation as a low occupation (mechanistic process) and translators as mere conduits (with no responsibility)?
- In the documents of associations, are translators regarded as responsible ethical agents or simple executors of clear, non-ambivalent and *a priori* defined tasks?

To answer these questions, one would like to look at the internal documents of associations, the discourse of which would reflect the power dynamics inherent in the professionalization process. I believe the code of ethics and/or conduct is the main document where answers to these questions can be discerned as it is the document which mostly reflects the associations' identity and policy. Codes of ethics may reflect the translator's self-concept, role(s) and status. They display the required conduct from translators in their work and their relations with colleagues and outsiders. On the one hand, they define *translation*; on the other hand, they regulate the 'professional' practice and establish 'ethical' and 'professional' *relations* between the translator and the other agents (in)directly involved in translation. And the analysis of these two latter aspects in codes of ethics is likely to show the translators' self-positioning in relation to the other agents. It can reveal whether the principles in codes of ethics are included for the sake of ethics or are meant to respond and cater to the interests of an agent against other agents' interests. In sum, the analysis can show how power dynamics inherent to the process of 'professionalization' are reflected in one of the main identifying documents of translator associations and one of the milestones in this process, that is, the code of ethics. Studying these codes will show whether and how they affect the translator's *capital* – using Pierre Bourdieu's notion – and reveal the *occupational control* mode – in Terence Johnson's (2016) analysis – that governs translation 'professionalization' processes, and ultimately identify the agent(s) that pay the economic, symbolic and ethical price for these processes.

Codes of ethics are the locus where we can discern not only the translator's power and recognition but also their level of ethical agency, by and large. Recognition and ethicality are very interconnected. The (symbolic) position of translators may affect their ethical choices, the main purported aim of the documents, and their study is, therefore, likely to reveal any paradoxes within them. Codes of ethics state and enforce principles and rules that supposedly aid the translator in making ethical decisions during different encounters in translation. But these pre-determined principles/rules may affect the translator's ethical judgment and autonomy – which, in turn, can have further impacts on themselves and other agents/people/species. I believe ethics and codes of ethics can barely be studied and understood without studying the status of practitioners as the two aspects impact on each other. The current work examines how the ethical principles/rules listed in the codes may be reflective of the status assigned to translators. It, likewise, explores how these documents symbolically and ethically affect some of the agents involved in the occupation and beyond.

With these considerations in mind, this work shows how the translator's *capital* and *moral self,* in Bourdieu's and Zygmunt Bauman's terminology, respectively, are reflected in, and affected by, the codes of ethics established by 'professional' associations, and proposes alternative ethics that are likely to enhance the translator's capital *and* moral self. The book reveals where and how codes of ethics position the translator vis-à-vis the other agents, namely large clients, corporate employers, authors and publishers, and, therefore, how some of the principles they underline affect the practitioners' control over their occupation and their ethical autonomy. To this end, the study explores the underlying narratives of translator codes of ethics, the translation theories that may have found resonance in them, and the concept of *translation* reflected in them. The book also discusses the ways in which these codes tackle the wider social and planetary ethical issues beyond the translation circle. Finally, it proposes pedagogical and ethical avenues that translators can pursue to empower themselves ethically and symbolically.

It is noteworthy that codes of ethics are not the catalyst/source of translators' (in)sufficient agency or capital, *per se*; they are rather a manifestation of their level of power/autonomy. My study of codes of ethics, therefore, examines their macro-context, including the professional claims and conceptual/meta-narratives in which they and their guidelines are embedded – i.e., where these guidelines are coming from. I delve into the deeper sources of this (de)valuing discourse about the translator/translation, and how it is propagated internally. At the end of the day, codes of ethics simply reinforce an already existing discourse of political, legislative, social and commercial institutions – a discourse which also has historical underpinnings. The book takes associations and their codes of ethics as a case study and brings to the forefront the global social, economic, political and historical factors as well as power dynamics in which the translator's activity is embedded – how the different agents (in)directly involved in the field of translation (including the translator and their representative associations) interact and influence each other and who ultimately imposes their terms and conditions. Therefore, the study does not propose changes in codes of ethics as they stand now but seeks mainly to shake some of the (internal and external) sources of this discourse, with the aim of bringing about a gradual change in the roots of this social discourse about translators/translation and their ethics. It seeks to deploy external resources of power (academia/education) to shake the established discourse about translation/translators (ethics). The book proposes an alternative pathway that revolves around the self to represent translation as a complex activity and translators as important social agents – of course, with the support of these external resources of power – and therefore, equip translators with enough power to exercise their (ethical) agency.

In this book, I describe and analyze codes of ethics of seven national/provincial translator associations, representing Africa, the Middle East and North Africa (MENA), Asia, North America, South America, Oceania, and Europe, in addition to two international bodies' charters/recommendations[9]. The national/provincial associations are generalist voluntary associations, Orders or unions that represent translators, regardless of specialization[10]. These are large associations, members of the FIT, which generally have some authority to speak on behalf of the 'profession,' to use

12 *Introduction*

Pym et al.'s expression (2013, 26). They, thus, purportedly seek market control and lobby political actors for favourable legislation at the regional, national and international levels. This variety allows a comparative perspective depending on their natures and functions. I hereafter briefly introduce the national/provincial associations, whose documents are studied.

- The Association of Translators and Interpreters of Ontario (ATIO), Canada[11] was founded as early as 1920, under the name 'Association technologique de langue française d'Ottawa' [French Language Technological Association of Ottawa]. It is now a regulatory body that controls the market through its legally sanctioned certification system. The ATIO is "the first translators' association in the world whose certified members are deemed professionals by law, for in February 1989 the Province of Ontario granted reserved title for certified members of ATIO through the *Association of Translators and Interpreters Act, 1989*."[12] The latest version of its code of ethics, which is examined in this book, was adopted in 2009.
- The Indian Translators Association (ITAINDIA) is a voluntary association that was founded in 2006. It is the only Indian member of the FIT. The association's main function is "to look after the interests of individual translators and Small Scale Agencies" (ITAINDIA Membership Information, Section B). Also, "it constantly acts as an interface between the government of India and the affiliates of the Translation Industry of India" (ITAINDIA Membership Information, Section A). Its Code of Professional Conduct contains two sections: one for Service Providers and another for Employers or Contractors.
- The Australian Institute of Interpreters and Translators (AUSIT) is a voluntary association, which was created in 1987, with the support of the National Accreditation Authority for Translators and Interpreters (NAATI), the only certifying authority for translators and interpreters in Australia[13]. The association "engages in dialogue with interpreting agencies, government and business entities, and makes submissions to government and to relevant inquiries about the work of interpreters and translators."[14] Its first code of ethics was adopted in 1995. The latest version of the document, established in 2012, consists of a Code of Ethics, a Code of Conduct, and two explanatory sections: Conduct Issues Specific to Translators and Conduct Issues Specific to Interpreters.
- The Société française des traducteurs [French Society of Translators] (SFT) was created as early as 1947. It is a founding member of the FIT. The SFT is a union that defends the interests of translators/interpreters in France and promotes the profession of translation/interpreting (SFT Deontological Code, About the SFT). "The SFT is an essential interface between translators of all categories, translation users and

public authorities" (ibid., my translation). The latest version of its Deontological Code was adopted in 2009.
- The South African Translators' Institute (SATI) is a voluntary association, which was founded in 1956. The SATI is "widely recognised in the industry" and "it offers the only professional accreditation available in South Africa."[15] Its main proclaimed function is to "promote excellence in translation and related fields, as well as clarity of thought and expression; ensure high standards of professionalism among its members through accreditation and the adoption of a code of ethics; and provide support for its members both in their occupational lives and as members of a multicultural and dynamic society."[16] The SATI also seeks to "promote the interests of the translation, interpreting, text editing and terminology professions." The SATI has three separate codes of ethics for individual members, language agency corporate members and language office corporate members, respectively. The latest version of these codes of ethics was adopted in 2013 (Kruger and Crots 2014, 148).
- The Asociación de Traductores Profesionales del Perú [Peruvian Association of Professional Translators] (ATPP) is a voluntary association, founded in 1992. The purpose of its establishment was "to institutionally strengthen the translation and interpreting profession in order to benefit translators and interpreters alike, as well as users of translation and interpretation services."[17] Its main claimed objectives are the promotion of translation and interpretation as "professional activities in Peru" and "the recognition of translators and interpreters as high-ranking professionals" (ibid.). The ATPP also aims to "[e]nsure that high ethical and quality standards are adhered to when performing professional translation and interpretation services" (ibid.).
- The International Association for Egyptian Translators (IAFET) is a voluntary association that has an accreditation system. Its purported aims are to "[promote the recognition of the translations and interpreting professions," "create and maintain standards of professional ethics, practices and competence," and work "constantly with universities and non-governmental and governmental Organization and other entities in such matters as the education and continuing education of translators and interpreters" (IAFET Bylaws, Article II). The IAFET's first code of ethics was adopted in 2017.

In addition to these provincial/national associations' codes of ethics, I examine documents of two international organizations – which have different natures and functions – namely the Translator's Charter of the Fédération Internationale des Traducteurs [International Federation of Translators] (FIT) and the UNESCO Nairobi Recommendation.

14 *Introduction*

- The FIT was founded in 1953 in France by only six national associations of translators and interpreters. Currently, it gathers more than 100 translator/interpreter/terminologist/linguist associations and institutes from 55 countries, representing more than 80,000 translators. The FIT is a consultative association of the UNESCO. The main goal of the Federation is "to promote professionalism in the disciplines it represents. It seeks constantly to improve conditions for the profession in all countries and to uphold translators' rights and freedom of expression."[18] The FIT adopted its first Translator's Charter in 1963. This charter was amended in 1994. One of the main aims of this document is to lay "the basis of a translator's code of ethics" (FIT Translator's Charter, Preamble).
- The Recommendation on the Legal Protection of Translators and Translations and the Practical Means to improve the Status of Translators[19] was adopted by the UNESCO during its nineteenth General Conference session in Nairobi, Kenya on November 22, 1976, thanks to the work of lobbying exercised by the FIT. The analysis of this document of an outsider agent helps in revealing the extent to which this international 'recognition' (in 1976) is reflected, or surpassed, in codes of translator associations. In the current project, I study the extent of this 'recognition,' i.e., where the UNESCO Nairobi Recommendation positions the translator in relation to the other agents. I also show how similar or different this positioning is to the other codes of ethics.

The current work is interdisciplinary. It draws on Michel Foucault's (1984a, 1984b, 2001a/1982, 2001b/1983, 2001c/1984, 2001e/1988) genealogy of ethics as well as Bourdieu's (1986, 1990a, 1990b, 1993, 1998a, 1998b) and Bauman's (1993, 1994, 2003a/1995, 2003b, 2007, 2008) distinct but complementary sociologies, in addition to Transformative Learning (TL) theory. To undertake the analysis of the translator's (self)positioning via the studied documents, I use Bourdieu's notion of capital – along with insights from TS – as a heuristic tool to identify and examine the clauses that empower or impoverish the translator's cultural, economic, social and symbolic forms of capital in their struggle for benefits and recognition with the other agents involved in the translation industry (mainly employers, large clients, authors, legislators/politicians and publishers). I also draw on Bourdieu's sociology in order to uncover and assess the labour relations between the involved agents. With the support of insights from the sociology of professions, the concept of capital ultimately helps reveal the mode of occupational control the translation practice is undergoing, and therefore, who of the agents is imposing their terms and conditions in this process of 'professionalization.' It is noteworthy that the term 'clients' here and throughout this book refers to large clients, and not to (vulnerable) individual clients. This is simply because the biggest portion of the translation market nowadays is with large clients/employers (such as international/regional organizations, governments, multinational corporations, localizers, giant translation companies and media outlets)[20].

I draw upon Bauman's notion of moral self, backed with insights from TS, to analyze the role and place of the translator's ethical autonomy/ responsibility in these codified ethics. This notion allows to identify whether the translator's moral judgment can play a role in their decision making or whether they are completely subjected to the preordained rules of codes of ethics. Ultimately, this part of the project will tackle the implications of the possible exclusion of individual morality, in the name of 'professionalism,' on the translator's ethics and on various societal/planetary issues. The concept of moral self and Bourdieu's notion of capital together allow me to examine the ethical, symbolic, cultural, social and economic power translators are endowed with or deprived of, and, thus, the extent to which their agency is enhanced or undermined in the documents under study.

Bauman's theory is used mainly as a critical tool with which to approach the current translation codes of ethics. His theory is complemented by Foucault's notion of *self-care*, which is used to propose ethical alternatives to the current codes, which may, in the name of ethics, be unethically disempowering individual translators. I propose a charter for ethics that overcomes the weaknesses of the current codes along with a pedagogical project inspired by Foucault's ethics and based on Transformative Learning theory. Drawing on Foucault's ancient ethics that are centred on the *self* stems from the fact that these ethical traditions allow us autonomy from the codified ethics modern thought has imposed. In MacIntyre's words, they enable us "to overcome the constraints on such self-knowledge that modernity, especially advanced modernity, imposes" (2007, vi). The epistemological and moral crises of modernity, manifest in its inability to continue the games of "illusions," in MacIntyre's (1977, 2007/1981, 1988) thought, may necessitate a return to ancient traditions – which modernity has interrupted and rejected – in order to look for ways that may help to respond to the current crises.

The book is expected to enrich the discussion on the thorny issue of ethics in TS, which, I believe, still needs more in-depth interdisciplinary investigations from different angles – notwithstanding the existence of quite a rich literature in the field. Adopting an interdisciplinary approach to studying codes of ethics, relying on insights from reflexive sociology, the sociology of professions, philosophical genealogy and pedagogy, besides TS, makes it possible for this work to examine the question of translator codes of ethics from different perspectives. Specifically, the book uses different conceptual lenses to explore the possible internal expressions of the corroborated law status of the translator (see, for instance, Liu 2013, Dam and Zethsen 2008, Gouadec 2007, Katan 2011, Sela-Sheffy and Shlesinger 2011, Dam and Koskinen 2016, and most, if not all, culturalists). It digs into the conceptual foundations of codes of ethics and the phenomenon of the 'professionalization' processes – the driving force behind this codification. More broadly, it contextualizes codes of ethics and links them to wider issues not only in the fields of translation and translator's/translation ethics, but in the complex social sphere and the diverse ideological, social, institutional, historical, economic, cultural and even geopolitical factors that affect the perception of the translator/*translation* in society and the partitioner's self-perception, as well as their ethical agency.

The current study complements the TS works that have problematized translator codes of ethics for being idealistic, decontextualized and insufficient or for undermining the translator's moral accountability, as reported earlier. The project also builds on the studies that underscore the power issues in codes of ethics, like the brief allusions made by Martín Ruano (2017) about the derogatory view of translation in codes of ethics, Lee and Yun's (2020) advocacy for symmetrical communication in codes of ethics, or the work of Inghilleri (2008, 2009, 2010, 2012) regarding the interpreter's ethics. It further investigates the power relations in which specific clauses of these codes may be embedded and how they impact on translators themselves. Importantly, the study gears the discussion on ethics in TS toward ethics of the self as a prior condition for ethics of the Other, distancing itself, thus, from the focus on otherness and social responsibility, which have been prevalent in TS, as I discuss in detail in Chapter 2. Also, this book proposes alternative ethical pathways that are non-coercive and purely personal. Previous TS publications have either proposed other similarly preordained ethics (e.g., Chesterman 2001, Gouadec 2007) or abstained from proposing any in the name of postmodern thinking that inherently refutes imposed prescriptions (e.g., Koskinen 2000a). This study will ultimately attempt to propose a middle ground between proponents of codes and their opponents. Following Foucault, I argue that charters for ethics can still co-exist along with self-constituted ethics and develop (as part of a gradual change) on the condition of being stripped of their coercive mantle. Hopefully, this research will be a nucleus for a critical approach to translator ethics that draws a new pathway for an ethically, culturally, symbolically and materially empowered translator of tomorrow.

0.4 Book Outline

The book includes four parts. Part I is devoted to professionalization, translation/translator ethics in TS, and *translation* understanding in codified ethics. Part II analyzes the translator's capital in the studied documents. Part III examines the translator's moral self in these documents, and Part IV proposes alternative ethical avenues.

In Chapter 1, I discuss the main models/theories in the sociology of professions with a special focus on what is known as the power approach. I show how the process of 'professionalization' is embedded in power dynamics and, thus, how the vulnerable agent (the practitioner or the client/consumer) involved in an occupation pays the price of this process. Then, I discuss how TS literature about translation 'professionalization' tackles this question of power dynamics. In Chapter 2, I give an overview on how translation/translator ethics have been approached in contemporary translation theories. I lay out the main views and explain their strengths and their usefulness for my research, and how their gaps informed the current project. Chapter 3 opens the analysis of the corpus. It analyzes the definition given to *translation* in each document. I put this chapter about the definition of *translation* in the studied documents in Part I, rather than Part II, because this definition serves as a background for both Part II and Part III and, to some extent, Part IV. It is used to account for how the view of *translation* affects both the translator's capital (Part II) and moral self (Part III).

In Chapter 4, Part II, I introduce Bourdieu's theoretical framework, on which I draw in my analysis of the translator's capital in the corpus. In Chapter 5, I analyze the translator's different forms of capital, namely cultural, social and economic forms. I show how the definition of *translation* (analyzed in Chapter 3) and the translator's self-concept as well as the relational aspects reflected in the studied documents affect the translator's different forms of capital and, therefore, their status. Chapter 6 is the central chapter in which I reveal whether and how the three forms of capital convert or not into symbolic power. Because translators can be seen as both occupation practitioners and cultural producers, I postulate that their cultural capital can be convertible into a symbolic capital that can take two main forms: recognition as autonomous *professionals* who self-govern their profession, and/or recognition as autonomous cultural producers (manifest in copyright). I show whether, and the extent to which, the translator is recognized as a *professional* and reveal how the current copyright law is reinforced or resisted in the studied documents and whether it can be considered as a symbolic recognition of the translator as a cultural producer. In the last section of the chapter, I discuss the symbolic violence translators may be subject to in case their capital is not recognized in any of the mentioned forms and I explore possibilities of their emancipation.

In Chapter 7, Part III, I present Bauman's notion of moral self and other issues related to morality in Bauman's postmodern theorization, as I use his insights to analyze the translator's moral self in codified ethics.

18 *Introduction*

In Chapter 8, I investigate the issue of *public protection* (highlighted by the studied codes of ethics), its understanding, its 'ethical' and 'professional' means as well as its limits and repercussions on the translator's moral self, before I analyze the issues of Otherness, representation and cultural sensitivity in the documents under study. In Chapter 9, I show how, and the extent to which, morality may be an institutional concern rather than an individual translator's responsibility in the studied codes, and how these documents designers claim universalism and well foundedness. I then delve into discussing the translator's morality in postmodern ethics and into tackling the ethical challenges posed by globalization.

In Chapter 10 of Part IV, I present an overview of Foucault's ethics of *Epimeleia Heautou* (self-care), on which I base my alternative ethics proposal. In Chapter 11, I show how the *culture of the self* can be enhanced within the institutions concerned with translation – namely TS, the translation occupation and translation pedagogy – and I propose an alternative charter for ethics that can be viable within the global approach of the culture of the self in the mentioned institutions. Being aware that this charter may be of little value if not adopted by empowered translators, I further explain in Chapter 12 how the empowering culture of the self can be embodied pedagogically and applied in the education of the translator. For this purpose, I resort to Transformative Learning (TL) theory as a complementary approach that is appropriate for the implementation of the ethics of self-care in translation classrooms. I present the core components of TL and ethical growth and explain how the translator's self-care through TL can be instantiated in a translation classroom.

Notes

1 www.youtube.com/watch?v=7etsh4HwG78 (Accessed on September 16, 2023).
2 All translations from French into English in this book are mine unless stated otherwise.
3 In this book, *translation* will be italicized when the term is used to refer to the concept.
4 I will still be using the mainstream terms, 'profession,' 'professional,' 'professionalism,' 'professionalization' in scare quotes. I will be using *profession, professional, professionalism, professionalization* (without scare quotes) only when an occupation is under the power or control of practitioners. The latter understanding/use of the terms will be discussed at length in Chapter 1.
5 I will be using the term 'codes' or 'codes of ethics' to refer to codes of ethics and codes of (professional) conduct/practice.
6 'Translator associations' or 'translator organizations' will be used interchangeably in this book to refer to different types of translators' networks such as orders (where translation is a legally regulated 'profession'), voluntary associations and unions (where translation is not legally regulated), and federations

(which gather regional/national associations). The exact nominations will be used when necessary.
7 Some other available studies related to interpreters' codes of ethics include Schweda-Nicholson (1994), Bancroft (2005), Hale (2007), Mikkelson (2000), Cokely (2000), Witter-Merithew and Johnson (2004), Valero-Garcés 2017, Baixauli-Olmos (2017), Ren (2020), Phelan et al. (2020).
8 See, for example, Kelemen & Peltonen (2001) and Kavaliauskas's (2011) studies on business codes of ethics; Holtzhausen's (2015) research on professional communication codes of ethics; Meijl's (2000) analysis of anthropological codes of ethics; and Johnson's (2016/1972) accounts of power dynamics in accountancy.
9 Although the focus of the current project is on codes of ethics, I occasionally resort to the organizations' other documents (e.g., bylaws, websites) when the former documents are broad or less clear about an issue and when more clarifications are needed to reach grounded conclusions.
10 The word 'translator' is used to refer to practitioners for whom translation is the main source of income and who are members of translator organizations. Some discussions may include interpreters as well. It is noteworthy that some studied codes of ethics are addressed to both translators and interpreters. Although I cannot claim the current study applies to interpreters as well as translators in every respect, it is probable that some conclusions apply to both, as they have many similar issues (see Lambert 2023 for details on the topic).
11 Note that the ATIO is a member of the FIT indirectly through the Canadian Translators, Terminologists and Interpreters Council (CTTIC), of which it is a member.
12 https://atio.on.ca/about (Accessed on July 5, 2018).
13 "NAATI is a not for profit company that is jointly owned by the Commonwealth, State and Territory governments. We are governed by a Board of Directors, who are appointed by the owners" (NAATI Website: www.naati.com.au/about/who-we-are (Accessed on May 10, 2018).
14 https://ausit.org/AUSIT/About/Who_We_Are_-_Our_History.aspx (Accessed on June 10, 2018).
15 http://translators.org.za/sati_cms/index.php?frontend_action=display_text_content&content_id=1 (Accessed on August 17, 2018).
16 www.translators.org.za/satis-mission-and-objectives (Accessed on August 17, 2018).
17 www.atpp.org.pe/association.php (Accessed on September 20, 2018).
18 www.fit-ift.org/about (Accessed on September 5, 2017).
19 Henceforth, the Nairobi Recommendation.
20 The figures of some giant companies of translation are quite revealing, in this respect. For example, the translation company Lionbridge alone concentrates a big portion of the global translation market. "We're fluent in 350+ languages, and we work from more than 5,000 cities [...]. Through our world-class platform, we orchestrate a network of 500,000 passionate experts around the world" (Lionbridge Website: www.lionbridge.com/who-we-are (Accessed on November 20, 2020).

Part I
Professionalization, Translation Ethics, and *Translation* in Codified Ethics

Part I of this book provides further context to the current study. It draws on sociological perspectives that allow situating codes of ethics within the general process of 'professionalization' of the translation occupation. It explains the power relations in which this process is embedded, and which might have an impact on the orientation of these codes of ethics. For this purpose, I first present some views from the sociology of professions before reviewing the existing literature in TS about translation 'professionalization.' In Chapter 2, I review some TS writings about translation/translator ethics and place the current project within this scholarly research. This first part also opens the analysis of the corpus in its Chapter 3 where I present the view of *translation* advanced by the studied documents, which serves as the background on which the analysis in the subsequent parts of the book is based.

1 Translation Professionalization and the Sociology of Professions

1.1 Professionalization in the Sociology of Professions

Scholarship that examines professions and professionalization started to appear under the umbrella of the sociology of professions in the 1950s as a response to the growing professionalization of some fields of practice. Social scientists have generally agreed that professionalization of some occupations is a major, if not, a defining characteristic of modern societies (Johnson 2016, 9).

The most classical approach in the sociology of professions is what is known as 'the trait model.' This approach considers that a profession is characterized by a set of attributes that differentiate it from an occupation. These attributes are: "1) systematic theory, 2) authority, 3) community sanction, 4) ethical code, and 5) a culture" (Greenwood 1957, 45). The trait approach advances that an occupation can be considered a profession only with the existence of a systematic knowledge specific to the field of practice, an authority of professionals in determining the client's needs, recognition from society for this authority, the establishment of a **code of ethics,** and the existence of a professional culture manifest in professional networks or associations.

Another approach is the functionalist model. This approach stresses systematic knowledge, disinterestedness and self-control of behaviour through the internalization of codes of ethics – all for the welfare of society. Its pioneers, Parsons (1991/1951, 1954, 1968), Goode (1960) and Barber (1963), claim that professions have a functional relevance for society and, therefore, need to be regularized in order to protect the general public from abuse and violations. Public protection is ensured mainly through the establishment and implementation of codes of ethics and practice (Saks 2016a, 72). Talcott Parsons (1954, 1968, 1991), the most influential proponent of functionalism, also stresses the cognitive rationality, functional specificity and universalism of professions.

DOI: 10.4324/9781032713557-3

Terence Johnson (2016/1972), a prominent figure in the sociology of professions, rejects both the trait and the functionalist models. He argues that the institutionalized form of occupational control is a management strategy that arises as a result of uncertainty and tension in the producer-consumer relationship, and aims to reduce the doubt between these agents in their transactions/interactions. This reduction of doubt is not achieved in an idealistic fairness to all agents. There is a price to be paid by one of the parties. 'Consensus' may be reached, but usually at the expense of one of the agents – and hence the determining role of power dynamics. Based on this postulate, Johnson argues that the trait approach is too atheoretical; it "too easily falls into the error of accepting the professionals' own definitions of themselves" (2016, 25). He contends that "[t]here are many similarities between the core elements as perceived by sociologists and the preambles to and contents of professional codes" (ibid.). The process of professionalization is usually restricted to an occupation's technicality and other self-attributes of practitioners in the trait approach, Johnson reports. Johnson rejects the assumption that the inherent qualities and nature of an occupation solely and autonomously determine its professional status. In his account of accountancy, he contends that this occupation is, in fact, not a profession despite its accumulation of many supposedly professional traits, and despite its mainstream perception as such. The reason, for to him, is that practitioners are not in a position of power and do not self-control their occupation, but are rather subject to the power of patrons/clients. In sum, the trait approach, for Johnson, ignores issues of power dynamics in the occupational control processes, like the lobbying that occupational groups engage in and the possible role played by governments and educational institutions or powerful patrons/clients in imposing their own definitions and contents of the practice on practitioners' representative bodies (ibid., 30).

Likewise, Johnson refutes the functionalist model for overlooking power dynamics. He criticizes Parson's assumption about rationality, functional specificity, universalism and affective neutrality in the content of practice as well as in interpersonal relations for its pre-determinism regarding such content and relations. These are, in fact, usually influenced by power relations beyond 'professional' criteria, as Johnson demonstrates:

> [w]here, for example, a physician or architect is subject to the whims of a single powerful patron as the sole client; where the client has the power to define his own needs and the manner in which they are to be met; then the relationships of affective neutrality and authority which Parsons claims are inherent in the professional role will be undermined.
> (Johnson 2016, 36)

Parsons's thought is embedded in modernist rational thought that underlines a neutral regularization of the interpersonal relations between practitioners and other agents. It is, also, embedded in a striking idealism as it stresses professionals' disinterestedness. Johnson corroborates Rueschemeyer's (1964, 17) critique of the functionalists' idealistic picture of professions, "conceived of as service occupations that (1) apply a systematic body of knowledge to problems which (2) are highly relevant to central values of the society." For Johnson, functionalism pays little attention to power dynamics and ignores the fact that the powerful agent may be in a position to dictate not only the nature of the relationship but also the practice content.

In a similar vein, Mike Saks classifies both the trait and the functionalist models under 'the taxonomic approach' and criticizes them for their uncritical view of professions. He refutes both models for being "more oriented towards legitimating professional ideologies" than "depicting how professions operate in practice" (Saks 2016a, 72; see also Saks 2015, 2016b). Bourdieu (1992), in a brief discussion of the concept of 'profession,' vehemently criticizes Parsons' functionalism, which he qualifies as a 'theoretical jumble.' Bourdieu refutes the notion of 'profession' as it is a constructed social category rather than a scientific concept – which, if unexamined, appears as neutral and commonsensical.

> The notion of profession is all the more dangerous because it has, as always in such cases, all appearance of neutrality in its favor and because its use has been an improvement over the theoretical jumble (*bouillie*) of Parsons. To speak of 'profession' is to fasten on a true reality, onto a set of people who bear the same name (they are all 'lawyers' for instance); they are endowed with a roughly equivalent economic status and, more importantly, they are organized into 'professional associations' endowed with a code of ethics, collective bodies that define rules for admission, etc. 'Profession' is a folk concept which has been uncritically smuggled into scientific language and which imports into it a whole social unconscious. It is the *social product* of a historical work of construction of a group and of a *representation* of groups that has surreptitiously slipped into the science of this group. This is why this 'concept' works so well, or too well in a way.
> (Bourdieu and Wacquant 1992, 242–243, italics in original)

Bourdieu, thus, rejects taking the concept of 'profession' "at face value" (ibid., 243). Rather, he stresses "the work of *aggregation* and symbolic imposition that was necessary to produce it" (ibid., italics in original). Bourdieu, like Johnson and Saks, therefore, stresses the play of power dynamics in advancing professions and professionalization. Following this understanding, he issues a call "to *replace* this concept [profession] with that of field" (ibid., 242, italics in original), i.e., to take it "as a structured space of social forces and struggles" (ibid., 243).

Bourdieu's brief remarks were taken up by Schinkel and Noordegraaf (2011), who, likewise, regard *professionalization* as the process of struggle over available stakes to attain scarce symbolic capital, that is *professionalism*. They argue that the notion of 'profession' is "a socially consecrated and legitimated concept within a field of differences" (2011, 77), and that it has been *naturalized* as non-arbitrary through power struggles that settled it as common sense (ibid., 78). The process of *professionalization*, as a symbolic control of content, deploys discursive resources and takes place within certain determining historical and structural contexts that give it shape.

> These contexts determine whether specific field can arise in which "professionalism" can function as symbolic capital. In short, when we take available conceptions of professionalism and connect them to Bourdieusian thinking, professionalism can be seen as *symbolically controlled content in autonomous but dynamic contexts of struggle*. Both content and context can be elaborated in order to understand professionalism-as-construction.
>
> (Schinkel and Noordegraaf 2011, 85, italics in original)

Johnson, Saks, Bourdieu, and Schinkel and Noordegraaf all argue that the idealistic image of professions as rationally regulated entities that promote the good functioning of society and the protection of the public, regardless of the agents' struggles for privileges and status, is fraught with problems. They can, thus, all be safely put under the umbrella of the power approach to the sociology of professions.

Under this approach also goes Eliot Freidson (1970, 1984, 1986, 1994), one of the most influential figures in medical sociology. Freidson critically defines 'profession' as a form of monopoly and control over one's practice and a securing of a highly regarded position in the division of labour, and autonomy from other agents. Despite its various uses,

> [i]t is possible to reserve the term "profession" for that form of occupational organization which has at once gained for its members a labor monopoly and a place in the division of labor that is free of the authority of others over their work. Work as such, and the skills it entails, while not irrelevant, are not the focus for discrimination so much as the organized place of an occupation in the labor market and in a division of labor.
>
> (Freidson 1994, 115)

Freidson rejects the trait approach for its overemphasis on the aggregation of certain attributes for professionalization. He argues that, despite the importance of the intrinsic qualities of a practice and the workers' actual skills or education level, these variables alone do not lead to professionalization. He rather stresses the role of political lobbying in securing favourable jurisdictions (ibid., 114–115). Likewise, he refutes the functionalist approach for being idealistic in advancing the altruistic function of professions to society, for taking professionals as *ipso facto* ethical and for advancing the efficiency goal of self-regulation through professional associations. In sum, following Freidson's thought, professional groups promote 'professionalism' ideology and engage in a (political) struggle to enhance the status of their occupations and reinforce or maintain exclusionary social closure that secures the boundaries of their proclaimed professional territories. Ultimately, their endeavours aim at privileging and empowering the practitioners and protecting their interests.

Although the two influential scholars in the sociology of professions both underline power dynamics in professionalization processes, Johnson (2016) differs from Freidson's approach as he does not tackle the question of power and self-interest in a one-dimensional way, as Freidson does. Instead, he shows that in many occupations that are conventionally seen as professions, practitioners do not actually possess the power to control and determine the content of the practice and its relations[1]. Johnson argues that professionalism is imposed only when practitioners gain support of a wider social power and their clients or consumers of their product are heterogeneous and divided.

> [i]t is only where an occupational group shares, by virtue of its membership of a dominant class or caste, wider resources of power that such an imposition is likely to be successfully achieved, and then only where the actual consumers or clients provide a relatively large, heterogeneous, fragmented source of demand.
>
> (Johnson 2016, 43)

Where there is a single powerful consumer/client or a unified body of clients/consumers, practitioners are usually unable to impose their own definitions of professional relations or professional content. The nature of practitioners' expertise and the inherent qualities of an occupation, although important, are not determining factors in its professionalization. It is rather *professionalism* – redefined as a mode of occupational control when professionals have external power resources – that is liable to lead to professionalization under the terms and conditions imposed by the professionals.

[p]rofessionalism, then, becomes redefined as a peculiar type of occupational control rather than an expression of the inherent nature of particular occupations. A profession is not, then, an occupation, but a means of controlling an occupation. Likewise, professionalisation is a historically specific process which some occupations have undergone at a particular time, rather than a process which certain occupations may always be expected to undergo because of their 'essential' qualities.

(Johnson 2016, 45)

Thus, similarly to Bourdieu's thought, Schinkel and Noordegraaf's view, and Freidson's account, Johnson contends that the imposition of the *belief* that the occupation is important and esoteric through lobbying and struggles is the main determining factor in professionalization. In other words, it is not about the actual expertise practitioners possess but about how this expertise is represented and, most importantly, how it is perceived. That being said, professionalism is only one mode of occupational control. This control can take other forms depending on whom, among the main agents involved in the occupation, possesses more influential power resources. Johnson concludes that occupational control can take three main forms: *collegiate control*, *patronage* and *mediation*.

Collegiate control or *professionalism* refers to the mode in which the professional defines the client's needs and the way they cater to these needs, advancing the mark of expertise – which is in fact only deployed as a tool of control. As stated earlier, this mode of occupational control emerges when the producer/practitioner community is homogeneous and enjoys some external resources of power, while the clientele/consumers are and fragmented, with divergent interests (ibid., 51). In this case, the expert's authority gives them the opportunity to create and/or exaggerate the clients/consumers' needs, in the name of professional counselling and guidance.

On the other hand, professional aspiration is usually weakened when practitioners have divergent interests or lack powerful external support, while clientele/consumer base is organized, powerful and homogeneous. Such situation gives rise to what, Johnson calls *patronage system*. This mode is characterized by the power of the client/patron to define both the content they need and the way they wish these needs to be catered to. "In such cases the members of occupations applying esoteric knowledge are themselves 'clients,' having neither exclusive nor final responsibility for their services; ultimate authority in the assessment of process and product lies with the patron or patrons" (Johnson 2016, 65). This form of occupational control, in turn, has three subtypes: oligarchic patronage, corporate patronage and communal control. *Oligarchic patronage* dates back to traditional societies when the aristocratic patron would define their wishes for their architects, artists, translators and craftsmen, and impose the ways they were to be fulfilled. *Corporate patronage*, on the other hand, develops when a few large-scale powerful corporations are the main consumers of practitioners' services while the latter are a heterogeneous community with divergent interests and no external sources of power (Johnson 2016). In this case, practice is not defined by the practitioners' knowledge or even theorists' understandings but is imposed by the client in line with their needs, definitions and terms. This mode "has been associated with the growth of bureaucratic organisation in industrial societies, creating conditions in which the demand for many occupational services comes increasingly from a declining number of large-scale corporations, both private and public" (ibid., 66). *Corporate control* mode is perfectly epitomized in the accountancy occupation – conventionally regarded as a profession – in today's industrial world where a large part of accountants' services is mainly demanded by large corporations (ibid., 46). "The influence of corporate patronage has always been felt in the governing bodies of the accountancy profession in so far as the public practitioner was oriented to the needs of business," Johnson tells us (ibid., 67). The last subtype of 'patronage' is *communal control*, which "refers to a situation where a community as a whole or a community organisation imposes upon producers communal definitions of needs and practice" (ibid., 46). This communal control can take the form of consumers' associations that try to control any 'deviations/abuses' of producers/practitioners. The proliferation of consumers' rights associations in many countries are good examples.

Under patronage systems, practitioners are expected not only to share the modes of practices of their patrons/clients and produce the contents the latter demand but also imbibe and reflect the (theoretical) understandings, value systems and 'ethical' orientations/practices of these patrons/clients. The ethical responsibility of practitioners may be confined to being *loyal* to the patron and faithful/adherent to their favourite mode of practice and their 'ethical' codes. The consequences of one's actions beyond this practitioner-client unidirectional relationship is, thus, probably not a concern for the practitioner. Repercussions their acts may have on society, environment, remote places/people and other species in general do not seem to be within their ethical concerns. This is because that may embarrass the patrons who may be involved in suspicious/unethical activities, as Johnson (2016, 71) underlines. The practitioners' concern for the patrons' value systems and their definitions of the practice foregrounds "an ethic of limited responsibility, contrasting with that of professionalism – a situation in which the 'professional' does not look beyond the consequences of his [sic] actions for the patron. Also, such practitioners tend to be apolitical, where the expression of political views or political action may embarrass the patron" (ibid., 71–72, italics in original). All these issues will be discussed as far as translation occupation is concerned.

The third mode of occupational control is *mediation* by a third party. This intermediary role has been played by states and other forms of political and/or religious regularization (e.g., the Church). In this mode of occupational control, neither the producer/practitioner nor the consumer/client determines the content of practice or the interpersonal relations between stakeholders. They are rather determined by the intermediary.

Regardless of its mode, the main characteristic of occupational control in modern times is the creation/existence of 'professional' associations that gather practitioners with similar status, expertise and identity. 'Professional' associations seek to "promote uniform policies by imposing a monopoly on practice in the field and regulating entry to it" (ibid., 54). They play the role of gatekeepers of the 'profession' by creating mechanisms of entry filtering based on strict conditions. In order to proclaim homogeneous identity and set standards for their practice, they legislate codes of practice and ethics and develop measures that ensure their members' compliance with the regulations. These codes mostly include defining clauses of the practice and relationship with peers, clients and the public. Their study may, therefore, reveal the occupational control mode that a certain occupation undergoes, and this is one of the objectives of this book regarding translation.

1.2 Translation Professionalization and Power Dynamics in TS

In most TS literature, the term 'profession' has been used in its mainstream sense to refer to the translation occupation and specifically to non-fiction/pragmatic types of translation. The question of professionalization started to attract the interest of scholars only recently, with the growing demand for translation services in the age of globalization. While some scholars still discuss the issue of the professional recognition of translation/translators quite atheoretically, a few others have started to discuss the question drawing on scattered ideas from the sociology of professions. Most of these studies have focused on the translator/interpreter's self-perception (professional) status, and internal and external struggles for recognition, as I discuss shortly.

In his work *Translation as a Profession*, Daniel Gouadec (2007) often discusses translation as a 'profession' in its mainstream meaning. By professional translation, he often means translating for "business" (2007, 3). In some parts of his work, however, Gouadec expresses his concern over the current 'professional' status of translation, regarded as "secretarial work" (ibid., 245). "[T]here still exists no official status for translation and translators and trying to get professional recognition and financial rewards for their skills and technical expertise is still basically a lone struggle" (ibid., 245–246). Gouadec argues that translators need to present their skills and technical expertise as important as they actually are and calls for an international recognition of their expertise (ibid., 246). In this analysis, Gouadec overlooks the fact that such recognition must be seized by translators using other external resources of power that may be available to them, as Johnson (2016) would have argued. Gouadec also seems to equate the legal status of translation/translators with professionalization when he cites the case of translation/translators in Canada as a model to follow in other parts of the world.

This same understanding of translation professionalization is held by Lynne Bowker (2005). The author equates the legal status of a reserved title for the ATIO's certified members with 'professional recognition.' Paradoxically, in the same publication, she argues that while translators value this 'professional recognition,' "it seems to be less well understood by the public" (2005, 29); employers seek and value less this 'professional recognition' and the majority of them are "unaware of or unconcerned" about it (ibid.).

Surveying translators/interpreters worldwide, David Katan (2011) investigates the translators' self-perception of their work and the traits of 'professionalism.' He reports that although translators perceive themselves as "satisfied professionals" when they focus on the limited text world, they, however, feel their work is undervalued and lacks "public recognition" when they look at the wider reality of their job. "[W]hen asked to focus on the wider reality they become acutely aware that they lack societal recognition, and that translators, in particular, lack status" (ibid., 84). Katan observes that very few translators, however, show an interest in responding to the requirements of the trait approach, and, thus, the accumulation of the necessary criteria for 'professional' recognition.

> [T]here is not really much mention or apparent awareness regarding wider professional autonomy or many of the key traits deemed necessary for the transformation from an occupation to a profession. In fact, control of output and its use in wider society is hardly mentioned, nor is the need for a recognized body of T/I [Translation/Interpreting] knowledge (rather than practice) or professional certification/qualifications.
> (Katan 2011)

Katan, subsequently, concludes that translation is still an occupation "rather than a fully fledged profession" (ibid.).

Another TS study that relies on the trait approach to measure the professional status of translators in Canada comes from Marielle Godbout (2012). The author argues that translation in Canada is still a "semi-profession," as some of its attributes of 'professionalism' are only partial. For instance, despite the existence of translation programs (as a trait of theoretical knowledge) all over the country, as well as a number of translator associations with established codes of ethics, not all provinces/territories accord translators a legal status or recognize their system of certification. But the main attribute that is seriously lacking, according to Godbout, is the recognition of the expertise of translators and/or their reserved title by society. The author, thus, like the authors discussed above, barely touches on the power issues, other than the fact that translators are "the authors of their own misfortune" (Godbout 2016, n.p)[2]. Godbout recommends that associations give access to Reserved Title only to translators with training in the field and that they "become proactive in publicizing the value of their work to the good functioning of society" (ibid.) – reflecting, thus, Parsons's functionalism, discussed earlier.

Not very differently, Sergey Tyulenev's (2015) relies on Flexner (1915), one of the first pioneers of the trait approach. He, thus, overlooks insights from the sociology of professions since the 1960s – except a few swift general remarks about Freidson – under the pretext that "the sociology of professions has been experiencing a crisis and it is felt that little progress has been made" (Tyulenev 2015, 15). He also justifies his dismissal of later developments in the field by the "lack of consensus" despite the richness of the literature (ibid., 16). Tyulenev argues that translation is an occupation that is still in the process of professionalization. He concludes that "translation cannot as *yet* claim the status of a fully fledged profession" as it fails some of Flexner's criteria of 'professionalism' (ibid., 24, italics added). Not so differently, Kafi, Khoshsaligheh and Hashemi (2018), based on "in-depth interviews" of different agents involved in translation in Iran, namely translation scholars, translators, translation agency managers and a head of a publishing house, found that the main obstacle to 'professionalization' is the lack of attributes of 'professionalism, such as a representative body, precise market entrance criteria for translators, an agreed-upon code of ethics, and the necessary skills for the newly graduated students from translation departments to succeed in the market.

Critical of the ethnomethodological studies about translation 'professionalization' (i.e., studies based on the translator's self-perception) prevalent in TS, Tyulenev, Zheng and Johnson (2017) conducted a comparative study of professionalization in Russia, China and Spain. They examined external views of translation, by analyzing the requirements of consulates/embassies, as well as internal views, by looking into the translation agencies' requirements of job applicants. The authors found that the Spanish authorities are more appreciative of the specificity of translation as they put higher demands on quality and adopt adequate mechanisms to measure quality. The Russian and Chinese authorities, on the other hand, while admitting the importance of translation, are not as strict regarding the establishment of methods to assess quality. Concerning the translation agencies' (internal) view, the authors conclude that the Spanish and Chinese agencies are stricter than the Russian agencies as far as skills and education requirements are concerned. Based on their findings, Tyulenev, Zheng and Johnson (2017) conclude that "translation is professionalized, yet not uniformly across countries" (ibid., 352). These authors' atheoretical ways of assessing professionalization in this study show, of course, a very reductive view of the process and the notion of 'profession,' compared to how they are viewed in the power approach in the sociology of professions.

A somewhat different approach is adopted in Baixauli-Olmos's (2017, 2021) publications, as he tries to use Bourdieu's notion of capital to understand the "professionalising power" of codes of ethics for interpreters. The author contents that codes "are intended to improve the public's perception of the profession" (2017, 265). He argues that representative associations enhance opportunities of recognition through these documents that underscore the necessity, importance and complexity of the translators' role, as well as coherence in performance (ibid., 265–266). Interpreters, for him, accumulate different forms of capital (social, cultural and symbolic) and "this accumulation of capital takes place in the context of professional conduct documents by making reference to notions that benefit the profession or the organisation by earning them recognition, trust, legitimacy" (ibid., 268). Baixauli-Olmos's (2017, 2021) understanding of professionalization is, of course, based on traits approaches, which emphasize the accumulation of some traits by an occupation to become a "fully-fledged profession" (2017, 250). Although he uses Bourdieu's capital, the author barely discusses the power struggle of interpreters in their interaction with the different stakeholders involved in the field of interpreting.

Wen Ren (2020), likewise, draws on Bourdieu's sociology to study the evolution of the status of interpreters in China over the last 70 years, and how that has changed the perception and application of some of the main principles found in codes of ethics (mainly the principle of 'fidelity'). The author argues that in the first phase (1949–1978), interpreters in China did not have enough cultural capital because of the lack of training/resources, and the political agent dominated the field. 'Fidelity,' for example, "was recognised as one of the cornerstones of professional ethics for interpreters, but it was understood that this notion should not be taken at face value" (ibid., 287), as political allegiance to the state usually overrode it. Ren contends that during the second phase of the studied period (1979–2009), interpreters gained internal control and had a stronger capital and better codified ethics, and other traits of 'professionalism.' She argues that 'fidelity,' then, "was given more importance" (ibid., 292) and became more achievable thanks to the high cultural capital of the interpreter – although she implies that it remained driven by the political agent. The third phase (2010–2019), characterized by the increasing growth of language service industry, makes Ren doubtful about whether the 'profession/professionals' will keep its/their autonomy and symbolic capital. Ren's conclusions and findings remain to be revisited by other studies about interpreting (codes of) ethics in China. In her article, the notion of autonomy and professionalism are taken at face value. Despite the use of Bourdieu's sociology, the author seems to see professionalization as a process of accumulating some traits, mainly the enhancement of the interpreter's knowledge/skills through training.

Interestingly, Rakefet Sela-Sheffy (2008, 2016) somehow examines the question of translation professionalization and the translator's recognition in the Israeli context through power struggle lenses. She investigates the way literary translators in Israel stand against any joint efforts of all categories of translators to collectively regulate the occupation, and rather advance their personal prestige through their self-representation as cultural agents in the media (Sela-Sheffy 2008, 610)[3]. Although her studies demonstrate certain awareness of power issues among different ranks of practitioners and subfields within the same occupation, Sela-Sheffy fails to see the external power struggles, in which practitioners engage. She equates professionalization with control of translation by any involved party (even if it is the government or the patrons).

> [W]hether or not an occupation undergoes professionalisation depends on market incentives and the interest of corporate or governmental bodies to control the given cultural production. However, the major impetus for this process comes from the practitioners themselves, who strive to capitalise on their specific abilities and monopolise them as their own exclusive assets.
>
> (Sela-Sheffy 2016, 56)

In the introduction to the same special issue of *The Journal of Specialised Translation* on the translation 'profession,' the editors, Helle Dam and Kaisa Koskinen (2016, 2) argue that despite attempts at transforming translation into "a fully-fledged profession" through the accumulation of traits of professionalization, "translation has not *yet* reached full professional status, and the boundaries of the field remain fuzzy" (italics added). Pym et al. (2016, 50), likewise, note that "[t]he kind of legally protected title that is based on an academic degree and membership of an association seems not likely to happen anytime soon in the case of translation." This situation is due to the high number of freelance and part-time translators and the fragmentation of specializations – and therefore the multiplicity of associations – as well the technological advancements, which have further disturbed the already disordered market. In the digital age, traits of 'professionalism' are less trusted as the occupation attracts many non-professionals (ibid., 2016).

In a study about *The Status of the Translation Profession in the European Union*, Pym et al. (2013, 76) advance that "[i]t may be that the modes of 'power' and 'control' associated with the image of a fully autonomous profession are simply not those that are operative in the field of translation." Translation does not endow its practitioners with the necessary power to be recognized by clients/consumers and society (ibid.). This same understanding is seen in Dam and Zethsen's analysis (2011), as the authors assume that "the barriers to full professionalization [in Denmark] are closely connected to status and prestige" of translators (2011, 979), which are not recognized by the clients and/or the public (2010, 207) (see Dam and Koskinen 2016 for similar assertions). Pym et al. and Dam and Zethsen rightly argue that since translators do not have the power and control of autonomous professionals, it follows that translation may not be self-controlled.

Pym et al.'s (2013) argument, however, seems to be paradoxical. While they seek to empower translators to allow them to set their terms rather than submit to their clients/employers' agendas, they endorse 'professionalization' based on a consensual effort with those very agents. They suggest that the desired 'professionalization' requires cooperation from everyone involved for the mutual benefits of all – thus, undermining the fact that these agents are engaged in permanent struggles to impose their different agendas, contents and definitions, and therefore, enforce their mode of occupational control. Not very different from Sela-Sheffy (2016), who equates professionalization with any kind of occupational control (i.e., collegiate or corporate control), Pym et al. (2013) are idealistic in their plea for 'professionalization' through patrons' consent on the translators' terms in a cooperative atmosphere. This is manifest in their recommendation that any action in this direction should be "*clear and recognisable for employers*" (Pym et al. 2013, 121) – implying the involvement of employers in processes of qualifications or certifications. Yet, Pym et al. (2013), like Sela-Sheffy (2016), overlook the fact that this mode – which may require the translator's inclination to patrons' terms – cannot lead to the translator's autonomy and, thus, to the occupation self-control.

The introductions of the two main recent volumes about translation professionalization/profession or translator status, namely the volume entitled *Identity and Status in the Translatorial Professions* (2011) and the special issue of *The Journal of Specialised Translation* (2016) – some of which contributions were discussed above – qualify translation as a "semiprofessional occupation" (Sela-Sheffy 2011, 3), which has "not *yet* reached full professional status" (Dam and Koskinen 2016, 2, italics added), respectively. Although some of the contributions are aware of the internal and external power dynamics in which the field is embedded and of the translator's struggle for recognition, the prevalence of terms like 'semi-profession' or 'partial professionalization' in TS literature shows that most accounts are based on the archaic "atheoretical" trait model – in Johnson's (2016, 25) qualification – and barely make use of the more plausible power approach in the sociology of professions. Most of these studies often count the accumulated traits and deduce that the 'professionalization' process is not complete *yet* as some of the attributes of 'professionalism' are still missing. Those scholars, therefore, urge for more work to be done to accumulate all the attributes. The best many TS scholars aspire to is a legal status (see for example, Gouadec 2007, Sela-Sheffy 2016, Pym et al. 2016), overlooking the fact that legal status does not guarantee collegiate control, in the Johnsonian sense (Johnson 2016). As Johnson shows, although accountancy has a legal status and all the traits of 'professionalism,' it still fails the test of professionalization and, hence, submits to the *patronage* system.

This book examines the power relations at stake in these attempts at occupational control through an analysis of the translator associations' codes of ethics and/or practice. Ultimately the study explores whether *professionalism* as a social construction of imposition that enhances the translator's symbolic capital (see Schinkel and Noordegraaf 2011), and, therefore, gives them the power to monopolize the "'official' definitions" (to borrow Johnson's term 2015/1977, 106) of *translation*, its content and relations – with the support of an external source of power – is within reach. Let us now turn first to a review of translation ethics in TS before moving to the analysis of the official definitions of *translation* in the studied codes of ethics.

Notes

1 I do not mean that Freidson does not, like Johnson, highlight the control of occupations by managerial agents (corporate capital) or the state (in some regimes), but he does not pursue a systematic analysis in this direction as Johnson does. This is probably due to the fact that Freidson's primary focus is the medical profession (traditionally controlled by professionals) while Johnson's primary focus is accountancy, which has always lacked practitioners' self-control.
2 www.circuitmagazine.org/dossier-131/lack-of-status-are-translators-the-authors-of-their-own-misfortune
3 Strikingly, this "anti-professionalization" culture among 'elite' translators contaminates even "non-elite practitioners" (Sela-Sheffy 2016, 68).

2 Translation Ethics in Contemporary Translation Theory

The question of translator/translation ethics has gradually come to the fore in TS over the years. In the last twenty years, a number of renowned journals devoted special issues to translator/interpreter ethics (see Pym 2001, Drugan and Tipton 2017, Hutchings 2021, Inghilleri and Harding 2010, Fiola 2004, Monzó-Nebot and Wallace 2020, Baker and Maier 2011a). Very recently, we saw the publication of *The Routledge Handbook of Translation and Ethics* (Koskinen and Pokorn 2021). Apart from these collective specialized publications and many other targeted studies that are centred around translator/interpreter ethics, there have been countless other publications that are indirectly related to translator/translation ethics. These studies gave rise to various and divergent views on the topic. The impossibility of agreement on the notion of ethics and its implications stems from the complexity and multifacetedness of the issue, as well as scholars' adherence to different conceptual traditions. Specifically, the different conceptualizations of *translation*, due to its *complexity* and *openness* (Marais 2014 and Tymoczko 2007, respectively), have provoked such differences.

Since the 1970s, hermeneutists have brought radically new insights to TS, making alterity a central ethical issue in translation – in an abrupt departure from the dominant objectivist linguistic-oriented approaches to translation, hitherto. By the 1990s, the cultural turn scholars further emphasized alterity but underlined the socio-political, ideological and cultural dimensions of translation, as well. Some of these scholars also highlighted the translator's ideological/political allegiances as an important variable that needs to be considered when studying translation. In parallel with these major developments, some TS scholars have continued debating ethics from an idealistic perspective, in the name of pragmatism and functionalism. In what follows, I sketch the main traditions in TS regarding translation/translator ethics, without claiming to be exhaustive, as translation is "intrinsically ethical" (Goodwin 2010, 26). Hence, any analysis

DOI: 10.4324/9781032713557-4

of ethics is also an analysis of some of the main theories and practices of translation in general – which makes it impossible to include every scholarly contribution that hints at ethical matters.

2.1 Hermeneutics and Translation Ethics

George Steiner's (1975) seminal work, *After Babel: Aspects of Language and Translation*, is one of the most extensive hermeneutic works in the history of reflections on translation. The author devotes significant space to discussing otherness in his hermeneutic motion, arguing that translation is an aggressive appropriation of the Other. He, therefore, calls for compensation: a restoration of balance, a reciprocity, for the translation cycle to be complete and ethical. Steiner quotes Massignon as saying: « pour comprendre l'autre, [...], il ne faut pas se l'annexer, mais devenir son hôte » [to understand the other, [...], one must not annex them, but rather become their host] (1975, 395). Steiner's interest in ethics of otherness can be seen as more focused on poetics, and less centred around issues of cultural dominance. The question of power relations is not a very central issue in his work.

Antoine Berman (1984, 1999/1985, 1999/1995), on the other hand, questions the dominant ethnocentric theoretical underpinnings of *translation* that are behind exclusionist translation acts. "Getting translation out of its ideological ghetto is one of the tasks of a theory of translation," Berman asserts (1984, 17, my translation). Similarly to Steiner, he argues that translation should be « l'auberge du lointain » [the shelter for the distant] (1999/1985, 76), i.e., an ethical translation must represent the Other in their otherness, refuting annexation methods, and advancing the argument that meaning may indeed be untranslatable. "Sense 'trafficking' that translation indulges in is a dubious, deceitful and unnatural operation," Berman tells us (ibid., 43, my translation). Following Benjamin (2000/1923), Berman argues that translation that seeks communication and the appropriation of the content is doomed to betray the form of the original (Berman 1999/1985, 71–72). At the opposite extreme from Chesterman (2016/1997) who seeks clarity for the sake of rational communication as one of the most ethical operations, Berman believes clarifications can be unethical (1999/1985, 71–72). His advocacy for the recognition and importation of difference in translation is reminiscent of Schleiermacher's affirmation that 'a good translator' is the one that "leaves the writer in peace as much as possible and moves the reader toward him" (2012/1813, 49).

Quite a plausible criticism that can be levelled against Berman is the elitism of his ethics, which are hardly applicable to all fields, genres and cases in the same clear-cut way (Gouanvic 2001). Pym qualifies Berman's ethics as "factitious" for being "devoid of two-way power relations"

(2012, 92). Pym rightly argues that Berman overlooks situations where powerful cultures impose their models/canons on receiving cultures, as is the case of colonial powers (ibid.).

Not far from Berman geographically and intellectually resides another renowned French translation critic, Henri Meschonnic. Meschonnic (1999) argues that translation ethics and translation poetics are two sides of the same coin; they both consist of preserving the ST's rhythm and discursive spirit. "The ethics and poetics of translation are one and the same pursuit: preserving the rhythm of the text" (ibid., 221, my translation). Meschonnic (1999) also argues that a good translation is done for good and all. A translation that calls for another translation is not a translation, for him. Berman (1999/1995) criticizes Meschonnic for being intuitively judgmental and negative in his critiques. The role of a pertinent critique is indeed to provoke a re-translation, as every translation calls for retranslation, Berman argues.

Although Berman and Meschonnic – like Steiner and other German precursors – fiercely defend respect for alterity in its aesthetics, forms and models, they hardly devote any room to issues of (political) agency, activism, social responsibility or colonial/patriarchal hegemonies. These issues and the central role played by the translator in reinforcing or contesting them will be among the prime concerns of the cultural turn.

2.2 The Culturalist Perspective on Translation Ethics

Since the early 1990s, the question of translation ethics has taken a central position in various debates, as TS scholars started to put the translating agent at the centre of enquiry. Many theorists have scrutinized the historical, ideological, political and social facets of translation, beyond the idealistic understanding of translation as a pacific transfer of a transcendent and stable signified (see for example, Tymoczko 2007; Venuti 1995, 1998, 2005; Baker 2006a; Drugan and Tipton 2017). These scholars have examined the notion of *translation* as a historical concept that evolved, taking different shapes and yielding different practices, depending on the agents involved in it. They generally argue that the socio-culturally constructed understanding of the concept of *translation* as faithfulness has mostly been created by dominant actors and cultures and has been imposed on the rest of the world (see Trivedi 2006; Tymoczko 2007, 2007; Susam-Sarajeva 2002). Most importantly, the cultural turn scholars have highlighted the importance of embracing ethics of difference, and ethics as a social responsibility and an engagement with just causes (see Venuti 1995, 1998; Davis 2001; Cronin 2003, 2006; Tymoczko 2010/2003, 2007; Baker 2006a, 2006b, 2007, 2008, 2010; Drugan and Tipton 2017; Drugan 2017; Harding and Ralarala 2017, to name a few).

Among the theorists that have denounced the "scandalous" translation practices issuing from the hegemonic conceptualization of *translation*, based on assumptions of equivalence, is Lawrence Venuti (1995, 1998). Drawing on Berman and German Romantics (mainly Schleiermacher 2012/1813), Venuti calls for "minoritizing translation" relying on "discursive heterogeneity" (1998, 12). Ethical translations should not adhere to the dominant standards but import minor foreign literatures – minor even at home – with all their archaisms, if any (ibid., 1998). This minoritizing strategy implies the creation of a heterogeneous discourse in and through translation, bringing the remote other as other. Venuti's vision of translation ethics consists of adopting foreignizing translation strategies that can "restrain the ethnocentric violence of translation" (ibid., 20), and create "possibilities for cultural resistance, innovation, and change at any historical moment" (1995, 68).

Venuti's vision is not, however, unanimously embraced by his colleagues from the cultural turn. Douglas Robinson (2003), for instance, is critical of what he calls Venuti's Marxist radicalism that advocates "principled action" to bring about abrupt change. Robinson rather proposes an evolutionary tactic "that nudges the reader gradually, cautiously, out of the hegemonic mindset that feels so natural, so real, so comprehensive, so complete, and into a confrontation with the leading edge of the repressed" (2003, 150). Also, although Venuti's position as a proponent of ethics of difference and plurality is important, he, nevertheless, fails to consider that his foreignizing option can be the very strategy used to unethically represent the Other as strange and primitive (see Faiq 2004, Carbonell 2004). As Tymoczko (2007, 2010) and Baker (2010) rightly affirm, Berman and Venuti's fight against cultural enclosure and assimilation to canonical fluent discourses is specific to the French and American contexts, respectively, and hence the difficulty to generalize them. A fierce criticism of Venuti's plea in favour of the translator's visibility and resistance, and therefore authorship, comes from Barbara Folkart, who considers his foreignizing strategy to be a "mindless word-for-word translation" (2007, 388). Folkart asserts that visibility, in Venuti's sense – the kind that produces "a 'resistant translation' – one that 'minoritizes,' or that shines and shocks merely by its graininess – is worlds away from authoring a text" (ibid., 385).

Not far from Venuti Berman, Tymoczko (1999, 2000, 2005, 2010/2003, 2006, 2007, 2010) refutes the dominant Western discourse about *translation* and questions the Eurocentrism of current translation theories – echoing Berman, as well. She seeks a reconceptualization of *translation* as a "cluster concept" that can encompass varied meanings and cultural models and push its boundaries to include a variety of types and styles. Tymoczko considers the current dominant concept of *translation* as being "limited and [...] also ideological," and therefore, unethical (2007, 6). Her reference to the ideological meaning of *translation* includes the work of missionaries, colonization and globalization nowadays, which all have conceptualized *translation* idealistically as a pacific cultural encounter, in an attempt to conceal the role it plays in the indoctrination and domestication of the dominated local populations (see also Niranjana 1992). Tymoczko (2007) stresses the important role translation/translators play in political agency and in challenging or fostering hegemonic discourses and political domination. "Translation has marked political dimensions, becoming a mode of spying or intelligence gathering used for the purposes of domination or, alternatively, a mode of counterespionage, resistance, and rebellion" (Tymoczko 2007, 197). In 2010, Tymoczko reiterates her position affirming that "in peace as in war, translation always has a potentially radical and activist edge, that it is driven by ethical and ideological concerns, and that it participates in shaping societies, nations, and global culture in primary ways" (2010, 19–20).

Along similar lines, Baker (2005) argues that the act of translation and the role of translators is either that of building bridges of peace or creating damage and destruction.

> No one questions whether bridges are always built for the (morally) 'right' reasons, nor the fact that just as they might allow us to cross over and make positive contact with a different culture, they also allow invading troops to cross over and kill, maim and destroy entire populations.
>
> (Baker 2005, 9)

Baker's (2006a, 2010) narrative framework – borrowed from social and communication theories – brings the ethical question to the fore. Drawing on the notion of "narrative reframing," she argues that some outwardly accurate translations may sometimes have "suspicious frames" (2010). Through *selective appropriation* and other features of narrativity, she examines how some translators and publishers select certain elements of the STs/cultures and not others with the aim of presenting a coherent story, which is in fact only a partial representation of reality. "[S]electing, and in some cases 'inventing,' texts that help elaborate a particular narrative of an 'enemy' culture, then, is a well-documented practice that often relies heavily on the services of translators and interpreters" (2006a, 75). Thus, Baker, like Tymoczko (2000, 2007), preaches the principle of activist interventions in support of just and ethical causes. Following her reasoning, neutrality is a *myth*[1] that conceals atrocities. Baker (2018) urges translators to approach their assignments not only as technical tasks, but mainly as ethical challenges/dilemmas that require critical skills (ibid., 290).

Not very different from Tymoczko and Baker, Michael Cronin (2003, 2006, 2010/1998, 2017) advocates the activist dimension of translation. He argues that in a globalized world, characterized by acute imbalance in translation traffic, the translator's responsibility should extend beyond taking translation only as a 'professional' activity to taking it as a cultural fact with political facets. "There must be an activist dimension to translation which involves an engagement with the cultural politics of society at national and international levels […] Indeed, the professional and the political are inextricably linked," Cronin argues (2003, 134). In his recent publications, Cronin (2017, 2021) reiterates his earlier positions and further stresses the collaborative, global and processual dimensions of translation. Most importantly, he adds an original dimension to translation ethics, taking it beyond political agency and social responsibility toward humans alone, to an awareness of inter-species relatedness and the preservation of biodiversity.

> If part of the struggle for justice in the colonial period was to give voice through translation to the oppression of the subaltern, to turn the colonised from positivistic objects of commercial exploitation and scientific enquiry to hermeneutic subjects of sentient experience and liberation […], then translation studies in a posthuman moment might finally turn its attention to the minoritised languages of the majority of beings on the planet.
> (Cronin 2021, 191)

Cronin (2017, 2021), thus, extends translator ethics to include responsibility to "the plight of living organisms with whom we share the planet" and to allow "shared sovereignty of the planet" in order to ensure an ecological balance and survival for all species – humans included (2021, 290). For collective survival, he argues that "[t]ranslation studies has to engage with planetary futurity as a guide to the priorities of the present" (2017, 92). Cronin believes that translators – along with other agents – should be called upon to evaluate the ecological price of certain translations in the digital age.

> As connoisseurs of language, culture and/or different specialisms, they would assist in the evaluation of the likely impacts or benefits of the translation of particular texts. In an era of anthropogenic climate change, it is no longer possible to abstract the 'externalities' of environment from the cost of engaging in or pursuing a particular activity and this includes translation.
> (Cronin 2017, 107)

Drugan and Tipton's (2017) special issue of *The Translator* constitutes another pillar of enlarging ethics to include social responsibility as an important aspect of translation/interpreting, beyond the service dimension of practitioners' work. "[A] professional focus on social responsibility may have an impact on individuals and society far beyond the narrow professional sphere" (2017, 120). The authors note the positive shift in TS from deontological approaches to the translator/interpreter ethics toward more differentiated approaches that consider the communicative encounter in decision-making. In this same issue, Harding and Ralarala (2017) study the reconstitution/reframing of narratives, which compromise social justice, while Drugan (2017) raises the issue of ethical training of translators/interpreters who work in sensitive social fields with care service agents and underlines the importance of having ethics training revolved around social responsibility.

Not differently from the view that emphasizes the responsibility of translators/interpreters working in sensitive fields with external agents stands Moira Inghilleri (2008, 2009, 2010, 2012). Inghilleri argues that political and ethical judgments in encounters of high tensions should be driven by the nature of the ethical encounter, rather than pre-determined by codified ethics that emphasize impartiality or neutrality rules. Drawing on philosophical and sociological insights, she embraces ethics of interpreting "that resists the wish to transcend the violation of the other through codes based in transcendent ideals and is instead guided by the nature of the ethical encounter itself where 'the right thing to do' cannot be calculated or predetermined, but can only ever be decided in the event itself" (2008, 222). Inghilleri questions preordained rules of codified ethics for being abstract, unrealistic and decontextualized – especially in contexts that are characterized by high tension. Most importantly, she warns against the fact that interpreters may be 'ethically' annexed to the military or political field they choose to serve, in the name of impartiality and neutrality (Inghilleri 2010, 2012). Inghilleri rather underlines situational ethics and the uncertainty of the interpreter's choices in asylum adjudication situations and war zones (Inghilleri 2012). I believe her invaluable insights need to be taken further by examining these codes of ethics, where they actually exist and where they are proclaimed as important internal official documents. This is especially important as these official documents probably impact on all interpreters/translators' ethical agency in most seemingly non-conflictual situations.

A tangible strategy to respond to ethical demands in translation is that of massive textual interferences, proposed by Appiah (2000/1993) and Sturrock (2010/1990). With the African context in mind, Appiah calls for 'thick translation' strategies; a rich textual and cultural contextualization of the remote literary production through annotations and glosses. Only this way can the translator challenge the reader "to undertake the harder project of a genuinely informed respect for others," and hence contribute to the repudiation of racism (Appiah 2000, 427). Sturrock, on the other hand, advocates 'interlinear translation,' which highlights the non-immediacy of the translation act and "allow[s] certain 'purely' untranslatable characteristics of the syntax and lexicon of the source to show through in the translation" (2010, 63).

2.3 Deconstruction, Postcolonialism and Gender Approaches to Translation Ethics

2.3.1 *Deconstructionist Tradition and Ethics*

The translation theorists discussed in the previous sub-section have, to different extents, been inspired by the poststructuralist thought that started to dominate in humanities after World War II. Outsider theorists, like Jacques Derrida, provide the most inspiring views that are later taken over and developed by TS deconstructionists concerned with 'ethics.' In 1985, Derrida writes a ground-breaking essay in which he discusses Walter Benjamin's (2000/1923) text 'The Task of the Translator.' Corroborating Benjamin's argumentation, the French theorist argues that translation is inherently *transformative*. In his comment on the German theorist's postulate, Derrida affirms that translation is impossible and necessary; it is an unachievable promise that is rarely accomplished (Derrida 1985, 174). "Translation becomes law, duty and debt, but the debt one can no longer be discharged" (ibid.). This is due to the plurivocality of linguistic signs and the constructivist nature of human knowledge. Translation, thus, is a fiction we live by, as Robinson (2003, 6) puts it. It is a symbol of the confusion that humans have been left to face, the uncertainty they have been destined to, since 'God' forbade the colonial violence of *one* universal tongue, *one* universal signified, *one* frame of reference, *one* structure, and ordered the deconstruction of the Babel Tower – the symbol of totalitarianism and uniformity. Discussing the Semites' ambition to totalization and completeness by building the Tower, Derrida contends that, by deconstructing the Tower, 'God' "ruptures the rational transparency but interrupts also the colonial violence or the linguistic imperialism. He destines them to translation, he subjects them to the law of a translation both necessary and impossible" (1985, 174). Derrida's deconstruction embraces the ethics of pluralism and awareness of the double-voicedness of discourse – to use Bakhtin's (1981) term – and the uncertainty based on the incompleteness and instability of meaning.

The other hardcore poststructuralist TS scholars who have played a major role in promoting 'deconstruction' and 'hybridity' principles in the field have followed Derrida's deconstruction ideas (e.g., Spivak 2000, 2005; Davis 2001). Davis, for instance, refutes the idea that meaning transcends language and that translation imports meaning smoothly and completely. Meaning is rather an effect of language. It is neither a stable nor a fixed entity. Davis (2001, 46) considers that "the desire for total translatability, which has always been the desire of Western metaphysics, is a desire to reign, or dominate." She, thus, refutes the Eurocentric translation theories for being exclusionist and limited. She implies that any 'code of ethics' drawn from the ethnocentric conceptualization of translation is impetuous. "An ethics of translation theorized according to such a definition would be irresponsible to that which it excluded in order to define itself. For this reason, deconstruction remains wary of 'ethics,' which in many contexts implies the application or establishment of an ideal code" (ibid., 92). Highlighting the notion of ambivalence, Davis argues that translation decisions that do not go through 'the ordeals of the undecidable' are not decisions. The ones that abide by the norms and pre-established 'passages' and 'programmes' are just mechanical accounts, for Davis (2001, 93), following Derrida. Ambivalent and uncertain passages should be envisaged. The translator should take into consideration the singularity of every event and should be aware of the impossibility of any complete grasp of the *Other*, in order to respond responsibly and ethically. Responsibility and ethics do not mean submitting the *Other* to one's own code of reference, i.e., one's assumptions and frames, but understanding the codes of the *Other* in their Otherness.

In tune with Davis's analysis, Spivak, another hardcore deconstruction and postcolonial theorist, argues that translation is an "unavoidable failure" (2005, 95). For her, cultural otherness is irreducible and inaccessible, and an ethical translator is one who is aware of these inherent limitations in translation. A translated text is a sort of "trace rather than of achieved translation: trace of the other, trace of history," says Spivak (ibid., 105). Staten (2005) exposes Spivak's radical conceptualization of the 'aboriginal Other.' The 'aboriginal' is "the one *most* alien to European culture, the one most securely expelled from the name 'Man'" (2005, 115, italics in original), and hence the impossibility of their translation. In Spivak's understanding, the 'aboriginal' as a representative of the extreme *Other* – that is unrepresentable by Western frames – stands in opposition to the 'native informant' that incarnates colonial ideology. Staten reproaches Spivak for the radicality in her conception of the "aboriginal." She ignores all others that exist on the "scale of degrees of closeness to and distance from the fully constituted 'metropolitan subject'" (ibid., 116). Staten argues that "[t]he transcendental or quasi-transcendental notion of radical alterity is the most severe constraint on our notions of ethical encounter, which Spivak conceives on this basis as both imperative and impossibility; *this notion, however, is meta-ethical and does not by itself provide us with any political point of application*" (ibid., 116–117, italics

46 Professionalization, Ethics and Translation in Codified Ethics

in original). Also discussing the problematic of the Other's representation, Eaglestone (2005) – drawing on Benjamin (2000/1923) – argues that translation reveals that one language is not enough. This 'failure to be enough' is what discomforts us, but at the same time, makes us aware of the ethical significance of respecting Others' uniqueness and mystery (Eaglestone 2005, 136). He points that, "it is only by approaching the neighbor, the other, as that which we cannot understand or comprehend, or translate, that we act ethically" (ibid.).

Arnaud Laygues's (2004) draws on Levinasian thought about the ethics of the Other and applies Lévinas's notions of "image" and "face" to translation ethics. Laygues rejects the view of *translation* as 'resemblance' or 'image' and embraces the view of *translation* as a site of encounter of the Other. "The possibility is thus offered of translation not as resemblance, image of the target text, but as an encounter open to the relationship: the translator on the lookout for the "face" of the other present in their text" (2004, 53, my translation). The notion of "the face of the Other" allows the translator to promote ethical relations to the Other as well as the reader, Laygues concludes. Similarly to Laygues, Christopher Larkosh (2004) underlines the relevance of Lévinas's philosophy to translation ethics. He underscores the supremacy of Otherness and the translator's role in shaping language, culture and society as well as in giving voice to the voiceless, in order to challenge the global structures of domination. Larkosh writes,

> the translator's presence as a theorizing subject, now more than ever, can be recognized as inseparable from this practice. Clearly, discussions of translational ethics must be concerned not only with the accurate transferral of meaning, but also the broader cultural significance and potential public spaces of the texts we translate and the institutionalized positions from which we do so. Translating ethically, especially from Global South to Global North, may well imply an interruption in official discourses by enabling voices not traditionally audible in present-day academic discussions of translational ethics to come forth, and thereby challenging the Eurocentric foundations of present structures of symbolic domination.
>
> (Larkosh 2004, 28–29)

Other notion widely adopted by poststructuralist TS scholars include *hybridity* and *in-betweenness*. Drawing mainly on Homi Bhabha (1994), Michaela Wolf has strongly argued in favour of 'in-betweenness' to "transcend dichotomizing notions of translation" (2000, 130). She contends that authoritative discourses can be undermined by polyphonic, hybrid and double-voiced constructions (Wolf 2000, 2002). New meanings that defy the fixed polar entities and generate new spaces can then emerge, Wolf argues. These new meanings are "located in the third space, a sort of in-between space located between existing referential systems and antagonisms" (ibid., 135). Thus, translation, for Wolf, is not a reinforcement of the original but rather a *transformation*. This is because "the 'original' is never finished or complete in itself. The 'originary' is always open to translation so that it can never be said to have a totalized prior moment of being or meaning – an essence," as Bhabha insightfully argues (1990, 210). Translation as generative of discursive multiplicity and the proliferation of signification, and therefore the adverse of control, delimitation and certainty is similarly advocated by Karin Littau (2010/1997)[2]. Desacralizing the original (text and author) – which are 'anoriginal,' in her terms – and valuing translation/translators, is a way of promoting the proliferation of meaning and multiplicity.

> [W]e have inferiorized translation, we have devalued it, because we fear it, since it is a flaunting manifestation of textuality's most 'uncontrollable aspects,' since it is an index of the 'cancerous and dangerous proliferation of significations.' By extension, we have inferiorized the translator, because we fear her or him, since he or she is the very initiator or proliferator of discourses, the multiplier of versions.
> (Littau 2010, 441)

Following Roland Barthes's 'death of the author,' Littau adds that "the faithful translation died with the author, with our faith in the Author-God" (ibid., 438).

Not very different from Wolf and Littau, Bachman-Medick (2006, 2009) introduces the notion of 'culture as translation.' Like Wolf, she draws on Bhabha (1994) in her argument that the dynamic nature of cultures and their hybridity in today's world necessitate newer approaches to this 'cultural encounter.' "Cultures constitute themselves *in* translation and *as* translation," says Bachmann-Medick (2006, 37, italics in original). For her, an ethical anthropology/cultural translation can and should move beyond essentialist cultural polarization to account for hybridity, shifts, displacements, transformations, heterogeneity and dynamism within cultures and between them. She embraces the exploration of a third space and border crossing, quoting Bhabha (1994, 39) as he says: "by exploring this Third Space, we may elude the politics of polarity and emerge as the others of our selves." In other words, she theorizes a new (cultural) translation/anthropology in today's global world, based on a rupture with the dichotomous conceptualization of cultures and civilizations. Bachman-Medick advocates anthropology/translation that can evade their traditional mire in authoritative discursive games that favor reading about the Other's mode of life instead of learning to live a new mode of life (Bachmann-Medick 2006; see also Asad 2010/1986).

The deconstructionist/poststructuralist tradition is drawn upon by TS scholars with postcolonial and gender studies orientations in revealing the abusive effects of colonialism and sexism in translation and textual production in general, respectively. Hence, the ethics of translation for these two traditions require the deconstruction of the totalitarian colonialist and patriarchal discourses that regard the West/Man as the sacred originals and Third World/Woman as translations – or deficient derivative copies – (see Spivak 2000, 2005; Niranjana 1992; Cheyfitz 1991, Rafael 1988/1993; Mehrez 1992; Bandia 2005, Flotow 1997, 2007, 2011; Simon 1996; Chamberlain 2012/1988).

2.3.2 Postcolonial and Gender Approaches to Ethics

For postcolonial scholars, "colonialism and translation went hand in hand" (Bassnett and Trivedi 1999, 3). Translation is a channel of empire, a technology of dominance and colonialism (Robinson 1997, 31). The ideology of objectivism of translation was one of the tools used to harness and domesticate the natives in many parts of the world.

The work of Eric Cheyfitz, *The Poetics of Imperialism: Translation and Colonization from the Tempest to Tarzan*, is one of the most comprehensive outlines of postcolonial theory of translation. In this publication, Cheyfitz examines the conquest of the New World. According to his analysis, the 'savage' natives were seen as inferior to Europeans, and genetically unable to negotiate, and, therefore, needed to be alienated and translated. Cheyfitz (1991, 16) writes: "[t]he failure of dialogue, figured as a genetic inability in the other, rather than as a problem of cultural difference, is the imperial alibi for domination." An important part of this translation process was the seizing and transfer of the natives' properties – since they had no sense of it – into the conquerors' hands. Translating the natives was, however, an extremely difficult, if not an impossible, task as they did not understand 'eloquent speech,' and were 'incoherent, non-objective and irrational.'

In the same vein, Tejaswini Niranjana (1992), in her seminal work, *Siting Translation: History, Post-Structuralism, and the Colonial Context*, raises the question of interpellating the natives by teaching them English and British ways (civilizing them), and thus translating and purifying the Indian heritage into British canons. "Translation produces strategies of *containment*" (Niranjana 1992, 3, italics mine). According to the scholar and translator William Jones, who was "responsible for the most influential introduction of a textualized India to Europe," translation had to serve "to domesticate the Orient and thereby turn it into a province of European learning" (Niranjana 1992, 12). Hence, translation was a means to 'gather in,' 'domesticate' and 'rope off' the Orient. The translation of Indian texts into English promoted Orientalist images for even the educated Indians, who started to perceive them as 'natural' and even truthful (Niranjana, 1992).

In a similar line of thought, Vincent Rafael (1993/1988) studies the interconnection of translation, conversion (to Christianity) and conquest in the colonization of the Tagalog society in the Philippines by the Spanish in the 16th century. He raises the questions of transformation and conversion of the population in order to guarantee their voluntary submission and even love and affection toward the conqueror/oppressor. To facilitate the conquest, the Tagalogs needed to be converted, translated and transformed. "The Spanish notion of translation as the reduction of native signs into a structure comprehensible in Spanish terms was very much at the root of the attempts to codify native culture" (1993, 106). Because the Christian signifiers ('God's words') were untranslatable – as there were no 'equivalents' in the pagan Tagalog vernacular to express the Christian 'truth' – they were retained as such and entered into the vernaculars (which also needed to be purified and moved closer to God's language). In a later article, Rafael (2010/2007) maintains that translation can be anything but objective and smooth. Instead, it can be "an instrument of surveillance with which to track and magnify the alienness of alien speech, decoding dangers, containing threats, and planning for interventions" (2010, 386).

According to postcolonial thought, translation was depoliticized (idealized as linguistic transfer) for centuries, thus, hiding its aggressive imperial role. According to this tradition, it is because of the understanding of *translation* within the realm of rationalism, objectivism, equivalence, transference of transcendental meaning, civilizing, converting to the divine original, that most atrocities and unethical transformations and domestications of local populations in human history have taken place.

Gender-oriented studies, drawing on poststructuralist thought, have, similarly to postcolonial studies, tried to reverse patriarchal hegemony that regards the Man as the active and creative original and the Woman as a translation, a derivative version (see Godard 1990; Chamberlain 2012/1988; Flotow 1997, 2007, 2011; Simon 1996). The association of translation with all that is recreation, derivation, faithfulness, loyalty is strongly rejected by Chamberlain (2012/1988). She rebukes the sexist and patriarchal terminology of *originality* associated with the male and the author, on the one hand, and *unfaithfulness* and derivation associated with translation and women, on the other hand. Sherry Simon (1996), for her part, debunks the prevalent binarist discourse about translation and women – which is, in fact, an extension of the binarist thought prevalent in society, culture, and languages, in general. "[G]ender is relational, and is in fact an extension of the binary, oppositional structure that pervades all our thinking" (ibid., 17).

Feminist TS scholars also highlight the necessity of challenging gender bias in textual material, and they, therefore, advocate translation as visible rewriting in the feminine. In this regard, Barbara Godard (1990) refutes the linguistic alienation of women and rejects the notion of equivalence in translation. The feminist translator, for her, is an *active* producer of meaning, not an invisible reproducer of 'original' meaning. She writes:

> *Womanhandling* the text in translation would involve the replacement of the modest, self-effacing translator. Taking her place would be an active participant in the creation of meaning, who advances a conditional analysis. Hers is a continuing provisionality, aware of process, giving self-reflexive attention to practices. The feminist translator immodestly flaunts her signature in italics, in footnotes – even in a preface.
>
> (Godard 1990, 94, italics in original)

Luise von Flotow (2011), for her part, argues that translation is inherently interventionist as it is an intentional and deliberate act exactly as is any feminist or other form of social activism. "Translation, it can be argued, is as intentional, as activist, as deliberate as any feminist or otherwise socially-activist activity" (ibid., 4). Flotow, hence, equates translation acts with activist acts, and in particular, with feminist acts.

Many of the contemporary translation theories and the views on ethics cited in the foregoing review have been developed based on data pertaining mainly to literary translation – with probably the exception of Cronin (2003, 2013, 2017), Baker (2005, 2006a, 2007, 2010), Inghilleri (2008, 2009, 2010, 2012), Drugan (2017) and Harding and Ralarala (2017). It may be argued that most of these views – which underscore politics, otherness, social responsibility and power dynamics – have little to do with today's 'professional' translation that is mostly pragmatic, and which is ethically less problematic and hardly involves otherness, power dynamics or ideological issues. However, as Davis (2001, 97) rightly points out, "translators always face decisions in their translation process (no matter how technical the text may be), as well as in the larger context of their work" (see also Tymoczko 2007, Cronin 2003, 2017). In the same line, I argue that many of these views do, in some ways, apply to today's pragmatic translation, although to different extents, depending on the nature of the document and the genre of the text. What applies to literary texts in fact applies quite similarly to politically oriented texts and news adaptation/translation, for example. These text types are the sites of representation, power dynamics and ideology, *par excellence*, and their impact is much wider than literary texts (probably read by fewer readers). As already explained, Baker (2005, 2006a, 2007, 2010) has mainly worked with media translations as her data. She has, on many occasions, shown how these (non-literary) pragmatic types of translation represent the others negatively, following certain geopolitical agendas. Studying the Canadian context, Chantal Gagnon (2006), in turn, shows that even the translation of the word 'Canada' in media/political texts is ideologically/politically driven. Gagnon (2006) observes some important shifts in the French translations of the lemma 'Canada' and surrounding words. These shifts, Gagnon concludes, reflect the different perceptions of the Canadian identity by the two major linguistic/cultural groups. In a similar vein, Hatim and Mason (1997, 12–20, 127–132) report on influential shifts that have ethical implications in a translated text carried out for the UNESCO. They reveal that a translation of a document about the historical heritage of Mexico published in the UNESCO *Courier* was reshaped in a way that undermines the indigenous people and culture of Mexico. These shifts, hence, result in the obliteration of otherness in the service of socio-cultural and institutional factors[3].

We know that the UN, its affiliate organizations and many such international and regional organizations and governments depend heavily on translation and, thus, employ large numbers of translators, who do a lot of sensitive (political) language work. We also know that in their daily work of adapting news/political texts to their specific audiences/cultures, journalist-translators encounter countless dilemmas similar to, or even more complex than, those identified in the studies of Baker, Gagnon, and Hatim and Mason. This is not to mention situations in countries which are bilingual or multilingual (and which depend on translations in every sector of life) with all the cultural sensitivities that may affect translations, as a result – as seen in the Canadian context.

Political/media texts are not the only types of texts affected by ethical dilemmas that have to do with representation and ideology. Any other type of pragmatic texts (used by other large powerful employers/clients) may include problematic stretches that have to do with ideology, power relations or representation. As we learn from Bourdieu (1991) as well as the pioneers of Critical Discourse Analysis (like Fairclough (2003, 2010) or van Dijk (1993)), language is a site of power asymmetries, regardless of its thematic content. In this respect, Gagnon and Kalantari (2017, 27–28) show that issues of identity in translation between French and English can also be identified in technical/commercial texts, as well. They report examples from the websites of two different Canadian brands, Tim Horton's café and Canadian Tire (which is a retail company). The English and French versions of the two brands' promotional texts, although purely pragmatic, reflect the identity perception divide between the two major linguistic/cultural entities. Although these texts are normally less ideologically loaded than political/literary texts, they may occasionally contain ideological/discursive elements that are not naïve and that require reflexivity on the translator's part. Commercials and all other audio-visual adaptations/translations may include ethical dilemmas related to the representation of minorities, otherness or women. This is not to mention translations/interpreting in sensitive service domains (see, for instance, Harding and Ralarala (2017).

Pragmatic translation may even be more ethically taxing and complex than literary texts, as the preservation of our planet stands as its primary ethical focus, especially in the face of today's ecological crisis, manifest in global warming and climate change. Purely technical documents may pose more dilemmas as they may have direct and discernable fatal consequences for ecological balance or survival of humans and other species in the present or the future. As Cronin points out "notions of climate justice and translation need to move beyond the strict purview of the human if they are not to be complicit in ecologically damaging forms of subjection" (2021, 290). For example, translating labels/documents of the products of the agrochemical corporation, Monsanto, may be the most ethically challenging since the American company has been involved in many ethical scandals, the latest of which is its herbicide, Roundup, which was found to be carcinogenic[4].

In addition, heavy reliance on automated translation poses many ethical issues related to pragmatic translation. Some studies, for example, have identified the issue of (gender, age, racial) bias in stored corpora (see, for instance, Bowker 2021; Vanmassenhove, Hardmeier and Way 2018). "Using corpora as training data for MT systems raises another question about social responsibility. A recent concern regarding corpus-based MT is that these approaches could suffer from so-called *machine* or *algorithm bias*" (Bowker 2021, 272, italics in original). And here comes the need to curate these corpora (see Bowker 2021). The very recent innovations with the launch of many applications/tools of what is now known as Generative Artificial Intelligence (AI), such as ChatGPT and Dall-E (developed by OpenAI company), followed by Bard (made by Google) and Bing Chat (by Microsoft), have not substantially changed the situation. All these AI tools have inherent issues related to privacy, security, ethics, accuracy, biased information, lack of contextual understanding, misinformation, and manipulation – as these tools designers themselves acknowledge[5]. They themselves warn users that overreliance on AI can lead to reduced critical thinking and independent decision-making, and that critical human intervention is essential to avoid misguided actions or errors. In sum, pragmatic translation has social, political/ideological and ecological dimensions (see, for example, Davis 2001; Cronin 2003, 2017; Tymoczko 2007; Baker

2006a; Gagnon 2006; Gagnon and Kalantari 2017) and has become more ethically demanding with its increasing reliance on automated output (see Bowker 2021).

Writings that advocate ethics of difference, uncertainty, resistance, hybridity, social responsibility and the recognition of otherness, as well as engagement with socio-political causes are significant in volume. However, planetary and ecological integrity remains an underexplored area. Most importantly, TS has barely responded to the question of equipping ethical subjects who are able to cater for all these challenges. Despite these gaps, one wonders if these postpositivist ideas have been adopted (or are even applicable) in the codes of ethics of translator associations. In the current study, I show whether any of these views have found resonance in different translator associations' code of ethics. Also, I examine how these codes of ethics might affect the translator's capital and, therefore, whether they allow practitioners any margin of manoeuvres or power in relation to other agents, and thus, any chance for visibility and agency that the scholars discussed above advocate.

2.4 Functionalist 'Professional' Ethics

In response to certain scholars' view of, and plea for, the translator's sovereignty or power, Anthony Pym (2012, 88) has stated: "[h]ow could we recommend a particular action, for example, to someone who has no agency at the level of that action? Asking a translator to save the world is sometimes like asking an infant to read." Although one may find it difficult to disagree with Pym's assertion about the current status of the translator, one, however, may not share his determinism. The 'infant' *can* still grow, learn to read and gain quite a good position in relation to the other agents involved in translation, and thus acquire some relative power and agency. Pym's comments stem from his disbelief in the agency of the translator in the complex social dynamics of the translation act. This is due to his understanding of the translators' responsibility as limited mainly to the immediate context and parties involved in the 'professional' translation circle. Pym claims that translators have no responsibility for the content of the translated work, seeing them – drawing on Goffman (1981) – as 'animators' or speech reporters (Pym 2012, 62). "Translators have no 'I'," he says (ibid., 63). Pym contends that the 'profession' "requires detachment rather than commitment" (ibid., 67) to the translated message, although he admits that "any supposed neutrality is a profoundly ideological professional construct" (ibid., 67). The question is whether the current 'professional' ideology also uses the alibi of 'neutrality' to foster 'professional detachment' and encourage indifference toward possible negative outcomes of a translated text in a target context[6]. Quite paradoxically,

Pym does not very much approve of the current 'professional' codes of ethics. These codes "do not help the translator solve the difficult decisions encountered while actually translating. If translators only followed professional recipes, they would not be responsible for anything that was really theirs. Their capacity to bring about change, their agency, would only be that of the profession" (ibid., 68–69).

Pym's ethical theory contains some seemingly contradictory, or at least confusing, statements. On the one hand, he underlines the impersonality of the 'professional' translator and their invisibility and gives the impression that he "does not want to see translators or translation scholars as social beings" (Abdallah 2013). On the other hand, he does not exclude their intervention. The ambiguous division between detachment and personal choices or 'professional' and personal ethics in Pym's account constitute "moments of doubt in his argumentation," as Koskinen (2000a, 75) rightly argues. Yet, one may understand that Pym considers 'professional detachment' as a social pretense or 'mask' to establish trust with the other stakeholders. But a more plausible reading of Pym may conclude that although the author admits that the translator's idiosyncratic decisions are inevitable, he seeks to limit their scope and, therefore, their influence, in the name of 'professionalism.'

Pym's (1998, 2012) idealist theorization is clearer in his argument that an interculture is a common ground that should be created by the mediating translator. For him, "translators *are* intersections" between cultures (1998, 182, italics in original). He claims that translators should translate only when and in such a way that translation fosters *cooperation* between the parties involved in a transaction (Pym 2012). If cooperation can be achieved by other means of communication (language teaching, for example), translation should not be undertaken, from an ethical point of view, Pym (2012, 157) proclaims. Pym, driven by pragmatic functionalism[7], seems to underestimate the possible adverse effects that non-translation may have on linguistic/cultural biodiversity, especially with the hegemony of English nowadays. Ironically, Pym (2023) argues that non-translation can teach us to respect linguistic diversity, overlooking today's linguistic/cultural and geopolitical dynamics, in which English has dominated the global communication sphere and, therefore, undermined multilingual communication. This current situation is in complete contrast to his case about the multilingual communication and the absence of translation between the different indigenous linguistic groups in Australia before the European invasion.

Pym's idealist 'cooperation' implies the goal of achieving mutual benefits for all involved parties in the transaction, which, in my view, overlooks the translating agent's permanent struggle with other agents for recognition (see Abdallah 2013[8]). His view also overlooks the wider social responsibility of the translator (see Drugan and Tipton 2017), and the fact that translators are embedded in narratives and ideological affiliations (Baker 2006a, see also Tymoczko 2010/2003), and can, therefore, be involved in cultural hostilities, as was the case in colonial contexts. Shockingly, Pym (2012, 139) argues, "both actors must try to predict what the other is going to do. The search for cooperation becomes a series of 'prisoner's dilemmas.' The calculations are now based on the probability of the other's investments, and on the management of that risk." Pym's *calculative* 'ethics' of cooperation are anything but ethics per se. As Lévinas (1991, 1995) conceptualizes it, morality is an *a priori, gratuitous* and *infinite* responsibility *for-the-Other* regardless of any *exchange, communication* or *cooperation*. Pym's (2012) assertions come as no surprise to his readers. Although aware of the power dynamics between cultures, the socio-political dimensions of translation in today's globalized world and the imperialist/colonial history of translation, he consistently seeks to mitigate these aspects by privileging the economic/commercial dimension of translation and its functional pragmatic uses (see Koskinen's critique 2000a).

Not very differently from Pym – and in contrast to Cronin who contends that "the political and the professional are inextricably linked" (2003, 134) – Andrew Chesterman (2001, 2016/1997) insists on a distinction between personal and 'professional' ethics. Like Pym, he gives primacy to 'professional' ethics in his *Hieronymic Oath* (2001)[9], and excludes the translator's engagement from the scope of these ethics. "This means that the political engagement of the translator, which may affect the choice of texts to be translated and also ways of translating them [...] lies outside the realm of professional ethics" (Chesterman 2001, 147). Chesterman's (2019, 2021) writings, however, show a certain hesitation regarding a clearcut divide between personal ethics and 'professional' ethics. "Are translators professionally responsible for working towards a fairer world, or just personally responsible? Or both?" (2019, 673). Chesterman argues that this depends on the translator's *telos* and translation *skopos*[10]. He contends that codes of ethics need to consider text types and situational contexts, i.e., "the extratextual world" of the text (2019, 672). Hence, he reiterates his plea for a revision of the current codes and calls for the inclusion of virtue ethics into them "such as the striving for excellence – even when this means breaking code guidelines and fidelity norms" (ibid., 673). Chesterman's proposal of an isolated *Hieronymic Oath* with no proposition of change in the translator's work environment overlooks the modern institutional, economic, political and legislative constraints of the translator's work that might affect the practitioner's virtue ethics. I believe the apparent confusion in Chesterman's thought regarding ethics stems from his reliance on divergent traditions of ethics: virtue ethics in the Greek tradition and MacIntyre's virtue ethics that seek "internal goods" to the practice, on the one hand, and modern, formalized 'professional' ethics that seek "external goods" to the practice – to use MacIntyre's (2007/1981) words – on the other hand. These two traditions are incompatible and may lead to conflicting actions in many situations.

Nord (2005/1988, 1991, 1997), on the other hand – in an attempt to overcome the criticism of functionalist approaches for being over-guided by the function of the TT – stresses the ethics of *loyalty*. This principle mostly entails responsibility toward the ST author's communicative intentions, the initiator and the expectations of the readers/consumers of the TT, thus, allowing little room for the translator's visibility or agency, if any. Even the shifts required by the TT *skopos* should be honestly reported to the other involved agents. "[I]n such cases, they [translators] would be obliged, in view of their loyalty towards the ST sender, to specify exactly which ST aspects have been taken into account and which have been neglected" (2005, 33). The determinism Nord expresses regarding the author's intentions to which the translator needs to be loyal, as well as the one-size-fits-all readers' expectations, makes her approach utterly problematic.

Although Pym, Chesterman and Nord concede that full impartiality in translation is impossible, their theorizing of ethics is still embedded in a reductive view of *translation* as an ideal cultural encounter. The subordination of the translator's socio-political agency for the sake of 'professional' ethics as well as their overemphasis on the limited 'professional' circle of the translation show that – along with *equivalence* and *neutrality* – these more recent conceptualizations about ethics probably inform many a 'professional' code of ethics.

To summarize the foregoing analysis about ethics of translation, Nord, Chesterman and Pym stand at the opposite end of the position taken by the culturalist, hermeneutic and deconstruction scholars (including postcolonial and gender studies scholars). These functionalist scholars seem to undermine the fact that there are differences in world views and underestimate issues of power relations inherent to cultural encounters as well as the important role played by all translators in contributing to a better/worse world. On the opposite pole, the hermeneutics, culturalist and deconstructionist scholars, all call for ethics of translation that respect *difference* and emphasize the *particular*. The focus and perspectives of culturalist, deconstructionist and hermeneutic scholarship are, however, slightly different. If Berman, Steiner and Meschonnic call for the recognition of otherness and resistance to ethnocentrism in translation, Venuti reacts against cultural domination and stands by a greater visibility of the translator. Appiah and Robinson seek self-reflexivity and gradual change, whereas Inghilleri, Tymoczko and Baker call for more proactive engagement with (political) causes, and Cronin adds the ecological cause. Deconstructionists and their followers – postcolonialists and feminists – highlight uncertainty, hybridity and deconstruction of dominant discourses.

Following this TS research review – which is in no way exhaustive – I argue that TS alone cannot account for the multifaceted nature of translation ethics. As Drugan (2019, 251) rightly argues, "[t]he blossoming of research on translation ethics has if anything underscored the gaps in knowledge. Chief among these is the need for broader perspectives to illuminate ethical issues and approaches." TS does not possess a strong and private conceptual apparatus able to cover all aspects of ethics or to study ethics from various perspectives. In TS, we possess only fragments of moral knowledge, and our conceptual understanding of ethics is still in its infancy[11]. In order to 'appropriate' and accumulate these conceptual tools, the foundations need to be sought in disciplines where the study of ethics has a strong historical and conceptual background, mainly, in philosophy and, to a lesser extent, in sociology. "[P]hilosophy can bring an informed understanding of ethics to bear on translation theory and practice, and assist Translation Studies in making connections between translation, other professions and other academic disciplines" (ibid., 252). It is true that many insights about ethics are already inspired by other intellectual traditions, like hermeneutics, cultural studies, anthropology, postcolonial studies and gender studies. However, I believe that we still need to reach further and dig deeper into philosophical and sociological insights on the topic. The sociological turn in TS invites us to study the question of translator ethics in relation to the internal institutions (representative bodies) and external ones (employers/clients/states) in which translators operate and to examine the codes of ethics' orientations from a relational perspective in order to understand how these orientations are socially, institutionally and ideologically/politically driven. Moira Inghilleri (2012) remains one of the rare scholars who have combined philosophical insights with sociological perspectives (especially Bourdieusian ones), in addition to other disciplines, in her study of some of these relational interactions, with respect to interpreters' ethics. I believe the need for an interdisciplinary approach is even more persistent when studying the codes of ethics and practice of modern 'professional' translation. And this is the direction the current study tries to take. In the following chapter, I analyze the definition(s) of *translation* in the studied corpus. The repercussions of these definitions on the translator's capital and moral self are tackled in Part II and III, respectively.

Notes

1 Roland Barthes (1989/1957, 231) argues that *myth* "abolishes the complexity of human acts, gives them the simplicity of essence, removes all dialectics, does away with anything beyond the immediately visible, arranges a world without

58 *Professionalization, Ethics and* Translation *in Codified Ethics*

contradictions because it is devoid of depth; a world laid out in obviousness. Myth establishes happy clarity; things appear to mean all by themselves" (my translation).
2 See Hermans (2010/1996) for a similar account on the ideology of translation control that seeks to prevent its generative power of meaning.
3 Of course, shifts are not always unethical. Often times – to be moderate – practical and ethical requirements do call for such interventions.
4 www.spiegel.de/international/world/monsanto-papers-reveal-company-covered-up-cancer-concerns-a-1174233.html (Accessed on March 1, 2019).
5 I asked ChatGPT the question: "what are the main ethical challenges of using ChatGPT for translation?", and I received the following answer from the chatbot:

Using ChatGPT for translation presents several ethical challenges:
- *Accuracy and Reliability:* ChatGPT might not always provide accurate or reliable translations, especially for complex or nuanced content. Relying on it without proper human oversight could lead to misinformation or miscommunication.
- *Bias and Cultural Sensitivity:* If not trained carefully, ChatGPT could produce translations that reflect biases or cultural insensitivity. It might inadvertently perpetuate stereotypes or generate offensive content.
- *Privacy and Confidentiality:* When using ChatGPT for translation, sensitive information could be shared with the model. Ensuring data privacy and security becomes crucial, especially when dealing with personal, legal, or medical content.
- *Quality Control:* Monitoring and maintaining translation quality is challenging when using automated systems. Proper mechanisms for review and correction need to be in place to ensure that translations meet acceptable standards.
- *Job Displacement:* Widespread use of automated translation could impact professional translators' livelihoods. Finding a balance between the convenience of automation and preserving job opportunities is important.
- *Loss of Human Interaction:* Relying solely on automated translation may erode opportunities for cross-cultural learning and human interaction that come with traditional translation methods.
- *Unintended Use:* There's a risk that the technology might be used for unethical purposes, such as translating hate speech or extremist content.
- *Dependency on Technology:* Overreliance on machine translation could lead to a decline in language skills and discourage efforts to learn and communicate in other languages.
- To address these challenges, it's important to combine the capabilities of ChatGPT with human oversight, maintain transparency in the use of AI, continuously train the model to be culturally sensitive and unbiased, and ensure that the benefits of automation do not outweigh the potential negative consequences. (30 August 2023).

6. Note that Pym (2012, 159–163), nevertheless, supports 'interventions' when the intention is to enhance *cooperation*.
7. I use *functionalism* here to refer not only to *Skopos* theory, but in a wider sense, to scholarship driven mainly by the pragmatic functional purpose of the agents involved in the professional circle and that stresses responsibility only to the agents involved in the 'professional' circle .
8. It is worth noting that Abdallah's reading of Pym is selective as she finds him an excuse for not including some publications that advocate the translator's agency and activism. "Regrettably, as the book is a translation of the French original based on lectures given in 1994, some more recent and interesting contributions regarding the subject at hand have not been included. Here I refer, among others, to Koskinen 2000, Tymoczko 2007 and 2009, Inghilleri 2009, and the 2011 special issue on ethics in The Interpreter and Translator Trainer edited by Baker/Maier." But Pym cites Baker (2006, 2009) – to whom he reserves inappropriate and unfair criticism alluding to her activism as comparable to neo-Nazism – and Abdallah (2013) knows that well as she affirms in her introduction that Pym has included updates in the current English version published in 2012.
9. It is clear that both Chesterman and Pym use the terms 'profession'/'professional' in the mainstream way, in this analysis.
10. Chesterman's distinction between personal and 'professional' ethics can be contrasted with Inghilleri's (2012) outwardly similar distinction between 'role morality' and 'ordinary morality.' But Inghilleri, unlike Chesterman, clearly underscores the problems associated with the former morality, as it seeks to maintain "structural hierarchies of power and knowledge," and encourages moral unaccountability and "moral closure" (2012, 57).
11. This situation reminds us of MacIntyre's (2007/1981, 2) criticism of the language of morality we have in Modernity at large (and not only in TS). He argues that this language is in a state of "grave disorder" and that what we have in our possession is only "simulacra" of morality or fragments of a conceptual scheme.

3 The Concept of *Translation* in Codified Ethics

Most modern codes of ethics include two main elements: the "'official' definition" of the practice – to reuse Johnson's (2015, 106) terminology – and the relational aspects of the occupation. The corpus under study is no exception, in this regard. It includes the definition of *translation* and the translator's relations with peers and the other agents. In this chapter, I focus only on the first element – the effects of which will be later analyzed in Parts II and III. But before I delve into the analysis of the definition of *translation* in this corpus, I make a few brief general remarks about the structure and content of the studied documents.

Although the codes of ethics share many rules/principles regardless of the association's nature, function or country of origin, some differences can, nevertheless, be discerned at the level of form and discursive approaches. As far as form is concerned, the main difference between different national/provincial organizations' documents is the extent to which they explain the rules/principles they state. While some codes are very brief and posit the translators' duties – and sometimes rights – in concise articles (ATPP, SATI, ITAINDIA), others tend to illustrate each principle extensively (AUSIT). Another difference is the presence or absence of a preamble. Some associations like the AUSIT, ATIO, SFT and ITAINDIA have preambles, in which they stress the associations' mission, function and objectives, whereas others, like the ATPP or the SATI, do not. As far as speech act categories are concerned – following Searle's (1976, 1983) classification of illocutions – some codes adopt 'directive' acts (i.e., direct instructions on how to follow certain orders and behave in certain ways) as is the case of the ATIO, SATI, SATI and the SFT, while some others adopt 'commissive' acts, by which translators commit themselves to take certain courses of action in their work (ATPP, ITAINDIA).

At the level of content, there are recurrent themes in all codes of ethics. The difference, however, lies in emphasis and approaches to duties and rights. While some codes of ethics are purely deontological, i.e., duty-based, others adopt a mixed approach of duties and rights. Besides this variation, differences are also discerned in the degree of centredness on the translator (or the other agents) as far as relational aspects of the documents are concerned, as I explain in detail in Part II.

The documents of the two international organizations, namely the UNESCO Nairobi Recommendation and the FIT Translator's Charter, share many principles/rules of codes of ethics as well as some thematic aspects. Nevertheless, the two documents are somewhat different in some other respects, given their nature as well as the function of their issuing organizations. Both documents contain a detailed preamble that contextualizes and states their aims. In addition to the preamble, the FIT Translator's Charter contains 40 articles organized under five sections. The first three sections are about the "General Obligations of the Translator," the "Rights of the Translator" and the "Economic and Social Position of the Translator," respectively. The fourth section is about the "Translators' Societies and Unions," in which the Charter shows the importance of translator organizations and their functions. The last section is devoted to "National Organizations and the International Federation of Translators," in which the FIT calls for gathering in larger national associations and joining the international organization (FIT). The Nairobi Recommendation, on the other hand, contains 16 paragraphs under seven sections. The document mainly stresses the translator's rights. It, however, does not fully exclude the translator's obligations – a fact which is paradoxical, in form, as the purported function of the document is "the legal protection of translators and translations and the practical means to improve the status of translators." The main specificity of the Nairobi Recommendation is its audience. While all the other documents purportedly address the translating agent, the UNESCO document addresses the Member States, i.e., the political agent.

The studied codes of ethics are directive or commissive text types that list the elements that guarantee a certain conduct of all (individual and corporate) members of the respective associations. The aim is to regulate not only the interpersonal relations between the association member and their peers, employers and clients, but also to determine how members should understand *translation* and how they have to apply this understanding in practice. The definition of *translation* is generally made explicit in every such code as the foundation on which the translator's other behaviours draw. In some of the studied documents, the definition of *translation* and its characteristics are introduced in only one article without further elaboration (ATPP, SATI, ITAINDIA, ATIO, SFT, IAFET). In others, the definition is further explained in subsequent articles/statements (FIT, UNESCO and AUSIT). In this section, I analyze the main recurrent themes in the definition of *translation* in the corpus of codes of ethics and the FIT Translator's Charter as well the Nairobi Recommendation before analyzing their influence on the translator's symbolic power and morality in parts II and III, respectively.

The articles that define *translation* and what its practice entails are as follows:

- FIT Translator's Charter
  - ✓ Translation, being an intellectual activity, the object of which is the *transfer* of literary, scientific and technical texts from one language into another, imposes on those who practise it specific obligations *inherent in its very nature*. (Article 1, italics added)

  - ✓ Every translation shall be *faithful* and *render exactly the idea and form of the original* – this fidelity constituting both a *moral and legal obligation* for the translator. (Article 4, italics added)

  - ✓ A faithful translation, *however,* should not be confused with a literal translation, the fidelity of a translation not excluding an *adaptation* to make the form, the atmosphere and deeper meaning of the work *felt* in another language and country. (Articles 5, italics added)

- UNESCO Nairobi Recommendation
  - ✓ [T]he term "translation" denotes the transposition of a literary or scientific work, including technical work, from one language into another language, whether or not the initial work, or the translation, is intended for publication in book, magazine, periodical, or other form, or for performance in the theatre, in a film, on radio or television, or in any other media. (Paragraph 1a)

  - ✓ [...] organizations or associations might undertake, where national law permits, in particular, the following specific activities:
    (a) promote the adoption of standards governing the translating profession; such standards should stipulate in particular that the translator has a duty to provide a translation of high quality from both the linguistic and stylistic points of view and to guarantee that the translation will be a *faithful rendering of the original*. (Paragraph 7a, italics added)

- SATI Code of Ethics for Individual Members

  All members of the Institute shall undertake:
  To endeavour constantly to achieve the highest possible quality in respect of accuracy of rendering, terminological correctness, language and style. (italics added)[1]

The Concept of Translation *in Codified Ethics* 63

- SFT Deontological Code
  The translator shall work in accordance with the rules of the art by *faithfully* rendering the message of the document entrusted to them.
  (Article b, italics added, my translation)

- ATPP Code of Ethics
  As an ATPP translator and/or interpreter, I pledge to: [...] Ensure the *accuracy* of the translation and the *most accurate conveyance* of the ideas expressed in an interpretation, which are both *moral and legal obligations* for translators and interpreters. (Article 2, italics added)

- ITAINDIA Code of Professional Conduct for Service Providers
  I will endeavor to translate or interpret the original message *faithfully*, to satisfy *the needs of the end user(s)*. (Article A, italics added)

- ATIO Code of Ethics
  Members shall *faithfully* and *accurately* reproduce in the target language the closest *natural equivalent* of the source language message *without embellishment, omission or explanation*.
  (Article 2.2.1, italics added)

- AUSIT Code of Ethics and Code of Conduct
  ✓ [...] the Code obliges members to: maintain *professional detachment, impartiality, objectivity* and confidentiality.
  (Preamble, italics added)

  ✓ Impartiality: Interpreters and translators observe *impartiality* in all professional contacts. Interpreters remain *unbiased* throughout the communication exchanged between the participants in any interpreted encounter. Translators do not show *bias towards either the author of the source text or the intended readers* of their translation.

  Explanation: Interpreters and translators play an important role in facilitating parties who do not share a common language to communicate effectively with each other. They aim to ensure that the *full intent* of the communication is conveyed. Interpreters and translators are *not responsible for what the parties communicate, only for complete and accurate transfer* of the message. They do not allow bias to influence their performance; likewise they do *not soften, strengthen or alter* the messages being conveyed.
  (Code of Ethics, Article 4, italics added)

  ✓ Accuracy: Interpreters and translators use their best professional judgement in remaining *faithful* at all times to the meaning of texts and messages.

64   *Professionalization, Ethics and* Translation *in Codified Ethics*

> *Explanation*: Accuracy for the purpose of this Code means *optimal and complete message transfer* into the target language *preserving the content and intent* of the source message or text *without omission or distortion.*
> (Code of Ethics, Article 5, italics added)

- IAFET Code of Ethics
  All IAFET members shall:
  Carry out translating or interpreting tasks *thoroughly* and *responsibly*.
  (Article 2.1, italics added)

As is clear, the main recurrent themes in this compilation of articles defining *translation* and translation practice are 'faithfulness' and 'accuracy.' 'Faithfulness' and 'faithful translation' as such appear in six documents (FIT, UNESCO, ATIO, AUSIT, SFT, ITAINDIA), while 'accuracy' occurs in four documents (FIT, ATPP, SATI, AUSIT). 'Accuracy' and 'faithfulness' occur, also, in other wording, such as 'render exactly' (FIT). 'Equivalence/equivalent effect' is also stressed in two documents (ATIO, FIT). 'Impartiality' and 'objectivity' are highlighted in one code (AUSIT), and the same goes for the rules of 'detachment' and 'clarity' (AUSIT and SATI, respectively). The 'end user/client' is highlighted in two codes (AUSIT, ITAINDIA), and 'responsibility' is featured only in one code (IAFET) (see Table 3.1).

The highlighted rules of *faithfulness* and/or *accuracy*, which appear in all documents (except in the IAFET's), seem to be unconditional, i.e., they are to be applied in all circumstances to all text types, as nothing indicates otherwise. The FIT Translator's Charter and the ATPP Code of Ethics go even a step further when they consider 'faithfulness/accuracy' a moral and legal obligation for the translator. The FIT retracts in article 5 and counteracts the first affirmation in article 4 – as Chesterman (2016/1997, 185) also observes – by clarifying that faithful translation may include "adaptation." Chesterman argues that "[t]he FIT formulation seems to be based on an implicit belief in the overruling priority of equivalence, formal and stylistic equivalence included ('the idea *and form* of the original'). However, […] clause (5) […] counteracts this interpretation" (ibid., italics in original). This "contradiction" between the two clauses "remains unresolved," in Chesterman's view (ibid.). I believe that *Equivalent effect*, in Nida's (1964) terminology, is also discerned in the last part of article 5, which brings the meaning of 'adaptation' in the FIT definition closer to this notion. The preceding article 3 contains another paradoxical affirmation. The article reads, "[t]he translator shall refuse to give to a text an interpretation of which he/she does not approve" (FIT Translator's Charter, Article 3). While the FIT charter assumes 'faithfulness' to a given stable meaning in the 'original' (in article 4), in this article,

Table 3.1 Rules stressed in the defining articles of *translation* in the studied documents

	Faithfulness (6)	Accuracy (4)	Equivalence/ equivalent effect (2)	Objectivity (1)	Impartiality (1)	Detachment (1)	Clarity (1)	End user/ client (2)	Responsibility and thoroughness (1)
FIT	✓	✓							
UNESCO	✓		✓						
ATIO (Canada)	✓		✓						
ITAINDIA	✓								
SFT (France)	✓							✓	
SATI (South Africa)		✓					✓		
ATPP (Peru)		✓		✓	✓	✓			
AUSIT (Australia)	✓	✓						✓	
IAFET (Egypt)									✓

there is an implicit recognition that meaning in the 'original' is subject to different interpretations and, therefore, to different translations – a fact which complicates the legal clearance of the translator, as I explain later in this project. The FIT, however, seems to see differences in interpretations as rarities and exceptions rather than usual or common phenomena.

Not so differently, the ATIO code stresses 'faithfulness' and 'accuracy' in order to ensure 'equivalence.' In order to achieve 'equivalence,' the code underlines that "embellishment, omission or explanation" are not allowed under any circumstances (see Article 2.2.1). The ATIO is clearer and more categorical about these rules than the FIT, as is reiterated in the guides for the Standard Certification Examination in Translation of the Canadian Translators, Terminologists and Interpreters Council (CTTIC)[2], which controls the certification examination on their behalf. The main general standard that guides the grading of the translations of candidates for the certification examination of the CTTIC is 'faithfulness.' "A candidate is judged competent if the translation provided is *faithful*, idiomatic and requires *little or no revision*"[3] (Marker's guide, italics added). One wonders whether there is a translation that is definitive and that does not call for, probably, endless revisions. In the section, 'DOs and DON'Ts for prospective candidates,' the CTTIC, similarly, stresses questions of omissions and faithfulness. "DON'T *over-adapt* the texts. In trying to demonstrate your skill in paraphrasing, you may well *alter the tone and meaning* to such an extent that the translation will no longer be considered *faithful*"[4] (Candidate's guide, italics added). This statement somehow implies that adaptations are, to a certain extent, still acceptable (or probably just tolerable). Adaptations may be allowed as far as they do not *alter the tone and meaning* of the text. But it is noteworthy that this is an internal document addressed to candidates for certification and evaluators whereas the code is addressed to all agents (including clients and employers). Among us, as translators, we know that adaptation is inescapable, but we still tell others what they want to hear. One wonders, however, how one can adapt a textual material without shifting the tone (or even meaning) of a text, or how one can be certain of transporting the exact same meaning load and tone of the 'original.'

The AUSIT code of ethics stresses unconditional 'faithfulness' "*at all times* to the meaning of texts and messages" (Code of Ethics, Article 5, italics added). It, likewise, stresses 'accuracy,' which implies "*optimal and complete* message *transfer* into the target language *preserving the content and intent* of the source message or text *without omission or distortion*" (ibid., italics added). Like the FIT, in its annex section entitled 'Conduct issues specific to translators,' the AUSIT tries to retract the statement made in its code of ethics with a seemingly more flexible statement, which may allow some margin for adaptation in some circumstances. The statement reads: "[t]ranslators deliver a translation that *completely* and impartially renders the meaning and intention of the source text *within the parameters and requirements of the target language and culture* and is in keeping with *the purpose* specified in the commission received from the client/initiator" (Article T3, italics added). The paradox in this statement lies in its emphasis on two conflicting principles, i.e., 'completeness' of ST meanings and intentions, on the one hand, and adaptation to the target language/culture (stylistic) traditions and the *skopos* of the TT, on the other hand. We all know that the *skopos* of a translation may obviously require highlighting some aspects of the foreign text and leaving out others, thus, breaking the rules of 'completeness' and 'faithfulness.' Even if one presupposes that 'faithfulness' and 'completeness' are possible, they cannot always be the guiding principles for translations, following *Skopos* theory. They can be guiding principles only if the ST and the TT have the same function and purpose. While the ST is given prominence in 'faithful' translations, in *Skopos* theory, it is the audience and function of the TT that are more important determinants of translation strategies. Thus, the immediate question that comes to mind is: should the AUSIT rule of 'completeness' be sought only as far as it does not disturb the linguistic/cultural canons and/or the purpose/function of the TT? Apart from this ambiguity, the AUSIT seems to take the intention and meaning of the ST as clearly measurable and can be transported entirely and safely without loss or distortion.

Reading through Ozolins's paper that reports about the process of drafting the AUSIT code by the responsible working group shows the reductive view of *translation* as an accurate transfer won over in some debates. And this starts with the declared orientation that the code adopts the 'conduit model' (see Ozolins 2014). One educator had suggested to the working group what may seem a flexible understanding of 'accuracy.' This had led to the drafting of the article about 'accuracy' as follows:

> Interpreters and translators shall endeavour to provide accurate and complete renditions of the original. It must be noted that the meaning of accuracy depends on the *context of the situation*; for example, the type of interpreting (conference or community), the *translation brief*, etc. The concept of accuracy is a complex one that is dealt with in detail in training. Interpreters and translators should strive to obtain formal training before practising (Rewritten code, Second draft).
> (Ozolins 2014, 364, italics added)

Unfortunately, this wording was objected to on the grounds that the article as such is "unhelpful" because the concept is left unexplained, as Ozolins informs us (ibid.). The final version of the article was more 'explanatory' and posited some criteria for accuracy (ibid.).

Very much like the AUSIT, the ITAINDIA urges its members to translate faithfully and to cater to the end user's needs, at the same time. Unfortunately, the impossible combination of faithful translation and response to the end user's needs make such statements utterly paradoxical. Faithful translation may not meet the end user's needs, in many cases – if it is attainable at all.

The principles of 'faithfulness' and/or 'accuracy' are equally stressed by the SFT, the SATI, the ATPP and the UNESCO Nairobi Recommendation in less paradoxical statements, but probably in a more problematic way. These organizations are unequivocal regarding their principles of 'faithfulness' and/or 'accuracy' unlike the FIT, the ATIO, the ITAINDIA and the AUSIT, which, at least, show some awareness of the relativity of those principles, although in paradoxical terms.

Other related requirements emphasized as defining features of translation by one of the code of ethics, namely the AUSIT's, are impartiality, objectivity and detachment. Article 4 of the association's code underlines that "[...] [t]ranslators do not show *bias towards either the author of the source text or the intended readers* of their translation" (Code of Ethics, italics added). But, as we have learned from Baker (2006a), translators are embedded in narratives as in-between grounds are impossible (Tymoczko 2010/2003), and they may well have allegiances toward the 'original' author or the target audience in some types of translation, like political or media texts. Article 4 of the AUSIT code explains that "[...] [i]nterpreters and translators are *not responsible for what the parties communicate, only for complete and accurate transfer* of the message. They do not allow bias to influence their performance; likewise they do *not soften, strengthen or alter* the messages being conveyed" (ibid., italics added). These rules are, again, unconditional, regardless of the situation or the translation/text type. "Professional detachment is required for interpreting and translation assignments *in all situations*" (Code of Conduct, Article 4.1, italics added). These articles replicate Pym's denial of any personal responsibility on the part of the translator regarding the content they transmit as they are mere reporters of other people's enunciations (2012, 62).

'Clarity' is another rule highlighted as a defining characteristic of *translation*, besides 'accuracy,' in one code of ethics, namely the SATI in its mission statement. The statement reads, "[...] the institute endeavours to: [...] [p]romote excellence in translation and related fields, as well as clarity of thought and expression." This proclaimed goal replicates Chesterman's (2001, 2016/1997, 2019, 2021) insistence on the virtue of excellence, as well as 'clarity' as a way of promoting 'rational communication.' But as Berman (1999/1985) argues, clarifications risk appropriating the Other to fit one's canons, and, therefore, distorting their representation. Also, 'clarity' may foster ease with one's frames of perception as the one and only (see Eaglestone 2005). Following the latter scholars, translating the Other as unclear and different is the most ethical decision. But both positions (Chesterman/AUSIT's and Berman/Eaglestone's) are overdeterminant. They both overlook the fact that the rules they advocate, respectively, are not *a priori* ethical or unethical. That all depends on the context and the encounter.

The IAFET is the only association that avoids defining *translation* or prescribing a way to translate. Its code describes *translation* as a 'thorough' and 'responsible' endeavour. However, it is not clear what the IAFET implies by these two qualities, nor whether the omission of the mainstream definitions (such as faithfulness or accuracy) is intentional. Reviewing the association's "Introduction to the IAFET Certification Examination," I found that the association requires that "*[e]verything integral to the source text is included in the target text* and nothing that is not implicitly or explicitly stated by the author is added" (italics added)[5]. In order to ensure this level of achievement, the examiners expect candidates to produce an accurate analysis of the ST. "Accurate analysis of the source text ensures that *the target text reflects the view, argument, or presented information on all levels (text, sentence, and word)*" (ibid.). As is clear, although the IAFET does not use classical terms (such as 'faithfulness,' 'accuracy' or equivalence) in its code of ethics, it requires complete transfer of the view, argument and information of the ST, even at the *word* level, regardless of the situation or the translation type. On the other hand, some of the wording used by the IAFET reflects a certain awareness of the problematic nature of the classical notions. For example, it clarifies that acquaintance with the different strategies of translation is demonstrated by the candidates if the "[v]iew, argument, and information are presented *appropriately* for the target culture" (ibid., italics added). Also, regarding the transfer of meaning, the IAFET seems less dogmatic about its completeness and sameness. "Idioms in the source text are rendered so as to convey a *comparable* meaning in the target text" (italics added). In sum, the contradictions in the IAFET statements clearly show that it is unable to dismiss the rule 'faithfulness,' despite some awareness to its implausibility at all times.

As discussed above, the studied documents generally emphasize the monosemy of the concept of *translation* and the measurability of the practice, which, therefore, "*imposes on those who practise it specific obligations inherent in its very nature*," as the FIT Translator's Charter indicates in Article 1. Translation has a clear nature and *one* meaning is (i.e., faithful transfer of meaning). Therefore, it yields clear and 'specific obligations,' following the mother organization of translator associations. The concept of *translation* as 'faithfulness,' 'accuracy' or 'equivalence,' adopted by the studied organizations, assumes the capacity to determine the exact meaning and intent of the ST in all circumstances. *Translation* is understood as a rendering of the author's intentions, in disregard of the polysemous nature of language and the differences in perceptions of reality in different cultures and by different individuals. The defining articles on *translation* overlook the difficulty of being certain about someone's intentions in their textual material, let alone being able to exactly transfer these intentions into a different context. These documents ignore the fact that the meaning of a text is an individual's construction and that the contexts of the ST and TT affect their (different) meaning constructions (see Tymoczko 2007). As Tymoczko (2007, 284) rightly argues,

> [b]ecause a source text and its translation emerge from and function within different contexts, it follows *ipso facto* that they have different meanings. If for no other reason than context, therefore, it is illusory to imagine that meaning preservation or transfer can or should be the goal of translation.
>
> (Tymoczko 2007, 284)

Since every text has a "surplus of meanings," the translator has to make decisions about which information to reproduce in the TT depending on their performative aims (ibid. 288). The responsibility of the translator, then, is the judicious selection of meaning, following these aims. According to Karin Littau (2010), this proliferation of meaning in translation is a gain in itself. Littau writes, "[t]his shift 'from the one to the many,' to borrow Matei Calinescu's (1991) phrase, is also a shift from loss to gain, a shift from an unattainable equivalence to an unstoppable proliferation" (2010, 440). Understood as such, the translator is a meaning constructor, rather than a meaning transferor. This is because there is *not* only one predetermined stable meaning to be transferred from the ST to TT. Every text is inexhaustible; it may have numerous interpretations and "a surplus of meaning," in Tymoczko's (2007, 288) words, and it, therefore, calls for, and can have, various translations. "Meaning in communication, and in translation for that matter, is therefore not an invariable, but always the result of a selective and reconstructive process determined by context" (Guldin 2016, 49). Translation, then, can be seen as a process of decision-making that involves the selection and construction of meaning in a TT that has a relation with a ST. In other words, it is a process of deconstruction and construction. The translator selects meanings following their own reading[6], according to the context of translation and its *performative* aims, and invests those meanings in the new context. "Translators both define the meaning of the source text and construct the meaning of the target text. In both roles translators are *meaning makers*" (Tymoczko 2007, 304, italics added). And, the translator, as a meaning maker, is, of course, influenced by many contextual factors, especially their own narrative and political/ideological orientations (ibid., 295-6-7-8). Hence, the best a translator can seek is *similarity in difference* (Tymoczko's 2007) as *sameness* is neither fully achievable nor always desirable. The IAFET gets a little close (although still timidly) to this understanding of *translation* as similarity in difference (to its 'original') when it stipulates that "[i]dioms in the source text are rendered so as to convey a *comparable* meaning in the target text" (Introduction to the IAFET Certification Examination, italics added). But unfortunately, this relativity awareness of untranslatability is contradicted by seeking to include in the TT "[e]verything integral to the source text"[7].

As meaning makers, translators are original creators who generate new meanings from two different matrices and distant views; they are bisociative thinkers and nomads, in Cronin's thought.

> Languages are uniquely constituted by their differences so that translation as an operation involving two or more languages has *ipso facto* considerable bisociative potential. It can be argued that, in teaching translation studies, more time has to be devoted to highlighting the epistemic specificity of translation as expressed in the concepts of distance, the nomadic and the bisociative.
>
> (Cronin 2003, 127)

Unfortunately, having ignored this bisociative potential of translation, all the definitions discussed above can be placed under the semantic fields of passivity, mechanicalness or transparency. Regardless of the interpretations the defining organizations might have of their own definitions, the vocabulary associated with *translation*/translators in those definitions may imply fixity, sterility and inactivity (e.g., faithfulness); invisibility (e.g., transfer, impartiality, detachment, objectivity); or transparency and certainty (e.g., accuracy) to the outside agents and the public at large. All the definitions neglect the translator's movement, nomadism, creativity and agency. Cronin writes, "[t]he vocabulary of 'fidelity' and 'infidelity' is after all strongly linked to the notions of licit fixity and illicit movement" (ibid.). And 'faithfulness' or 'equivalence' is linked with an understanding of *translation* as "a mechanistic process," in Koskinen's view (2000b). As such, translation is seen as "an invisible practice" (Venuti 1992, 1), which is stigmatized by "likening it to manual as opposed to intellectual labor" (ibid.). And with such an understanding of *translation* "are effaced the translator's dual activities of reading and (re)writing. The translator is understood to be a servant, an invisible hand mechanically turning the words of one language into another. The translation is considered to be a copy and not a creative utterance," as Barbara Godard tells us (1990, 91).

Theories of meaning and reception theory as well as postpositivist TS pronouncements, which all demonstrate that translation is a much more complex process than the reductive definition imposed in the studied documents, may seem too 'abstract' (for some translators) or may seem specific to only certain types of translation, mainly, literary translation. One may argue that these organizations are mainly concerned with translation of pragmatic texts and, thus, advance only the definition that concerns these types of texts/translations. But many pragmatic translation practices are anything but faithful to the 'original.' Localization, multimodal translation, legal translation, news adaptations, news translation are all instances of practices that require *adaptation, change* and *transformation*. The stark evidence that translation is transformative – far from 'abstraction' and far from other historical/cultural evidence – comes, thus, from today's practices, in which many translators are involved and which many clients/employers demand.

The principles of faithfulness, accuracy, equivalence, detachment and so on highlighted in most studied documents all show that these documents are source-oriented. But, as mentioned, many practices today are clearly target-oriented and anything but faithful. These new practices involve *transformation* in order to adapt to cultural, ideological and technical constraints (in Diaz-Cintas's (2012) terms about audiovisual translation), and to the performative functions they seek. Tymoczko writes,

> at present translation does not necessarily constitute reported speech but can be a new utterance whose primary purpose is an independent statement about or reference to the subject matter itself. Thus translation is often *performative, productive* and *discursive*. Localizations, advertisements and other types of contemporary commercial translations exemplify this shift, as do many news reports, political statements and official translations of nations or governmental bodies [...] It is in this sense that translation practice is shifting from the interpretive to the *performative* in many circumstances.
> (Tymoczko 2009, 404, italics added)

The recent technological developments have shown that this conceptualization of *translation* as a faithful transfer is utterly problematic. Tymoczko argues that "terms like *localization* indicate a movement away from the old transfer hypothesis that has dominated Eurocentric thinking about translation since the late Middle Ages" (2009, 401, italics in original). These new practices – which are not rare or insignificant in 'professional translation' – indicate that a big portion of translations made today entail considerable shifts from the source material, and therefore, go beyond the illusions of equivalence, accuracy, faithfulness or impartiality highlighted in the studied corpus. As Koskinen (2000a, 14) rightly puts it, "contemporary understanding of the process of translation is [...] strikingly different from the dichotomy of faithful versus free translation: choice, conscious or not, is now rather seen as an essential feature of *all* translation" (italics added). Processes of decisions, shifts, selections, choices, strategizing are all part of the translation process regardless of its type, Koskinen argues.

Choices and transformations for *pragmatic* reasons are, of course, not the only types of shifts found in contemporary non-literary translation practices. Shifts and transformations are prevalent in some types of translation (beyond literary translation) for (un)*ethical* reasons. Translation of political texts and news adaptation, for example, undergo transformations due to issues of ideology, power, representation and ethics. These types of translations are even more ethically taxing than literary texts as they may, of course, be more ideologically loaded. Also, the most technical text may undergo important shifts for ethical reasons if they, for example, seem to have hazardous implications on life on this planet.

Another aspect of today's translations ignored in the definition of *translation* in the studied corpus is the shift in the translator's role and identity, resulting from their interaction with emerging technologies. In many of today's practices, the translator's very self-concept is changing. With Machine Translation (MT) and Computer-Aided Translation (CAT) tools, the translator may be seen as a (post)editor (see Ignacio Garcia 2009). Cronin (2003) has argued that the translating agents in the new millennium should be construed

> as translational cyborgs who can no longer be conceived of independently of the technologies with which they interact. In other words, it is not simply a question of translators dealing with material from technical and scientific disciplines; it is that their very identity is being altered by an externalization of translation functions.
> (Cronin 2003, 112)

In addition to overlooking these identity shifts in their defining articles of *translation*, the documents under study ignore the fact that the classical source/target dichotomy is itself now being challenged. For example, many national and international multilingual employers obliterate this distinction. The documents of the European Union (EU), for instance, stand as equal 'originals' in the languages of all Member States in order to advance the ideal of 'linguistic equality' (Tymoczko 2009, 404, Koskinen 2000b). Similarly, in localized content, the distinction between ST and TT is not always easy, nor relevant (Tymoczko 2009, 402).

Against these new realities (as well as old/other practices[8]), i.e., the proliferation of transformative practices, the shifts in the translator's identity and the increasingly blurry line between the ST and TT, the studied organizations insist on considering *translation* a faithful transfer of meaning. Faithfulness and its associates (like equivalence, accuracy, impartiality, and objectivity) imply order, control and clarity of standards. And we know that the very existence of such organizations is to set boundaries, control the 'profession/professionals' and establish order and unity of practice. Hence, any change in these (old new) realities would imply the questioning of this fictitious order. The recognition of plurality of practices would make the principle of *accountability* (one of the main means of self-control) implausible as this would always give the translator means to evade institutional control. Faithfulness is, thus, a myth that disguises this disturbing plurality and this inherent 'pathological' disorder of the translation 'profession.' It is, thus, a mere scarecrow for the containment and control of the translator, on the one hand, and an insurance policy to the outsider agents, on the other hand. This is, of course, due to the suspicion of wrongness in 'unfaithfulness' and the fear of the non-containment of the 'free' translator's behaviour and choices. Fidelity is reassuring while transformations and choices are threatening as they allow 'disorder' and 'dishonest' practices. Cronin (2003) writes,

> [i]f translation has been faithful to anything over the centuries, it has been to the notion of fidelity itself. From Philo Judaeus to Vladimir Nabokov, the company of the faithful has been numerous. The stock commonplaces of literary pundits all bear on the dubious textual morals of translators. The ritual invocation of *belles infidèles, traduttori, traditori* and the omnipresent dictum of poetry being what gets lost in the translation suggest that translators are basically not to be trusted and that translation is a somewhat dishonest enterprise.
> (Cronin 2003, 68, italics in original)

Discussing the historical origins of this imposition of 'faithfulness,' Koskinen (2000a), similarly, argues that

> [f]aithful translation was the one and only, while free rewritings were many, and all of them 'wrong' and suspect. The assumption that free will always produces [sic] wrong choices, that unmonitored freedom always verges on licentiousness, led to the conclusion that translators' freedom needs to be bridled in order to prevent them from using it to do wrong. To start making choices would lead to infidelity.
> (Koskinen 2000a, 13)

But choices are demanded by contemporary patrons/clients, although they may not admit that out loud. Like translators, localizers, media patrons and audiovisual translation patrons, for example, all know very well that what they need are transformative translations rather than faithful ones. But the irony is that the illusion of 'faithfulness' is not only claimed by patrons/clients – many of whom oppose it in practice – but reinforced by translators and some translation scholars/critics as well. Tymoczko (2009, 404) contends that "many translators and translation scholars also perceive these shifts as threats and sources of anxiety because they seem to undermine all that people have learned about translation as transfer, as well as about the importance of fidelity, the concept of equivalence, the sacredness of the word, and so on." In a Barthian sense, these shifts constitute threats to the established happy *myth* about *translation*. They are a source of ambivalence, confusion, disturbance and uneasiness for many agents (including translators), as I discuss in Parts II and III. Contemporary developments have unveiled these illusions without proposing alternative myths that can get established easily and embraced unanimously. Translators are rather left to face this perplexing complexity and to get accustomed to its perpetually shifting demands. The paradox is that, in their discourse, they abstain from voicing it and rather claim to follow the myth of 'faithfulness.' 'Faithfulness' seems to be more relaxing to the other agents as it is a *shared myth*. Disorder and plurality are (temporarily) disguised as they are unduly seen as embarrassing.

A plural open concept, like Tymoczko's (2007) "cluster concept" – which can encompass varied meanings of *translation* and, thus, include a variety of types and styles of translations – may seem very problematic to translator associations. On the one hand, this indeterminate, fuzzy concept may be seen as unable to sell the *uncertain* (possibly deviant) manufactured product (that is, translation). On the other hand, it may not guarantee allegiance to supreme principles shared by all members of the institution. Most importantly, an open concept of *translation* may make the translator associations unviable. We know that these associations' very raison d'être is to control the practitioners and establish order in the occupation. Openness to other definitions is synonymous to plurality in practices, and may, therefore, imply 'disorder.' This 'out of control' situation is liable to create messiness and chaos – which the associations were, in fact, created to contain, to begin with.

Regardless of their different natures, functions and geographical locations, the studied organizations all underline the rule of 'faithfulness' and/or other associated rules in their documents. This is despite the recent upheavals in the translation industry. The major shifts in today's practices and in the role of the translator as well as the irrelevance of the ST/TT dichotomy in some cases, in addition to the cultural/historical differences in the practice of translation stand as stark proof of the inadequacy of the definition imposed in the studied documents. This is not to mention the fact that this understanding of *translation* obscures its ideological, political, ethical and socio-cultural dimensions – which the cultural turn has underlined. Problematizing the principles of 'faithfulness' and its associates does not mean, however, that they are *a priori* unethical or always completely inappropriate. What I mean is that they are illusionary ideals that are hardly achievable. Also, fidelity is problematic as it "makes claims about its exclusive relationship with moral correctness, when other approaches are also ethically viable" (Clifford 2004, 110). Also, in many cases, fidelity and its associates are undesirable as they either do not accomplish the *performative* function of the translated material (as required by the commissioner) or they fail in ethical appropriateness. This reductive definition will definitely have repercussions on the translator's perceived status in the eyes of other agents as well as their own self-concept, and will ultimately affect their moral self. These issues will be discussed thoroughly in parts II and III, respectively.

Notes

1 The articles of the SATI code of ethics are not enumerated.
2 The CTTIC gathers seven provincial associations of translators in Canada, among them, the ATIO, and adopts a national standardized examination on their behalf.
3 https://atio.on.ca/wp-content/uploads/2019/03/CTTIC-Markers-Guide-En-2019.pdf/ Accessed on September 25, 2019.
4 https://atio.on.ca/wp-content/uploads/2019/03/CTTIC-Certification-Exam-Candidates-Guide-2019.pdf/ Accessed on September 25, 2019.
5 https://iafet.cyrillabs.com/wp-content/uploads/2019/01/Text-placeholder-1.pdf/ Accessed on October 25, 2019.
6 If we follow reader-response or reception theorists, translation as reading involves the reader/translator's active supplementation and generation of meanings (see for example Barthes 1984/1968, Iser 1978, Eagleton 2008, Hall 1980).
7 https://iafet.cyrillabs.com/wp-content/uploads/2019/01/Text-placeholder-1.pdf/ Accessed on October 25, 2019.
8 See Tymoczko (2007) for a review of practices of translation from different cultures and times that involve transformation (see also Trivedi (2006) for a review of Indian practices of translation).

Part II
The Translator's *Capital* in Codified Ethics

This part investigates the ways in which the translator's *capital* is affected by the discourse of codes of ethics. It examines the different forms of the translator's capital as reflected in the corpus under study and analyzes the extent to which they convert (or not) into symbolic recognition, manifest in *collegiate control* of their profession or in *copyright* as cultural workers. The following chapter lays out some of the basic tenets in Bourdieu's reflexive sociology that will be deployed later on in the chapters devoted to the translator's (self)-positioning in the studied documents.

4 Basic Tenets of Bourdieu's Reflexive Sociology

Of particular interest to my analysis is the concept of *capital* and its intertwined concepts of *field* and *habitus*. Although the focus is on the notion of capital, it is impossible to dissociate it from the other two notions.

4.1 Habitus

Following Pierre Bourdieu (1990b), *habitus* is a set of durable embodied dispositions that the individual internalizes in their living history and that informs their choices and actions – or in Bourdieu's terminology – organizes their 'social practice.' He defines *habitus* as

> systems of durable, transposable dispositions, structured structures predisposed to function as structuring structures, that is, as principles which generate and organize practices and representations that can be objectively adapted to their outcomes without presupposing a conscious aiming at ends or an express mastery of the operations necessary in order to attain them. Objectively "regulated" and "regular" without being in any way the product of obedience to rules, they can be collectively orchestrated without being the product of the organizing action of a conductor.
>
> (Bourdieu 1990b, 53)

Bourdieu's understanding of *habitus* is, thus, characterized by its structuring and structured nature. But practices that are informed by *habitus* are not conscious or calculated. By this, he means that while choices can be made, the principles that determine the choices are already in place, i.e., the game is played following pre-established rules. The apparent determinism of Bourdieu's *habitus* may be disappointing to proponents of individual transformations and the reshuffling of social relations. However, a careful reader of Bourdieu's concepts soon realizes the transformational

DOI: 10.4324/9781032713557-7

potential in the *habitus*. Bourdieu (1990b) does not rule out rational decisions altogether but rather reduces their significance, in reaction to "rational actor" theory. Responding to the criticism of his determinism, Bourdieu (1990a, 13) affirms: "I wanted to emphasize that this 'creative,' active, inventive capacity was not that of a transcendental subject in the idealist tradition, but that of an acting agent." Answering Loic Wacquant's question in *An Invitation to Reflexive Sociology* about whether the notion of *habitus* rules out "strategic choice and conscious deliberation," he replies, "[n]ot at all. [...] The lines of action suggested by habitus may very well be accompanied by a strategic calculation of costs and benefits, which tends to carry out at a conscious level the operations that habitus carries out in its own way" (Bourdieu and Wacquant 1992, 131). Times of crisis constitute a good example of circumstances where "rational choice" may reign, Bourdieu points out (ibid.).

4.2 Field

The second important notion for my analysis is *field*. This concept can be understood as the structure that defines the rules of the game as well as the relations between the agents within its arena. Bourdieu defines the notion of field as follows:

> In analytic terms, a field may be defined as a network, or a configuration, of objective relations between positions. These positions are objectively defined, in their existence and in the determinations they impose upon their occupants, agents or institutions, by their present and potential situation (*situs*) in the structure of the distribution of species of power (or capital) whose possession commands access to the specific profits that are at stake in the field, as well as by their objective relation to other positions (domination, subordination, homology, etc.).
> (Bourdieu and Wacquant 1992, 97, italics in original)

Bourdieu insists on the conflictual nature of the field and the play of power dynamics as a result of the agents' permanent competition over the available stakes within it. "When we speak of a *field* of position-takings, we are insisting that what can be constituted as a *system* for the sake of analysis is not the product of a coherence-seeking intention or an objective consensus [...] but the product and prize of a permanent conflict" (1993, 34, italics in original). A very important notion in Bourdieu's analysis is what he calls "the field of power." By this, he refers to the field located at the top of the hierarchy of other fields in the general social world.

The field of power is a field of forces structurally determined by the state of the relations of power among forms of power, or different forms of capital. It is also, and inseparably, a field of power struggles among the holders of different forms of power, a gaming space in which those agents and institutions possessing enough specific capital (economic or cultural capital in particular) to be able to occupy the dominant positions within their respective fields confront each other using strategies aimed at preserving or transforming these relations of power.
(Bourdieu 1996, 264–265)

The forces of these struggles depend on what Bourdieu (1996, 265) calls "'exchange rate' (or 'conversion rate')" of the different forms of capital into symbolic power, i.e., they depend on which form of capital (economic, social or cultural) is more valuable when converted into symbolic power. For instance, intellectual producers or professors, who have considerable cultural capital, on the one hand, and industrialists, who have considerable economic capital, on the other hand, compete in the field of power for domination, each of them using their own powerful capital. The struggle is settled in favour of one side depending on whose capital (economic or cultural) converts at a higher rate into a symbolic power. Most importantly, the struggle is over the very representation of these different forms of capital or the value attributed to each of them, i.e., the competition is over which capital should be imposed as more important. It is a struggle over the "power to dictate *the dominant principle of domination* [...] a struggle over *the legitimate principle of legitimation* and, inseparably, the legitimate mode of reproduction of the foundations of domination" (ibid., italics in original). Power, thus, does not seem to be "a brute force" that is arbitrary; it is justified, and is, thus, *recognized* as legitimate and natural. In other words, in obliterating its arbitrariness, power becomes well established. The role of social science is, thus, to uncover its arbitrariness or "pathological character" (Bourdieu 1996, 3).

4.3 Capital

The notion of *field* is inextricably linked to the notion of *capital*, for it is the struggle for the latter and its use in subsequent struggles that characterize the dynamics within the field, and hence determine the different agents' positioning within it. Bourdieu defines capital as "accumulated labor (in its materialized form or its 'incorporated,' embodied form) which, when appropriated on a private, i.e., exclusive, basis by agents or groups of agents, enables them to appropriate social energy in the form of reified or living labor" (1986, 241, italics in original). The competing agents in a field mobilize their forces to either maintain or transform the established relations of force depending on their position in the field. "[E]ach of the agents commits the force (the capital) that he [sic] has acquired through the previous struggles to strategies that depend for their general direction on his [sic] position in the power struggle, that is, on his [sic] specific capital," Bourdieu (1990a, 143) points out when discussing the literary field. The appropriation of a significant (rare) capital endows the appropriating agent with the power to impose their agendas and laws which, in turn, guarantee the reproduction of this capital within a certain field. Bourdieu (1986) proposes three forms of capital: economic, cultural and social. Any of these three forms of capital can convert into a title of nobility or prestige, which Bourdieu calls "symbolic capital."

Economic capital is purely material and the most tangible and clearest form of capital. It can simply take the form of money or property.

Cultural capital, on the other hand, is more complex and "can exist in three forms: in the *embodied* state, i.e., in the form of long-lasting dispositions of the mind and body; in the *objectified* state, in the form of cultural goods (pictures, books, dictionaries, instruments, machines, etc.) [...]; and in the *institutionalized* state," in the form of educational qualifications (ibid., 243, italics in original). The *embodied cultural* capital is acquired in a long process of *personal* embodiment that is usually costly in terms of emotions and economics. It is a labour of acquisition/learning and enculturation that involves sacrifice and costs a lot of time. This long time "must be invested personally by the investor [...] it cannot be done at second hand" or delegated (ibid., 244, italics in original). The embodied state of cultural capital – when significant and scarce – has the specificity of being easily recognized and, thus, easily convertible into symbolic power. Besides, it may yield important economic profits.

The *objectified cultural* capital, on the other hand, refers to the material objects and media of cultural production that an agent possesses. Its value, however, largely depends on the agent's embodied cultural capital (ibid., 246–247). Legal ownership of means of production (like machines, computers, instruments, books, paintings) requires simply economic capital. Their use, nevertheless, requires means of consumption, i.e., technical knowledge on how to appropriate them and efficiently operate them to one's benefit. "Thus cultural goods can be appropriated both materially – which presupposes economic capital – and symbolically – which presupposes cultural capital" (ibid., 247). Therefore, the owners of mere economic capital need access to embodied cultural capital by *proxy* to appropriate and use cultural goods. These agents need to secure this form of capital by paying its holders for their services. The latter use their scarce expertise and esoteric knowledge to increase their *collective* power. However, the holders of economic capital may manage to set them in competition with each other through the very logic of recruitment competition, and, therefore, may decrease their imposing power (ibid.).

The *institutionalized cultural* capital, distinctively, has the power to "secure belief" and "impose recognition," as Bourdieu puts it (1986, 248). It is a "legal," "conventional" and "constant" "certificate of cultural competence" for its holder (ibid.). "It institutes cultural capital by collective magic, just as, according to Merleau-Ponty, the living institute their dead through the ritual of mourning" (ibid.). Academic qualifications are, in many cases, the measurement tool of the economic worth of any cultural capital (ibid.).

The possession of a complex cultural capital can convert into a significant symbolic and material power not only within the field of cultural production but also within the field of power. Holders of a rare cultural capital like cultural producers, professors and professionals (e.g., doctors and lawyers), when recognized and consecrated, hold a position within the field of power, and are, therefore, dominant agents within the larger social field. Intellectuals as cultural producers are recognized thanks to their ability to uncover zones of mystery and make people believe their revelations.

> Cultural producers hold a specific power, the properly symbolic power of showing things and making people believe in them, of revealing, in an explicit, objectified way the more or less confused, vague, unformulated, even unformulable experiences of the natural world and the social world, and of thereby bringing them into existence. They may put their power at the service of the dominant. They may also, in the logic of their struggle within the field of power, put their power at the service of the dominated in the social field taken as a whole.
> (Bourdieu 1990a, 146)

Despite their positioning within the field of power, cultural agents (like professors or writers) are dominated in the higher social field as their cultural capital converts to symbolic power at a lower rate than the capital held by the economic or political agents (Bourdieu 1990a, 145, Bourdieu 1998b, 44, see also Bourdieu 1986, 1993, 1996). Thus, they have unstable and sometimes divided allegiances to either the dominant or the dominated depending on their own interests and positions (1990a, 145).

A less concrete type of capital than cultural capital, in Bourdieu's analysis, is *social* capital. It is less tangible, at the outset, as it does not depend on the individual's material possessions or knowledge, but on their "possession of a durable network" or "membership in a group" (1986, 248). Bourdieu defines social capital as "the aggregate of the actual or potential resources which are linked to possession of a durable network of more or less institutionalized relationships of mutual acquaintance and recognition" (ibid.). Thus, being part of an influential group enhances an individual's power. It provides the member with "the collectivity-owned capital" (ibid., 249). Network membership has the power of a "multiplier effect" on the individually owned capital (ibid.). These social relations are usually consolidated and sustained through "material and/or symbolic exchanges" (ibid. 249) – gifts being the clearest example of these mutual exchanges. Networking is, thus, a set of conscious or unconscious "investment strategies" in useful relationships, which may – in the short or long run – secure material and/or symbolic profits. The available resources and (symbolic and/or material) benefits, however, depend on the size of the network *and* on the volume of capital each of the agents in this network possesses (ibid., 249). If the network is large and its members prestigious, the benefits are usually significant. In contrast, if the network is small and its members uninfluential, the benefits are insignificant. Bourdieu also points out that social capital, as a network of relations, does not provide the necessary power or the sought services instantly. It "cannot act instantaneously, at the appropriate moment, unless they have been established and maintained for a long time, as if for their own sake, and therefore outside their period of use" (ibid., 252). Unlike the transparency and immediacy of economic exchange, investment in sociability is usually long-term and the reaping of its benefits requires a time lag and concealment of self-interest. Because of these properties of social investment, the results are never guaranteed or certain. Social investment "necessarily entails the risk of ingratitude," Bourdieu tells us (ibid. 254).

Social networks have consensual boundaries and identities, which are the responsibility of all members to protect and respect.

> Each member of the group is thus instituted as a custodian of the limits of the group: because the definition of the criteria of entry is at stake in each new entry, he [sic] can modify the group by modifying the limits of legitimate exchange through some form of misalliance.
>
> (ibid. 250)

Conditions of entry are, thus, restricted because of the fear of "redefinition's, "alteration" or "adulteration" of this identity and/or boundaries by any new entrant.

Networks tend to have "institutionalized forms of delegation" (ibid. 251), i.e., one agent or a small group of agents represents the entire group and therefore possesses the concentrated capital that they supposedly use to defend the group's interests. The aim of this diffuse delegation is for the delegate member to defend the weak members' 'honour' as a way of defending the group's 'collective honour' and also to expel the 'wrongdoers' or the 'embarrassing individuals' as a way of shielding the group from disrepute (ibid.). The representative agent(s) may function in an exclusionist manner against some of their peer members. "One of the paradoxes of delegation is that the mandated agent can exert on (and, up to a point, against) the group the power which the group enables him [sic] to concentrate" (ibid.).

Conversion of the Different Forms of Capital into Symbolic Power

The three forms of capital (economic, cultural and social) may convert into symbolic capital, which is in turn reconvertible into economic and social forms of capital. In *Practical Reason: On the Theory of Action*, Bourdieu defines symbolic capital as

> any property (any form of capital whether physical, economic, cultural or social) when it is perceived by social agents endowed with categories of perception which cause them to know it and to recognize it, to give it value. [...] More precisely, symbolic capital is the form taken by any species of capital whenever it is perceived through categories of perception that are the product of the embodiment of divisions or of oppositions inscribed in the structure of the distribution of this species of capital (strong/weak, large/small, rich/poor, cultured/uncultured).
> (Bourdieu 1998a, 47)

Symbolic capital is granted as a "credit" and a "credence" by those agents who *recognize* the value of a certain property (or capital) as rare and valuable (1990b, 120). It is a "doxical submission" of the granter to certain propositions that are in total agreement with their (mental) predispositions (1998a, 102–103). Bourdieu (1998a) underlines the "magical power" of shared beliefs and categories of perception between the grantee and the granter in the efficiency of symbolic power. Symbolic capital acts like "a veritable *magical power*: a property which, because it responds to socially constituted 'collective expectations' and beliefs, exercises a sort of action from a distance, without physical contact. An order is given and obeyed: it is a quasi-magical act" (ibid., 102, italics in original). Because symbolic capital derives its power and efficiency from the shared *doxa* – which is the taken for granted, pre-reflexive beliefs – between the beneficiary agents and the bestowing agents, Bourdieu (1990b, 1996, 1998a) warns us that this form of capital may generate what he calls "symbolic violence."

> Like the theory of magic, the theory of symbolic violence rests on a theory of belief or, more precisely, on a theory of the production of belief, of the work of socialization necessary to produce agents endowed with the schemes of perception and appreciation that will permit them to perceive and obey injunctions inscribed in a situation or discourse.

86 The Translator's Capital *in Codified Ethics*

The belief I am describing is not an explicit belief, possessed explicitly as such in relation to a possibility of nonbelief, but rather an immediate adherence, a doxical submission to the injunctions of the world which is achieved when the mental structures of the one to whom the injunction is addressed are in accordance with the structures inscribed in the injunction addressed to him. In this case, one says that it went without saying, that there was nothing else to do.

(Bourdieu 1998a, 103)

Those who hold symbolic capital may use it as a means of dominating the other agents, who submit voluntarily and take the hegemonic relationship as natural and commonsensical. Bourdieu (1998a) writes, "soft relations of exploitation only work if they are soft. They are relations of symbolic violence which can only be established with the complicity of those who suffer from it. [...] The dominated collaborate in their own exploitation through affection and admiration" (ibid., 111). In short, symbolic violence is efficient because the dominated contribute to its "efficacy" (1996, 3)[1].

In this project, I use Bourdieu's notion of capital to account for the status accorded to the translator in their struggle for recognition from other agents in the field of power (mainly, large corporate clients/employers, authors, publishers, legislative/political powers and scholars/educators) and how that status is reflected in a collection of codes of ethics, the FIT Translator's Charter and the UNESCO Nairobi Recommendation. Bourdieu's concept, along with insights from the sociology of professions, allows me to evaluate whether these documents allow the translator to impose their content and relationship terms or whether they simply reinforce the translator's low status voluntarily[2]. Internal competition among individual translators for capital (in a different delimitation of field) is not accounted for, as it does not shed light on the status of translators compared to that of the other agents involved in translation. I have chosen to focus on these external agents because the struggle for symbolic power in occupational fields is mainly external. The stake is "externally shielding-off professional practices from external influences," as Schinkel and Noordegraaf put it (2011, 69). An occupation becomes a profession and its practitioners acquire symbolic power only when it is auto-regulated by practitioners themselves, without any external interferences, and recognized by other surrounding agents and the general public as of value. As Schinkel and Noordegraaf (2011, 87) rightly affirm,

Bourdieu's field analysis is often used and interpreted "internalistically." In such an analysis, one would point out that the *field-specific content* of "professionalism" or the very *reference* of the idea of a specific "profession" is continuously at stake within a specific professional field. But the idea of a "profession" marks not only a field in itself but at the same time a *difference* within a larger relational system of positions. Bourdieu's notion of the field of power enables us to see professions as fields of positions nested *within* a general field of power.

(Schinkel and Noordegraaf 2011, 87, italics in original)

Such a perspective allows us to measure the extent to which the documents under study position the translator as an autonomous cultural producer (similarly to the author). It also makes it possible to reveal whether they promote translators' collegiate control over their occupation. Ultimately, the study shows how close or distant the translator is from setting foot in the field of power, like any other cultural producer or professional[3]. In this study, I also draw on Bourdieu's notion of symbolic violence to show how the established order and discourse within the field of translation (as reflected in codes of ethics) impact on the translator's autonomy. In Chapter 5, which follows, I present the translator's different forms of capital as reflected in the corpus under study. In Chapter 6, I analyze their degree of conversion into symbolic recognition.

Notes

1 See a similar view of Althusser (1971) about what he calls, 'self-subjugation' or 'interpellation,' which results in the reproduction of the relations of dominance in the labour order *with no cost*.
2 The translator's low status is corroborated by many empirical studies (see, for instance, Liu 2013, Dam and Zethsen 2008, Gouadec 2007, Katan 2011, Sela-Sheffy and Shlesinger 2011, Dam and Koskinen 2016).
3 Schinkel and Noordegraaf (2011, 68), and (Bourdieu 1996, 267) argue that professionalism can be regarded as a form of symbolic capital in the 'field of power.'

5 The Translator's Forms of Capital in Codified Ethics

Translation practice is primarily an intellectual endeavour, and, therefore, a cultural production. Cultural capital is, thus, the translator's most convertible form of capital into symbolic imposition. It is the form of capital that can advance the translator's professionalism or entitlement to authorship. And this symbolic capital, if achieved, is, in turn, convertible into economic capital "as the earning power of a profession increases" (Jackson 2017, 798).

The translator's cultural capital can convert into symbolic power when it is recognized as significant, esoteric and rare. The other agents' view depends partly on the translator's self-perception and promotion of their cultural capital but is most importantly guided by the external resources of power that translators can mobilize to advance this view (see Johnson 2016). If the translator represents their cultural capital as being high and this representation is backed up by powerful resources, the other agents are more likely to believe it to be so. In sum, if the other agents share the translators' own *belief* of their practice as a complex endeavour that requires high cultural capital, this will lead to the acquisition of considerable symbolic capital. Should this be achieved, relational aspects will be shaken up and translators will gain more prestige and value. On the other hand, if translators adopt a low view of their own cultural capital, their symbolic capital will not only be impoverished but they may be subjected to symbolic violence. The contribution of social capital to economic and symbolic forms of capital is not completely irrelevant for translators who are members of large associations. But social capital is itself partly dependent on cultural capital, which can play an important role in creating valuable social networking, as I will demonstrate shortly.

Next, I discuss the translator's cultural capital in its three states, as presented in the documents under study before discussing their social and economic forms of capital.

5.1 The Translator's Cultural Capital

Cultural capital takes three forms: the embodied, the institutionalized and the objectified states (Bourdieu 1986). In the case of the translator, the embodied cultural capital can refer to their theoretical knowledge about the field of translation, practical experience in the field, "long-lasting dispositions" – in Bourdieu's (1986, 243) terminology, general knowledge and knowledge in a specialized field, as well as expertise in using objectified cultural capital (machines, tools, references, sources). The translator's institutionalized cultural capital, on the other hand, refers to the translator's educational qualifications, degrees, certificates and the nature of their institutional training. Their objectified state of cultural capital refers to their materials, books, articles, technological tools, machines, computers, and so on.

5.1.1 The Embodied State of Cultural Capital

The acquisition of embodied cultural capital related to translation takes a long time and a great deal of effort and material cost. Usually, having a bachelor's degree takes four years on average in many countries. Likewise, having some experience takes a few years. The translator also devotes their life to the acquisition of two or more languages. This is in addition to their whole (school) life dedication where they go through the long process of "incorporation" and "labor of inculcation and assimilation" to accumulate the necessary knowledge (general and specialized) "in the form of what is called culture, cultivation, *Bildung*" (Bourdieu 1986, 244). This bodily and cognitive investment in embodied cultural capital requires painful efforts, relative deprivation and renunciation of pleasure. "[O]n paie de sa personne" [One gives of oneself], as Bourdieu puts it (ibid.). Besides time and effort, this type of capital requires a considerable economic investment in the form of miscellaneous fees that students pay for their schools, probably throughout their school life in the age of increasing privatization of education in many countries.

This form of cultural capital, which consists of the dispositions acquired in one's life through various sources and tremendous efforts, presents a problem for those who want to acquire it instantly. This is because it "cannot be transmitted instantaneously (like money, property rights, or even titles of nobility) by gift or bequest, purchase or change" (ibid., 244–245). However, powerful agents can acquire this form of capital by *proxy* (ibid., 247) as they have the economic means to buy it from its holders (i.e., translators) whenever needed. On top of that, they may be able to impose their terms and conditions on translators in return for the fees they pay. Bourdieu warns us that powerful agents seeking to acquire cultural capital by *proxy* may, in fact, buy the practitioner themself. He wonders, "[h]ow can this capital, so closely linked to the person, be bought without buying the person [...]?" (ibid., 245). In our case, we wonder: how can translators keep their (ethical) autonomy when selling their services to powerful patrons/clients? I will return to these questions in this Part II and Part III, respectively.

The translator's embodied cultural capital is never fully acquired by the acquisition of institutionalized forms of cultural capital, i.e., graduation. Translation undergoes continuous and rapid changes, evolution, novelties, updates and shake-ups. Hence, translator associations and other organizations of interest (like the UNESCO and the FIT) stress life-long learning and/or 'professional' development in their defining documents. These organizations emphasize the continuous updating of one's knowledge, the acquisition of new skills required by the advancements in technology and research, and the deepening of one's knowledge about the socio-cultural contexts of working languages. The UNESCO Nairobi Recommendation, for example, urges Member States to provide and develop opportunities for continuous learning and 'professional' development (Paragraph 11). It also stresses the importance of translator exchange policies/programs between countries to improve the linguistic knowledge of the source language and the sociocultural contexts of the STs (Paragraph 13). Similarly, all national associations' codes of ethics urge the translator to seek continuous (self)-learning and/or 'professional' development opportunities – which ultimately promote the translator's embodied capital. While some codes' statements are general and broad (SATI, ATPP, IAFET and SFT), other codes are more explanatory on the issue (ITAINDIA, AUSIT). The explanations in the AUSIT's code of ethics are the most detailed. Article 8 further stresses continuous "life-long learning" in order to update one's knowledge and skills to the evolution and changes in the field. It explains that this includes the continuous upgrading of one's language, 'transfer' skills, and "contextual and cultural understanding," as well as keeping up to date with technological advancements. Likewise, the ITAINDIA is explicit and detailed about the translator's continuous development in its introductory section. And rather than including this requirement as the duty of only the translator, the ITAINDIA stresses the role of the association in "providing adequate guidance and orientation to its members so that they meet the professional standards of the industry" (Section A). The association commits to "the up-gradation of knowledge and capabilities of its members by organizing workshops, creating quality awareness and following the code of professional conduct" (ibid.). Also, with national and international partnerships and collaborations, the ITAINDIA underlines its active involvement in information exchange as well as development of "relations that help in up-gradation of translation as well as technological skills of its members" (ibid).

Another issue related to 'life-long learning' that comes up often in some of the documents under study is 'knowledge sharing' among association members. The FIT Translator's Charter stresses that one of the functions of translator associations is to collect sources and share them with translators, as well as organize seminars and meetings (Article 32). Three national/provincial associations (IAFET, ATIO and SATI) are explicit about the importance of knowledge sharing and cooperation among association members.

While this is a productive tradition to sustain and promote as it enhances the translators' cultural capital, knowledge sharing is restrained by the principles of 'disclosure,' 'confidentiality' and copyright law. When there are innovative practices, protocols and software, they are usually protected by nondisclosure agreements that secure the patrons/clients' exclusive ownership and, thus, prevent the translator from sharing them with peers. As Tymoczko rightly points out,

> [m]any cutting-edge responses to contemporary challenges now occur behind closed doors. Corporations and governments develop innovative translation protocols, software and team structures to respond to the new demands on translators, but anti-disclosure contracts make it difficult or even impossible for translators in these closed spheres to share their innovations with the profession as a whole.
> (Tymoczko 2009, 418)

In this respect, the SATI code limits 'knowledge sharing' among its members by strictly applying the rule of 'confidentiality' in regard to the client/ employer's resources and information. Other codes, although not as explicit as the SATI, stress the principle in separate articles, devoted to copyright and confidentiality, which I further discuss in this Part II and Part III.

Another important component of embodied cultural capital that all studied documents stress, to different degrees, is 'competence.' The term 'competence' appears in four documents (FIT, AUSIT, ATIO, SFT). In some codes, it appears multiple times (10 times in the AUSIT document, for example). Other elements implying or regarded as part of 'competence,' such as the mastery of languages, translation skills, (specialized) knowledge and translation standards, are highlighted. All documents (except the IAFET's) stress the mastery of languages as part of the translator's competence. Some of them (UNESCO, FIT, ATPP, ITAINDIA, SFT) categorically urge practitioners to translate solely into their native language or to a language in which they are highly proficient.

92 The Translator's Capital in Codified Ethics

In sum, the studied organizations stress, to different degrees, lifelong learning, 'professional' development, competence and/or knowledge sharing to enhance the translator's cultural capital. The question remains: do these organizations represent *translation* as a creative and complex practice that requires all these intellectual efforts/competences? In Chapter 6, I discuss how the definition of *translation* affects the translator's cultural capital and, by extension, their symbolic imposition and, therefore, why these calls to boost the translator's embodied cultural capital may be inefficient.

5.1.2 The Institutionalized State of Cultural Capital

In line with the claim of *professionalism* that translator associations aspire to, they would supposedly stress institutionalized forms of knowledge, i.e., the possession of a specialized degree in translation from a postsecondary recognized education institution as a condition of entry. The institutionalized form of cultural capital is what differentiates the cultural capital of an amateur or a 'non-professional' "autodidact" from that of a bearer of legally recognized academic and/or 'professional' qualifications (Bourdieu 1986, 247–8). Regardless of whether the translator possesses the knowledge and skills associated with a degree/certificate, the institutional recognition wields the magic power that represents their embodied cultural capital as high and significant. Degrees/certificates are the only visible assurance of a translator's competence for the other agents (employers/clients) dealing with them for the first time, especially when the latter do not possess the necessary knowledge on how to assess their embodied cultural capital and cannot delegate that to a senior translator. In Bourdieu's words, this institutionalized form of cultural capital has the power to "secure belief" and "impose recognition" (1986, 248). In 'professional' networks, it could have a double function: it would protect the homogeneity of the social group by eliminating 'intruders' and advertise the claims of 'public protection' by forbidding access to the 'incompetent.'

Education in the field of translation promotes the possession of systematic knowledge *specific* to the field. The UNESCO Nairobi Recommendation emphasizes the distinct character of 'translation' as a field of study and recommends that it be separated from the departments of languages in educational institutions. "Member States should recognize in principle that translation is an independent discipline requiring an education distinct from exclusively language teaching and that this discipline requires special training" (Paragraph 11). The call of the UNESCO is an international recognition that the exercise of this occupation requires specialized training and should come with high cultural capital. It

The Translator's Forms of Capital in Codified Ethics 93

acknowledges how important the institutionalized form of cultural capital is as a protection from the aberrations bilingual 'amateurs,' coming from language departments, might produce.

The Nairobi Recommendation suggests that it would be wise for the UNESCO Member States (as well as individual students) to invest in this precious cultural capital. The translation industry is expanding rapidly in today's globalized world and its non-regulation or non-institutionalization may be 'chaotic' and 'open to all risks.' Should Member States implement this recommendation, more learners will invest in this specialization and seek to join translation departments/schools, which may secure good jobs. Ultimately, one could imagine this important field being organized and limited to highly trained individuals. From a student's perspective, however, securing a good job these days may not be guaranteed by joining these departments/schools. As we learn from Bourdieu (1986), the value of this investment all depends on the state of the market at the time of graduation. The economic and symbolic values of an academic capital (i.e., a certain degree) fluctuate depending on its rarity and on clients/consumers' perspectives of it. Unless the latter agents are convinced of the high value of this kind of capital, the investment of time, effort and money in such institutionalized cultural capital may be less profitable than desired or expected (Bourdieu 1986, 248). Although demand for translation is skyrocketing, the current conditions of employment of many translators are difficult, as evidence shows. Low rates of pay, poor working conditions, unfair management practices, unclear contracts about job specifications and vulnerable social security all attest to the degrading working conditions of many translators around the globe[1]. This is not to mention bouncing cheques and scams[2]. These conditions attest to the low value assigned to this institutionalized form of capital (degree in translation) and probably its irrelevance in the eyes of many beneficiary agents. As such, this institutionalized form of cultural capital may not be worth investing in, according to many governments, institutions and students.

The FIT Translator's Charter and all the national/provincial associations' codes (except the IAFET's) make indirect allusions to the importance of possessing a proper institutionalized form of cultural capital to join the associations. Their allusions are mostly inexplicit and mentioned in passing as the codes explain other duties, such as quality, competence and truthfulness about one's qualifications. Reading through the associations' websites and the requirements for access – where such general statements of the codes are specified – it becomes clear that some associations (ITAINDIA, SFT, ATPP[3]) are content with experience (embodied cultural capital) when the candidate does not possess institutionalized cultural capital. Some other associations require neither institutionalized

94 *The Translator's* Capital *in Codified Ethics*

(degree) nor embodied cultural capital (experience) for ordinary membership (SATI[4], IAFET[5]) (see Table 5.1).

Although the studied associations refer to the importance of possessing some sort of institutionalized cultural capital, their membership is quite open, and *social closure* – to use the Weberian term (1978/1922) – is not as solid and strict as in many other known professions, such as the legal and the medical professions, or even the accountancy occupation. Overall, the studied associations seem to prefer the enlargement of membership rosters and the collection of as many fees as possible to a strict control of admissions. But the inflated membership size, which may appear to be beneficial to the social capital of some translators, may in fact have the side effect of undermining the association's reputation in the eyes of other agents and the public, as I demonstrate in Chapter 6.

5.1.3 The Objectified State of Cultural Capital

The majority of the studied documents do not emphasize the possession of objectified cultural capital (i.e., material objects and tools of cultural production, such as translation softwares, for example). They do not underline the "means of production," which are generally possessed only by holders of economic capital, in Bourdieu's thought (1986, 247). These means of production may be *provisionally* and *conditionally*[6] provided to translators by third parties (the beneficiaries, the employer or the representative association).

Only two national associations (ITAINDIA and AUSIT) and the two international bodies (UNESCO, FIT) refer to this form of capital in their documents in one way or another. The Nairobi Recommendation emphasizes that both the beneficiaries of translation and the UNESCO Member States provide the necessary "means of production" for the translator to facilitate their tasks and ensure high quality (Article 14b). It also recommends that Member States establish terminology databases/centres and make them available to translators. Quite similarly, the AUSIT urges its members to secure access to the various materials, devices, aids, reference information and physical environment needed for the task at hand (Code of Conduct, Article 7). The FIT calls on translator associations to invest efforts in making some "cultural goods" – to use Bourdieu's (1986) term – available to translators (Article 32).

Although sophisticated "means of production" are generally possessed only by holders of high economic capital, translators may possess two types of affordable objectified cultural capital: hardware materials (such as books, dictionaries, glossaries and computers) and virtual accesses (such as access to books/articles, some terminology databases, some CAT tools and other resources), in addition to contents created by the translator

Table 5.1 Institutionalized cultural capital required for access to the different translator associations

	Educational qualification/ certification AND experience	Educational qualification OR experience	Experience only	Educational qualification only	No requirements
ATIO (Canada)		✓ Specialized education or experience			
ITAINDIA SFT (France)		✓			
			✓ Exercising translator		
SATI (South Africa)			✓ Experience for accreditation		✓
ATPP (Peru)			✓		
AUSIT (Australia)	✓ "OR other acceptable qualification"				
IAFET (Egypt)					✓

themself (like glossaries, publications, personal corpora and Translation Memory). The ITAINDIA is the only code of ethics that mentions the creation and production of the translator's own "cultural goods." It affirms that the association offers its members the "[o]pportunity to publish articles in ITINDIA's [sic] publications."

When clients/employers provide translators with "cultural goods," they do so either because they do not have time to utilize them themselves (as in the case of translators owners of translation companies), or because they do not have the required embodied cultural capital to use them efficiently. In the latter case, they possess them only materially but not symbolically. Following Bourdieu's analysis, if translators (holders of embodied capital) are desperately needed to put objectified cultural capital (different devices/materials) into effective use – in other words, if their expertise is needed for the functioning of the institutions of the powerful beneficiary agents – their economic benefits are liable to increase. This form of capital, when recognized as rare, esoteric and accessible to only a limited number of professionals can be used as an important tool in the translator's struggle to "obtain profits proportionate to their mastery of this objectified capital, and therefore to the extent of their embodied capital" (Bourdieu 1986, 247). Economic profits proportionate to their complex expertise would not be the only outcome of the mastery of objectified capital. Symbolic gains would also be achieved – as I discuss thoroughly in Chapter 6. In sum, the mastery of technological tools and large databases, or even better, their creation and ownership or the authoring/translation of books/articles, or simply the ownership of a considerable number of books supposedly enriches the translator's objectified and embodied cultural capital simultaneously.

That said, there is a problem with these "means of production" in the case of translators. First, translation tools/materials are not seen as complex as machinery used by other specialized professionals. Unlike engineers, for example, who are the only people able to initiate the use of certain machinery (to be used later on by technicians), translation tools/materials may be seen as manipulable by anyone, including the owner/client/patron, did they have the time to do so. The few technological tools that may be seen as mysterious are not built by translators but by tool designers, who may get all the recognition. The translator's use of these tools may, therefore, be seen as quite mechanical. They may be seen as only selling secretarial services using the already established and fully functional means of production supplied by their employer/client. Such a situation may have the effect of reducing the translator's economic capital significantly. For example, the translator may be paid only for the words/sentences that are not translated by the Translation Memory (TM), despite the work of editing and textual/intellectual work on the entire text. On the symbolic level, these new technological tools may undermine the value of the translator's work, as their *ethical/intellectual* effort and the ambivalent process of choice/decision-making (selection of the right stretches of text for the right situation, addition, rephrasing, adapting), which is at the core of intellectual and ethical positionings, may be reduced to simple post-editing. "Rather than seeing a translator who interprets a source text's meaning and intention and renders these in an appropriate target text, clients may perceive the language professional as a copy editor who simply makes minor revisions to the 'real' work that has been largely done by a machine" (Bowker 2021, 167–168). This, of course, includes the denial of their work in creating parallel corpora used in this machine, in the first place. Kenny (2011, 9) argues that "at a time when machine translation has never been as reliant on human translation as it is now, it is ironic that the role of translators in the creation of parallel data is often obscured" (see also Kenny 2019). Technology has undermined the translator's role and perception in translation workflows, and therefore, affected their empowerment (see Kenny and Doherty 2014). Technology has, therefore, not only made the already existing assumptions about translation/translators more dominant but more 'commonsensical' and 'proven,' as technology is seen as to be doing the main part of the job, thus, ignoring its reliance on human translations for its data as well as its legitimacy, in the first place. These assumptions overlook the fact that these data, made of parallel corpora, "is assumed to contain good answers to translation problems; and they are assumed to contain good answers precisely because they contain translations performed by human beings" (Kenny 2011, 2; see also Kenny 2019).

Regardless of the type of organization and its proclaimed function, all the documents under study underline some constituents of the embodied form of cultural capital. They generally suggest – to different degrees – lifelong learning, 'professional' development and competence. Most importantly, they present their views of what *translation* is and what translators' roles are – as I discussed in Part I – which are the sites where the translator's perceived embodied cultural capital mostly displays. Also, most of them make allusion to institutionalized cultural capital without, however, imposing it as a strict requirement for entry. Only a minority of documents refer to the possession of objectified cultural capital, or "cultural goods." I discuss the implications of the positions of the organizations under study regarding the translator's cultural capital in Chapter 6. I measure the rate of conversion of the presented cultural capital into symbolic power. In the following section, I present the translator's social capital.

5.2 The Translator's Social Capital

According to Bourdieu (1986), social capital is generally acquired by belonging to large and/or prestigious networks. The network members usually identify with each other on social, ethnic, political, ideological, occupational or economic bases. Translators try to acquire this capital as they invest in relations with peers by joining their 'professional' associations. But to what extent does the translator's investment in these networks pay off in the short and long run?

In the documents under study, all translator organizations underscore the importance of networking and enumerate the benefits of joining associations for the individual translator. The FIT – which is the mother organization of all national associations – devotes two entire sections (4 and 5, which is 16 articles out of 40) of its Translator's Charter to highlight the importance of gathering in national associations and networking with other organizations with similar interests, as well as joining the international federation. The Translator's Charter claims that the main task of these local/national translator associations is to defend their members' "moral and material" interests and improve the conditions of their 'profession' (Article 26). These organizations "exert their influence on public authorities in the preparation and introduction of legal measures and regulations concerning the profession" (Article 27). The FIT emphasizes that these associations have the task of establishing relations with the organizations that represent users of translation/translators, including "publishers' associations, industrial and commercial enterprises, public and private authorities, the Press, etc.) for the purpose of studying and finding solutions to their common problems" (Article 28). In order to assure high standards of quality, they also "keep in touch with cultural organizations, societies of authors, national sections of the Pen Club, literary critics, learned societies, universities, and technical and scientific research institutes" (Article 29). Furthermore, translator associations "give advice on the training and recruitment of translators, and [...] co-operate with specialized organizations and universities in the pursuit of these aims" (Article 31). The FIT Translator's Charter also stresses that associations shall endeavour to provide resource materials for translators (Article 32).

As for its own mission, the FIT highlights its role in lobbying for, and defending, the translator's "material and moral rights" on the world stage as well as in keeping informed on the latest "theoretical and practical" developments in the field and spreading 'civilization' (Article 37). The charter underlines the role of networking with other organizations/governments at the international level as well as engaging in international gatherings and activities for translators in achieving the above aims (Article 38). In sum, translator organizations, according to the FIT, have two main roles to play. First, they have the role of self-regulation and internal control in order to improve the standards of the practice. Second, they have the external role of opening up and engaging with their environment to ensure continuous dialogue and negotiations with all agents (in)directly involved in this practice (i.e., employers/clients, publishers, politicians/legislators, educators/researchers, critics, authors, journalists). The ultimate aim of this openness is to defend the translator's rights and interests and address potential issues.

The UNESCO reiterates the FIT aims[7]. The Nairobi Recommendation urges Member States to allow and encourage the establishment of translator associations that "define the rules and duties which should govern the exercise of the profession" and "defend the moral and material interests of translators." These associations should ultimately negotiate on practitioners' behalf and promote the profession, as well as establish a culture of dialogue and exchange between translators and 'original' authors (Nairobi Recommendation, Paragraph 7).

Like the FIT and the UNESCO, national/provincial associations underline the importance of membership for translators. They list the actual and potential benefits of belonging to their networks in their documents (namely codes of ethics, bylaws and websites). These translator networks ostensibly aim at creating an atmosphere of solidarity that fosters cooperation and assistance through "material and/or symbolic exchanges," to borrow Bourdieu's terminology (1986, 249). The associations list the following benefits, among others, in their internal documents:

- the defence/protection of the translator's material and symbolic rights or interests (SFT, ITAINDIA, AUSIT, ATPP, IAFET, SATI);
- the exchange of knowledge (ITAINDIA, IAFET, ATIO, SATI);
- solidarity, mutual assistance, support and cooperation (ITAINDIA, ATIO, IAFET, SATI, ATPP, SFT, AUSIT);
- the use of the association logo/name (ATIO, IAFET, ITAINDIA), and
- representativity with clients, authorities or other agents (ITAINDIA, SFT).

While a comparison of the different associations' codes and documents shows similarities between these associations regarding many actual and potential benefits, it yields slight differences as to the degree of emphasis on the translator's interests, depending on the nature and function of the association. The SFT, given its unionist nature, is unsurprisingly the most explicit association in stressing the defence of the translator's interests in its code. In the very introduction, it stipulates: "the French Society of Translators (SFT) is a professional union that defends the interests of translators and interpreters and promotes translation occupations in France" (About the SFT, my translation). On the other hand, the ATIO, being a 'professional' order, overemphasizes elements that are of interest mainly to the beneficiaries of translation, such as "professional accountability," "quality of service" and "the protection of members of the public." The only tacit allusion to the translator's "collective voice" appears timidly on its website. "The ATIO Secretariat provides clients and the public with information on the various aspects and working conditions of the professions represented by ATIO. We actively advocate for our members and publicize the role performed by our members in society."[8] The other voluntary associations are closer to the SFT position than to the ATIO's in this policy. On its website, the AUSIT highlights, among other services, "advancing the professional interests, standing, rights and recognition of members within and outside Australia."[9] Similarly, the SATI underlines that it is "the only association that looks after the interests of all in the language practice profession in South Africa."[10] The ITAINDIA stipulates that it aims "to look after the interests of individual translators and Small Scale Agencies" (Membership Information/B). The ATPP claims that it aims "[t]o support its members through the Association's prestige"[11] and "[p]romote the recognition of translators and interpreters as high-ranking professionals."[12] In its bylaws, the IAFET, similarly, states that it seeks to "[p]romote the recognition of the translation and interpreting professions."[13]

All studied organizations highlight some of the material and symbolic benefits/resources of membership in networks with colleagues. But the available resources and benefits depend largely on the *size* of the network and mainly on the size of capital of each of the network members, as we learn from Bourdieu (1986, 249). The larger and more prestigious the network, the more resources and benefits there are. For this reason, translator organizations seek to enlarge their networks' size and influence. The FIT Translator's Charter encourages associations of specialized translators and regional associations within the same country to join efforts and gather in larger associations that can be more powerful and more influential (Article 33)[14]. On its website, the FIT takes pride in representing more than 100 translator/interpreter/terminologist/linguist associations and institutes from 55 countries, representing more than 80,000 translators[15], and in having a consultative status with the UNESCO[16].

The national/provincial associations, likewise, underscore their (large) size and their influence. Some of them also take pride in their long history, connections and achievements (by proxy).

> Established in 1947, [...] The SFT is also a founding member of the International Federation of Translators (FIT), a non-governmental organization that maintains official relations with the UNESCO. This partnership of consultation led the UNESCO General Conference to adopt the Nairobi Recommendation in November 1976, which recommends that the translator be assimilated to the author and that their name be prominently featured on all published copies of their translations.
>
> (SFT Deontological Code, About the SFT, my translation)

Not very differently, the AUSIT underlines its connections, reputation and influence. It underscores its active membership within the FIT and the fact that it hosted its World Congress in 1996 (where its original code of ethics was presented to the mother organization). It also rejoices in the fact that the accreditation institution (the NAATI) adopts its code of ethics and closely collaborates with it. Besides, the AUSIT reminds the readers/members that its very establishment was a response to a call from the NAATI. It also underscores the fact that its code of ethics "was adopted by NZSTI, the national association of interpreting and translating professionals in New Zealand (est. 1985), at its Annual General Meeting in 2012" (AUSIT Code of Ethics, Preamble). Importantly, the AUSIT shows pride in the adoption of its code of ethics by many beneficiary agents in Australia, who require it as the basis of the translator's work (ibid.).

On its website, the ATIO emphasizes the fact that it is part of the Canadian Translators, Terminologists and Interpreters Council (CTTIC) – itself part of the FIT. The ATIO, likewise, takes pride in its size as well as its long history as the oldest Canadian organization of its kind, founded as early as 1920. Most importantly, it underlines the fact that it is "the first translators' association in the world whose certified members are deemed professionals by law, for in February 1989 the Province of Ontario granted reserved title for certified members of ATIO through the *Association of Translators and Interpreters Act, 1989.*"[17] The ATPP, similarly, takes pride in its membership growth and achievements[18], as it is "an institutional member of the ATA (American Translators Association), is affiliated with the FIT (Fédération Internationale des Traducteurs) and is a founding member of the Latin America Regional Center (CRAL) of the FIT."[19] The IAFET, which has a short history, does not mention the size of its membership but takes pride in "being *the only and the first* Egyptian association member of the International Federation of Translators FIT"[20] (highlights in original). The SATI also takes pride in its long history (since 1956), its leadership and recognition in the field of language practices, as well as its accreditation monopoly in South Africa[21]. And like all other associations, the SATI stresses its affiliation with the FIT[22] (see also ITAINDIA taking pride in being part of the FIT in its Introduction, Section A).

All associations take pride in belonging to the FIT. Belonging to the international organization naturally bestows more social capital on these national/provincial associations – which are smaller in size and influence. The FIT is sought after for its social capital as it is "well known" and "worthy of being known," in Bourdieu's words (1986, 250). Its "work of sociability" is "highly productive" (ibid.). The FIT has an international presence and has direct connections with an international body (i.e., UNESCO) that makes recommendations to its Member States in the fields of education, culture and science. Indirectly, national/provincial associations are linked to the UNESCO. Ultimately, recommendations made by the FIT to the UNESCO end up being imported back to the national level. Some of these recommendations may be much more advanced than those of national legislation/regulations. National/provincial associations would probably have not even suggested them locally as they are beyond reach. When these recommendations come 'from above,' however, they are liable to, at least, shake up the local regulations – which is already a gain for national association members.

In sum, the studied associations (whether in their codes of ethics or on their websites or on both) highlight similar areas of sociability but with differences in emphasis, depending on their key strengths. Such emphasis ranges from membership size, through networking and influence, to their (long) histories and legal status – which are all important elements in enriching their members' social capital. The aim of highlighting these elements is, of course, to advertise their social capital, which may attract newer members to join the network.

Ideally, assembling translators in 'professional' associations should enhance their social capital and thus empowers members who may be weak as isolated individuals. These large bodies should get involved in lobbying the other agents (mainly in the field of power) to advance their weak members' interests. The most important example at hand is the FIT lobbying the UNESCO to adopt its Nairobi Recommendation. As Bourdieu (1986, 248–249) tells us, such networks provide individual members with "the backing of the collectivity-owned capital, a 'credential' which entitles them to credit, in the various senses of the word," thus benefiting not only the translator's social capital but all other forms of their capital. These networks of like-minded practitioners are a ground of "useful relationships," in all respects (ibid., 249). For instance, benefiting from colleagues' diverse knowledge enhances the individual translator's skills, and, therefore, their embodied cultural capital. Likewise, defending the members' material and symbolic rights improves their economic and symbolic capital. In addition, there are times when the economic yield of the institutionalized form of cultural capital "depends on the social capital [...] which can be used to back it up" (ibid., 244). Belonging to a reputable network known to comprise highly competent practitioners multiplies the chances of attracting more business or better jobs. Some jobs that are sought after may require certification provided by a 'professional' association or consider it an asset, at least. Also, income is liable to increase through the delegation of some jobs or recommendations from more 'known' colleagues who have better connections. Importantly, social capital can sometimes even be more important than cultural capital. Some clients may prefer a translator recommended by a trustworthy translator, or a translator who belongs to an association known for its rigour in conditions of access and certification, over one who has a more interesting résumé. In this case, it is not only about what the translator knows (embodied cultural capital) but mainly about who they know (social capital), i.e., who recommended them and/or which association they belong to.

That said, with the boom of the translation industry in the digital era, the value of this traditional social capital may have decreased. Social capital is taking the form of a virtual social capital. The increasing number of online platforms and social networks of translators is seemingly impacting on the value of institutionally sanctioned social capital, embodied in belonging to 'professional' associations – which are limited in their geographic coverage. Besides, increasing numbers of clients/employers are subcontracting work to online freelance translators in other countries and at lower cost. In this case, the embodied cultural capital of the translator may be more relevant in attracting jobs than the institutionalized cultural capital and the authentic social capital together as most potential clients test freelancers before hiring them. Virtual social capital may, however, be paradoxically inefficient, or even turn into a source of vulnerabilities. Holders of economic capital (mainly clients, including translation companies) succeed in setting freelance translators into a fierce worldwide competition, and some practitioners become willing to accept any conditions imposed on them as far as they get the job (see Bourdieu 1986). Abdallah and Koskinen (2007, 675) argue that the translation companies have dominated the freelance sector and "have firmly established themselves as the intermediary between the client and the translator," whereas the role and position of the translator as an expert seems to have diminished. In such cases, the individual translator has limited means to impose better fees or gain decent working conditions (ibid. 678). This *status quo* opens the door to further vulnerabilities among freelance translators, or "telemigrant translators," as Cronin calls them, as these are many times dismissed right after task with a simple "push-button" action (Cronin 2021, 182). "The pay-per-view model of employment where workers are hired for specific tasks and fired once they are done offers little in the way of guarantees or social protection. A world of liquid labour favours employers but leaves employees routinely exposed," Cronin argues (ibid.). Researchers from the WZB Berlin Social Science Center and the University of Oxford found that major platforms and companies, like Gengo, Lionbridge, Scribie, TransPerfect, GoTranscript, SmartCat and Rev – whose clients include global businesses, such as AirBnB, L'Oreal, Spotify, Netflix, Google, and Facebook as well as prominent universities such as Princeton University, the University of California in Berkeley, the University of Washington, and Yale University – do not respect basic working standards for translators[23]. Added to these problems are differences in standards of pay in different countries – a fact which makes the competition very unequal and very demeaning to translators around the world.

Being part of a 'professional' association (and benefiting from its collective social capital) is not freely bestowed on the translator. In return for the actual and potential advantages (social networking, cultural/professional development and material profits) discussed earlier, translators are called on to adhere to strict rules, duties and practices that maintain and reinforce the social group they belong to. They are urged to abide by the obligations that help make the benefits available and possible. They are also compelled to contribute their share of knowledge, money (membership fees), effort of assistance and support in return for the knowledge and assistance they get from the association. In sum, the individual member is required to contribute their material and symbolic share of involvement to guarantee the enhancement of the entire group. In other words, the translator acquires "the aggregate of the actual or potential resources" of the whole group (Bourdieu 1986, 248), i.e., the collective capital of the association, only if they contribute to it and help preserve the 'power' and image of the association by complying with its rules and duties and enhancing its symbolic and financial power.

The studied codes of ethics underline that members are representatives of the association and that the quality of their work, ethics and conduct are the credit of the association and the 'profession' they represent. The individual translator's behaviour and conduct are "the business of the whole group" – in Bourdieu's (1986, 250) words. The AUSIT code, for instance, stipulates that "[i]nterpreters and translators respect and support their fellow professionals, and they uphold the reputation and trustworthiness of the profession of interpreting and translating" (Article 9). It further explains, "[p]ractitioners have a loyalty to the profession that extends beyond their individual interest. They support and further the interests of the profession and their colleagues and offer each other assistance" (ibid.). In a similar vein, the SATI calls on translators "[t]o take part in the activities of the Institute and always to conduct themselves in such a way that their conduct and the quality of their work will be to the credit of the Institute and translation as an occupation" (Code of Ethics for Individual Members). The ATPP, in turn, urges its members to "[r]efrain from any act which may be detrimental to the Association's interests" (Code of Ethics, Article 9), and to "[c]ontribute, in general, to the advancement of the translation and interpreting profession" (ibid., Article 11). The ATIO code devotes an entire section to "promoting the profession" (Section 4). It stipulates that "[m]embers shall promote a positive image of their profession and endeavour to make it more widely known, through their actions and the quality of the services they provide" (Article 4.1.1). It adds that "[m]embers shall refrain from any activity that could tarnish the image of their profession or the Association" (Article 4.1.2). The ITAINDIA, likewise, warns members not to "indulge in activities, which are prejudicial to the Aims and Objectives and/or the Rules & Regulations of the Society" (Membership information/B). The SFT devotes section 6 of its code to the question of "Respect for the profession and for the SFT." "The translator must refrain from any conduct that is likely to undermine the dignity of the profession or any act that is likely to bring the SFT into disrepute" (Article 6a). The IAFET code of ethics calls on translators to "[r]efrain from any and all sorts of conduct that might in any way harm or undermine IAFET's interests" (Article 1.2). It, also, urges its members to "[c]ontribute to upholding the good standing of their professions by means of offering services of the highest possible standards" (Article 3.3). The code stresses the appropriate use of the name of the association in a way that is not detrimental to its image (Article 3.7).

In sum, the codes of ethics under study underline the member's duties toward their 'profession' and their association, as they list the membership benefits. These duties include, of course, compliance with the code of ethics, among other obligations. And to guarantee fulfilment of the mentioned duties, some associations may at the outset set conditions of entry that ensure "undisputed, pre-reflexive, naive, native compliance with the fundamental presuppositions of the field" (Bourdieu 1990b, 68). Hence, in return for the associations' potential support and the potential benefits they may offer to translators, these organizations ensure that members follow "the rules of the game" of the network, have "practical faith" in the "presuppositions of the field" – including the definition of the practice and the instructions of the code of ethics – and offer actual financial and symbolic contributions.

Arranging the conditions (of entry) that guarantee the translator's "practical faith" is not always enough to ensure compliance of all members with "the fundamental presuppositions of the field" (ibid.). That is why associations adopt other policies that seek to deter potential violators after entrance. In this regard, some codes of ethics under study call on different agents to report on any kind of misconduct. The IAFET code urges members to "[r]eport to the IAFET Good Practices Commission or to any other relevant organization on any *colleague* whose conduct appears to be detrimental to the profession and, furthermore, contribute toward the investigation into such conduct" (Article 3.8, italics added). The IAFET limits its call to members and doesn't open the possibility to file a complaint to any outsiders. Not very differently, the SFT limits its intervention to requests made by translators (Internal Regulations (2018); Article 3.2. Discipline). "Regarding disciplinary issues, the Steering Committee can rule only on the request of a directly affected translator"[24] (my translation). Quite differently, the AUSIT code indicates that "[c]lients or other parties who work with interpreting and translating practitioners should bring any breach of this Code to AUSIT's attention [...]" (Preamble). The AUSIT thus incites third parties (mainly beneficiaries) to report on translators' possible misconduct. Somewhat similarly, the ATIO seems to open doors to anyone to make a complaint. "Complaints with respect to members who contravene this Code of Ethics or in any way damage the reputation of language professionals may be submitted to the Discipline Committee of the Association [...]" (Article, 5.1.2).

As is clear, the reported associations adopt two different approaches as to the agents who are eligible to report on a translator's potential misconduct. While the IAFET and the SFT call on colleagues to watch one another (internal control), the AUSIT and the ATIO open doors to clients and any third parties to report on members' misconduct. Clearly, positions such as the AUSIT's and the ATIO's may make the translator subject to the clients/employers' whims and inclinations and, therefore, subject to external control. This may put translators under continuous pressure to respond to these agents' wishes, fearing their reporting of any possible 'lapses.' Such incitement of outsiders to police association members may ultimately affect the translator's autonomy and, therefore, symbolic capital, as I discuss thoroughly in Chapter 6.

Reports on a translator's misconduct may result in disciplinary actions taken by the delegate(s), i.e., disciplinary committees and/or board members. The delegate translating agent works to protect the image of the translator association from disrepute, by taking disciplinary measures against the members who do not comply with the collective rules, especially codes of ethics. They ensure the purification of the group and the preservation of its 'honour' by expelling the 'wrongdoers,' or the "embarrassing individuals," in Bourdieu's (1986, 251) words. In this respect, the IAFET code stipulates that any misconduct or breach of the code of ethics is subject to disciplinary action.

> Becoming a member of IAFET implies acceptance of this Code of Ethics and commitment to fully respect it in practicing the translating and interpreting professions. Any and all forms of conduct contrary to this Code of Ethics shall be subject to the sanction deemed proper by the IAFET Good Practices Commission, depending on the circumstances surrounding the case in question and in accordance with the provisions of IAFETs Bylaws.
>
> (Code of Ethics Conclusion)

Similarly, the ATIO stipulates that "[a]ny breach of this Code of Ethics will constitute an act of professional misconduct and members may be subject to discipline by the Discipline Committee of the Association" (Article

5.1.1). The procedure set out in the ATIO's *By-laws* (2014)[25] allows the Discipline Committee to take different punitive actions that range from revoking membership in the association to a reprimand, among others.

Not so differently, the SFT in its "Internal Regulations" (2018) enumerates the cases which are considered serious misconduct and, thus, may lead to expulsion or a warning.

> The following constitute gross misconduct for all members – leading to a warning or expulsion:
>
> a. *failure to comply with the applicable By-Laws, Internal Regulations or Deontological Codes*;
> b. undermining the material or moral interests of the union or the profession;
> c. using the membership status of the SFT in association with a company name, business name or other name and delegating this status to a third party such as an employer, employee, company or any other entity or organization;
> d. using the visual identity or the name of the SFT outside the conditions and rules governing the use of the membership title without the consent of the Steering Committee.[26]
>
> (Article 3.1, italics added, my translation)

What is surprising in these internal regulations is the fact that the code of ethics of a *unionist* association like the SFT is a binding rather than a guiding document. 'Non-respect' of this document is considered a 'faute grave' [gross misconduct] that leads to a warning or expulsion. The SFT, on the other hand, highlights its arbitration function when it comes to disputes between translators and users of translation (Article 13)[27]. Astonishingly, members (and other disputing parties) are required to pay for this arbitration. Typically, in a unionist organization, membership fees and other various contributions would be enough for a member to benefit from such a 'service' – which is supposedly a sort of "gratitude" for the previous efforts and money invested by the member (see Bourdieu 1986, 252). The SFT does not seem to recognize the debt it has toward its members when they need a service like 'arbitration.' In sum, the SFT adopts differentiated positions regarding the translator's compliance with internal regulations, on the one hand, and their disputes with outsider agents, on the other hand. While it shows firmness as far as the former is concerned, it adopts arbitration policy for the latter.

Similarly to the SFT, the ITAINDIA code stresses arbitration in cases of dispute. "I will notify my clients of any unresolved difficulties. If we cannot resolve a dispute, we will seek arbitration" (Code of Professional Conduct for Service Providers, Article D). On the other hand, the ITAINDIA is very firm as to the 'violation' of internal regulations.

> [t]he Governing Body of the society shall have the powers to expel/terminate any member(s) from the membership of the association on the following grounds:
>
> (a) On becoming insolvent or of unsound mind
> (b) On written resignation
> (c) If found to be involved in any anti-social activities
> (d) If adjudged by any court of law to be a criminal offender
> (e) If found guilty of indulging in propaganda against the Aims and Objectives of the society,
> (f) If he/she fails to pay the subscription,
> (g) If he/she has not attended three consecutive meetings of the general body without informing the secretariat, and
> (h) *If he/she disregards Rules & Regulations or disobeys the decisions of the Governing Body.*
>
> (Section B, italics added)

While some of the grounds of expulsion may be plausible, such as (d), it is quite striking that the ITAINDIA may expel a member because they failed to comply with the decisions of the governing body (h). This autocratic tone is alienating and rather incomprehensible from a voluntary association.

Although it calls on third parties to report on translators' misconduct, the AUSIT warns them that its Board of Professional Conduct has a mere guiding and consultative function; it "has no power of enforcement." The Board, however, maintains its prerogative to expel members found guilty[28]. This is despite its seemingly lenient attitude when it proclaims that punitive action is only taken as a last resort.

The SATI, in turn, adopts the arbitration process. It urges its Language Office/Agency Corporate Members "[t]o be bound by an arbitration process established by the SATI in the event of a dispute between themselves and any clients, employees, subcontractors or fellow members" (Code of Ethics for Language Agency Corporate Members). Surprisingly, this article disappears from the Code of Ethics for Individual Members. The SATI makes a brief mention of 'disciplinary procedures' on its website when laying out the "Benefits of SATI Membership." It stipulates that the SATI "[e]nsures that best practices are followed in the profession through our Codes of Ethics for individual members, for agencies and for offices, and our Disciplinary Procedures."[29] It remains unclear what these disciplinary procedures are. But this statement is an indication that the SATI goes beyond informal arbitration or mediation.

All translator associations discussed above stress the 'honour' of the organization and/or the 'profession,' despite their different natures and functions. They all take disciplinary actions against 'embarrassing' or dissident members who do not abide by the regulations and codes of ethics (with the exception of the ATPP, which omits any mention of adjudication procedures in cases of dispute with users of translation or breach of the code of ethics)[30]. That said, minor differences are identified as far as strictness of application is concerned. The ATIO (order), the ITAINDIA, the IAFET (voluntary) and the SFT (union) are the strictest in their disciplinary measures while the AUSIT and the SATI (voluntary) appear to be less strict. On the other hand, some associations emphasize their arbitration nature in cases of dispute with external agents – a fact which may also suggest their inability to support vulnerable members when they need support. And this leads one to doubt whether investing in such social networks is worthwhile, given the limited support a member gets in moments of distress in contrast to the sanctions that apply if they ever 'lapse.' One wonders, thus, whether isolation and *autonomy* are not more advantageous than *alienating sociability*.

Adopting disciplinary measures, associations' delegates (board or committees) run the risk of abusing their power when judging accused members. Those who hold the totality of the social capital of the association and act and speak on behalf of the whole group may misappropriate the "collectively-owned capital" – in Bourdieu's (1986, 249) terms – and misuse this delegation in various ways, including in the adjudication procedures (ibid., 251). This is because judging a certain conduct of a certain translator is not as easy as it appears. Translators make different decisions depending on their personal judgment. A decision that may displease a certain party may be well justified on other ethical or practical grounds. A delegate may misjudge a translator's behaviour or decision and unjustifiably accuse them of misconduct just because their ground is different than that of the translator[31]. This does not even include cases in which some delegates may intentionally work against the individual members' interests and abuse "the power which the group enables ... [them] to concentrate" (ibid.). Such a situation might arise when some employers (corporate translators, i.e., representatives of translation companies) are influential board members of an association and work mainly to respond to the clients' or employers' requirements[32]. Thus, the social capital sought by joining the professional network may turn into a collective interpellation of members by a small number of delegates – who get their power from these same individual translators.

In addition to all the actual and potential restraints on social capital, discussed above, the accumulated amount of it thanks to membership in a large association may be significant *only* in relation to other peer translators who do not have that membership, and not in relation to the other agents with whom translators struggle for prestige. Following Bourdieu (1986), the social capital of a translator who is a member of an association depends not only on the size of the association but also on the volume of (economic, cultural or symbolic) capital its individual members possess. Thus, although the size of some translator associations may be larger than, say, some leagues of authors or associations of publishers[33], the volume of symbolic capital of each member translator may be lower than that of the author/publisher – as I discuss in Chapter 6. The members' low prestige may not help empower the network and, therefore, may not feed the social capital of individual translators. In short, it is not only about the number of members an association has but mainly about the 'quality' of those members: i.e., the symbolic size is more important than the material size (i.e., quantity/number).

All studied associations underscore the importance of membership and networking with like-minded practitioners. They also all take pride in being part of a larger international network, which is the FIT, a consultative body of the UNESCO. To be part of such large networks and benefit from their useful relations and resources, individual members are required, of course, to contribute materially and symbolically. Most importantly, members are urged to comply with the collective rules of the game and work in a way that upholds the reputation of the association and the 'profession.' Most associations implement coercive measures in order to guarantee 'appropriate' conduct of their members. In contrast, they provide little support to them in cases of dispute with other agents. Worse, some associations incite outsiders to report any translator's action/behaviour they deem inappropriate. These associations, therefore, leave the door open to external pressures on individual members and risk the intrusion of these agents in internal affairs, as I further demonstrate in Chapter 6. But before delving into the discussion of this issue, I next analyze the translator's economic capital in the documents under study.

5.3 The Translator's Economic Capital

Economic capital is purely material and can simply take the form of money or property. In the case of the translator, economic capital can be instantaneous in the form of remuneration earned immediately in return for a service, or eventual in the form of deferred benefits, like social insurance, job security, retirement, copyright and the translator's share in subsequent use/success of their translations.

5.3.1 Instantaneous Economic Profits

Many organizations purportedly defend the economic/financial interests of translators. As far as remuneration is concerned, the UNESCO recommends that contracts governing relations between a translator and a "user"[34] "accord an equitable remuneration to the translator whatever his or her legal status" (Nairobi Recommendation, paragraph 5a). Likewise, the FIT Translator's Charter reiterates the translator's right to fair remuneration for their commissioned work (Article 22).

Some national associations' codes follow the Nairobi Recommendation and the Translator's Charter as to the emphasis on the translator's *right* to equitable remuneration. The IAFET's code of ethics calls on translators to "[e]nforce and defend the right to receive pay that permits their profession to be practiced in a decent and effective manner" (Article 3.1). Likewise, the SFT underlines that "the translator is entitled to remuneration for their services, determined mainly on the basis of their experience, training, special skills, the complexity of the document to be translated, the research required, the deadlines and any expenses, investments and charges that may be incurred" (Article 4b, my translation). The ITAINDIA Code of Professional Conduct addressed to employers or contractors, on the other hand, calls on employers/contractors to "not require translators or interpreters to do unpaid work for the prospect of a paid assignment" (Article D). Articles tackling remuneration, however, disappear from the section of the ITAINDIA code of professional conduct addressed to service providers (i.e., translators).

Three of the organizations that underscore the translator's right for fair remuneration, likewise, forbid unfair competition that results in lowering rates (FIT Translator's Charter, Article 8; SFT Deontological Code, Article 4b; IAFET Code of Ethics, Articles 3.4, 4.2). This issue is especially pressing in today's fierce competition between translators globally, due to "job displacement' to "telemigrants," in Cronin's words (2021). These organizations, probably aware of the power of large clients to negotiate/ impose low rates, aim to restore order and thus preserve the dignity of the occupation and practitioners.

Some other national/provincial associations' codes tackle the economic issue quite differently. They rather urge their members to refrain from applying excessive fees. The SATI code, for example, urges translators "[t]o be guided in negotiating remuneration by the principle of equitability, and in particular to refrain from charging excessive rates." The ATIO code, purportedly seeking 'Protection of the Public,' stipulates that "[m]embers shall set fair and reasonable fees for their services [...]" (Article 3.4.1). It adds that "[m]embers will bill clients *only for services provided* unless otherwise stipulated between the parties" (Article 3.4.2, italics added).

Outwardly, the content of the latter article seems redundant for it goes without saying that one cannot charge others for services not provided. However, the article may be understood as a call for translators to bill clients only for the number of words 'actually' translated, and not for the 'repetitive' elements already available in TM. Although this interpretation is not certain nor the only one because of the ambiguity of the article, some clients and translators may, however, adopt this understanding, which, of course, constrains the practitioner's economic capital.

In sum, some organizations emphasize fair remuneration as a *right* to be gained and defended by translators. These organizations call on the other agents to respect the effort of translators and pay them accordingly. They, therefore, impose *duties* on clients and employers. Some of them also underline unfair competition as a translator's duty to abide by. This orientation indicates a collective engagement – with all the power this may generate for the translator community – to impose their terms on the other agents in the translation industry field (namely clients and employers), who would then have no choice but to positively respond to the translator's demands for fair pay. However, other associations highlight the excessive charges that translators may impose on beneficiary agents. The latter associations ignore the fact that translators do not have enough power that allows them to engage in equitable negotiations with powerful agents, as I further discuss shortly, as many of the latter are able not only to protect themselves but to impose their rates on translators (or even abuse them, as is the case with Able company[35]). We all know that most translation transactions nowadays are with large corporations and institutions (like the EU, the UN, national government institutions, localizers and multinational corporations).

5.3.2 Potential Economic Benefits

In addition to immediate remuneration as one of the main components of the translator's economic capital that yield fixed economic benefits, the two international bodies underline social and fiscal benefits like those "generally applicable to the authors of literary or scientific works" (UNESCO Nairobi Recommendation, Section 4) or "intellectual workers" (FIT Translator's Charter, Article 24). The SFT is the only national association that mentions the social insurance and fiscal situation of the translator in its code of ethics, but addresses it to corporate translators (i.e., self-employed translators) to "comply with the welfare and taxation regimes" in place (Article 2).

Social and fiscal benefits are not the only potential sources of income for translators. Copyright on their work supposedly adds income to their fixed remuneration. Since the Paris Act (1971) of the Berne Convention and the UNESCO Nairobi Recommendation (1976), more emphasis started to be put on the translator's copyright. "Contracts since the 1980s show an increasing recognition of the translator's crucial role in the production of the translation by referring to him or her as the 'author' or 'translator' and by copyrighting the text in the translator's name" (Venuti 1995, 12). The 1980s developments have supposedly had positive impacts on some translators' economic capital (notably literary translators, and non-literary translators who manage to sign contracts that contain such 'recognition'). For the translator, to institutionalize part of their economic capital in the form of property rights (in Bourdieu's terminology 1986, 243) – or copyright, to be exact in this case – may be beneficial in the long term. Nevertheless, the Paris Act did not accord translations full copyright. "Translations, adaptations, arrangements of music and other alterations of a literary or artistic work shall be protected as original works without prejudice to the copyright in the original work" (Article 2, Paragraph 3). Following this article, the translator enjoys copyright for their labour and skills (namely form/expression), but this copyright is subject to another layer of protection, that of the 'original' author. The translator's work, although owned in a 'similar' way as that of an 'original' author, it is only *partially* owned. The translator shares ownership of the translation with the author, a fact which reduces their economic benefits substantially. "[T]hese limitations carry some troubling consequences, both economic and cultural. By subordinating the translator's rights to the author's, the law permits the author to shrink the translator's share in the profits of the translation" (Venuti 1998, 47).

From the corpus under study, the Nairobi Recommendation reiterates the Berne Convention provision regarding the translator's copyright.

> Member States should accord to translators, in respect of their translations, the protection accorded to authors under the provisions of the international copyright conventions to which they are party and/or under their national laws, *but without prejudice to the rights of the authors of the original works translated.*
>
> (Paragraph 3, italics added)

The Paragraph, thus, sets out that the translator's ownership of their translations is subject to the author's copyright and, therefore, partial. In its preamble, the Nairobi Recommendation states that despite the legal advancements in intellectual property protection, the practical implementation of the existing provisions/laws is "not always adequate." Thus, practical measures are "justified to ameliorate the effective application of existing laws." Of course the UNESCO would not question the appropriateness of the law; it rather questions the inadequate implementation of the international convention in many national laws. For this purpose, the Nairobi Recommendation lists "measures to ensure the application in practice of protection afforded translators under international conventions and in national laws relating to copyright" (Article III, paragraphs 4, 5, 5.a, 5.b, 5.c). These paragraphs emphasize not only the immediate economic entitlements (fair remuneration for salaried translators or advance pay for non-salaried translators for their services regardless of the commercial success or failure of the project) but also proportional economic benefits for subsequent uses and potential success of their works. But paragraph 5.h once again reminds us that the translator's economic rights are *proportionate* to the 'original' author's economic rights.

The FIT adopts a mixed approach of duties (Articles 11 and 12) and rights (Articles 13, 19, 21, 22) as to the question of copyright and any subsequent economic benefits. But, like the Nairobi Recommendation, the Translator's Charter is embedded in a paradox. On the one hand, it underlines that the translator's (economic) rights in the subsequent uses of their translation are similar to those accorded to any intellectual worker. On the other hand, it emphasizes the subordinate status of the translator – whom it considers a 'secondary author' (Article 11) to the 'original' author, who continues to hold copyright even in translation – a fact which substantially diminishes the translator's economic benefits.

Following the international organizations, codes of ethics of some translator associations underline the obligation to respect copyright law. These organizations adopt three different approaches; some of the codes urge translators to respect the 'original' author's copyright, with no mention of the translator's copyright, like the SATI code of ethics; others call on members to respect intellectual property laws, without specifying whether that includes one's own copyright as a translator, as is the case of the ATIO (Article 3.3.2). A third approach taken by the SFT and the AUSIT documents includes the observation of both the author and the translator rights, following the international organizations (SFT, Article 5; AUSIT, Conduct issues specific to translators, Article T10, respectively). The SFT code, nevertheless, makes a vague (and probably misleading) affirmation that the Nairobi Recommendation "recommends equating the translator with the author and placing their name prominently on all published copies of their translations," without specifying the partiality of the translator's right (About the SFT, my translation).

Contrary to the codes of ethics of the associations from developed countries (where copyright law may have become commonsensical) and the SATI, codes of most associations from developing countries (namely the IAFET, the ITAINDIA and the ATPP) omit any explicit reference to the question of author's copyright. Interestingly, the ITAINDIA emphasizes *only* the translator's copyright – in contrast to the SATI and the associations from developed countries. It calls on employers or contractors to "give the translators the recognition traditionally given to the authors" for translations which are published and/or performed and over which they have direct control (ITAINDIA Code of professional conduct for Employer or Contractor, Article F). A position like this is hardly surprising as many developing countries – in addition to countries whose languages/cultures are not central, like the Scandinavian countries – have been resisting the current copyright law, especially the articles that restrain translation. The current copyright law is detrimental to small economies/countries, where translation is one of the main instruments of knowledge dissemination and economic development (Sadek 2018, 441; see also Basalamah and Sadek 2014).

Despite the "small increments" in the translators' economic conditions thanks to certain later amendments in copyright law, namely in the Paris Act, which "signal a growing awareness of the translator's authorship," Venuti asserts that "they do not constitute a significant change in the economics of translation, and it remains difficult for a freelance translator to make a living solely from translating" (Venuti 1995, 12). Also, the Special Provisions Regarding Developing Countries in the Paris Act still do not meet the aspirations of developing countries. Thus, the omission of any reference to this law from some codes of associations from developing countries (which are all signatories of the Berne Convention[36]) may be said to reflect a sort of resistance and/or a lack of copyright tradition in many of those countries – although these same codes paradoxically reinforce the very premises behind this law, as I explain shortly in Chapter 6.

In sum, although many associations underline reasonable remuneration for the translator, some of them reinforce the current copyright law – which favours the 'original' author and negatively affects the translator economic capital – as a common sense law. In addition, the calls for fair remuneration may be paradoxical as these associations represent translation in ways that may not increase its economic or symbolic value. In the following chapter, I discuss how ineffective and incoherent the positions of translator organizations regarding the translator's economic, cultural and social forms of capital in fact are, and the extent to which they affect the translator's symbolic capital.

Notes

1 https://fair.work/en/fw/blog/most-freelancers-on-translation-and-transcription-platforms-face-poor-working-conditions-according-to-new-fairwork-research (Accessed December 17, 2023).
2 As an example, an investigation of the Canadian CBC News Network published on February 13, 2019, revealed that Able Translations company, "once one of

the biggest companies of its kind in Canada," has been involved in a "vast extent" of "financial delinquency." "Court and financial records, company emails, and interviews with more than 50 translators — overwhelmingly immigrants — show Able has bounced at least two dozen cheques, defaulted on dozens of court orders, possibly misrepresented facts in court testimony and broken a litany of promises to pay its freelancers," CBC reports. All in all, "more than 200 people have sued for nearly $1.8 million in unpaid earnings and other damages," according to the report. Over the last two decades, this company, according to the same report, provided "medical interpreters for Alberta and Ontario hospitals, document translation for Fortune 500 firms, and language services to every level of government." The Able company subcontracted work to freelance translators, who were mainly vulnerable immigrants, with all the complexity of their (legal) situation. www.cbc.ca/news/canada/able-translations-interpreters-lawsuits-cra-debt-1.5016014(Accessed on March 20, 2019).

3 www.atpp.org.pe/membership.php (Accessed on August 20, 2019).
4 www.translators.org.za/categories-of-membership (Accessed on October 25, 2019).
5 https://iafet.cyrillabs.com/memberships (Accessed on October 15, 2019).
6 In cases where beneficiaries (namely clients and employers) provide CAT tools or any other "means of production" to the translator, they set strict limitations on the conditions of use as is expressively emphasized in all documents under the 'confidentiality' principle.
7 This is not surprising when we know that the FIT is a consultant to the UNESCO.
8 https://atio.on.ca/membership (Accessed on September 25, 2019).
9 https://ausit.org/AUSIT/About/What_We_Do_-_AUSIT_Services.aspx (Accessed on July 25, 2019).
10 www.translators.org.za/background (Accessed on October 25, 2019).
11 www.atpp.org.pe/association.php (Accessed on August 20, 2019).
12 www.atpp.org.pe/association.php (Accessed on August 20, 2019).
13 https://iafet.cyrillabs.com/wp-content/uploads/2018/09/bylaw-1.pdf (Accessed on October 25, 2019).
14 Of course, the FIT does not overlook the particularities of different specialized groups of translators as well as their regional specificities as it reminds them of preserving their identity within the central organization.
15 www.fit-ift.org (Accessed on September 25, 2019).
16 www.fit-ift.org/unesco (Accessed on September 25, 2019).
17 https://atio.on.ca/about (Accessed on September 25, 2019).
18 www.atpp.org.pe/asociacion.php (Accessed on August 20, 2019).
19 www.atpp.org.pe/asociacion.php (Accessed on August 20, 2019).
20 https://iafet.org/about (Accessed on October 25, 2019).
21 www.translators.org.za/background (Accessed on October 25, 2019).
22 www.translators.org.za/benefits-of-sati-membership (Accessed on October 25, 2019).
23 https://fair.work/en/fw/blog/most-freelancers-on-translation-and-transcription-platforms-face-poor-working-conditions-according-to-new-fairwork-research (Accessed December 17, 2023).

24 www.sft.fr/reglement-interieur.html#.XS3eqehKjIU (Accessed on October 25, 2019).
25 https://atio.on.ca/wp-content/uploads/bsk-pdf-manager/RGL-Anx2ENFINAL1420.pdf (Accessed on September 25, 2019).
26 www.sft.fr/reglement-interieur.html#.XS3eqehKjIU (Accessed on October 25, 2019).
27 It is noteworthy that the SFT, nevertheless, is very strict as far as respect of internal regulations is concerned, as discussed above (see Internal Regulations 2018, Article 3.1).
28 https://ausit.org/AUSIT/About/What_We_Do_BOPC.aspx (Accessed on July 25, 2019).
29 www.translators.org.za/benefits-of-sati-membership (Accessed on October 25, 2019).
30 The ATA, which is not part of the current study, even publishes the cases with the names of sanctioned translators in the section about 'ethics' on its website www.atanet.org/governance/sanctioned_members.php (Accessed on December 30, 2020).
31 As an example, the ATA reports on its website that one of its members was censured for violating the article about the requirement of 'faithfulness.' "An individual member (July 2017) was censured privately for violation of the first tenet in ATA's Code of Ethics and Professional Practice: 'to convey meaning between people and cultures faithfully, accurately, and impartially.'" I do not know the exact circumstances of this case, but I believe that judging a translator based on this rule is unfair in many cases. www.atanet.org/about-us/code-of-ethics/sanctioned-members (Accessed on January 12, 2021).
32 This is an important avenue for research to (un)corroborate the hypothesis.
33 For example, while the ATIO currently has 1,000 members in the province of Ontario, the Canadian Authors Association has had 25,000 members *from all over Canada in all its history* since its creation in 1921 (https://canadianauthors.org/national/history/). The Writers' Union of Canada has only 2,100 members *from all over Canada* (www.writersunion.ca/about), The Association of Canadian Publishers has no more than 115 publishers (https://publishers.ca/about/). Websites accessed on April 23, 2019.
34 "[T]he term "users" denotes the persons or legal entities for which a translation is made" (UNESCO Nairobi Recommendation, Paragraph 1.C).
35 www.cbc.ca/news/canada/able-translations-interpreters-lawsuits-cra-debt-1.5016014 (Accessed on March 20, 2019).
36 Signatories to the Berne Convention can be found at: www.wipo.int (Accessed on March 8, 2019).

6 The Translator's Capital Conversions

As we learn from Bourdieu, symbolic capital is "a capital of recognition or consecration" (1990a, 141). It consists of the *recognition* of any form of the three other forms of capital, namely economic, social or cultural capital. This recognition results from an accord between the categories of perception of the granter of symbolic capital and the property or quality being perceived – an accord which allows the granter to see it as valuable and worthy of admiration (Bourdieu 1998a). The agents concerned with translation, or the public at large, would regard translation practice and translators' qualities as valuable and worthy of recognition if, and only if, they are endowed with categories of perception and prior experience that allow them to regard them as such. Of course, these categories of perception correspond to socially constructed beliefs and "collective expectations" (Bourdieu 1998a, 103). In the case of translation and translators, if agents and the public recognized anything in the translator's qualities, they would recognize and appreciate their intellectual/cultural qualities. Like any other cultural worker, the translator would derive most of their symbolic capital from their cultural capital, following Bourdieu's thought. The translator's other forms of capital (social and economic) would be fed by the cultural capital were it converted into symbolic capital. Symbolic capital secures "useful relationships" – to use Bourdieu's (1986, 249) terminology – with the other agents in the field of power. They run after you when you are 'useful' to them. The economic capital is also mainly fed by this form of capital. One gets high remuneration if one is *recognized* as possessing complex and rare knowledge/competencies. In one word, for translators, cultural capital is the source, the nucleus and the orbit of all other forms of capital.

As practitioners of an occupation and as cultural producers, the translators' symbolic capital – if granted – would/should consist of a recognition for their *esoteric knowledge as professionals* (similarly to doctors or lawyers), or a recognition for their *creative cultural production* (similarly

DOI: 10.4324/9781032713557-9

to 'original' authors), or ideally *both*. Hence, their symbolic capital would/ should be manifest in *collegiate control* over their profession – to use Johnson's terminology (2016) (especially for translators of non-literary works) – or in a recognition of the translators' *authorship*, manifest in full intellectual property rights (especially for – but not limited to – literary translators). This is because *professionalism* implies the recognition of their esoteric expertise in a highly specialized field and because, on the other hand, copyright is one of the most tangible signs of recognition and consecration of cultural producers.

In Section 6.1, I discuss the extent to which the translator's cultural capital, as represented by the codes of ethics under study, may lead to collegiate control or professionalism, as a mode of occupational control (Johnson 2016). In Section 6.2, I discuss the symbolic value of the translator's copyright and how that is represented and reproduced by the documents under study. In these two sections, I further analyze articles from the corpus that reflect the translator's symbolic status. Meanwhile, I occasionally discuss the extent to which their level of symbolic recognition, if any, feeds or not their social and economic forms of capital. In Section 6.3, I discuss the symbolic violence the translator may undergo and the possibilities of their liberation.

6.1 The Translator Is (Not) a Professional

This section discusses the symbolic capital of translators as *practitioners of an occupation*. It examines the power relations at stake in the translators' attempts to self-control their practice. This section shows what mode of *occupational control* is being developed, following Johnson's typology (2016/1972), i.e., who is paying for the process of regularization and how that is reflected in the translator associations' identifying document(s), namely their codes of ethics. In other words, this section examines whether *professionalism* as a social construction that enhances the translator's capital[1] and gives them the power to impose the "'official' definitions"[2] of *translation*, its methods/strategies and interrelations is within reach.

As we learn from Bourdieu, a *profession* is a field of struggle over available stakes and is the product of "the work of *aggregation* and symbolic imposition" (Bourdieu and Wacquant 1992, 243, italics added). Yet, professionals within the same field have internal as well as external struggles. On the one hand, they compete with neighbouring/sister occupations to demonstrate their distinctiveness and impose their occupation as the one and only profession. On the other hand, they struggle in the larger social field to secure a position within the field of power[3]. Mike Saks argues that Bourdieu's work may actually be synergistically useful in understanding professionalism as a form of symbolic capital, the substance of which is challenged and subject to regular struggle and negotiation in power-driven contexts. Here, professional fields may be seen as embedded within other fields in what Bourdieu views as a general field of power – in which professionalism can be seen as a legitimated way of acting and interpreting.

(Saks 2016b, 13)

Translators, seeking *professionalism*, struggle with outsider agents to impose the definition and terms of their practice and ultimately to assign themselves a position within the field of power alongside other professionals and cultural producers.

As is the case with other professionals (e.g., lawyers, doctors), cultural capital is the form of capital that is liable to feed the translator's symbolic capital and, therefore, allow them to impose their *professionalism* and shield against external impositions. "Cultural and symbolic capital are especially important to professionalization, as professionalism itself may be described as the conversion of cultural capital (knowledge) into symbolic capital (status)" (Jackson 2017, 798). This conversion of cultural capital into symbolic power is possible only if the translator's embodied cultural capital is regarded as complex and valuable, and their institutionalized cultural capital is seen as high, especially by holders of symbolic and economic capital. Should this be the case, translators may be able to impose their conditions on the holders of large economic capital (namely clients and patrons) in what Johnson (2016/1972) calls "collegiate control" of one's occupation. This, of course, entails the establishment of labour, economic and symbolic relations that may be favourable to practitioners. On the other hand, if the translator's cultural capital is seen as mechanical and low, translators will be subject to *corporate patronage* and, therefore, undergo disadvantaged labour and economic relations. For recognition to happen, translators need to be united, and most importantly, they need to mobilize powerful external resources that can boost the value of their cultural capital in the minds of the other agents. In addition to the two conditions that need to be secured by translators themselves, the consumers of their services, i.e., clients/employers, should represent a "relatively large, heterogeneous, fragmented source of demand" (Johnson 2016, 43).

The studied translator organizations all claim, or at least seek to promote, 'professionalism.'[4] They all advance, to different extents, a few purported attributes of 'professionalization,' such as the organization of translators in an association, their reliance on systematic knowledge, the possession of educational qualifications and the establishment of a code of ethics – as seen in the discussion of the different forms of capital.

However, advancing these attributes is never enough to claim *professionalism*, following the power approach in the sociology of professions. What is more important is having control over one's practice and imposing one's terms and conditions on outsiders. In parallel, some articles in some of the documents under study purport to defend the translator's rights and interests and seek a *professionalism* that implies collegiate control. They highlight the fact that translation should be an autonomous profession and that translators should be recognized as professionals, who autonomously define its rules. In this respect, the FIT lays out a strong advocacy for the translator's autonomy and recognition. The FIT Translator's Charter highlights the importance of translation and its widespread impact in today's world, and calls for its recognition as "a distinct and autonomous profession" (Preamble). It, likewise, stresses the autonomy and dignity of the translator as a professional (Articles 3, 9). "The translator shall refuse to give to a text an interpretation of which he/she does not approve, or which would be contrary to the obligations of his/her profession" (Article 3) and "shall neither seek nor accept work under conditions humiliating to himself/herself or his/her profession" (Article 9). The Charter emphasizes the need to affiliate the translation 'profession' to other professions in terms of protection and the right to establish associations or unions (Articles 23, 25). It also underlines the importance of lobbying public authorities to adopt regulations and legal measures that are favourable to translators. "They [translators] shall exert their influence on public authorities in the preparation and introduction of legal measures and regulations concerning the profession" (Article 27). These articles clearly show that the FIT is well aware of the power relations at stake and that recognition is gained through struggles and lobbying.

Some national associations stress the question of translators' recognition, dignity and autonomy in similar ways as the FIT. The SFT code stipulates that "the translator shall advise their clients on the methods and techniques that are best suited to the accomplishment of the tasks they entrust to them"[5] (Article 3d, my translation). The document, likewise, underlines that "the translator shall not accept instructions from a client or employer that may constitute a breach of this Deontogical Code" (Article 6b, my translation). The union, thus, implies that the 'professional' translator is an expert and counsellor in the field and that they adopt different strategies and methods depending on the task at hand and its situation/context. It also advances the specialization, autonomy and self-control of the translation 'profession.' The translator as a 'professional' autonomously decides what constitutes their practice and its ethics. They do not accept impositions from any other agent (namely clients or employers). Not very differently, the IAFET urges members to "[n]either offer nor accept jobs that are improper in terms of deadline, environment or method." This statement shows that the association is aware of the power play and the possible impositions that can be inflicted on translators in terms of methods/strategies of translation as well as working conditions. Similarly, the AUSIT code stresses 'professional' relations and adequate working conditions for the translator. It also calls for the recognition of the translator's status. "International recognition of the status of interpreters and translators becomes even more important as they achieve greater prominence through media, international affairs and local political issues, attracting increased scrutiny of their standards" (Preamble). The AUSIT is, therefore, like the FIT, the SFT and the IAFET, aware of the power relations at stake and, therefore, seeks the translators' collegiate control over their occupation.

Somewhat differently from the above mentioned organizations, the SATI stipulates that the association seeks to "[e]nsure high standards of professionalism among its members through accreditation and the adoption of a code of ethics" (Mission Statement). The SATI does not show awareness of the power relations at stake as it simply stresses some traits of 'professionalism' that it claims ensure "high standards of professionalism." Consistent with its other articles, the SATI code seems to support the mainstream understanding of 'professionalism' (as the skill, the good conduct and the skills of a practitioner). This same understanding of 'professionalism' can easily be deduced from reading the ATIO code of ethics. The terms 'profession' and 'professional' are repeated 24 times out of 876 words in this code, all as a neutral concept that is devoid of conflict and power struggles. The mainstream sense of the terms can be discerned, likewise, in the ATPP and the ITAINDIA codes.

In sum, all translator organizations highlight the element of 'professionalism' in one way or another in their documents. Some understand it in its mainstream sense and ignore the power relations at stake. Others see it as a form of recognition that involves power dynamics. The latter group of organizations, however, overlook the fact that recognition and autonomy require the creation of many favourable conditions, the most important of which is the promotion and imposition of a favourable definition of the translator's practice. As we know from Johnson (2016), professionalism implies a struggle over the very definition of the practice. The importance of this battle lies in the fact that the definition of the practice affects all the other relational aspects of the practice. If translators imposed their understanding of their work, they would subsequently trace not only its trajectories and internal laws, but also their relational rules on outsiders. Conversely, when the clients/patrons impose their definition of the practice, they "circumscribe the translators' ideological space" (Lefevere 1992, 7), and impose all its interlinked relational aspects.

The more complex a definition is, the more imposing it may be. Esoterism, complexity and mystery are important qualities that make an occupation a wonder to its beneficiaries and the other surrounding agents. Unfortunately, as discussed in Part I, the way *translation* is presented and defined by all organizations does not make it appear as possessing these qualities. In this definition, the primary role assigned to the translator is to be a subservient 'faithful' copier, who follows the original text and the purpose of the client/patron, period. Creativity and initiative as part of the translator's work are neglected or probably even regarded as 'unprofessional' and/or unethical. In this mainstream definition, *translation* is not regarded as requiring esoteric knowledge in the categories of perception of the other agents and the public nor is it seen as requiring different and complex decisions in different situations. It is rather represented as a practice that is clear and evident to everyone. This implies that translation requires mere mechanical skills and, therefore, does not need high cultural capital – or at least so it seems to outsider agents/large public, who may (intentionally or unintentionally) ignore the nuances and the different interpretations that members of the translating community may hold of 'translation as faithfulness' – if they do, at all.

Powerful agents (users/consumers of translation) seem to have the same view of *translation* as the one advanced in the documents under study. They perceive of the translator's work as a practice of copying/faithful transfer that hardly provokes any admiration or appreciation. Koskinen states that the Translation Services of the European Commission, the largest employer of translators in the world, for instance, does not perceive translators "as experts in intercultural communication" (Koskinen 2000b, 54) – adopting a policy that highlights faithfulness, equivalence and equality between the different languages of the EU Member States. "Translating is only perceived as a mechanistic process best over and done with quickly and cheaply" (ibid.). Similarly, Stecconi, in a joint presentation with Theo Hermans, confirmed that translation as faithfulness is the prevalent view at The Translation Services of the European Commission, a fact which reinforces the mechanistic perception of the translator's work (Hermans and Stecconi 2002, 13). "Terminological issues and faithfulness play a large role in the discourse about translation at the SdT [Service de traduction (Translation Services)]; it's as if we never overcame Jerome's concerns" (ibid., 4). Stecconi also observes that little importance is attributed to translation despite its decisive contribution to the functioning of the European institution. "[I]t has been observed that translation figures very little in the wider communication within the Commission and the other institutions; in fact, it seems we are taken very much for granted" (ibid., 3). Not very differently, the UNESCO, a large employer of translators along with its mother organization, the UN, takes *translation* as a mere "faithful rendering of the original" (Nairobi Recommendation, Paragraph 7a), despite its claim to improve the status of translators in its Nairobi Recommendation. In another context, Annie Brisset (2008) criticizes the decision of Canada's federal Translation Bureau for not hiring candidates who hold an M.A. in translation (with a B.A. in a different specialization) under the pretext that M.A. level is "trop théorique" [too theoretical] (2008, 151). She argues that the decision reflects a 'taylorist' and 'technical' conception of the translator's work. This position of the Translation Bureau reflects the view of translators as 'subordinates.' It reinforces "a demeaning perception of translation, ingrained in the minds of translators as well as in society" (ibid., 156, my translation).

The perception of translators as mere mechanical executors (with little embodied or institutionalized cultural capital), and of translation as an unimportant activity is, indeed, softly reinforced by these giant employers. The fact that translator organizations reiterate the views of these industrialists/political agents in their definitions of *translation* in their internal documents, and do not demand higher education for access (an M.A. for example, as translation practice *is* based on theorizing) is a clear example that translators take the same position as those who dominate them. And as Stecconi rightly points out, when discussing the status of translation/translators at The Translation Service of the Commission of the EU, "[t]his mechanistic view of our craft is not exactly the best way to win professional respect" (Hermans and Stecconi 2002, 13). In this widespread sense, *translation* is mainly seen as a question of dictionaries, terminology, technological tools and language correctness. Other agents (namely users) know exactly what they want from their translators, and the latter simply execute their demands. And, "[o]f course, one of the most common reasons for a failure to appreciate the *complexity of translation* is that it is viewed as the activity of the *hack,* a kind of *slavish copying of the original*," as Cronin tells us (2013, 139, italics added). As importantly as not realizing the *complexity* of translation, the other agents and the public (and probably some translators themselves) do not realize the *importance* of translation (as discussed by Hermans and Stecconi 2002). According to Cronin, "[i]t is possible to get others interested in an area not by telling them how complex translation is (which it is) but *why it matters*" (2003, 3, italics added). The studied codes highlight neither the *complexity* nor the *importance* of translation.

In the case of the recognized professions, the situation is quite different. The consumer is usually vulnerable and knows very little compared to the professional – who is regarded as possessing a complex knowledge of a mysterious practice. The vulnerable 'ignorant' patient, for example, informs the professional doctor about what is hurting them and lets the expert make the hard decision about the cure. Likewise, the lawyer's client is 'ignorant' of the intricacies of law, its gaps and evasions; only the lawyer knows its mysterious pathways. Most importantly, patients and clients, in these two cases, are highly convinced by *how important* these two professions are for themselves and for society. The translator, on the other hand, executes what is already clear to everyone, including the client/employer. Unlike doctors and lawyers, who make different decisions depending on the patient's/client's case, they have the same prescription (i.e., faithfulness) ready for everyone and every context, following the mainstream view of *translation* that the organizations under study reproduce. They do not experience the pain of innovating/creating different solutions to different situations, nor do they use a special jargon that is not clear to clients/users. The discourse around *translation* is nothing special or perplexing like the discourse of doctors, lawyers or engineers. And unlike patients, who are at the mercy of their doctors' expertise and who rarely challenge their doctors' decisions, the translator's clients are, in most cases, more powerful and far from being passive recipients of a mysterious treatment. Instead, they are the ones who impose their treatment/ views – which are already reflected in the associations' codes of ethics.

The perceived low embodied cultural capital of the translator that results from the proposed definition of *translation* is aggravated by the fact that none of the studied associations require *institutionalized* cultural capital as a precondition of entry – despite the UNESCO's emphasis on specialized training in translation in educational institutions (Nairobi Recommendation, paragraph 11). Hence, the translator's supposedly low qualifications hardly convert to any symbolic capital. We know that recognized professionals are appreciated and respected mainly for the long years they spend at higher education institutions where they accumulate very specialized knowledge in their field of study. The fact that they possess a higher degree is the stamp of security and trust for users. Translators, not regarded as getting this long and specialized education, lose recognition from the public and the relevant agents. In the public and other agents' eyes, any bilingual with a few years of experience can join these associations, and therefore, become a (certified) translator. And there are millions of them! Everybody is bilingual nowadays. Godbout (2016, n.p.) is right to argue that "the authority of translators within society is questionable. Most people still believe that bilingualism is the only requirement necessary to be a translator." Thus, even the translator with high institutionalized cultural capital may be perceived as a bilingual autodidact who acquired the mechanical translation skills through some practice.

In sum, the fact that the documents under study represent translation as a work that requires neither specialized studies (institutionalized cultural capital) nor complex knowledge/skills (embodied cultural capital) feeds the public image of translation/the translator as a mechanistic practice/practitioner unworthy of recognition. This has an impact on other relational aspects, of course, including the economic aspect[6]. Following Bourdieu's thought, the translator's institutionalized cultural capital doubtless plays a role in establishing rates of pay. The educational qualification "makes it possible to establish conversion rates between cultural capital and economic capital by guaranteeing the monetary value of a given academic capital" (1986, 248). The low cultural capital, reinforced by the studied organizations, definitely serves the other agents' economic agendas. Clients, customers, patrons and the public may consider translation as worth little disbursements, proportionately with the mechanical skills it requires (faithful transfer) and the non-educational qualification required for its practitioners. As Cronin tells us, "[t]he less highly a culture values translation, the less it is going to want to pay its translators" (2003, 134–134). If their practice is not perceived as esoteric enough, the pay translators will receive is not as high as the pay received by, say, doctors or engineers, who are perceived as possessing rare esoteric knowledge, which users/consumers/clients desperately seek and for which they are ready to pay whatever price the expert professional imposes – I do not know of a patient who has negotiated the rate of a medical examination with their doctor! This state of affairs makes the calls for reasonable remuneration that are issued in some of the codes under study relatively useless and in vain, and somewhat paradoxical. The associations ignore the fact that economic capital is fed mostly by the translator's perceived cultural (and symbolic) capital.

The translators' possession of complex knowledge and high qualifications would never be enough for the professionalization of translation. These qualities need to be recognized and valued by translators themselves, first and foremost. Translators cannot persuade other agents if they themselves are not convinced of the complexity of their practice and its high value for society. As Godbout suggests in her discussion of the translator's lack of status or prestige, translators are "the authors of their own misfortune" (Godbout 2016, n.p.). "In order to gain public recognition, translators will need to increase their self-esteem, trade their image of subservience for one of a highly skilled professional service and come out of the shadows into the limelight" (ibid.).

This *productive* self-promotion is supposedly done through one's official channels. Unfortunately, analyzing these channels, mainly codes of ethics and/or practice, one can discern the omnipresence of the other agents' voice. Most codes seem to address competing agents. In the translation industry field, the documents seem to address both the individual translators and the *corporate* translators/employers, in a sort of *double-voiced* discourse, to use Bakhtin's term (1981). Even in the associations that claim to address individual translators and corporate translators separately through separate codes – as is the case of the SATI and the ITAINDIA – individual translators' codes still clearly include the corporate translator/employer's voice. The question is, therefore, whose voice is foregrounded? The power asymmetry between the two translating agents allows the dominant one (i.e., the corporate translator) to impose (some of) the internal regulations either *directly* or *softly*[7]. In the case of the AUSIT, for example, Ozolins (2014) states that the AUSIT committee that revised the code received agencies/employers' feedback/suggestions that reflect the (ethical) problems they have had with translators/interpreters. Some suggestions were, however, resisted by the committee in order to ensure the translator/interpreter's autonomy, Ozolins reports (2014, 365). But even if we accept Ozolins's assertion that there was no direct imposition, the committee certainly embraced many suggestions *softly* because they correspond to its members' categories of perception. Not surprisingly, Ozolins reports that, overall, the views of the translators/interpreters' representatives (designing the code) and the views of the other agents seem to agree on the translator/interpreter's roles (2014, 361). The translators/interpreters are already playing the roles desired by employers/clients very well *by themselves*. The reinforcement of the mainstream definition of *translation* (which serves the powerful agents economically in the short term, at least) is one of the most important examples, in this respect.

The tone of most codes gives the impression that not only are corporate translators' requirements addressed by these documents but outsider stakeholders' (other clients, employers, publishers, authors, legislators) needs as well – despite the variation in the extent of the presence of this voice in the different documents. Some codes are blunt about the protection of these agents, *exclusively*. In many articles, these documents direct some ethical principles toward protecting the rights and *interests* of clients, employers and authors, while they remain silent about others' rights. The ATIO code of ethics, for instance, stipulates that "[m]embers shall practise their profession with *honesty* and *integrity*, respecting the rights and *interests of their clients and/or employers*" (italics added). In another article about non-discrimination, it underscores the following:

- Members shall approach professional services with *respect and cultural sensitivity towards their clients*.
- Members shall not discriminate in the services which they provide on the basis of race, ancestry, place of origin, colour, ethnic origin, citizenship, creed, sex, sexual orientation, age, marital status, family status or disability.

(Articles 2.4.1, 2.4.2, italics added)

As is clear in the articles, even the call for non-discrimination is specific to, and *limited* to, the client to whom the translator provides services, while other potential forms of discrimination *in text* are overlooked. Of course, this limited responsibility to the payees is manifest in many other principles propounded by these documents such as the unconditional rule of 'confidentiality' to clients (regardless of the content), as is the case of the ATIO, ATPP, FIT, SATI and ITAINDIA[8]. This is in addition to other (virtue) ethics that are oriented solely toward clients, as I discuss thoroughly in Part III. These *a priori* principles, if embraced unconditionally and unquestioningly, may simply be used as tools to manipulate the translators so that they serve their clients/patrons submissively and unquestioningly, whatever the ethical matter is. Translators who abide by the principle of 'confidentiality' unconditionally and unquestioningly may, of course, not disclose information that is illegal/threatening or harmful in the translated material. Worse, they may disseminate this information. This is, of course, not to say that there is anything wrong with guaranteeing certain rights of the client to have their sensitive information protected. But the fact that these rights are *unconditional* and *exclusive* to these agents, in disregard of the other vulnerable agents or species' rights, is fraught with problems. Second, they are problematic as they are *unconditionally* secured regardless of the translator's dignity, autonomy and ethical judgment.

The double-voiced codes of ethics may, however, be seen as seeking promotional ends (See Lambert 2018). Koskinen writes about codes of ethics seeking such ends.

> One can ponder who is the primary addressee of the codes of practice, charters, quality standards and oaths of fidelity: are they truly intended as guidelines for translators or are they rather directed to the clients and readers of translations, and is their hidden function to create an atmosphere of trust and thus facilitate cooperation.
>
> (Koskinen 2000a, 82)

Following this view, the codes seek to reduce or eliminate the clients' possible suspicion and doubt (see Johnson 2016/1972, 41) and to promote cooperation. This view holds that the translators' documents include the desires of the external agents strategically in order to gain these agents' trust and, therefore, secure more jobs for the associations' members, all to enhance their economic profits. I argue that the assumedly promotional articles in some codes have adverse consequences. The presentation of the translator as unconditionally willing to abide by the wishes and demands of the client/patron ultimately undermines their prestige as autonomous experts and, consequently, reduces their economic profits. Jobs would come anyway, and with good rates, if the agents who need the translators' expertise recognized them as valuable experts. Translators could sell their valuable service more expensively if their cultural capital were recognized (i.e., converted into symbolic capital). Effective promotion, thus, means the advancement of the image of the autonomous professional rather than that of the subservient executor.

Softly imposing the other agents' wishes and interests in the associations' documents that purportedly support the translator's professionalism clearly shows that collegiate control is far out of reach. These agents' voice/interests reflected mainly in sharing their denigrating doxa about what *translation* is, and consequently, in its relational aspects, can be said to place the control of the occupation in the hands of outsiders. To somewhat shake the *status quo*, the translator would need to transform their self-perception and impose their view(s) in their defining documents and ultimately in the actual relations with the other agents. They need to transform the understanding of *translation* – over which the struggle is now softly settled in their disfavour – into a more complex practice and favourable concept. Taking these actions, however, is not an easy endeavour. Even when aware of the reductive definition of their practice and the demeaning relations it yields, translators may be unable to shake off the *status quo* for fear of negative reactions from the other agents. These agents may object to any change (even in the translator's self-perception) that might contradict their perception of this practitioner and that might ultimately jeopardize their economic and symbolic interests. Translators are, thus, compelled to adhere to the established rules of the game unless they mobilize more external support from the field of power itself, namely the scholar – a topic I thoroughly discuss in Section 6.3.

The influence of *corporate patronage* is clearly felt in the documents of the studied translator associations. The principles of faithfulness, impartiality and confidentiality are guarantees of security for the client/patron, author, publisher and politician. These notions dissipate the clients/patrons' suspicion and uncertainty because (creative and autonomous) interventions are suspicious, and, therefore, fearful. They may embarrass the client/patron or give away their potentially unethical or illegal behaviour. Interventionist and subversive translators could counter their patrons' desires or agendas. With these principles reinforced, translators are themselves "clients," as Johnson (2016, 65) puts it, because they have "neither exclusive nor final responsibility for their services; ultimate authority in the assessment of process and product lies with the patron or patrons" (ibid., 65). Many of the rules highlighted in the documents under study are, in fact, principles that require translators to adhere to the client/patron's (economic) interests and/or ideology exclusively and unconditionally. Their effectiveness stems from the fact that they are shared beliefs between the translator (through their internal documents) and the powerful users of translation.

The prospects for the professionalization of translation, among many other occupations – including those whose representative bodies promote complex skills and higher education – are less favourable nowadays, if we follow Freidson's thought (1994). The domain is already well controlled by "managerial agents of either the state (in socialist nations) or corporate capital" (ibid., 116). Schinkel and Noordegraaf (2011) argue that managers have started to take control even over recognized professionals. Translators, of course, are not immune to these developments, which posit further challenges to their attempts at collegiate control, especially with the technological advancements related to translation and the creation, expansion and concentration of giant translation corporations that internationalized the industry and monopolized it.

Patronage imposition, reflected in the document under study, is not a new form of imposition that is characteristic of only modern control of occupations but is as old as translation itself. Oligarchic patrons, like monarchs, princes or lords defined the paths/rules for their translators/servants in ways similar to those of today's capitalist patrons (clients, employers, publishers). The translator's 'success' in both forms of patronage (oligarchic and corporate) is conditional on their abiding by the patron's perimeters and desires. André Lefevere (1992, 6–7) writes:

> If translators do not stay within the perimeters of the acceptable as defined by the patron (an absolute monarch, for instance, but also a publisher's editor), the chances are that their translation will either not reach the audience they want it to reach or that it will, at best, reach that audience in a circuitous manner [...] the Earl of Roscommon reflects a shift in patronage in his description of the (hack) translators of his own time: "I pity from my Soul unhappy Men/Compelled by Want to prostitute their Pen,/ Who must, like Lawyers, either starve or plead,/ And follow, right or wrong, where Guineas lead."
>
> (Lefevere 1992, 6–7)

The image of a translator as prostituting their pen reflects the very same unfortunate situation both in the past and in the present. The only difference is that oligarchic patronage usually worked case by case and direct orders from the patron whereas modern patronage works via the translator's own institutions, with no direct 'intervention' from patronage[9]. Current patronage is *working by itself*; it is collectively reinforced and reproduced by the practitioners' associations. Another difference is that the motives of oligarchic patronage seem to be mainly ideological whereas modern corporate patronage is driven by both ideological and economic factors.

Despite the relative awareness demonstrated in some of the studied organizations' documents regarding the power dynamics involved in professionalization when they empathize the autonomy of translators as professionals, these organizations fail to secure internal self-control of their practice. All studied organizations include clauses that mainly serve powerful external agents, especially the clauses defining *translation*. The *status quo is*, of course, due to the power and concentration of many of these agents involved in translation and the fragmentation of translators and the little external support they enjoy. The following section analyzes how the translator's symbolic status as an author is addressed in the documents under study, with reference to copyright law.

6.2 The Translator Is (Not) an Author

Copyright attributed to translators under the Berne Convention as stipulated in Article 2, Paragraph 3 (cited in the Economic Capital section), may, at first glance, be seen as a sort of consecration – an international recognition of the high worth of the translator's intellectual work and, therefore, their authorship. However, a careful reading of the article in question dashes these hopes. In this article, the translator's 'gained symbolic recognition' – like their economic capital discussed earlier – is proportionate to the 'original' author's, and not, in any way, equivalent to it. This *partial* recognition cannot even be acquired without the author's *will* to permit the translation, first and foremost. And once acquired, it remains subordinate to its donor, the author, because its object (translation) is only a derivative form of the 'original' that the author owns. The translator, thus, shares ownership of their own translation with the author.

This copyright law reflects the view external agents have of the translator's cultural capital and cultural production, i.e., translation. In the eyes of the legislator and the political agent (the signatory States of the Berne Convention), partial copyright is proportionate to the derivative copying work translators do. The understanding of *translation* that underlies this view is reproduced and reinforced by the concerned agent themselves (the translators) through their representative bodies. Although most codes under study call for life-long learning, 'professional' development and competence as a way of promoting the value of the translator's cultural capital, as I discussed in the Cultural Capital section, these same codes represent *translation* as a mechanistic and fixed practice in their definition of *translation*. Hence their former calls for recognition remain ineffective because the definition of the practice is the site where cultural capital is mostly reflected. Worse, most of them reinforce the current copyright law as commonsensical.

Six out of the nine documents I examined reproduce the image of the translator as subordinate to the author when highlighting the question of the author's and the translator's respective copyrights. The translator's low symbolic status is reinforced by a discourse that purportedly protects them but, in fact, continuously reinforces their subordination to the author. The Nairobi Recommendation section entitled "measures to ensure the application in practice of protection afforded translators under international conventions and in national laws relating to copyright" and Paragraph 5, Section III are just examples of this paradoxical discourse.

- Member States should accord to translators, in respect of their translations, *the protection accorded to authors* under the provisions of the international copyright conventions to which they are party and/or under their national laws, *but without prejudice to the rights of the authors of the original works translated* (Paragraph 3, section II, italics added).
- As a general rule, a contract governing relations between a translator and a user, as well as where appropriate any other legal instrument governing such relations, should: [...]
   (g) stipulate that, *subject to the prerogatives of the author of the original work* translated, no change shall be made in the text of a translation intended for publication without seeking the prior agreement of the translator;
   (h) assure the translator and his translation similar publicity, *proportionately to that which authors* are generally given, in particular, the name of the author of the translation should appear in a prominent place on all published copies of the translation, on theatre bills, in announcements made in connexion with radio or television broadcasts, in the credit titles of films and in any other promotional material;
   (Paragraph 5, Section III, italics added)

While the Nairobi Recommendation stresses the translator's right to copyright that 'resembles' that of the author, in line with the Berne Convention provisions, these paragraphs "seem to denigrate the translator more than other texts, precisely because they are more explicit and detailed" (Sadek 2018, 90). Even changes to an already translated text are "subject to the prerogatives of the author of the original work translated." The author's intervention in the translator's work is apparently permissible without the translator's consent[10]. Besides, it seems that *only* textual changes are subject to the translator's 'agreement' – in case these textual changes are not requested by the author. The translator's view about paratexts does not seem to be of interest[11].

The FIT Translator's Charter, similarly, parrots the Berne Convention provisions on the question of copyright. In the very definition of *translation*, the Charter insists on bringing in the legal aspects of 'translation.' Articles 4 and 5 stipulate, respectively, that,

- ✓ Every translation shall be faithful and render exactly the idea and form of the original ï¿½ [sic] this *fidelity* constituting *both* a *moral and legal obligation* for the translator.
- ✓ A faithful translation, however, should not be confused with a literal translation, the fidelity of a translation not excluding an adaptation to make the form, the atmosphere and deeper meaning of the work felt in another language and country. (italics added)

Besides the problematic conceptualization of *translation* – discussed earlier – these two articles deepen the ambiguity about the *legal* definition of *translation* and the uncertain, if not insecure, legal position of the translator because of this definition. The FIT stresses that 'faithfulness' is not only a 'professional' obligation but a moral and legal duty – as Basalamah also observes (2004, 76). The translator is, thus, continuously under legal threat if they do not transfer the ideas and forms of the 'original' 'faithfully.' The FIT, seemingly aware that 'faithfulness' is fictitious, retracts and illustrates that 'faithfulness' may imply adaptation (Article 5). Yet, the extent to which adaptation can be considered a 'modification' or 'distortion' is always open to interpretation – hence the ambiguity of the question of 'faithfulness' or 'fidelity' as a moral and legal duty. Many thorny questions issue from these two articles: to what extent is an adaptation desirable, moral and legal? How does a translator measure the limits of a 'faithful' adaptation? How can one morally and legally decide that a translation is an infringement on the author's right? Who decides the extent of the allowed adaptation? And who guarantees that an adaptation or even a 'faithful' translation – does not unintentionally modify the 'intent' of the original work? Respecting the author's 'moral and legal right' in translation is, thus, a complex issue – if possible at all – and the FIT remains unclear about its boundaries or measures. It does not only severely constrain the translator's creativity and agency but also causes perpetual legal insecurity because of a possible charge of 'unfaithfulness.'

> [d]erivative works like translations could conceivably provoke a legal action under this last right [...] In principle, legal protection against distortions endows authors with enormous power over every aspect of the translating process, permitting them to develop their own idea of what constitutes the integrity of their work in a foreign language.
> (Venuti 1998, 52)

The translator, therefore, has to be careful not to distort the author's image and should probably ultimately seek the author's benediction of their work in order to secure a moral and legal clearance. Being submissive to the author or faithful to their work never guarantees the translator legal clearance, due to their perpetual uncertainty even when they desperately seek 'faithfulness' to the 'original' work.

The other articles of the FIT Translator's Charter that address copyright are found in two different sections. The first section is about "General Obligations of the Translator" and the second about "Rights of the Translator."

Section I: General Obligations of the Translator

11. Being a "secondary" author, the translator is required to accept special obligations with respect to the author of the original work.
12. He/she must obtain from the author of the original work or from the user authorization to translate a work, and must furthermore respect all other rights vested in the author.

(Articles 11, 12)

Section II: Rights of the Translator

13. Every translator shall enjoy all the rights with respect to the translation he/she has made, which the country where he/she exercises his/her activities grants to other intellectual workers.
14. A translation, being a creation of the intellect, shall enjoy the legal protection accorded to such works.
15. The translator is therefore the holder of copyright in his/her translation and consequently has the same privileges as the author of the original work.
16. The translator shall thus enjoy, with respect to his/her translation, all the moral rights of succession conferred by his/her authorship.
17. He/she shall consequently enjoy during his/her lifetime the right to recognition of his/her authorship of the translation, from which it follows, inter alia, that

    (a) his/her name shall be mentioned clearly and unambiguously whenever his/her translation is used publicly
    (b) he/she shall be entitled to oppose any distortion, mutilation or other modification of his/her translation
    (c) publishers and other users of his/her translation shall not make changes therein without the translator's prior consent

(d) he/she shall be entitled to prohibit any improper use of his/her translation and, in general, to resist any attack upon it that is prejudicial to his/her honour or reputation.

18. Furthermore, the exclusive right to authorize the publication, presentation, broadcasting, re-translation, adaptation, modification or other rendering of his/her translation, and, in general, the right to use his/her translation in any form shall remain with the translator.

(Articles 13, 14, 15, 16, 17, 18)

Consistently with the defining article 4 discussed earlier, articles 11 and 12 reiterate that the translator's copyright is subject to the initial rights owned by the author – who, thus, continues to hold a symbolic power over the translator. This power is manifest in the permission process through which the translator needs to secure authorization to translate 'the author's work' – in accordance with Article 8 of the Berne Convention devoted to the "Right of Translation"[12] – and in the extension of the latter's ownership to the translation they did *not* create.

In the translator's rights section – which is ironically larger in size – the FIT reiterates the position of the Nairobi Recommendation about the translator's right to oppose any changes to their translations (made by publishers and/or other users) without their permission (Article 17b, 17c). But again, like the UNESCO, this seems to exclude paratexts. The difference from the UNESCO document, however, is that the FIT refrains from giving the 'original' author an exemption from this clause. Even the author is not allowed to make changes without the translator's consent, if we follow the article verbatim. One more slight difference between the FIT Translator's Charter and the Nairobi Recommendation is that the former underlines the translator's *moral rights* in a way that may appear similar to how the author's moral rights are addressed under the Berne Convention[13]. Articles 16 and 17 (b) highlight the translator's moral rights as an 'author.' But again, this remains ineffective as the translator's moral rights are subject to the author's moral rights. Although the FIT elaborates on the translator's rights in a way that might astonish a hasty reader of articles 13 through 18, articles 11 and 12, in fact, make the latter articles redundant and useless, if not deceptive. This is because all the enumerated rights are constrained by articles 11 and 12, which qualify the translator as a "secondary author."

Both international bodies (UNESCO and FIT) reinforce the Berne Convention provisions regarding copyright. Although the UNESCO's position on the matter is no surprise and understandable as it represents the political field and is based on the Berne Convention (ratified by many of its own Member States), it is within our right to question the reproduction of a discourse that nurtures the translators' inferior status by the FIT, the translator's representative body. As Basalamah (2009, 324) rightly argues, "the translator is not only minorized by the world of copyright, but they seem to be almost even more so by the organization [FIT] gathering all the associations defending their rights" (my translation).

Codes of ethics of national/provincial associations take different stances as far as copyright is concerned, as discussed in the Economic Capital section. The SATI code, for example, emphasizes almost everyone's right (the client's and the employer's rights and the author's copyright) except the translator's. It calls on the latter to "respect all rights of the author and the client/employer, and specifically copyright" (Code of ethics for individual members). Not very differently – although in vaguer terms (i.e., with no mention of beneficiaries) – the ATIO urges its members to "observe and respect copyrights and any other intellectual property rights" (Codes of Ethics, Article 3.3.2). These two codes, thus, refrain from reiterating a right recognized and bestowed on translators by other agents (politicians/legislators), as is manifest in the Berne Convention and national legislations about copyright. The SFT and the AUSIT take a middle position, similarly to the UNESCO Nairobi Recommendation and the FIT Translator's Charter, by stressing both the translator's rights and their obligations. On the other hand, three codes of associations from developing countries, namely the IAFET, ATPP and the ITAINDIA, refrain from urging the translator to abide by copyright law. As already discussed, the adverse economic and cultural repercussions of the current copyright law on developing and least developed countries are significant.

It is not surprising that the documents of the UNESCO, the FIT and the associations from developed countries (AUSIT, ATIO and SFT) all stress the duty to respect the author's ownership of their material, while the codes of some associations from developing countries refrain from reproducing this as a commonsensical law. Copyright culture that sacralizes the 'original' has become a solidly anchored piece of common sense in hegemonic countries, and questioning it may be seen as nonsensical. As we know, historically, powerful countries originated and imposed the protection of intellectual property rights as they were the major exporters of 'original' cultural goods (Basalamah and Sadek 2014, 398). Because these powerful countries 'created' more and translated less (in a time of imperial expansion), they lobbied for translation to be considered as reproduction – which in turn requires that the rights owned by 'original' creators (in the 'original' First World) be secured. On the other hand, developing countries and countries whose cultures/languages are not central resisted this orientation during the meetings in preparation of the Berne Convention.

During the nineteenth century, France pushed to see translation considered as reproduction because that was to its advantage as one of the rare exporters of literary works. At the same time, nations whose language was not central (such as Russia, Brazil, Sweden, India, etc.) rejected the idea and voiced considerable concerns, in light of the importance of translation for their cultural (and economic) development.

(Basalamah and Sadek 2014, 398)

Because of (cultural, political or economic) power asymmetries, *translation* is perceived differently by these two poles. While it is seen as a 'derivative second-order' work in central cultures/countries, it is perceived of as an important source of knowledge and a means of building national literatures in peripheral cultures/countries, especially under colonial and postcolonial conditions. Venuti rightly argues that the difference in how *translation* is perceived in hegemonic countries and dominated countries has metaphysical, cultural, economic and geopolitical roots.

[T]he cultural authority and impact of translation vary according to the position of a particular country in the geopolitical economy. In the hegemonic countries, metaphysical concepts of authorial originality and cultural authenticity denigrate translation as second-order writing, derivative and adulterated, so that especially in the United States and the United Kingdom it receives relatively little attention from writers and critics, scholars and teachers. In developing countries, translation accrues cultural as well as economic capital. The need to communicate between major and minor languages has spawned translation industries and training programs. Translation is seen as a significant intervention into the polylingualism and cultural hybridity that characterize colonial and postcolonial situations, a source of linguistic innovation useful in building national literatures and in resisting the dominance of hegemonic languages and cultures.

(Venuti 1998, 187)

In sum, most of the documents under study reinforce the image of the translator as "a symbolic derivation" of the 'original' author – to use Sadek's (2018, 189) terminology – by reproducing copyright law unquestioningly. They reproduce the view that the translator is entitled merely to the author's *symbolic residue* or *remainder*. The translator is perceived as a copying/second-degree author who is permanently in debt to the 'original' author, a debt they can never pay off – to use Derrida's (1985) term about 'translation' – a debt that the author is entitled to (economically and symbolically), for eternity. Salah Basalamah (2004, 76), analyzing the position of the translator in copyright law concludes: "the translator, like translation in copyright law, which qualifies it as a 'derivative work,' is an author in the second degree, or literally an emanation of the author, a kind of excretion that is not enough to be an accessory as it considers itself 'subject' to the author" (my translation). In such a case, the author endows the translator with a small share of their symbolic recognition for subserviently helping disseminate their work to other languages/cultures. And for that work – which requires only attention not to spill any of its content or add to it on the way – they deserve a reward that is proportionate to that little effort.

> Thus conceived, the translator was bound to become the repressed product of the symbolic and discursive swelling that defines an author. They were literally condemned to have status only in relation to those incorporating the new sacredness (Bénichou, 1973). The symbolic value of the translation and its author was therefore reduced to the small portion that would remain in the shadow of the author of the original work: a representation.
>
> (Basalamah 2004, 78, my translation)

Although the author's moral right argument behind the current copyright law has been 'similarly' applied to the translator for their authorship in the Paris Act, the translator's moral right remains utterly paradoxical and legally incoherent. On the one hand, 'translation' is protected as it constitutes an intellectual effort and involves an *original creativity* in the form/expression of a work (see Berne Convention, Article 2, Paragraph 3). On the other hand, it is seen as a *derivative* work in which the translator should do "justice to the expression of his [the author's] thinking, giving it a style and phraseology which allows the second language readers to take in as much as possible of the original" (Article 8.1). The recognition of the effort involved in creating original expressions/wording should have made translation an autonomous creation. Its original expression (i.e., different words and probably style) owes nothing to the author's expression or style. Translation owes something only to the author's content – which is not a criterion for copyright. This recognition would give translators exclusive copyright on their work, independently of the author's copyright. Venuti questions the ambiguity and contradictions in the legal definition of *translation* as both original and derivative. "In copyright law, the translator is and is not an author" (1995, 9). Venuti writes, "[t]he Berne Convention (Paris 1971) at once assigns an authorial right to the translator and withdraws it" (ibid.). In a similar vein, Basalamah (2007, 122) wonders, "how can the original remain present within the translation, when the change in language constitutes a major change in form, and it is the form alone – the expression – which is protected under copyright?"

Venuti argues that the recognition of translators as authors for their labour and expression coincided with the prominence of the author's *droit moral*, a fact which dooms translation to "the ambiguous legal status that it currently occupies" (1998, 58). This is because the *droit moral* consists of the obligation to respect the author's *person* by avoiding any modifications/distortions of their work, i.e., the duty to abide by the 'faithfulness' rule.

The fact that the current copyright law is based on moral grounds makes it doubly binding – i.e., morally and legally – and therefore unshakeable. Since Jeremy Bentham (2000/1781), we have become aware that legislation is not to be equated with morals (Rosen 2010, 149). A law can be a bad or unjust law, and, therefore, changeable. As John Stuart Mill (1969/1861) argues, law is *not* the ultimate criterion of justice as there may always be unjust or immoral laws. Mill distinguishes *moral rights* from *legal rights* for there may be a bad law that gives legal rights to agents who do not deserve them and deprives others of rights they deserve (1969/1861, 241–242). Therefore, there are opinions that say bad laws should be disobeyed (ibid., 242). But the current copyright law has a solid 'legitimacy' as it is based on a moral argument. This is probably why it is emphasized in some associations' codes of ethics, normally concerned with ethical rather than legal issues.

Against the moral argument, which claims that an author's work is a unique embodiment of their person and, thus, must not be distorted or modified, we now know that translation is a distinct form of creation. Every translation is a distinct form of reading; "an act of interpretation, based on individual experience and cultural conditioning" (Polizzoti 2018a, 92) and an act of transformation *par excellence* (see for example, Derrida 1985). Reception theory has shown that the reader (in this case the translator) plays an active role in constructing meaning and supplementing text with the influence of their background and schemata (see for example, Hall 1980, Iser 1978, Eagleton 2008). From literary theory, we now know that meaning is unstable and uncertain, and subject to interpretations. The ideas of the 'death of the author' (Barthes 1984/1968) and intertextuality (Kristeva 1969) have convincingly shown that authorship is a *collective* endeavour. Textual creation derives from stretches of other pre-existing materials and the pre-established discourses of other people, contemporaries and past.

> The copyrightable form in a work, then, is not self-originating, but uniquely derived: the precise selection, arrangement, and elaboration of materials that already exist in a culture, not merely the lexicon, syntax, and phonology that define a particular language, but the structures and themes that have accumulated in the various cultural discourses of that language – literary, rhetorical, political, commercial, and so forth. It is

from these materials, never raw or natural, always culturally coded by previous uses, that an author produces a form determined by an address to a particular cultural constituency.

(Venuti 1998, 61)

If we accept that 'original' creation is a collective and derivative work from previous materials in a source language/culture that is shaped by a specific audience as is translation derivative from materials in the target language/culture (in addition to materials from the source culture) to target a different audience, it follows that "the translation and the foreign text are distinct projects because they involve different intentions and contexts" (ibid.). Therefore, 'faithfulness' is neither always desirable, nor fully achievable/possible. Since translations are created from different cultural repertoires/discourses and from a different language repertoire of forms, the translator should be accorded a copyright protection which excludes the author. As Venuti concludes his third chapter about 'copyright,'

> copyright would be grounded on precise formal features which show that similar procedures are involved in creating the foreign text and the translation, and these procedures occur with sufficient autonomy, in different linguistic and cultural contexts, to allow the works to be viewed as independent.
>
> (Venuti 1998, 66)

Venuti's conclusion is, of course, based on empirical evidence. Caroline Summers (2017), for instance, corroborates his statements. Studying the translations of the East German writer Christa Wolf's novel *What Remains*, Summers shows how the translations, carried out in different discursive contexts, involve reframing and rewriting and should, therefore, be seen as new forms of authorship.

> The most recent translations therefore show how each is marked by the discourse that produces it, and suggest that while her translators have come much closer to an effective replication of her style, the framing of her authorship in translation continues to prioritise compatibility with target-culture narratives, resulting in a rewriting of her authorship.
>
> (Summers 2017, 222)

The evidence that translation is a form of rewriting in the target language is not new in TS. André Lefevere (1992) has convincingly argued that translation is a form of rewriting that is impacted by poetical, ideological, discursive and patronage factors in the target context. But, with the understanding of intellectual property as an individual property and as a moral right of the 'original' producer, the translator may remain creatively restrained, textually and socio-politically invisible, ethically neutralized[14], and legally insecure.

The high symbolic capital of authors, in contrast to that of translators – manifest in the current copyright law – arises, in fact, from the historically and socially constructed difference between the two intellectual workers. The socio-historical construct (doxa) that associates authors with genius creativity and translators with *copying* and *invisible transmission* has taken centuries to be internalized as common sense. This collective belief has become unshakeable as it hardly has any competing views (except a few publications in TS). On October 16, 2019, when the American President Donald Trump made what was widely seen as inappropriate and inaccurate remarks about Syria and Italian-American relations[15], respectively, the interpreter's facial expressions of shock went viral on social media. The interpreter's *visible* reaction was also reported by some news outlets as an unusual act that shows the absurdity of Trump's declarations (see, for instance, Newsweek[16], National Post[17]). Even the very experienced interpreter, who is supposedly *invisible* in the people's collective imagination, showed her astonishment and discontent. But despite her 'unusual' act, the interpreter "*has won sympathy* from those who say not even a seasoned interpreter, a *neutral* professional figure *par excellence*, can refrain from being horrified by Trump's rambling speeches" (Giustini 2019, n.p., italics added). Hence, this 'unusual' act of showing one's emotions was *exceptionally* forgiven and sympathized with even though it broke the rules of the game. The translator's normal and 'successful' behaviour consists of adhering to the 'collective' categories of perception 'in force,' i.e., to be *invisible*, or to be more precise, to claim invisibility[18]. It is just the way it is; the *nature* of this work; there is nothing else to do (see Bourdieu 1998a, 103). Tim Parks (2010) has written about this denigrating dominant view.

> The translator should do his [sic] job and then disappear. The great, charismatic, creative writer wants to be all over the globe. And the last thing he wants to accept is that the majority of his readers are not really reading him. His readers feel the same. They want intimate contact with true greatness. They don't want to know that this prose was written on survival wages in a maisonette in Bremen, or a high-rise flat in the suburbs of Osaka. Which kid wants to hear that her JK Rowling is actually a chain-smoking pensioner? When I meet readers of my own novels, they are disappointed I translate as well, as if this were demeaning to an author they hoped was "important".
>
> (Parks 2010, n.p.)

This social construct, being reinforced with the complicity of translators themselves, prevents the recognition of their value (manifest in authorship) by the other agents' schemes of perception. Beatriz Zeller exclaims, "[w]hy not grant authorship of a translated book to its author *and* to the person responsible for the translation? The reason, I fear, is that translation is perceived as a mere transfer of an author's vision from his language into another language" (2000, 134–135, italics in original). This image of the translator implies that their work (and, therefore, their cultural capital) is far from being influential in the social arena. Translators, unlike the other cultural producers, who have "the power of naming, in particular of naming the unnameable, that which is still unnoticed or repressed" (Bourdieu 1990a, 149), do not name-create or enlighten the public but simply parrot other 'creators' "naming." Following Bourdieu, the authoring agents belong to the field of power, i.e., the field of dominant groups in the social field (although dominated within this field) (Bourdieu 1993, 37–38; 1998b, 44). Their power stems mainly from the prestige gained by 'creating' ideas, clarifying what was unclear, and, overall, orienting social action and social structure. Although Bourdieu does not mention translators as part of the category of intellectual producers, translators should supposedly be on an equal footing with other intellectual creators in the field of power since they are influential agents, as we understand *translation*/translators since the cultural turn. However, the view of *translation*/translators (as a spin-off product/producers), reproduced in legal terms by international conventions about intellectual property and disseminated under 'moral' and 'professional' conduct umbrellas by translators themselves through their associations, prevents the translator from gaining any proximity to the field of power, and thus, from joining other intellectual creators, namely authors.

The current copyright law was originated and imposed by 'original' countries – which dominate the global geopolitical/economic scene – and 'original' creators and publishers – who dominate the cultural production field and establish its internal laws – in order to reproduce the same power relations that had existed between developed and developing countries and between the translator and the powerful agents involved in the translation industry, despite the efforts to obscure these motives by moral and legal arguments (see Venuti 1995, 1998; Basalamah and Sadek 2014; Sadek 2018). The law tacitly reflects the idea that 'original' developed countries and 'original' authors/publishers are the source/original divine creators and, thus, the ones that deserve better (economic, cultural and symbolic) conditions. On the other hand, it reinforces the derivative, subordinate, submissive, follower and second-copy images of translators and developing countries and, therefore, further aggravates their socio-economic and symbolic vulnerability. As we learn from

Bourdieu, power is used "to impose the laws of functioning of the field most favourable to capital and its reproduction" (Bourdieu 1986, 246). And despite an increasing awareness of the implausibility, ambiguity, contradictions and unfairness of the current copyright law in regard to translation/translators and developing countries, some translator organizations seem to accept the laws (and, therefore, the translator's partial rights) as common sense. Worse, they impose it as an ethical matter in their codes of ethics. Three associations from developing countries refrain from reproducing this law in their codes of ethics. But unfortunately, they still reproduce the very Eurocentric premises behind the law, especially in their definition of *translation* as a faithful copy of an 'original.' From a postcolonial perspective, these associations' epistemological space has been conquered (see for example, St-Pierre 2000, Niranjana 1992, De Kock 1992). The apparent resistance is to the tip of the iceberg, i.e., to what is visible from the relations of exploitation but not to its deeper frames of thought. Therefore, their resistance using the very reasoning, ideologies and concepts of the dominator to disguise their domination is incoherent and, therefore, inefficient. "They're within the hegemonic discourse, wanting a piece of the pie, and not being allowed, so let them speak, use the hegemonic discourse," to use Spivak's statement in her interview with De Kock (1992, 46). For Tymoczko, this uncritical adoption of Western *translation* understanding in other parts of the world is an example of a hegemonic form of knowledge (2007, 77). This is what Susam-Sarajeva (2002, 198) calls "self-colonization."

The lack of recognition of translators as cultural producers (or authors), manifest in the *partial* copyright reproduced by most documents under study, is due to the low rate of conversion of their cultural capital into symbolic capital. Their embodied cultural capital self-represented and seen as mere dispositions to faithfully transfer meaning does not prompt any admiration from the surrounding agents or the public at large. The current copyright reduces the translator's economic revenues in favour of the 'original' author and the publisher. The translator's 'derivative' work (insignificant cultural capital) is worth less economically and is, thus, acquired cheaply by the authoring and publishing agents, who have substantial symbolic and economic forms of capital, respectively.

> Without a greater recognition of the collective nature of authorship, translators will continue to be squeezed by unfavorable, if not simply exploitative, contracts. Individualistic notions of intellectual property will continue to seem pious fictions used by authors and publishers to add a patina of legitimacy to their money grabs.
>
> (Venuti 1998, 66)

The translator's low symbolic capital affects their social capital as well, despite the efforts of recruiting as many translators as possible to enlarge the network[19]. Authors (with whom competition over interests is fierce), or even publishers, have better social capital than translators because they have better symbolic capital, despite the fact that their representative bodies may be smaller in size. This is because social capital is not only about the size of the network but mostly about the symbolic 'quality' of its individual members. The individual author or publisher, member of a league/association, can mobilize more qualitative and useful relations than the translator can in their own network. More importantly, author leagues or publisher associations may have better external support from influential agents/networks in the field of power (e.g., the political agent or the legislator), who may help them advance their agendas in return for some other kind of (political, ideological, electoral) support. In the case of author leagues, this is often the case thanks to the noble names that may be part of these leagues. If a renowned or consecrated author is leading the league, it is very likely that their name will attract better connections, and thus better prestige and more influence for their league.

An improvement of the legal status of translation and translators would lead not only to an improvement of the translator's symbolic, economic and social forms of capital but also to a more open access to knowledge around the world, especially in developing countries. This would lead to a democratization of access to information and knowledge between all countries and individuals in the digital era of the Knowledge Society (Basalamah and Sadek 2014, Sadek 2018). "It is the sheer global reach of translation, its strategic and irreplaceable value in negotiating cultural differences, that lends urgency to the need for a clarification and improvement of its legal status" (Venuti 1998, 66). The current copyright regime that restrains translations hinders the aspirations of developing countries to catch up with scientific/economic development since translation plays a major role in these countries' access to knowledge. The paradox of the current copyright law is that it is based on moral arguments while it may itself be unethical, preventing knowledge from reaching populations that are economically vulnerable and culturally peripheral in the least developed countries[20]. The fact that many of these developing countries adopt the current copyright law and that such a law is reinforced in the documents of some translator associations as a moral and 'professional' obligation makes its subversion quite impossible unless the translator gets significant external support and their own views of their work is transformed.

6.3 Symbolic Violence Against the Translator and Opportunities for Empowerment

Reiterating the powerful agents' views and wishes in the translators' own documents not only undermines the creative value of their practice and shrinks their economic and symbolic benefits but also affects their autonomy and control over their work. Reproducing the mainstream understanding of *translation* as a standard routine of faithful transfer of meaning and unreflexively reinforcing copyright law and the unconditional duties toward the other powerful agents in the associations' documents lead to what Bourdieu (1998a) calls relations of *symbolic violence*. Freidson (1994, 124) made an excellent remark about how the ideas of 'professionalism,' protection of the public, dedication to service, work commitment and devotion to serving clients are used as tools of interpellation. "The ideology may be used by political, managerial, and professional authorities to distract workers from their objective lack of control over their work, to lead them to do the work assigned them as well as possible, and to commit them to means and ends others have chosen for them" (ibid., 124). Many of the rules/principles reinforced in the codes under study are indeed ideologies of distraction and subjugation. The protection of the public, for example, is, in fact, a protection of the client/employer, as I further explain in Part 3. Indeed, it is a rule that distracts the translator from their subservience to the client/employer, whose interests actually precede the interests of the large public. The ideology of 'faithfulness' – or the "possession" by 'faithfulness,' to borrow Bourdieu's term (1996, 3) – is a tool of subjugation that blinds them from seeing the complexity of their practice.

This doxa about *translation*/translators shared by both the translator and the other powerful agents remains the most important factor in the former's *soft domination*, to use Bourdieu's terminology (1990b, 128). It is a tool that undermines the value of the translator's work in the heads of all agents (including the translator themselves) and therefore facilitates exploitation. This dominant rule implies that this 'simple' and 'little' effort, that is translation, requires little pay and little recognition, if any. Some translators themselves (like their dominators) may accept the fact that they do not deserve high pay or recognition as they do a mechanical work of meaning transfer. They thus become complicit in their own domination, helping its "efficacy" (Bourdieu 1996, 3) by reinforcing it internally.

This low cultural self-image of the translator (as a copier) that hardly converts to any symbolic capital took centuries of fossilization to become an "ordinary evidence," in Bourdieu's terminology (1996, 3). The image of the translator has been reinforced throughout history through the practices of translators, writings about translation, translators' descriptions of their work, their biographies, translation critiques, knowledge about translation in educational and religious institutions, theories of translation, language and metaphors surrounding *translation*/translators, and the moral/legal arguments about the originality of creation, as well as the Western notion of property. Today, this image is reinforced and reproduced internally by translator organizations through their codes of ethics, websites, publications, seminars, meetings and conferences, as well as externally in the field of education, and the field of power. Translators are, thus, historically inclined to embrace this view as it is in conformity with their "socially constituted dispositions" (Bourdieu 1996, 3). Conversely, they are liable to recognize and value the symbolic capital of authors/publishers, patrons/clients, legislators/politicians and scholars. Authors are admired for being 'original' creators, and their word deserves all due respect. The legislators who adopted this copyright law know what they are doing; they especially know better than the general public and their law is commonsensical and beyond discussion. Publishers, clients and patrons are also appreciated for their economic power. Translators are compelled to help them achieve their objectives and, therefore, 'help' themselves. They must, thus, adapt to their ethical, aesthetic, stylistic and 'professional' orientations in their translations. They must be loyal to them because they make their living thanks to them. Scholars are admired for their cultural capital. Those among them who make 'sense' endorse the commonsensical principles underpinning *translation* in their publications and, most importantly, in their teaching and textbooks (see Maier and Baker 2011b, Arrojo 2005, respectively) and, thus, help translators thrive and get prepared for the market. Translators seemingly follow the latter scholars/educators' findings/teachings as they know better. In sum, the above dominant agents softly exploit dominated translators as the latter may be under the magic power of numbing. Shaking this cultural image of *translation* as a mechanistic endeavour may not only be resisted by its beneficiaries, but also by its victims, who are complicit in their own submission.

In his criticism of the current copyright law, which emphasizes the derivative nature of translation, and, therefore, reinforces the subordination of the translator to the 'original' author, Gaafar Sadek (2018) criticizes the law for its external nature, as it is imposed by external international bodies, i.e., the World Intellectual Property Organization and the UNESCO. He observes the absence of any representatives of translators during the meetings of these bodies to discuss translation rights.

> The *Berne Convention* and the *Nairobi Recommendation* are both important legal documents having an undeniable role in forming the image of the translator in the collective imagination. They can be both interpreted as stemming from an external authority to the translator, which may explain, though not justify, constantly relegating the latter's status to submissiveness to that of the author. In all of the minutes of the international meetings that I studied where translation rights were discussed over the last century and a half, not once was there a mention of someone representing translators. So it may be justified to view some of the language and provisions of *Berne, Nairobi,* and other texts as the

result of the absence of an agent representing the interests of translators, when they are in direct competition with other interests that are much better represented at such meetings.

(Sadek 2018, 191)

Sadek suggests that the relegation of the translator's status to submissiveness to the author is fully and *rationally/strategically* calculated and is, thus, of course, deplorable. What Sadek (and proponents of classical class conflict theory) overlook is that these organizations simply reproduce that collective *doxa* about *translation*/translators that translators themselves defend. Hence, even if translators had been directly present or represented, things would probably not have been any better. The proof is that many national/provincial associations' codes of ethics reinforce the copyright law unquestioningly. The best some other associations did was to remain silent about the issue. Also, we all know that the FIT is a counsellor to the UNESCO, and I, therefore, assume that the provisions of the latter were recommended, or at least, negotiated with them, which is quite clear from the resemblance between the FIT articles about copyright and those of the Nairobi Recommendation. The other reason is that none of the studied associations has a better representation of the translator's practice. Worse, the UNESCO (a representative of a different agent and itself an employer of translators) advances provisions that are seemingly more advanced than some of the latter associations (SATI, ATIO, SFT, AUSIT) in this respect and many other respects. Thus, submissiveness to the author is not *only* the result of an external imposition, but also a result of the unreflective *dispositions* of the concerned agent, i.e., the translator, in the first place.

Authors/legislators (and all the other agents) are not all and always intentionally and consciously complicit in the domination of translators. They do not meet in dark rooms to design conspiratorial plans against translators. The situation is a product of *natural* relations of power and the collective beliefs about where translators and authors belong. In sum, the symbolic imposition by dominant agents is not all rationally calculated, following Bourdieu (1996); it is merely the natural rule of the game. This is how things are! Of course, this does not mean that lobbying is irrelevant and that calculation is never on board, but rational calculation is not as efficient as the *magical power* of voluntary submission from distance (Bourdieu 1998a). It is not as decisive as the role played by interpellation resulting from the conformity of the translator's categories of perception with their dominators' ideas about them and their practice. In other words, concealed *natural* exploitation through symbolic violence (taken for granted) is cheap and much more efficient; *it works by itself.*

The interpellation of translators is, of course, never complete or all-encompassing. There are always resisting voices as in all relations of power (Foucault 1975). Or, there are individuals who are, at least, aware of the hegemonic relations in which their work is embedded. However, in the case where a translator is aware of the complexity of their work and the power relations in which it is embedded, they may be tempted by the immediate material profit and, therefore, defer to the wishes of the powerful agent. On the other hand, if the dissident translator engages in resisting/subversive tactics, they may face exclusion not only by the more powerful employers/clients but by their peers. It is not difficult to find that some associations stress the fact that members who do not abide by codes/rules will be excluded (as discussed under the Social Capital section). Thus, symbolic violence is complemented by coercive tools. Those who evade symbolic violence are treated by economic deprivation, or material violence, as well as social exclusion. They lose membership in the association as well as their clients, considering that their reputation becomes 'tainted.'

Resistant translators need to mobilize more peers who are aware of the demeaning labour relations and lack of control of their occupation should they aspire for a gradual change in their self-image and the view of their practice. But this is not all; for translators to impose (new) alternative and competing vision(s) in their documents and in the heads of other agents, and ultimately gain control over their occupation and/or have full authorship rights, *external resources* need to be mobilized. Translators need allies from the field of power who are *disposed* and *willing* to support them/their definition of their practice and advocate their rights/interests. As Johnson tells us, "[t]he resources of power available to any single occupational group are rarely sufficient to impose on all consumers its own definitions of the content of production and its ends, except where these resources are articulated with *other and wider bases of social power*" (Johnson 2016, 42, italics added). Because the agents in the field of power have contradicting interests on different levels, issues and domains, some of these interests may intersect with those of the translator, who could, thus, benefit from the support of one of those agents. The 'original' cultural producer (author), the industrial agent, the scholarly agent and the legislative/political agent – who are all part of the field of power, following Bourdieu's thought – have competing ideas about *translation*, and the roles and positioning of translators in the cultural field or the professional arena. The industrial/publishing field and the legislative/political field, who have their own (business/political/ideological) orientations, seem to be comfortable with the mainstream definition of *translation* (and the interpersonal relations this entails) as it is compatible with their frames of thought, and mainly their economic interests. *Translation* as such does not disturb; it is neither costly nor suspect. The translators' ethical and 'professional' orientations are, thus, unlikely to embarrass because the regulations associated with the said definition do not allow that. 'Original' cultural producers (i.e., authors) – who are also part of the field of power – side with the dominant agents (large clients/patrons, publishers) as their interests conflict with those of translators. They are part of the same game and any support for the translator would mean conceding some of their economic and symbolic stakes to their competitors (translators) in the cultural production field. Bourdieu argues that cultural producers, although generally disposed to align with the economically and culturally dominated in the social world, "remain loyal to the bourgeois order" when their position, interests or capital are threatened (Bourdieu 1990a, 145).

The only potential ally that translators might mobilize from the field of power is the scholar. Many scholars already line up with the dominated translators to elevate their status into *authentic cultural producers* or *recognized professionals* (e.g., Venuti 1995, 1998). Koskinen, Hermans and Stecconi, and Brisset's reactions to, and criticisms of, the powerful agents' policies with respect to translation (namely the Translation Services of the European Commission and the Translation Bureau Canada), discussed earlier, are tangible examples of a very direct and open conflict in the field of power between the scholarly agent and the industrial/political agent over *translation* and the translator's roles. Some of these scholars who line up with translators have shaken the reductive concept of *translation* and proposed a much more complex or cluster concept, which ultimately shows the complexity and value of the translator's cultural capital (e.g., Tymoczko 2007). The scholarly/educational ally is especially important as their institution is the main site where the translator acquires or transforms their understanding of *translation* and nurtures their embodied cultural capital. Furthermore, this institution is supposedly immune from the interplays of the market and the intervention of the other agents in the field of power as it is "at the service of *societies*, rather than markets" (Kearns 2008, 200, italics in original)

The scholars' support for translators is, however, problematic in many ways. First, they are themselves dominated in the field of power, as their cultural capital converts into symbolic capital at a rate that is lower than the rate of conversion of the economic capital of industrialists and sponsors of training programs into symbolic capital (see Bourdieu 1993). Thus, they themselves may be subject to the impositions of the other dominant agents in the field of power. These more powerful agents may easily overturn their vision about *translation*. Some scholars/educators may, therefore, become subject to market influences and the power of their employer (either governments or private entities) seeking to 'make sense' to students and to meet their expectations and the requirements of the market. Hence, despite the increasing research findings/theories and academic voices that advocate the complex nature of *translation*, the education institutions are still reluctant to engage in a new educational enterprise that may become costly and risky for the life of their unit (TS or translation program). These institutions fear losing students who wish to be trained according to the wishes of the powerful potential employer/client – who seems to be comfortable with the myth of 'faithfulness.' After all, students are paying to acquire the embodied capital that can mostly convert into economic capital, i.e., good jobs. In the age of "increasing commercialization of education" (Kearns 2008, 195), universities tend to adopt approaches that respond directly to the needs of their clients and clients' clients, i.e., students and their potential clients/employers. University departments (like any corporation) are under pressure to attract certain numbers of students to ensure their longevity, as governments increasingly cut their funding in many countries (especially in the Anglosphere). In the name of pragmatism and realism, many of those institutions and scholars are compelled to adapt to industry demands – a situation which may ultimately jeopardize their very autonomy. Work-based approaches, now very popular in many parts of the world, cater to employers' immediate needs and requirements – sometimes in disregard of research findings and educational aims. "As such, commerce allies with academic rationalism, embattling Progressivist and Social Reconstructionist positions alike," says Kearns (2008, 197).

Given this situation, TS scholars are divided as to which side to take. While some scholars/educators still resist all the mentioned constraints and align with translators, and even hire new recruits to their camp, many others (inadvertently) underestimate the complexity of translation and the value of translators, or even question the need for translation in some situations. Koskinen, Brisset, Hermans and Stecconi, Tymoczko and Venuti, for example, align with the translator, as discussed earlier, but other established scholars align with the powerful agents, as they perceive that their position, interests or capital are at stake (see Bourdieu 1990a). In this regard, I strongly believe that Anthony Pym, one of the most prolific and influential TS scholars, stands as a strong ally of the powerful. Pym (2012) denies authorship to translators and claims that translation can be replaced by other means of 'cooperation,' like language teaching. He argues that translators should translate only when and in such a way that translation fosters cooperation between the parties involved in the transaction (Pym 2012). If cooperation can be achieved by other lower-cost means of communication (language teaching, for example), translation should not be undertaken, Pym bluntly proclaims. But lower cost for whom? Powerful beneficiaries of translation, of course, for whom Pym seems to care the most among all involved agents in translation. Pym, driven by pragmatic functionalism, of course, underestimates the possible adverse effects that non-translation may have on linguistic/cultural diversity, and on the translator's/TS scholar's occupations' sustainability (see Hutchings 2021) – which is itself an ethical issue (see Kenny and Doherty

2014). Pym (2023) ironically contents that nontranslation can enhance respect for linguistic diversity, overlooking the fact that English, being a dominant language, does not allow for multilingual communication. And today's world linguistic/cultural and geopolitical dynamics are, of course, in sharp contrast to his case about the multilingual communication (and therefore, the absence of translation) between the different indigenous linguistic groups in their different aboriginal languages in Australia before the European invasion.

In collaboration with Grin, Sfreddo and Chan, Pym has worked for the European Commission – the largest employer of translators in the world, which reinforces the mechanistic perception of translation as work that should be done quickly and cheaply (Hermans and Stecconi 2002, Koskinen 2000b) – to produce a 'make-sense' document to the powerful both in content and form (Pym et al. 2012)[21]. In this document, Pym et al. contend that translation professionalization should be in a cooperation spirit and should make sense to the employers, overlooking the power dynamics in which translation is embedded (Pym et al. 2012). Capitalists and powerful agents in the social field, of course, spend billions of dollars funding scholarship, media, schools and universities that promote such a myth of cooperation and 'this is for the interest of all,' to stabilize the *status quo* and the rules of the social game and its functioning parameters in their favour. Pym is, of course, well aware of the paradoxes of his idealism and tries to present it as 'this or nothing else – this is the best and only way that's out there,' given the circumstances. He has no issue admitting that cooperation is a fictitious aspiration.

> I hasten to add that cooperation, as a model, is also a fiction, a story we tell in order not to get lost in the thousands of other psychological drives, tensions, and conflicts that form society. Cooperation, as a model, by no means accounts for all the causes that may from time to time affect the reality of translation. For all that, this idea of cooperation, however fictional it may appear, identifies a noble ethical purpose; it envisions a future that is better than the present; it operates as an abstract principle that can be filled with multiple contents, time and again.
> (Pym 2012, 138)

Pym pleads, in what he ironically calls 'ethics of cooperation,' low-cost translations that benefit the corporate agents against the professional translator, who loses that market to the amateur used by these powerful agent to do the work for free.

> We thus find some advantages in low transaction costs, and this should include low-effort translations. Facebook, for example, could have used

high-quality professional translation services to localize into perhaps ten languages. Using low-cost collaborative translation, it has localized into more than 83 language varieties (in 2012 – the list includes English Pirate Language and Upside Down English), with a correspondingly wider range of potential cooperative situations. The volunteer translators exchange their labor for the cultural value of seeing their language used and their experience grow, while the client company extends its revenue base (in this case the cooperation ultimately involves users clicking on advertisements so that the company generates revenue).

(Pym 2012, 141)

Privileging the economic interests of the powerful employers/clients, Pym is a good example of scholars who align with the field of power and not translators. Pym never seeks to shake the *status quo* but usually calls to adapt to it, in the name of ethics sometimes, as in the example of teaching English instead of translating when the first is less costly. Pym's advice is applicable, of course, to governments' spending on translation (for newcomers, for example) instead of spending on teaching English, fostering, therefore, the Babelian totalitarianism of one tongue[22].

Pym's obvious alignment with the powerful and the dominant has culminated in his fierce attacks and discrediting – sometimes very inappropriately – of his opponents who stand for the translator's agency, the vulnerable in the social field or the dominated on the world stage (see his attacks on Mona Baker's person, for example, that exceeds her scholarship) (Pym 2012, 2016). In this 2016 paper, he offensively (not to say something else) argued that Baker's work is cited by students from Africa to Indonesia, a statement which is full of shocking insinuations.

Because of the sharp division between TS scholars over whom to align with, in addition to the powerful agents impositions, the myth of 'faithfulness,' reiterated by all studied organizations, is thus maintained and reinforced by many education institutions. The recent research findings/theoretical advancements have been restricted to discussions among scholars and barely affect or reach the teaching curricula and methodologies (see Maier and Baker 2011b). Many translator trainees are still trained to be "meek"; i.e., to be "humble servants or handmaidens obeying their masters, as discreet, unobtrusive and self-denying facilitators, mediators, enablers, go-betweens, bridge-builders and the like," to borrow the words of Theo Hermans (Hermans and Stecconi 2002, 1). Although some educators may be teaching translator trainees to deploy all their creative skills to appropriately engage in the contemporary translation types that require skills of adaptation, transformation and shifts (ironically required by some employers themselves), they may, however, still inculcate the ideology of 'faithfulness' in their students' heads. It is not easy to transform some educators' long-held doxa about *translation*. Cultural capital "always remains marked by the earliest conditions of acquisition," as Bourdieu (1986, 245) tells it.

The internal fragmentation within the academic/educational corps does not help the translator's position. But worst of all, the translator themself is (inadvertently) conspiring in their own misrepresentation. Translator organizations (at least in this study) do not embrace the reflexive scholar's views. They, therefore, implicitly reject, or at least ignore, the scholars' support for their empowerment and recognition and rather indirectly align with their dominators and with these dominators' ally scholars. Katan (2011) has found that translators understand 'professionalism' as responsibility only to the text and, therefore, to the 'original' author with little awareness of the wider society or of their own autonomy and empowerment. "Their voluntary servitude does seem to be a prominent part of their world" (2011, 84). The scholarly views that advocate the reductive definition of the practice are usually embraced by the translator because they are less abstract and, especially, because they correspond to their perception of themselves and their vision of their practice, first and foremost. The non-empowering scholar and the translator share the same *doxa* of submission. Second, the latter scholars' presence and involvement with translators and their organizations is probably more influential[23].

Rather than interacting with the supportive scholar/educator in order to include some of their insights into one's documents and general views, some translator associations may want to see their (unreflexive) ideas reflected in education institutions' curricula. In the studied corpus, the FIT, the mother organization of all national associations, stresses the right of translation associations to give advice on the training of translators. "They [translators' societies and unions] shall have the *right* to give *advice* on the training and recruitment of translators, and to co operate with specialized organizations and universities in the pursuit of these aims" (Article 31, italics added). One wonders which institution, the translator organization or the university department, is in the right position to give advice to the other as far as training is concerned. The FIT statement implies that translator organizations want to act as messengers of the other agents and warrantors of their demands. Instead of implementing pedagogical approaches and methods that are discipline-based, the FIT seems to be asking universities to listen to the requirements of the market and their clients and other stakeholders. Such a tripartite institutional alliance (i.e., the translator institution, education institution and the institutions representing the other powerful agents involved in translation) appears to give translators little chances of liberation. "This institutionalized disavowal impinges on how translation is viewed and how translators are trained and supervised," as Tymoczko puts it (2009, 413).

In addition to the scarcity of external resources of power, translators are internally fragmented and heterogeneous. The lack of concentration and the lack of consensus over the title of 'translator' (i.e., the standards of being a translator) are among the main issues facing translators. This internal fragmentation is again due to the fact that the powerful agents (some employers/clients) further throw into confusion those standards by setting quite diverse criteria for recruitment. Some of them seek certified translators, some seek translators with education in translation and others are content with anyone who is proficient in the two languages required for translation. These agents ultimately succeed in setting translators in competition with each other (see Bourdieu 1986, 247), especially in today's digital era, characterized by a global competition in the global market of translation – add to this the proliferation of associations and the increasing specialization in translation/interpreting (see Pym et al. 2016). On the other hand, the other agents with whom translators struggle over stakes seem to be more homogeneous and more influential. Authors and publishers, whose representative bodies may be smaller in size, may have better external support and may be more influential, as I discussed earlier. Potential clientele/employers, although not single or structurally homogeneous, are usually large, concentrated and powerful. Multinational corporations, governments, continental/regional groups and regional/international organizations are among the main potential employers/clients of translators in many parts of the world. For example, the European Commission of the EU is the largest employer of translators in the world. In Canada, the Translation Bureau is the largest employer of translators in the country. Furthermore, in the digital era, large corporations of translation/localization services have been established. These corporations concentrate jobs and subcontract work to freelancers. They, therefore, become the only direct contact with clients (see Abdallah and Koskinen 2007). Some of these companies are likely to seek immediate economic profits rather than lobby for the recognition of the individual translator.

Despite the complex hurdles discussed earlier – which are natural obstacles in all struggles – and the difficulty, if not the impossibility to subvert the rules of the social game, the project of the translator's relative empowerment can still be viable, today, if it is a collective commitment of the entire body representing translators with the engagement of more academics forming/training them. And this is not to say that individual action is undesirable or useless. Change within institutions starts with individual voices before they get adopted by bigger groups and before they get to "reconstitute the social," to use Inghilleri's term (2012).

> Attempts by role occupants to define or redefine their positions within a given profession are likely to be oriented toward the correction or

adaptation of their individual practice rather than overt strategies designed to challenge or resist the official codes that guide them. However, the actions of individuals within an established practice can also serve to reconstitute the social.

(Inghilleri 2012, 57)

The reconstitution of the translator's (internal) laws can be arduous and long. The centuries-old assumptions about *translation* and translators are too fixed to be easily shaken. Their arbitrariness has been completely obliterated.

Although the role of strategic calculation to modify the conditions of the game and subvert domination is generally not stressed in Bourdieu's thought, he does not deny its relevance in moments of crisis (Bourdieu & Wacquant 1992, 131). I believe that today we are in a moment of crisis in the field of translation. The mainstream understanding of *translation* has been clearly shown to be fraught. Many contemporary practices of translation nowadays have shown that this understanding is an ideological shibboleth or a myth because all these agents (including the translator) know that translation involves transformation. These new practices have challenged the whole law of the field, which is based, primarily, on this definition. And the role and identity of the translator have substantially changed. The new and permanently changing role(s) of the translator are now obvious to everyone. Besides, the ubiquity of translation in the "translation age" (Cronin 2012) in today's global era is more than ever before calling for an elevation of the translator's status for them to do their work autonomously and ethically for the welfare of the public and the planet. Faithfulness – if possible, at all – does not always guarantee the protection of the public and our planet in the age of serious environmental, pandemic and human rights challenges. 'Faithfulness,' 'detachment' or 'confidentiality' can result in the dissemination of endangering products that may have fatal consequences for the environment and humans. Such concepts can also help disseminate racist, gendered or xenophobic language in an age of multiethnic and open societies.

We are in a moment of crisis because we can no longer ignore these challenges or keep ignoring the new/old stark evidence about *translation* as *transformation*. The empowerment of translators alone prepares them to face these new challenges. But despite all the evidence of crisis, I believe gradual change that is supported from one of the agents in the field of power is more secure and more realistic than calls for, or attempts at, abrupt subversion by translators alone with no external support. At the forefront of this possible change stand scholars who support the translator's autonomy. The educational/academic agent is the only one capable of seizing the opportunity presented by this crisis and the tremendous and unprecedented upheavals in the field to shake the current structure of the field by shaking the definition of *translation*, first and foremost. This is possible for them because they have the power of "naming"/defining and they are the translators' potential ally from the field of power. Following Bourdieu, the power to impose the laws/codes of functioning of a field rests within the powerful agents (Bourdieu 1986, 246). The hope is that these scholars may exert more pressure and, especially, deploy more energies (i.e., recruit other colleagues and implement the newer understandings of *translation* in their own curricula) in this period of crisis so as "to mobilize the potential strength of the dominated" translators in order to "subvert the order prevailing in the field of power" (Bourdieu 1993, 44). To mobilize translators to shake the established rules of the game, scholars/educators especially need to train the new generations on the complexity and multifacetedness of *translation* as well as the autonomy of translators as cultural creators and practitioners. Importantly, they need to publicly disseminate these ideas in order to gradually shake the public's/powerful agents' categories of perception of translation/translators. Of course, this is not a project without its hurdles as I explained earlier, due to the low position scholars/educators have within the field of power, compared to the agents who fund education institutions and research programs. But a realistic and gradual project of minimization of hegemony is not impossible. Educators/scholars still have enough margin of autonomy to include newer ideas in their teaching programs, research projects and public communications. In parallel, there needs to be internal work within translator associations. This work starts from gradually changing the self-denigrating discourse in their documentation (among them codes of ethics) and rather embrace the findings of empowering academics.

6.4 Conclusion

As cultural producers and/or practitioners of an occupation, the translator's cultural capital is the nucleus of all forms of capital – drawing on Bourdieu's thought. It feeds their social, economic and mostly symbolic capital. In the case of translators, social and economic forms of capital do not convert to symbolic capital but are rather fed by it.

All the studied organizations present translators as possessing low cultural capital. When seen as cultural producers, this perceived low embodied capital of the translator assigns them a limited copyright. Most studied documents reinforce the current copyright law that is denigrating to the translator. Two codes of association abstain from emphasizing this law, but paradoxically reinforce the discourse that underlines the derivative nature of translation that underpins this very copyright law.

Analyzed as practitioners who seek collegiate control of their occupation, translators are far from achieving this aim. Most associations' documents reiterate many of the powerful agents' demands unquestioningly and unconditionally. This *status quo* is due to three main reasons. First, they (inadvertently) present themselves as having low cultural capital. Second, they are internally fragmented, while the beneficiary agents are concentrated and powerful. Finally, they have limited external resources of power. Not only do translators lose control over their practice to the powerful agents but they also undergo a sort of symbolic violence. They themselves reproduce the devaluing views about their practice (shared by the powerful agents), defend the demeaning rules of their practice and their roles and take labour relations that issue from them as natural and commonsensical. They contribute to their own "misfortune" – to reuse Godbout's term (2016, n.p.).

Although some associations under study purportedly defend the translator's interests and rights in some articles of their codes, they paradoxically reinforce the very principles/rules that undermine these rights/interests in other articles. Many codes under study, for example, refer to 'professionalism,' which supposedly implies the autonomy of the practitioners, their high expertise and/or the claim of recognition. All of the codes, also, underline many constituents of the translator's embodied cultural capital such as competence, 'professional' development and lifelong learning. Some, likewise, defend the translators' rights to reasonable economic benefits. However, the conceptualization of *translation* – which affects the translator's perceived embodied cultural capital – and the non-requirement of high institutionalized cultural capital abort any attempts to convert these two forms of cultural capital into symbolic power.

The FIT Translator's Charter seems more advanced than many national/provincial codes. Adopting a mixed approach (rights and duties), it is the most explicit and detailed in laying out many of the translator's rights (of course besides duties). But like the latter associations, it fails in the main battle, i.e., the definition of the practice, a fact which makes its attempts toward collegiate control inefficient and vain.

The document that may be seen as representing the outsider agent (governments of the UNESCO Member States) is, surprisingly, more progressive than most associations' codes of ethics. Although adopted in 1976, much earlier than probably all studied codes/charters[24], the Nairobi Recommendation advances statements that are more appreciative of the translator's work. Most strikingly, this document of an organization that is itself (with its mother organization the UN) an employer of a large number of translators, and a union of most world states (which are also potential employers/clients of translators) assigns practitioners rights they themselves do not claim – or at least do not state as explicitly in their own documents. The Nairobi Recommendation is the document that mostly emphasizes high specialized training (institutionalized cultural capital) – a crucial element that is convertible into symbolic power. This demonstrates that submission is mostly voluntary and not always coerced by legal force and material violence. It is worth mentioning, however, that the Nairobi Recommendation is, like the other documents, embedded in a paradox as it reinforces the reductive definition of *translation* and the *partial* copyright of the translator. This is not to mention the mere symbolic nature of this document as it is not legally binding to signatory Member States, a fact which may make its provisions have little impact on translators in many countries.

Symbolic violence that translators undergo is not something that is easy to shed as this is, I believe, nurtured by the translator's disposition toward *subservience* (see the discussions of Simeoni 1998; Inghilleri 2003, 2005a; Buzelin 2014 and Katan 2011). And as we know from Bourdieu, the relational aspects in a field and its functioning are imposed by the powerful agents and reproduced by the dominated. That is why this project is a modest one. It only seeks a relative and gradual shaking up of the current *status quo*, taking advantage of this time of crisis characterized by major upheavals in the translation field. The scholar, an agent within the field of power and the translator's potential resource of external power, can seize the opportunity and help shake up the *status quo* by gradually injecting the new visions of *translation* into the field of power (especially to policymakers) and into their curriculum, should they deploy all their energies. In short, although complete reshuffling of power relations can never be achieved because of the concentration and the power of the other corporate/political agents and the historicity of the discourse on translation/translators, power asymmetries can certainly be reduced. And the battle starts in education institutions – a topic I tackle in Part IV.

Codes of ethics reinforce a discourse that does not only affect the translator's economic and symbolic forms of capital but may also affect their morality. The translator's impoverished capital may have an impact on their moral autonomy. This is what I address in Part III.

Notes

1 See Schinkel and Noordegraaf (2011).
2 Johnson's term (2015/1977, 106).
3 Of course, professionals do have internal competition with one another, but this is not the focus of the current project.
4 It is noteworthy that 'profession,' 'professionalism' and 'professionalization' are used in their mainstream sense by many articles in the studied documents. However, in some other articles, we occasionally discern tacit or direct allusions

to *professionalization* in the sense of internal and autonomous self-control, as I will discuss shortly.
5 This article appears in the html format of the Deontological Code on this link: www.sft.fr/code-de-deontologie-des-traducteurs-et-interpretes.html, but disappears from its pdf format. (Accessed on July 5, 2018).
6 Impact on social capital is discussed in the next section.
7 Companies of translation may be represented by individual members who may be owners or managers. Or in some cases, designers of codes of ethics request these companies' suggestions in order to include them in these documents (see Ozolins 2014 about suggestions received from these agencies/employers).
8 There are documents that condition the rule of 'confidentiality' like the IAFET (Article 2.5), the Nairobi Recommendation (Paragraph 5f), the AUSIT (Article 2.4, Code of Conduct/Obligations towards Recipients of Services) and the SFT (Deontological Code, Article 1c).
9 This is not to say that the religious/political institution did not influence the translators' choices and methods of translation but that the rules were not self-imposed through one's institutions the way they are today.
10 The author's intervention in the translator's work may sometimes be flagrant. Marilyn Booth (2008) argues that, in many cases, the translator "may not have the final word" on their work (2008, 201). She vehemently criticizes the author and publisher's domesticating revisions made to her translation of Raja' al-Sani's *Banat al-Riyadh* (Rajaa Alsanea, *Girls of Riyadh*, Penguin, 2007) without her consent.
11 We know that paratextual elements play a crucial role in (re)framing texts in many different ways and, thus, in orienting reading and weaving desired narratives of the other (Baker 2005, 2006a, 2007, 2010) or the self (Boukhaffa 2018).
12 "Authors of literary and artistic works protected by this Convention shall enjoy the exclusive right of making and of authorizing the translation of their works throughout the term of protection of their rights in the original works."
13 Article 6*bis*, paragraph 1 of the Berne Convention about the author's moral right reads, "[i]ndependently of the author's economic rights, and even after the transfer of the said rights, the author shall have the right to claim authorship of the work and to object to any distortion, mutilation or other modification of, or other derogatory action in relation to, the said work, which would be prejudicial to his honor or reputation."
14 I discuss in Part III how the translator may be ethically neutralized.
15 In the presence of the Italian President, the American President Donald Trump said that the cultural relations between the USA and Italy "[d]ate back thousands of years to Ancient Rome" (Giustini 2019, n.p., italics added). He also said that in Syria, "[t]hey've got a lot of sand over there. So there's a lot of sand they can play with" (ibid.). It is noteworthy that Trump was defended by some historians and journalists claiming that what he meant are the cultural values that bind Italy and the U.S.A. and which go back to Roman cultural and political traditions (Brennan 2019, n.p.). Of course, whether Trump was right or not about the first claim has no effect on my argument.

16 www.newsweek.com/donad-trump-translator-perplexed-comments-syria-lot-sand-italy-sergio-mattarella-twitter-1465903 (Accessed on November 2, 2019).
17 https://nationalpost.com/news/world/donald-trumps-perplexed-italian-translator-reminded-us-why-some-jobs-are-best-kept-invisible (Accessed on November 2, 2019).
18 We know that many contemporary practices indeed demand the translator's visibility, as I discussed in Part I.
19 The policy of wide-open doors to all autodidacts (with no educational requirements), which seeks to enlarge the network and increase the social capital, inadvertently impedes the translator's symbolic recognition. The external agents and the public may perceive of all translators as not having high degrees (cultural capital).
20 The latest development in Artificial Intelligence (AI) tools have also made the current copyright law valueless, as those tools presumably use copyrighted data, and it has become almost impossible to hold them accountable, because of the difficulty of traceability. Recently, we started to hear about some lawsuits, in this regard, however. The *Times*, for example sued OpenAI and Microsoft over the use of their copyrighted materials to train AI chatbots. See www.nytimes.com/2023/12/27/business/media/new-york-times-open-ai-microsoft-lawsuit.html (Accessed January 8, 2024).
21 The document deviates from scholarship publication structure and is very close to a business report, starting with an executive summary. Of course, the executive summary was removed in the book published a year later addressed to a different audience, namely academics and students (Pym et al. 2013).
22 He thus reinforces the hegemony of dominant language/culture, as well.
23 This is a hypothesis that needs to be corroborated by future research.
24 In the FIT Translator's Charter revised in 1994, i.e., 18 years later than the adoption of the Nairobi Recommendation, one hardly feels any tangible progress over the latter. And since 1994, i.e., 27 years later, strikingly, there has been no revision of the Charter although there has been tremendous evolution in the field, especially with the digital revolution and globalization. Hence, since 1976, there has been no advances, probably because of the continuous weakening of translators with the emergence of very powerful clients in the digital era.

Part III
The Translator's Morality in Codified Ethics

This part examines the extent to which the translator's *moral self* is neutralized by the principles/rules highlighted in institutionalized codified ethics, drawing on Bauman's postmodern morality. It also explores the opportunities that postmodern perspectives on ethics offer, especially in the age of globalization.

7 Bauman's Postmodern Morality
Beyond Rational Codification of Ethics

7.1 Modernity and Rational Codification

In his works on postmodernity and ethics, the Polish sociologist and philosopher, Zygmunt Bauman (1993, 1994, 2003a/1995, 2003b, 2007, 2008), presents a novel analysis of the thorny issue of ethics and morality[1]. Refuting modernity's lean toward rational 'control of chaos' and the imposition of ethical order through codified ethics and laws, he argues that postmodernity presents both a bane and a chance for the moral person (Bauman 1993, 16). Modernity has foregrounded the meta-narratives of Science, Progress, Industrialization, Enlightenment as its main guiding themes (see also Lyotard 1979, Baudrillard 2005, Somers and Gibson 1994) and sought to create a 'commonsensical' reality using the rhetoric of these metanarratives. Rational science, bureaucratic institutions and technologies have especially served as modernity's main instruments to create the perfect ordering of reality (Bauman 1993, 1994, 2003a/1995, 2003b, 2007, 2008). For Bauman, the aim of modernity and its ideological underpinnings has been the creation of a rational, flawless and efficient (social) order.

Since Kant, modern thinkers and legislators have tried to "compose and impose an all-comprehensive, unitary ethics – that is, a cohesive code of moral rules which people could be taught and forced to obey," Bauman points out (1993, 6). In the modernist project, both thinkers and legislators claim the universality of their prescriptions and rules. No law or rule is to be felt incomplete, wrong or contradictory by any rational human being. The modern philosophical prescriptions are also presented as "well founded" in the sense that they are based on the likeliness that rational persons will embrace them. The answer to the question 'why should I be moral' seems to underlie these rules. The heteronomous ethical prescriptions, backed and enforced by powerful social/political institutions, ultimately 'assist' individuals in making the 'right' decisions and 'save' them from the uncertainties of hesitations and ambivalence. It is an alleviation of personal responsibility, an erasure of the pain of uncertainty, and a 'preventer of evil.' By substituting autonomous moral responsibility of the self with 'non-contradictory' ethical duties, modern thinkers and legislators have purportedly aimed at preventing wrong from happening by giving the agent an *a priori* certainty of the consequences of their actions. "[T]he moral thought and practice of modernity was animated by the belief in the possibility of a *non-ambivalent, non-aporetic ethical code*" (Bauman 1993, 9, italics in original).

The non-ambivalent, complete and rational codes of ethics that cater for both the rational individual and the whole community are the basis of the *illusion* that modernity stands on, Bauman asserts (1993). The postmodern perspective "means above all the tearing off of the mask of illusions" (Bauman 1993, 3). It has the task of revealing the cruelty of modernity, manifest in its elimination of the unclear, the residual, the unfit, the exceptional, the particular, the rare and the out-of-order. And the task of the current project is to reveal the problems within the translator codes of ethics, embedded in this illusive discourse of modernity.

7.2 The Postmodern Ambivalent *Moral Self*

The unmasking of the illusions of uniformity, efficiency, universals and (near)completeness is exactly what is meant by postmodernity in Bauman's sense (1993, 1994, 2003a/1995, 2003b, 2007, 2008). Postmodernity is the critical reflection of modernity on itself; the realization that objectively founded universals are an unattainable myth. In other words, postmodernity is modernity that is aware of its paradoxes; it is modernity that is conscious of its own impossibility as such. Therefore, it should not be understood as an after-modernity era in a chronological sense since modernity is still around. Postmodernity is about debunking the theoretical absolutes and certainties of theoreticians, and the rejection of 'all-embracing' regulations imposed by bureaucratic institutional bodies.

> What the postmodern mind is aware of is that there are problems in human and social life with no good solutions, twisted trajectories that cannot be straightened up, ambivalences that are more than linguistic blunders yelling to be corrected, doubts which cannot be legislated out of existence, moral agonies which no reason-dictated recipes can soothe, let alone cure. The postmodern mind does not expect any more to find the all-embracing, total and ultimate formula of life without ambiguity, risk, danger and error, and is deeply suspicious of any voice that promises otherwise [...] The postmodern mind is reconciled to the idea that the messiness of the human predicament is here to stay. This is, in the broadest outlines, what can be called postmodern wisdom.
> (Bauman 1993, 245)

Following Bauman's argument, the postmodern individuals accept their fate and face their reality with all its contradictions, dilemmas and 'ills.' They are agents that are ready to live without or beyond the preordained rules, established by superior institutional powers. Postmodern individuals are autonomous beings, ready to assume full responsibility for their uncertain choices, willing to face the frustrations of decision-making and able to renounce the 'comfort' of choices made for them.

While the modern project has aimed at sidelining ambivalence and containing the bad, from a postmodern perspective, humans are neither inherently good nor bad. They are rather *morally ambivalent.*

> [A]mbivalence resides at the heart of the 'primary scene' of human face-to-face. All subsequent social arrangements – the power-assisted institutions as well as the rationally articulated and pondered rules and duties – deploy that ambivalence as their building material while doing their best to cleanse it from its original sin of being an ambivalence.
> (Bauman 1993, 10)

It is clear that in postmodern thought, no code of ethics can be absolute or comprehensive. Moral ambivalence remains uncleansed of its original sin despite the modern rationalist attempt to contain it in perfect coercive codes. Bauman argues that "morality phenomena are inherently 'non-rational'" (ibid., 11). They are beyond calculations, as they are ambiguous and unpredictable. For Bauman, moral impulse, inherently contradictory and ambivalent, cannot be eradicated, once and for all by rational codification; "at the most, it can silence it and paralyse" (ibid., 10).

Bauman rejects ethical prescriptions as they are rule-governed, uniform and bureaucratically imposed. Rational ethics that unfoundedly "shift[s] moral phenomena from the realm of personal autonomy into that of power-assisted heteronomy" try to dismiss the moral impulse, and silence the *moral self*, which is, in essence, "constituted by responsibility" (ibid., 11) toward Otherness. At the other extreme from *ethics*, morality is personal and "incurably *aporetic*" (ibid., italics in original). Situational choices are ambiguous and uncertain. Most of them are made between contradictory impulses. Endemic uncertainty is, thus, a *moral condition*. "I believe that the frustration of uncertainty is morality's gain. Not the kind of gain we would wish, perhaps, and have been looking for – but the greatest gain that one can reasonably hope for, while remaining a moral person" (ibid., 223). This frustration of ambivalence is a defining characteristic of the moral self. The latter, 'unarmed' with imposed regulations, is left bare to face the tyranny and burden of moral decisions. There is no guarantee that the moral impulse will always guide the individual to make the right moral decisions. The incurable ambivalence of morality as a fate of moral selves, thus, makes moral life more difficult and more complex, as the self no longer hides behind legislated ethical rules.

Postmodern morality, for Bauman is, thus, "[a] jungle deprived even of the jungle law, morality without ethics" (1994, 25). It is neither a good thing nor a bad thing; it is a boon and a bane. It just puts us in front of a real (natural) reality that is far more complex than the reduced one we have been invited to think and embrace. Postmodernity has unmasked the illusions that we have lived by and that have made our lives and paths sound perfectly clear, pre-planned, unified, managed, and under control. Postmodernity does not give *one* definitive answer to moral questions. It allows us to face the unknown, the unfamiliar, the unpredictable, the unclassifiable, the uncategorizable, the unformalizable and the uncontrollable; all constituting the essence of the human moral condition. Unlike modern codified duties that target the whole, the group or society and negate difference and particularities, postmodern morality gives individuals a chance, but a chance of which the results are *never* assured in advance.

> [M]oral *responsibility* exists solely in interpellating the individual and being carried individually. Duties tend to make humans alike; responsibility is what makes them into individuals [...] One may say that the moral is what *resists* codification, formalization, socialization, universalization.
> (Bauman 1993, 54, italics in original)

Morality does not need ethical codes as it predates all legislation or social norms; a world without codified ethics cannot be equated with a world without morality.

7.3 The *Pre-social* Being FOR the Other vs. The *Social* Being WITH the Other

Drawing on Emmanuel Lévinas, Bauman argues that "moral responsibility – being *for the Other* before one can be *with* the Other – is the first reality of the self, a starting point rather than a product of society" (Bauman 1993, 13, italics in original). As Lévinas (1991, 1995) conceptualizes it, morality is an *a priori* and *infinite* responsibility *for the Other*, a commandment to the *I*, an interruption of being, a vow, a non-indifference, an allegiance, or a hostageship to the irreducible Other, *independently of* and *prior* to any sociability, reciprocity, dialogue, or relationship.

> [T]he otherness of the other man towards the self is first of all – and if I dare say, is "positively" – the face of the other man obliging the

self, which, at the outset – without deliberation – is responsive to the other. *From the outset*, that is, the self answers "gratuitously", without worrying about reciprocity; it is the gratuitousness of the *for the other*, the response of responsibility that is already present in the greeting, in the *hello*, in the *goodbye*. Such language is prior to statements of propositions communicating information and narratives.

(Lévinas 1991, 184, italics in original, my translation)

Lévinas conceptualizes morality as a "gratuitous" responsibility devoid of any benefits, reciprocity, understanding, or even communication. Following Lévinas, Bauman (1993, 1994, 2003a/1995, 2003b, 2008) contends that morality has a primitive and existential status; it predates society with all its conventions, educational/philosophical discourses and legislations. It precedes imposed ethical regulations shared by society members. Morality is above rational calculations and purposefulness. It "is a mystery contrary to reason" (Bauman 1993, 13). Being *for* the other is pre-modern, pre-social, limitless and unconditional. It is driven solely by the proximity of *the Face of the Other*. Moral responsibility is "absolute, pristine, extemporal, and exterritorial, unsoiled by the products of societal cycling and unadulterated by illegitimate, heterogeneous, accidental, and dispensable admixtures" (Bauman 2008, 40). The *Face of the Other*, by its uniqueness, transcends any impersonal rules or ethical codes that treat all Faces as collective abstracts, with no unique or individual traits. Otherness is also irreducible to the self. Every Other is singular and different from Self and other Others. The encounter with the Other is individual (only Self and Other) with no interference of any other (social) variable that can taint, affect, or cast a shadow over the pure uncalculated and unpragmatic meeting.

Entering Levinas's moral space requires taking time off from the daily business of living and leaving aside its mundane norms and conventions. At the 'moral party of two', both I and the Other arrive disrobed, without our social trappings, stripped of status, social distinctions, and socially concocted or socially imposed identities, positions, or roles.

(Bauman 2008, 42–43)

The *Third* that intervenes in these twosome encounters is what worries Lévinas and Bauman most. *Thirds* are parasites that are everywhere to mediate or to orient the relationship. As soon as "the 'other' appears in a plural," i.e., in a social being, the moral impulse becomes a 'poor guide.' Once it becomes disoriented by external (social/economic/ideological/cultural) variables, moral responsibility loses its unconditional essence.

7.4 Social Spaces

Bauman (1993, Chapter 6) analyzes proximity/distance between the self and the Other in the social sphere. In this space, he makes a distinction between three discrete but strongly related processes: the *cognitive*, *aesthetic* and *moral* spacings.

The *cognitive* space is the rational construction that seeks control and order. Drawing on reason, it creates non-ambivalent signposts for the social behaviour that is deemed appropriate and acceptable by rational beings. Therefore, the stranger who is unable to assimilate these social signposts is seen as an alien. Because "the strangehood' has become a permanent condition" (ibid., 159) of the modern world and its urban cities (due to immigration, refuge, exile), the cognitive control over social spacing is being sought more than ever before in order "to confine and regiment freedom of the strangers and altogether 'keep them where they belong'" (ibid.). In today's cosmopolitan metropolises, the strategy of 'mismeeting' or indifference is modernity's answer to the physically close but socially distant strangers. The cognitive administration of the social space uses *proteophobia* (i.e., perceiving the other as dirty and alien) as its main resource and driving force (ibid., 165–168). This keeps the stranger at a social distance and builds an insurmountable fence that makes them inconceivable to the structured rational mind and the social/cognitive order.

Differently from the cognitive space, the *aesthetic* space is based on the attention given to the Other. This attention is affectively driven by curiosity and pleasure seeking. "The strangers, with their unknown, unpredictable ways, with their kaleidoscopic variety of appearances and actions, with their capacity to surprise, are a particularly rich source of spectators' pleasure" (ibid., 168). Unlike the cognitive space, which draws on *proteophobia*, aesthetic space relies on *proteophilia*, i.e., amusement and enjoyment experienced from the presence of the Other. The cognitive and aesthetic spaces are interwoven, however. The former is the controlling framework under which the latter functions. The aesthetic is a *play* space, a spectacle and a theatre; it is not real. As far as the game/spectacle is ordained by strict rules (i.e., by cognitive space) that keep the social space under control, the amusement offered by the aesthetic space continues/is allowed. The 'spectacle' of the Other, which is enjoyed in the aesthetic space, can take place as far as the cognitive space polices and administers the social space in a way that prevents any unexpected dangers or uncontrollable rebellion that may render the game serious; a fact that may endanger the cognitive ordering. The *flâneur* "can go on drawing the strangers around into his private theatre without fear that those drawn inside will claim the rights of the insiders. Social/cognitive spacing has created distances which aesthetic spacing can transgress only playfully, only in imagination, only inconsequentially" (ibid., 172).

At the other extreme of the aesthetic process – which cannot actually transgress social/cognitive rules – the *moral* space

> takes no notice of the rules that define the social/cognitive space. It is oblivious to the social definitions of proximity and distance [...] it engages no human intellectual capacities – such as examination, comparison, calculation, evaluation. By the intellectual standards proper to cognitive spacing, it looks abominably 'primitive': a cottage industry compared to a scientifically managed factory.
>
> (Bauman 1993, 165)

Moral space is, thus, an enemy of cognitive space in the sense that it threatens its security and non-ambivalence and challenges its universal categorizations and established order that are based on reason. The concern of the cognitive space is, thus, the mitigation, or if possible, the effacement of the moral effects of the moral space – perceived as pathological, chaotic and scandalous. The moral spacing also challenges the aesthetic spacing, which is based on mobile (and perhaps pushy) affectivity. For the aesthetic spacing, attention to the Other fades away once the enjoyment turns into boredom, novelty into familiarity (ibid.). Moral spacing, on the other hand, maintains the mystery, the difference, the unknown and the ungraspable aspects of the Other intact. The aesthetic can, however, lead to the moral spacing on condition of respecting the Other's difference and mystery for *eternity* and moving from the space of amusement for its own sake to the moral condition of caring *for* the Other. "To accomplish such a feat, the seeker of aesthetic satisfaction must be, however, also a moral person" (ibid., 181). Bauman concludes that both the cognitive and aesthetic spaces, as such, are inhospitable to the moral space.

> In both, moral urges are alien bodies and pathological growths. In the social/cognitive space – because they sap the lofty and indifferent impersonality of rules and soil the purity of reason with unwashable stains of affection. In the social/aesthetic space – because they tend to fix and arrest and immobilize things which draw their seductive powers solely from being on the move and ready to disappear once commanded.
>
> (Bauman 1993, 180)

7.5 The Ethical Challenges of Globalization

If Bauman's theorization seeks to free the individual from coercive modern ethics, it, however, does not provide a viable process that individuals can embrace or base their actions and decisions upon, in order to face the ethical challenges of *distance* in the new age of digital globalization. Although his morality is based on *proximity*, following Lévinas, he understands that "distances matter little now," as local actions may have global consequences (Bauman 2008, 71). Moral beings, in the globalized age, need to be aware of the far-reaching repercussions of their actions not only on people's lives in other corners of the planet but also on generations to come. Bauman recognizes that in our contemporary technological society,

> the scale of possible consequences of human actions have long outgrown moral imagination of the actors. Knowingly or unknowingly, our actions affect territories and times much too distant for the 'natural' moral impulses which struggle in vain to assimilate them, or abandon the struggle altogether. Morality which we inherited from pre-modern times – the only morality we have – is a morality of proximity, and as such woefully inadequate in a society in which all important action is an action on distance.
>
> (Bauman 1993, 217)

Bauman recognizes that pre-modern morality has short hands, as it is a morality of proximity. Therefore, the postmodern moral self is facing the challenge of stretching out their moral visualization to reach as far as possible, in the digital age. In this globalized era, humans need to adapt their moral imagination to think beyond the foreseeable, beyond the unseen, to reach far *distant* Others.

Bauman's conclusions may sound unrealistic and too abstract for those seeking grounded and gradual change. Despite the pertinence of his argument regarding "gratuitous" morality devoid of economic or ideological considerations, his concept of *morality* as primitive, innate and pre-social may seem problematic. Bauman's morality as an instinctive impulse that precedes society seems too radical, and thus, difficult to be taken wholesale at the practical level. As Bos and Willmott (2001) put it, Bauman's analysis is embedded in a sharp dualism between reason and emotion, and ethics and morality, and his absolute rejection of the interference of rationality in the moral space is quite untenable. I argue that modern citizens are embedded in modernist rational discourses and institutions that are hard to abruptly subvert to embrace an impulsive morality that may make very little sense to many of them (see Kelemen and Peltonen 2001 for a similar conclusion). I believe Bauman should have convincingly proposed how the moral individual could learn to work on themselves to *de-modernize*, and, therefore, recover from modernity's ills and regain their initial moral condition – if recoverable at all.

The other related issue at stake in Bauman's work, I believe, is that he does not suggest any ways to stretch moral imagination beyond its pre-modern state (of proximity) to adapt to the responsibility toward *distant* others and respond to the problems and challenges of globalization.

Bauman, himself aware of this problem, does not seem very optimistic about the potentiality of this morality of *distance* when he affirms that "[i]t remains to be seen, if at all, whether the intuitively evident need for a 'morality of spatial and temporal distance' may be translated into effective social interests, and consequently into tangible political forces" (Bauman 1993, 222). This is because Bauman knows that, at the end of the day, the question is whether or not the discourse of *distant morality* can attract supporters and be powerful. "Superior morality is always the morality of the superior," of the 'victor,' he points out (ibid., 228).

Leaving aside these gaps – some of which Bauman himself acknowledges – his work on ethics/morality presents a very interesting critical stance toward the ills of modernity and its moral crisis. His account of modernity's rational codification of ethics, alongside TS insights, is used to analyze the underpinnings of translators' codes of ethics. More importantly, Bauman's critical thought is used to analyze the role and place allotted to the translator's moral responsibility in these codes of ethics. His concept of moral self makes it possible to identify whether the translator's moral judgment can play any role at all in their choices. In other words, it makes it possible to see whether codes act as substitutes for the moral self. Finally, this part of analysis explores the implications not only for the translator's moral self but also for various societal issues if individual morality is excluded in the name of 'professionalism.' The following chapter examines the impact of some highlighted principles/rules in the documents under study on the translator's moral self. Chapter 9 discusses the nature of these institutional charters/codes of ethics and their repercussions on the translator's moral responsibility. The chapter also discusses alternative postmodern ethics. Finally, it presents a brief discussion of the ethical challenges of globalization.

Note

1 In Bauman's understanding, morality stands for the personal responses/actions that are gratuitous and uncalculated toward others whereas ethics refer to those socially constructed, or legislated codes and rules that people are forced to follow. In this book, I use the two terms with this understanding only in my references to Bauman.

8 The Translator's *Moral Self* in Codified Ethics

Throughout much of the history of Europe at least, translation has been seen as a suspicious activity and the translator as an untrustworthy practitioner. The widespread adage *Traduttore, traditore* (Translator, traitor) is an expression that attests to this mainstream view of translation/translators. "Furthering this attitude is a tenacious prejudice in favour of the original, or 'source', as undisputed master in the text-translation duo" (Polizzoti, 2018b, n.p.), as discussed in Part II. Thus, it is not surprising that this 'copying' and 'suspicious' activity and its 'deceitful' practitioner/'copier' are subject to processes of regulation and control in modernity, the age of ordering and containment *par excellence* (Bauman 1993).

Like all modern enterprises, the codification of translator ethics claims to contain the aberrant and secure the user or, to be more accurate, to advance the illusions of order and control. "These codes of conduct aim to regulate acceptable professional performance to match and obliviate the sticky fear" of the translator's clients and to gain their trust (Koskinen 2020, 96). Translator associations elaborate codes of ethics and/or codes of 'professional' conduct with the aim of 'regulating' the inherently 'suspicious' nature of the translator's behaviour/conduct in their practice and toward their environment. These codes are meant to avoid and prevent chaos in practice, establish the *boundaries* of the translation *system*, and create *a code* for the system, to borrow the terminology of Niklas Luhmann (1992). Through these documents and other regulations/bylaws of associations, translation practice is purportedly self-regulated and self-governed by the practitioners themselves. The ultimate aim is to reduce the doubt and suspicion of the potential clients/employers and to advance 'professionalism.'

As discussed in Part II, the translation occupation is, in fact, not self-governed by the translator, and their capital is significantly impoverished in the studied documents. But the translator's capital is not the only aspect that may be affected by a code of ethics. Their moral self may also be largely impacted by the very idea of ethics codification. Next, I look back on translator codes of ethics through Bauman's lens. In the following section, I discuss 'public protection,' one of the main objectives highlighted by all studied documents, its scope and the tools deployed to achieve it. Without being exhaustive, I lay out the main principles/rules that supposedly aim at 'public protection,' and I show how they enable or neutralize the translator's moral self. In Section 8.2, I reveal how the documents tackle the issues of representation and cultural awareness and, therefore, how that impacts on Otherness.

8.1 Protection of the Public and its Means

McDonough Dolmaya (2011) rightly affirms that translator codes of ethics are similar to those of other professional associations of service providers. They advance principles such as confidentiality, competence, impartiality, conflict resolution, respect of the profession and the association, among others, which purportedly aim at the protection of the public. These rules and principles are not very interesting to investigate "because they do not apply exclusively (or nearly so) to the translation profession," according to McDonough Dolmaya (2011, 32). She, thus, limits her in-depth investigation to the principles directly related to translation as *text*, namely "accuracy," "working languages," and "illegal/immoral/unethical texts," and excludes principles related to the translator's interpersonal relations with other agents. She, thus, overlooks the impact of the relational aspects of the translation practice on ethical decisions in textual material. Yet, as shown in Part II, some of these principles have direct and immediate implications for the translating agent's autonomy in text and beyond. And this section shows how these interrelational rules (that may seem unrelated to texts) and the other principles related to text complement each other in constraining the translator's moral autonomy as well, in the name of public protection.

8.1.1 Public Protection

Like codes of ethics of many other occupations and professions, the studied associations' codes/charters are centred on the principle of 'public protection.' The ATIO claims in the very preamble that the principles laid out in its current code aim to "protect members of the public." Section 3 contains four sub-themes as components of this protection, namely integrity, advertising one's qualifications, confidentiality and fees. For integrity, the code emphasizes honesty and respect for the clients/employers' rights and interests (Article 3.1.1). As for advertisements, the document obligates the translator to behave with integrity in advertising their qualifications and services (Article 3.2.1). The advertised qualifications should correspond to the member's actual language combination and their earned degrees from recognized academic institutions. The third principle, confidentiality, includes – beside the respect for the clients' or employers' privacy (Article 3.3.1) – respect for the author's intellectual property rights (Article 3.3.2). The last element, 'fees for services,' stresses fair and reasonable' fees (3.4.1), which also means that translators should "bill clients only for services provided" (3.4.2) (and probably not for the work of editing TM products). Most other articles are also oriented toward the protection of the immediate agents. Further, the ATIO has a sub-section in its website entitled, 'how we protect the public.'[1] In this section, 'public protection' is ensured through "professional, high stakes exam" or dossier examination to ensure high qualification, "a strict code of professional ethics and conduct," and the sanctioning of members "who fail to adhere to the code of ethics or conduct." Thus, neither in their code nor in the section devoted to 'public protection' on ATIO's website is there a hint to the larger public (i.e., responsibility to, and protection of, one's world).

In its preamble, the SFT advances that the current code "offers to *all stakeholders, service providers as well as clients*, a guarantee of reliability, competence, honesty and *morality* in their transactions" (About the Code, italics added, my translation). The code is thus presented as the means of establishing and guaranteeing a sound and ethical relationship between translators and clients. Hence, not very differently from the ATIO, the SFT limits the scope of its moral coverage to the relationship between the immediate agents involved in translation, as is even clearer in Section 3 entitled 'Respect of Clients,' where there is not a single allusion to the public interest in its wider sense. The ATPP and the ITAINDIA codes, likewise, omit any mention of the wider society. They limit their instructions to the preservation of the immediate agents' interests, namely the clients' and patrons'.

The SATI code, on the other hand, stresses the wider public in one of its articles. It urges translators "[n]ot to accept any work that, in their opinion, is intended for unlawful or dishonest purposes or is contrary to the public interest" (Code of Ethics for Individual Members). An investigation of the nine other articles of the SATI code shows, however, that, once again, clients/patrons and authors are the main agents concerned by this protection. Clients/employers are explicitly named as beneficiaries of the required protection in five articles (Articles 2, 3, 5, 8, 9), and authors' protection is stated in one article (Article 8).

The position of the AUSIT is rather unclear. Its code, like the previously cited codes, stresses the immediate agents' interests and rights mostly and makes no explicit reference to the 'public,' 'society' or 'the world' as such. However, in a few instances, it passingly alludes to larger ethical issues that concern the wider public. For example, in the explanation of article 1, the code makes a brief mention of 'cultural sensitivity' – although with no further explanation. The AUSIT also alludes to personal ethics and, therefore, supposedly sets up conditions for the other agents' protection. "Interpreters and translators complete assignments they have accepted, unless they are unable to do so for ethical reasons (see 3.4 and 4.2 below)" (Code of Conduct/Obligations towards recipients of services, Article 1.3). Article 4.2 further stipulates that "[w]here impartiality may be difficult to maintain because of personal beliefs or other circumstances, interpreters and translators do not accept assignments, or they offer to withdraw from the assignment." The AUSIT also refers to the question of 'discriminatory language' (among other issues) – an issue which indeed concerns the protection of the general public (T6 Conduct issues specific to translators). That said, the code does not seem to allow the translator any agency regarding such language without a return to the client/patron (ibid.). Further, the AUSIT does not allow its members to express their views on any matter during an assignment. "Interpreters and translators do not voice or write an opinion, solicited or unsolicited, on any matter or person *during* an assignment" (Code of Conduct/Obligations towards recipients of services, Article 4.4, italics added). The article allows the translator/interpreter to speak out only *after* the completion of the assignment, in contrast with the 1995 version, which forbade that under all circumstances (Ozolins 2014, 363). It remains, however, that it may be too late to voice such an opinion after an assignment. In sum, although the AUSIT codes allude to some wider public issues, they still prioritize the immediate agents' interests. They allow for little margin of action for the translator.

The IAFET, on the other hand, urges its members to "[n]ot take part in practices that might favor actions which are detrimental to the public interest, the law or the interests of their profession" (Article 2.4). Most of its other articles are centred on the translator and the 'profession.' They allude to the clients' interests only in relation to guaranteeing proper quality (Article 2.2) and respecting the principle of *conditional* confidentiality (Article 2.5), as I explain shortly.

Like most national/provincial associations, the mother organization, the FIT, does not seem to orient the translator toward ethical issues/relations beyond the immediate circle of the translation transaction. In none of its articles is there a clear reference to the broader public or society. Despite its emphasis on "the social function of translation" (Preamble) manifest in allowing the exchange of intellectual products among nations and, therefore, enriching their lives and contributing to "a better understanding amongst men [sic]" (ibid.), and its contributing "to the spread of civilization throughout the world" (Article 37), it refrains from underlining any ethical issues that may tag along these idealistic objectives[2]. The FIT underlines the translator's autonomy regarding their production in some of its articles (e.g., Article 3, 9, 17) but remains inexplicit as to the extent of such autonomy in ethical terms and how it should be approached when the ethical orientations of the direct beneficiaries or agents contradict with the general public's interest.

The UNESCO reiterates the 'social function' of translation underlined by its counselling organization, the FIT. The Nairobi Recommendation stresses the role of translation/translators in promoting "understanding between peoples and co-operation among nations by facilitating the dissemination of literary and scientific works, including technical works, across linguistic frontiers and the interchange of ideas" as well as the "international exchanges in culture, art and science" (Preamble). Given the nature of the document, it is not surprising that the protection of this very exchange between nations from aberrations that may harm certain other agents or species beyond the 'professional' circle is not a concern of the Nairobi Recommendation[3]. Although the purported aim is the economic and symbolic empowerment of the translator in order to serve *society* in the best possible ways, the UNESCO does not show awareness of the possible harmful side effects of this service if the translator's moral self is not empowered in a way that serves society in all respects.

As can be seen in the above analysis, *public protection* is approached in two different ways. For some documents, this implies mainly the protection of the clients and patrons' interests and, in some cases, authors and publishers (SFT, ATPP, ITAINDIA and ATIO codes). Other documents (namely the IAFET, the SATI, the AUSIT, the FIT and the UNESCO's) highlight the interests of the 'public' in both a limited sense (i.e., immediate agents), and a wider sense. However, in most of the latter documents, such emphasis on the 'public' is disproportionate, i.e., articles/principles oriented to the immediate agents outweigh the ones directed to the large public. Besides, responsibility to the limited circle seems to have priority over responsibility to the public interest in its wider sense, as I further explain in the following sub-section. Next, I show how some principles that purportedly advance the protection of the public may in fact constrain the translator's ethical/social responsibilities and affect their autonomy and their dignity.

8.1.2 Means of Public Protection

8.1.2.1 Faithfulness and Associates

One of the main purported means of 'public protection' that recurs in all the documents under study (except the IAFET's) is 'faithfulness' or its associate rules, such as equivalence, accuracy, impartiality, detachment and objectivity. But 'faithfulness' is, in fact, a crucial component of the 'protection of the public' in its restrained sense. In the folk view, *faithfulness* is meant to protect the clients, patrons and authors from unsolicited interventions of the translator who may distort the original content. Thus, according to some documents, *faithfulness* is not only a 'professional' method and an 'ethical' principle but also a *legally* binding rule, for which non-compliance may result in prosecution (e.g., FIT, ATPP).

The rule of faithfulness and its associates may be seen as distracting tactics for the translator to ignore their wider ethical/social responsibilities (see Tymoczko 2009, Drugan and Tipton 2017). Translation as a faithful transfer of meaning rather shelters the translator from the burden and ambivalence of decision-making as translation decisions are *not* their responsibility. Responsibility, which requires creativity and intervention, is not a translator's concern.

Faithful transfer of meaning in translation – reiterated in the corpus under study – is based on a Eurocentric assumption and practice that consider the word 'sacred' and the 'original' prestigious and is retraining to the translator's agency.

> Dominant Western views of translation as transfer – transfer of meaning in particular – undercut the ethical agency of the translator. The idea of transfer of the sacred Word derived from Bible translation keeps the focus on the microlevels of textual fidelity. It is no accident that professional codes of ethics also stress these microlevels, as well as the translator's immediate obligations to the employer, effacing larger spheres of responsibility to communities and the world.
> (Tymoczko 2009, 413–414)

The return to this historical concept by the studied organizations seeks the enforcement of 'order' and the containment of possible aberrations and disloyalty – objectives which are not incompatible with modern aspirations. It is a seal of assurance to the immediate powerful agents. Interventions in translation imply disorder and is a threat to translation beneficiaries as well as recipients and, therefore, to the social order. These translator organizations, thus, exclude other practices dating from other pre-modern eras in Europe's history and (old) practices in other parts of the world (Tymoczko 2007). Unfortunately, even associations from non-European countries adopt this universalized definition of *translation* unquestioningly and disregard their own local/particular (historical) practices (ITAINDIA, ATPP, SATI, ATPP).

Tymoczko, Susam-Sarajeva and others have questioned this dominant conceptualization for practical and/or ethical reasons (see Baker 2006a, Koskinen 2000a, Davis 2001, Clifford 2004, Trivedi 2006). This definition oppresses the multiplicity and pluralism of discourses about *translation*. Kathleen Davis writes, a claim to define the unique characteristics of translation (or even of language) forms a concept of "translation" – its essence and its boundaries – through the exclusion of that which is other to this essence or is outside those boundaries. An ethics of translation theorized according to such a definition would be irresponsible to that which it excluded in order to define itself. For this reason, deconstruction remains wary of 'ethics', which in many contexts implies the application or establishment of an ideal code.

(Davis 2001, 92)

This exclusionist definition unethically excludes other cultures/times that have different definitions and practices. The definition is "limited and [...] also ideological," and therefore, unethical, in Tymoczko's words (2007, 6).

The unethical conceptualization of *translation* has, of course, unethical implications at the practical level. Faithfulness and its associates, mentioned above, may imply that the translator's practice does not allow any transformative strategies and that the translator's (ethical) agency is unwelcome. Ultimately, faithfulness and its associates disallow the translator's moral self any room for intervention to counter acts/materials they may deem inappropriate, unethical or illegal. By stressing these duties as *a priori* rules, the codes ignore the fact that many principles, as decontextualized as they are, may have unethical/dangerous consequences or promote/disseminate illegal practices/discourses in many contexts if applied unquestioningly. They may harm the wider public (humans and non-humans, in the present and in the future). Tymoczko writes:

> [s]tatements of translators' professional ethics promulgated in these contexts typically focus on *textual fidelity, responsibility to the patron* (client, employer), *legal responsibilities*, and the like. One discerns here a dispersal of ideology, a strategy to turn translators' attention away from larger ideological questions of ethical engagement and geopolitical concerns that might mobilize the translators' independent agency in activist ways.
>
> (Tymoczko 2007, 219, italics added)

From TS literature, we have learned that the Eurocentric understanding of *translation* as faithfulness has indeed been used as an unethical tool of hegemony, domination and misrepresentation in the past and the present.

> This Western model of translation has been particularly useful for bureaucracies of various sorts, including commercial organizations, governments, colonial regimes and even religious institutions [...] it has much to do with the technical, economic, military and political

supremacy of Westernized countries, driving expansionism and various other forms of dominance.

(Tymoczko 2009, 405)

Similarly to Tymoczko, Mona Baker (2010) shows that 'accuracy' is sometimes used as a tool that helps represent the Other in negative ways. She found that the Middle East Media Research Institute (MEMRI)[4] translates various texts emanating from Arab and Muslim countries in accurate ways but uses other reframing strategies (such as selective appropriation, causal emplotment, temporality and relationality) to "generate dehumanising narratives of Arabs and Muslims" (Baker 2010, 347).

The studied translator organizations, which adopt 'faithfulness', accuracy and associate rules in their codes of ethics and, therefore, restrain the translator's choice, simply oblige their members to respond to the whims of the powerful patrons/clients and their (un)ethical orientations. These rules are "modes of control" and may be alibis that justify or ignore unethical acts/materials. "[T]he most effective way to ensure translator loyalty is to efface choice [...] and to *undercut ethical initiatives* associated with reinterpretations of meaning (Tymoczko 2009, 413, italics added).

Associations ignore the multifacetedness of *translation*, which allows the translator to respond to ethical matters contingently. Because of the legal, moral and 'professional' stamps attached to 'faithfulness,' translators may be unable to break through and stand up against unethical practices/materials as the dogma/myth of 'faithfulness' denies them any margin of choice. It is not surprising that Kruger and Crots (2014) have found that more experienced translators tend to lean to 'faithful' translation when dealing with ethically charged texts. Over the years in the occupation, and because of the indoctrination with this hegemonic discourse of 'faithfulness' to meaning and 'impartiality' as well as the symbolic violence of employers (and perhaps of some delegate associations themselves), translators have taken on the 'impartial' position, maybe without even thinking about the consequences of their actions on others.

8.1.2.2 Quality Service

Quality is one of the main themes emphasized in all the documents under study. The emphasis of quality service is a message of reassurance to the clients/patrons. In some codes, a full section is allotted to the theme, while in others, it is tackled in various sections.

The ATIO code of ethics reiterates the question of 'quality service' throughout the document. The preamble states that quality is one of the main objectives of the code. The association devotes an entire section to "Quality of Service" – divided into four sub-sections, namely 'professional' competence, faithfulness and accuracy, responsibility and non-discrimination (Section 2.0). Clearly, 'faithfulness' and 'accuracy' are key components of 'quality,' in the ATIO's instructions. Therefore, transformations, adaptations, omissions and explanations do not lead to 'quality' and are, thus, categorically 'unprofessional' and immoral regardless of context if one follows this section verbatim (see especially Article 2.2.1).

The SATI code stresses 'quality' in three articles out of ten. Like the ATIO, it associates 'quality' to "*accuracy* of rendering, terminological correctness, language and style" (Code of Ethics for Individual Members). The SATI code also stresses 'self-improvement' as a way to enhance the quality of the translator's work and the fact that the quality of their work does credit to both the association and the occupation (ibid.).

The SFT code approaches the question of 'quality' with the same rigour as the ATIO and the SATI. Under the section entitled 'Respect of Clients,' it explains the measures that guarantee quality work and, therefore, respect for clients. The section urges members to refrain from doing work for which they cannot guarantee good quality and from subcontracting work to third parties without the client's consent (Article 3.a). Further, it calls for truthfulness in advertising one's qualifications and competence (Article 3.b). In order to achieve quality work, the translator is required to translate only to their native language or a language in which they are fluent (Article 3.c. I). They are, likewise, required to possess knowledge and competence in the specialized field of the work (c.II), and to do research and acquire information relative to the task (3.c.III). The association members are also called on to improve their 'professional' knowledge/competence through continuous training (3.c.IV). Finally, they are urged to decline any deadlines that are incompatible with the entrusted task (3.c.V). Unlike the previous two codes, which explain what quality entails by clearly associating it with 'faithfulness' and/or 'accuracy,' the SFT leaves 'quality' quite undefined – which is not a bad thing – and simply lists the measures that may lead to it. However, it is unfortunate to realize that the SFT indirectly considers 'faithfulness' as a standard of 'quality,' as is clear in the defining article of *translation* (Article 1b).

The ATPP code stresses the issue of 'quality,' in similar ways. Related to competence, it calls on translators to accept only jobs for which they are properly trained and for which they have the necessary knowledge (Article 4). The ATPP also urges its members to continually strive to improve their 'professional' skills and upgrade their knowledge (ibid., Article 6). In practice, it calls on the translator to "perform *high-quality* work from both a language and a stylistic point of view" (Article 1, italics added) as part of the main "regulations that govern the profession" (ibid.). In order to achieve 'high quality,' the association members are required to work exclusively into their mother tongue or into a language they command as their mother tongue, except in cases in which the non-fulfillment of this requirement does not sacrifice quality *and* accuracy (Article 3, italics added). The ATPP code does not only regard 'accuracy' as a criterion of 'quality' but also as a moral and legal obligation (Article 2).

The ITAINDIA code highlights the question of 'quality' and 'excellence.' The preamble states that the association members commit themselves "to the *highest standards of performance*, ethical behavior, and business practices" (italics added). In order to achieve these 'highest standards of performance', the translator should "endeavor *to translate or interpret the original message faithfully*, to satisfy the needs of the end user(s)" (Article A, italics added). And "this level of excellence," i.e., translating the original message faithfully in order to satisfy the needs of the end user(s), requires mastery of the target language (Article A.1), "up-to-date knowledge of the subject material and its terminology in both languages" (Article A.2), access to resources/references, knowledge of the tools of the 'profession' (Article A.3), and continuous self-development (Article A.4). Not very differently from the previously analyzed codes, 'excellence' and 'quality' are, thus, clearly equated with 'faithfulness.' The paradox in article A lies in the fact that 'faithful' translation may be at odds with the needs of the end user(s). There are many types of contemporary translation where 'faithfulness' – if achievable at all – needs to be 'sacrificed' just to satisfy these very needs of the end user(s), as discussed in Part I.

The AUSIT directs its instructions to the conduct that leads to 'quality.' The concluding part of the preamble reads,

the code obliges members to: [...]

- strive for excellence through continuous regular professional development
- decline work beyond their competence
- promote working conditions, relationships and an understanding of roles that facilitate collaboration and quality service delivery [...].

These regulations are explained mainly in article 3, devoted to 'competence,' especially in regard to language mastery; article 7 about the securing of satisfactory working conditions that can guarantee quality service; and article 8, devoted to 'professional development' that leads to the provision of "quality service." Like all the previous codes, the AUSIT Code of Ethics links 'quality' to 'faithfulness' and 'accuracy.' To achieve this ultimate purpose, the translator remains "faithful *at all times* to the meaning of texts and messages" and accurate, to ensure "optimal and complete message transfer into the target language preserving the content and intent of the source message or text without omission or distortion" (Code of Ethics, Article 5, italics added). Thus, like the ATIO, the AUSIT stresses faithfulness and accuracy as constant standards of quality and considers omissions as being 'unprofessional' and unethical, regardless of circumstances.

The IAFET, quite differently, calls on translators to "[o]nly accept jobs for which they are able to guarantee a *proper* standard of quality to their clients" (Article 2.2, italics added). Unlike all previous associations' codes, the IAFET defines neither *translation* nor *quality*. It does not take 'faithfulness' or any of its associated terms as standards of translation quality or translation ethics. It rather highlights 'thoroughness' and 'responsibility' (Article 2.1.), and "*proper* standard of quality" (Article 2.2.) when carrying out translating or interpreting tasks. The fact that 'quality' is without pre-established boundaries in the IAFET code – as is *translation* – can be seen as a sign of awareness about the contingency of 'quality' on many situational factors, including, of course, the client's needs. However, these encouraging signs regarding 'quality' (and many other issues) are countered by the reductive definition of *translation* in the IAFET's other internal documents, as discussed in Part I.

The FIT Translator's Charter addresses the question of 'quality' very briefly. The term 'quality' as such appears only once in the entire document (Article 29). The article underlines the role of the translator associations in "watching over the quality of all works translated in their countries." For this purpose, "they shall keep in touch with cultural organizations, societies of authors, national sections of the Pen Club, literary critics, learned societies, universities, and technical and scientific research institutes." The question of 'quality' is, thus, co-determined with other social groups and agents. It is, therefore, *not* the area of expertise of the translating agents or their networks exclusively. The theme of 'quality' is also tacitly referred to in articles 6 and 7. Article 6 stresses the mastery of the target language and the possession of a sound knowledge of the source language. Article 7 highlights the possession of a broad general knowledge and sufficient knowledge of the subject matter of the translating task and calls on the translator to refrain from undertaking translations in a field beyond their competence. Although nowhere in the code is 'quality' clearly defined, it is implicitly linked to 'equivalence' and 'faithfulness' – which is not only a 'professional' obligation but also a legal and moral duty for the translator (Articles 4, 5).

The Nairobi Recommendation, although not a 'professional' or ethical guide *per se*, highlights the theme of 'quality' in many of its paragraphs. In order to improve translation quality, the UNESCO urges its Member States to establish and develop specialized programs in the field of translation (Paragraph 7h), to encourage translators' continuous education through writing programs, seminars and workshops in translator organizations and educational institutions (Paragraph 11), to create terminology centres (Paragraph 12), and to facilitate exchanges of translators between different countries (Paragraph 13). Also, in order to guarantee quality service at the practical level, the recommendation lays out some principles and measures that should govern the relation between the translator and the beneficiary. These include the allocation of reasonable time and resources to accomplish the work, the avoidance of retranslations as far as possible, and the translation to one's native language or a language in which one is as proficient (Paragraph 14). In addition, paragraph 7 urges the UNESCO Member States to encourage the establishment of organizations of translators with the aim to

(a) promote the adoption of standards governing the translating profession; such standards should stipulate in particular that the translator has a duty to provide a translation of *high quality from both the linguistic and stylistic points of view and to guarantee that the translation will be a faithful rendering of the original*; [...]
(b) set up procedures to assist in the settlement of disputes arising in connexion with the *quality* of translations.

(italics added)

The UNESCO emphasizes two main standards in paragraph (7a), namely translation of high *quality* from both the linguistic and stylistic points of view *and* '*faithful* rendering of the original.' These two standards are interlinked. Translation should be stylistically and linguistically acceptable from the target language/audience perspective but also faithful to the ST. These two standards sought together by the UNESCO are illusionary as they are barely, if ever, achievable together.

All studied documents associate 'quality' with 'faithfulness' and/or 'accuracy.' Some documents are explicit in this association (Nairobi Recommendation, and ATIO and ITAINDIA codes). Others tacitly link the two rules (FIT Charter, SFT, ATPP, IAFET and AUSIT codes). *Quality* interlinked with faithfulness – if ever achievable or even desirable – may have all the ethical problems associated with the latter principle, as discussed earlier.

But besides the possible ethical implications of equating 'quality' with 'faithfulness,' such standardization of quality is also fraught for practical reasons. Ironically, 'quality' in this understanding may indeed affect quality. In today's globalized world, 'quality' as 'faithfulness' may be undesirable, and can, therefore, be seen as low quality, in many types of translations, which require different strategies of transformations, adaptations, omissions, additions. And these strategies that are *unfaithful* to the 'original' are an important standard of quality for many clients/

employers. This is not to mention that some of the latter agents may sometimes want to make do with just "good enough" translations (O'Brien 2012, 112), or "indicative translation," to use Alan Melby's words (1997).

Translation 'quality' is a relative and open principle, just like the cluster concept of *translation* itself. It is contingent on other external/contextual variables that determine its shape and scope. It has no stable standards nor pre-determined boundaries at all times, in all places and for all uses, as the studied organizations imply. Translation strategies/methods that lead to high quality in one situation may lead to low quality in another, and vice versa. 'Explanations' that the ATIO code (Article 2.2.1), for example, seems to regard as symptomatic of poor quality or unethicality may be not only a quality standard but an ethical endeavour in some situations (see for example, Appiah 2000/1993). Adaptations, including omissions, in a commercial translation, likewise, may be seen as a standard of high quality given the nature of the material, which may require such transformations for technical, ideological or ethical reasons (see Diaz-Cintas's 2012 discussion of adaptation in audiovisual translation that follow technical and/or ideological constraints).

Quality standards fluctuate depending on the purpose of the translation, its context and its (immediate and far-reaching) consequences as judged by the translator's 'professional' view and moral self. The standardization of quality as faithfulness is, thus, illusionary as it leaves out or, at least, ignores many other types of translation to claim its possibility.

8.1.2.3 Confidentiality Rule

Confidentiality is another tool purporting to advance 'public protection' that is stressed in all documents. The documents under study differ, however, as far as its limits and conditions are concerned. While some emphasize unconditional confidentiality, others underline its conditionality. Two codes, namely the SFT's and the AUSIT's, clearly emphasize that 'confidentiality' excludes illegal matters (Article 1c of the Deontological Code and Article 2.4 of the Code of Conduct/Obligations towards recipients of services, respectively). The SFT adds another interesting exception, which is the disclosure of information for the translator's self-defence (Article 1c). Of course, this is not a very surprising exception from a unionist organization, which aims, first and foremost, to defend the translator. The IAFET, on the other hand, stipulates that disclosure of information is unavoidable by "reason of force majeure" without, however, being explicit about what can constitute a "force majeure" (Article 2.5). Similarly, the UNESCO is not explicit as to the conditions of 'confidentiality.' It simply underlines that the rule has to be observed "when appropriate" (Paragraph 5f). It remains, however, un-understandable how 'observing the confidentiality rule' contributes to 'the legal protection of translators and translations and the improvement of the status of translators,' the main objective of the Nairobi Recommendation.

In contrast to the previously mentioned documents, the FIT, the SATI, the ATPP, the ITAINDIA and the ATIO documents stress the 'confidentiality' rule *unconditionally* (Article 10; Code of Ethics for Individual Members; Article 5; Section for service providers, Article C; Article 3.3.1, respectively). These documents remain silent about cases where disclosure is mandated or authorized by law and refrain from encouraging the translator to speak up. Although it is not clear whether the unconditional confidentiality is intentional, it remains very probable that this omission seeks to reassure the shady agents against whistleblowers, or why does the ATIO, for example, stress the issue in its bylaws (an internal document that barely reaches the other agents) and omits it in the code of ethics (partly addressed to those other agents)?[5] Confidentiality, in the case of these organizations, is another tool that aims at protecting and being loyal to the immediate public. The unconditional emphasis on this rule seems to annul wider responsibility toward one's world. The most a translator can do is refrain from accepting work that "is intended for unlawful or dishonest purposes or is contrary to the public interest," in the case of the SATI members, at least. Nowhere is there a single call, or even permission, to report such unlawful activities.

In none of the studied documents is there an exemption from observing *confidentiality* in such cases where information in documents to be translated is unethical or harmful to others, and/or where its unlawfulness is unclear. Even the SFT, the AUSIT, the IAFET and the UNESCO documents, which conditionalize confidentiality, do not encourage a more proactive stance of translators beyond what is legally required (SFT, AUSIT), useful for self-defence (SFT), or required by some vague "force majeure" (IAFET). In sum, 'confidentiality' as advanced in all studied documents may silence translators from speaking about unethical practices/discourses of their client/patron. And if the rule is followed verbatim as it appears in some of these documents, it may silence translators even from reporting illegal practices/discourses.

8.1.2.4 *Virtue Ethics*

All the national/provincial associations under study highlight some virtues tacitly or explicitly in their codes[6]. 'Trust,' 'probity,' 'integrity,' 'commitment,' 'truthfulness/honesty,' 'fairness,' 'good faith,' 'loyalty,' 'selflessness,' 'solidarity,' 'diligence,' 'excellence' and 'respect' are some of these ethics, to name a few.

The SFT code emphasizes the ethics of 'probity' and 'integrity' toward clients, as they are the main ground of trust for clients. These virtue ethics

186   The Translator's Morality in Codified Ethics

allegedly preserve the translator's dignity and the dignity of their 'profession.' "The translator shall undertake their work with probity and integrity – which are the basis of the client's trust. The translator shall not accept any work that would require them to undermine their dignity or that of the profession" (Article 1a, my translation). The article entitled 'Probity and Integrity' appears, along with two other articles devoted to 'faithfulness' and 'confidentiality,' in the first section entitled 'General Principles,' as the four main principles that guide the translator's work. Section 3, devoted entirely to 'Respect of Clients,' again tacitly alludes to the virtues of integrity, probity and respect, which, like many other recommended principles promulgated by the SFT, seek to gain the trust of clients.

The ATIO code of ethics underlines 'integrity' as one of the principles that seeks to guarantee the 'Protection of the Public' (Section 3). "Members shall practise their profession with honesty and integrity, respecting *the rights and interests of their clients and/or employers*" (Article 3.1.1, italics added). 'Integrity' is especially required in advertising one's qualifications and services (Article 3.2.1) and when dealing with colleagues (Article 4.2.4).

'Integrity' and 'selflessness' are present in many articles of the ATPP code of ethics, as well (e.g., Articles 3, 4, 5, 7, 8). Members pledge to accept only work for which they have the right qualifications and knowledge, not to disclose or use any information for their own benefit and to provide moral and 'professional' support to colleagues.

The SATI, in its mission statement underlines, among other things, that "the institute endeavours to: [...] Promote *excellence* in translation and related fields, as well as *clarity* of thought and expression" (italics added) – importing, thus, Chesterman's ethical ideals (2001). The code also highlights ethics of 'trust' and 'integrity' in relation to the client/employer in at least 6 out of 10 articles. On the other hand, the SATI calls on the translator to refrain from accepting "any work that, in their opinion, is intended for unlawful or dishonest purposes or is contrary to the public interest." It thus shows that the public interest in its wider sense is not completely ignored even though the virtues of trust and integrity that it pursues are exclusively directed to the client/patron. This attention to the public is, however, disproportionate to the attention paid to the immediate agents and is, at best, limited to calling on the translator to decline suspicious work (in order to seem trustworthy to these agents) rather than inciting them to be more proactive.

The AUSIT, likewise, calls on the translator to "strive for *excellence* through continuous regular professional development" (Preamble, italics added). It also stresses ethics of 'honesty,' 'fairness,' 'diligence,' 'commitment,' 'respect,' 'integrity' and 'empathy':

> Interpreters and translators take responsibility for their work and conduct; they are *committed* to providing quality service in a *respectful*

and culturally sensitive manner, dealing *honestly* and *fairly* with other parties and colleagues, and dealing *honestly* in all *business practices*. They disclose any conflict of interest or any matter that may compromise their impartiality. They observe common professional ethics of *diligence* and *responsiveness* to the needs of other participants in their work.

(AUSIT Code of Ethics, Article 1, Explanation, italics added)

Following the AUSIT's instructions, the translator should be committed to do quality work and be diligent, responsive, honest and fair with colleagues and other agents involved in their work. They, for example, have to "represent their credentials honestly" (Code of Ethics, Article 3). They also have to show disinterestedness and selflessness toward their 'profession' and their colleagues. "Practitioners have a loyalty to the profession that extends beyond their individual interest. They support and further the interests of the profession and their colleagues and offer each other assistance" (Code of Ethics, Article 9, Explanation). It is clear, thus, that the stated ethics are exclusively aimed at the agents in the occupational circle. That being said, the AUSIT emphasizes that members should "maintain their *integrity* and independence *at all times*" (Code of Conduct/Obligations towards recipients of services, Article 1.1, italics added). It, also, allows its members to withdraw from some assignments for "ethical reasons" (Article 1.3), such as when it is difficult to maintain 'impartiality' because of "personal beliefs or other circumstances" (Article 4.2). But the call for 'integrity' at all times remains too vague as it does not explicitly orient this virtue toward wider issues beyond the translation transaction. This is why this isolated article may be better explained by the other clearer articles that limit the scope of virtue ethics toward the immediate agents. The limitedness of the translator's agency and responsibility becomes especially clear when we know that the only recommendation made in the case of a conflict between one's ethics and the material content means withdrawal from the assignment.

Not so differently from the AUSIT, the IAFET stresses the principles of 'good faith' and 'respect'. 'Good faith' is the guiding principle of all the other obligations in the code of ethics. "It shall be the basic duty of every member to: [...] Exercise the translating and interpreting professions on the basis of good faith, which encompasses, principally, the duties included in the following articles" (Article 1.3). As section 4 explains, 'respect' and 'good faith' are mostly directed toward colleagues.

Finally, the ITAINDIA highlights 'excellence' (Article A), 'truthfulness' about one's qualifications (Article B) and 'trustworthiness' (Articles C-F). The ITAINDIA virtues are the most client-oriented of all the codes under study. They are not 'ethical principles' *per se* as they are directed merely to "good business practices," as Chesterman observes (2001, 151)[7]. Not even the translator's colleagues/peers are considered in this code.

Virtue ethics as presented in this account focus on the other. They are barely centred on the self in the Aristotelean sense, except in very few instances, such as the AUSIT's and the SATI's brief calls for 'striving for excellence'. Most highlighted ethics in the codes of ethics are directly oriented toward the other, i.e., with little emphasis on enhancing oneself as a virtuous self, who seeks to attain *eudaimonia* in order to be enabled to be "more godlike to attain it for a nation or for city-states" (Aristotle 1973, 42). This is not surprising as the value of virtue ethics toward the community or the Other are given more prominence in modern virtue ethics (e.g., MacIntyre 2007/1981, Slote 2010). Taking virtue ethics from this modern perspective, one easily discerns that all virtues underlined by the different codes are oriented mainly to the immediate circle of translation, i.e., either to colleagues and the occupation itself or to clients/patrons. Most codes orient virtues much more directly toward the clients/patrons than to the translator themself (except for the IAFET, which is more translator-centred) to ensure trust in business transactions. And the wider public/community is barely within the moral coverage of any of these ethical principles.

This regulation of virtue ethics that restricts them to a certain limited circle make them lose their essence as virtues that first and foremost revolve around the self and that ultimately have an unlimited, *gratuitous* and *uncalculated* moral coverage (see Lévinas 1991, Bauman 1993). Following MacIntyre, a virtue is a quality that enhances social practices by enabling us to *"achieve those goods which are internal to practices"* and *not* goods which are external to them, such as money or prestige (2007/1981, 191, italics in original). But by highlighting these 'virtues' in the way they do, translator associations seem to seek goods that are external to the practice of translation (such as attracting more jobs/pay by winning the client/patron's trust), rather than internal goods, i.e., excellence in the practice regardless of external variables or profits. This is not very surprising. MacIntyre has warned us that virtues are vulnerable to "the corrupting power of institutions" and acquisitiveness as modern institutions are "characteristically and necessarily concerned with [...] external goods" (ibid., 194). 'Virtues' in the studied codes are, thus, tainted by the ideological and economic calculations of the institution that is promoting them, i.e., the translators' association. They are used as tools that guarantee the translator's loyalty and dissipate the client's suspicion. Restrained ethics as such seek the success of the business transaction regardless of its consequences. Accordingly, the moral self becomes selective and calculating, if not sellable. But translators are not merely responsible to clients, patrons and authors; they are also responsible to the world. They need to act responsibly as *citizens* of their world (see Baker and Maier 2011b). When the two responsibilities conflict, the global aspect should probably win over. And as we learn from MacIntyre (2007/1981), an apparent virtue may turn into a vice in some contexts, and vice versa. For example, the virtue of integrity toward a client may conflict with responsibility toward one's community, just as the vice of untrustworthiness (as in the case of whistleblowing) may turn into a virtue toward one's community. That is why virtues, even when gratuitous, need to be *contextualized*.

> Consider as an example such qualities as ruthlessness and relentlessness and distinguish them from the phronetic quality of knowing when to be ruthless or relentless. Clearly there are practices – the exploration of wilderness is one example – in which the ability to be ruthless and relentless in driving oneself and others may be a condition not just for achievement, but also for survival. Such an ability may require as a condition of its exercise the cultivation of a certain insensitivity to the feelings of others; caring about their feelings may get in the way of caring about their survival. Transpose that complex of qualities into participation in the practice of creating and sustaining the life of a family and you have a recipe for disaster. What seemed to be a virtue in the one context seems to have become a vice in the other.
>
> (MacIntyre 2007/1981, 275)

All studied codes highlight the idea of 'public 'protection' and adopt internal rules/principles (like faithfulness, confidentiality, quality service and virtues) that purportedly help achieve this main objective. Like other occupations and professions, they highlight disinterestedness and functional relevance of their 'profession' to society. However, allusions to responsibility to the public in its wider sense are rare and brief and present only in a minority of associations' codes (SATI, IAFET, AUSIT). Further, they come well after the responsibility owed to the immediate agents. Also, the documents emphasize decontextualized principles/rules and ignore the fact that some of them may be contradictory in many situations and that the translator may be obliged to transgress one of them in order to follow the other. We know from Paul Ricoeur (1990, 2000), for example, that deontological rules sometimes conflict and that the moral agent needs to resort to virtue ethics – which have primacy over the former – in order to solve such dilemmas. But in the studied codes, even virtue ethics are tainted by business and ideological considerations – not to mention the possibility of their conflict, and, therefore, the obligation "to choose between their rival claims," to use MacIntyre's words (2007/1981, 202). The emphasis on the useful notion of 'public' – which for most associations/organizations refers exclusively to 'clients and patrons' – probably aims at giving this

190 *The Translator's Morality in Codified Ethics*

rule an acceptable moral dimension. This is because the protection of the client/patron's interests may be perceived as a billable morality, at best. But in fact, this conception of the 'public' limits 'morality' to the part of the public that pays. It is a service – and a 'morality' – that has a price. Clients not only pay the translator in order to secure their 'professional/business' loyalty but also to alienate them morally, i.e., to make them adopt the patrons/clients' moral and 'professional' orientations/agendas, or at least turn a blind eye to possibly suspect practices/materials. This is achieved through the 'professional' rules of detachment, impartiality, confidentiality and neutrality. In the name of 'professionalism,' translators "are not responsible for what clients say or write," as the AUSIT bluntly puts it (in article 4.3). Unfortunately, the term 'professional' in many codes of ethics is used as a tool that legitimizes the exclusion of the translator's responsibility for any consequences their decisions might have for the world. Now that we know the ideological underpinnings of the notion of 'profession,' we know this claim is fraught, and that the assumed separation between 'professional' ethics and personal ethics is untenable.

Of course, one cannot posit that the advanced principles/rules are *all* and *always completely* irrelevant morally. In the case of the documents under study, they are fraught because they are presented as *a priori* duties that serve in all situations at all times, without taking into account the specificity of the encounter, its circumstances, the use of the translation, its possible consequences, its users, the client, its direction and the (cultural, political, social) positions of the source and target cultures[8]. The presentation of these principles as universal maxims is "an illusion and an illusion with painful consequences," as MacIntyre (2007/1981, 221) puts it, as little choice, if any, is given to the individual's moral assessment of the particular situation at hand. In Koskinen's words, codes of ethics as such "could thus be seen to consist, in short, of the requirement to refrain from choosing" (Koskinen (2000a, 13). Ironically, most of these codes' rules/principles do not disallow the dissemination of any discourses or practices regardless of their immoral or even illegal content – as long as the translation is 'faithful' to the 'original' text. These principles/rules are ideologies that neutralize the translator's moral self regarding their wider ethical/social responsibilities.

8.2 Representation and Otherness in Codified Ethics

Some may argue that codes of ethics are mainly designed for translators of pragmatic texts, in which the impact of translation on the larger public is insignificant and the representation of Otherness is rare, limited or unimportant. They may claim that there is not much to represent as the texts are usually dry and their terminology is mainly technical and specialized.

But as we all know, the range of pragmatic translation is wide and heterogeneous. It includes all types of texts that are non-fictional, from media texts to commercials to simple leaflets, which, as I have argued in Part I, also involve representation, identity and many power dynamics issues. This is not to further insist on the fact that all types of texts may, to varying degrees, involve such issues (see Gagnon and Kalantari 2017 for examples of such technical/pragmatic texts).

Not surprisingly, in all the documents under study, there is one brief reference to 'cultural sensitivity' that appears in the AUSIT code of ethics.

> Interpreters and translators [...] are committed to providing quality service *in a respectful and culturally sensitive manner*, dealing honestly and fairly with other parties and colleagues, and dealing honestly in all business practices. They disclose any conflict of interest or any matter that may compromise their impartiality. They observe common professional ethics of diligence and responsiveness to the needs of other participants in their work.
>
> (Article 1, italics added)

This reference to 'cultural sensitivity' and 'respect' when providing quality service is anything but clear. All we can discern is that it is linked with other ethical principles (such as honesty, fairness, impartiality and diligence) which are clearly directed to the immediate agents. The AUSIT tackles as briefly the issue of 'representation,' but in a much clearer way, when it addresses the question of 'discriminatory language.'

> If the source text contains particular elements that need to be taken into account in carrying out the translation, translators use their best endeavours and apply professional judgement to bring this to the attention of the client (except where the translated document is expected or required to be an exact reproduction of all source text content, meaning, style and language and needs to be thus certified). Such elements may include ambiguities, factual inaccuracies, linguistic errors, imprecise terminology, *language that in the judgement of the translator is discriminatory*, or wording or references that would jeopardise achieving the purpose of the text in the target language culture.
>
> (Conduct issues specific to translators, Article 6, italics added)

Discriminatory language in the translator's personal judgment (along with the other problems highlighted in the article) should be brought to the attention of the client, who ultimately decides on how to address it – which implies that the translator has no say over this type of language. They cannot decide to counter it or even euphemize it unless the client demands that. Translators, thus, simply have to follow the ethical orientations of their payees. If the client/employer judges, for example, that the discriminatory expressions are unproblematic, the translator has no agency except to "offer to withdraw from the assignment" (Article 2.4) and *let someone else do it*.

Other than the AUSIT's vague and quite disappointing statements, no other code makes the simplest allusion to representation or cultural awareness to otherness in the translator's texts. The ATIO code, however, raises the issue of 'discrimination' and 'cultural sensitivity' from quite a different perspective.

- Members shall approach professional services with *respect and cultural sensitivity towards their clients*.
(Article 2.4.1, italics added)
- Members shall not discriminate in *the services* which they provide on the basis of race, ancestry, place of origin, colour, ethnic origin, citizenship, creed, sex, sexual orientation, age, marital status, family status or disability.
(Article 2.4.2, italics added)

The two articles imply that respect and cultural sensitivities are reserved for those who pay for it. Cultural sensitivity toward remote others represented in the translated material, and who do not belong to the business network, are not a concern of a purely business-oriented code like the ATIO's. This position is quite untenable in a multicultural society and an officially bilingual country such as Canada, known for cultural sensitivities between its different linguistic/cultural groups, mainly the two rival ones, the French and the English. Of course, the two articles make very good sense in the case of individual vulnerable clients (like immigrants, refugees, minorities and disabled). But the largest quantity of translation transactions today is with large powerful clients/employers, who can not only defend themselves but also impose their terms on translators. Besides, the issue of cultural (discriminatory) representation in the translation field is mostly textual rather than relational.

I am well aware that some associations from non-English-speaking countries (like the ATPP and the IAFET) may have omitted any mention of otherness or cultural representation because of their members' profiles, working mainly from English. But it is surprising that these issues are ignored by the FIT, whose charter lay "the basis of a translator's code of ethics" (Preamble), or the SFT, the AUSIT and the ATIO, whose countries all have a growing immigrant population and a strong geopolitical presence and contact with peripheral countries and cultures. In the languages of countries where these associations are based, *pragmatic* translation projects that represent the Other negatively are not insignificant (see for example Baker 2006a, 2010; Rafael 2010; Boukhaffa 2017). Some of these translations demonize the Other using the very principles of accuracy and faithfulness, preached by all studied documents, and, therefore, help shape a negative public opinion about others (ibid.).

Ignoring the question of cultural representation and cultural sensitivity by the SATI and the ITAINDIA is also unjustified. We all know that South Africa is a very multilingual and a multiethnic country (with 11 official languages), a fact which requires large numbers of translations and, therefore, multiplies the ethical challenges translators encounter. More importantly, this country has a painful history of racial discrimination in which English (the current powerful language and the language of the past rulers and colonizers) has been a tool of apartheid and cultural oppression for a long time. The SATI, ignoring the specificity of the country, stresses principles such as "accuracy of rendering" and "clarity of thought and expression," unconditionally. I wonder how ethical it is to follow such principles unconditionally when translating discriminatory expressions from a historical text, for example. Unfortunately, Kruger and Crots (2014) have found that experienced translators in South Africa adhere more to 'faithful' translation, following the 'professional' code of ethics. "It therefore seems as if greater experience corresponds to a greater likelihood of the narrower professional, codified view of ethics being used as a frame of reference for translation decisions" (2014, 178). Regrettably, the authors have also found that that "translation strategies premised on faithful translation are by far the preferred choice of the translators [in South Africa] [...] when faced with ethically challenging material" (ibid., 177). Similar concerns can be raised regarding India where the ITAINDIA operates. This country is also very multilingual and multiethnic, and thus, a fertile land for translation and its inherent (ethical) challenges. And, similarly to South Africa, India has a long and painful history under British colonialism and, therefore, under the hegemony of English over local languages up to the present day.

In sum, the studied codes of ethics abstain from extending moral responsibility toward remote otherness or raising the translator's awareness to their responsibilities toward cultural diversity. The principles and rules highlighted in their documents are entrenched in rational calculations and purposefulness – in contrast with Bauman's morality, which is "a mystery contrary to reason" (1993, 13). Following Bauman's distinction between being *with* the Other and being *for* the other, 'professional' relations based on respect of the other agents involved in translation are within the being *with* the other sphere. It is a pragmatic calculated respect based on 'mutual' interests. However, being *for* the other, as conceptualized by Lévinas (1991, 1995) – who Bauman (1993, 2008) draws on – is inherently *before* mutuality, reciprocity or benefits. It is even *before* society and the socialization of the self. If we follow Lévinas's (1991) *encounter with the Face of the Other* concept in translating the Other, the translator should 'disrobe' themselves of any other social dressing, norms and conventions or any economic or ideological considerations/calculations that can taint or affect the pure translation act. Socially imposed identities, positions, roles, inclinations and economic considerations are outsider variables, or 'Thirds' – in Bauman's (2008) terminology – which taint ethical translation. They are parasites that orient the translation into taking a certain desired shape that may not be moral. The employer, client, consumer's orientations, norms and ethical codes of translation and pre-established discourses and concepts of *translation* are all Thirds that do exactly that in the translation act. They disorient the moral self of the translator. Translation as a moral task becomes conditioned by, and contingent on, these external factors, including other agents' (unethical) desires. Because the translator seeks economic profits, for example, their moral judgment may be well guided by loyalty to the paying agent's (un)ethical orientations rather than their moral self. The remote, invisible or 'unimportant' Other that is present only through the translated texts barely finds a place in these documents – some of which reserve 'cultural sensitivity' to clients exclusively, as does the ATIO code. The individual translator, in these codes, can be seen as a *cognitive calculative self* that focuses on the relational aspects of the translation business but not a moral self that is disrobed of these considerations.

I argue that responsibility to Others is nowadays more indispensable than ever before. With the increasing movements of people (especially those fleeing atrocities or dire economic conditions), the Other is now within sight in the host territories. You see others from different races, origins and ethnicities in large numbers, on a daily basis. They are now one's neighbours and co-workers. And even where they are not physically close, they are virtually neighbours in today's global village. Metropolises as well as online platforms are now mixed. Asylum seeking, mass refuge and immigration as well as technological advancements in the age of globalization have made everyone neighbour to everyone. The other is next door disturbing and shaking one's easiness with one's frames of reference and canons. That is a relevant reason why one would expect attention to Otherness in any association code of ethics, especially in host countries.

Bauman presents an obstacle to loving one's neighbour that he calls *Ressentiment*. This sentiment is nourished by insecurity and fear of the other, who is always a suspect and a threat to one's "symbolic cohesion," to borrow Jean Baudrillard's term (2005). The danger nowadays is so imminent and so close. Images of destruction and human casualties we used to see on television are no longer surreal or too remote from us to feel their impact. The perpetrators have come from far distances and 'illegally' penetrated our territories through our 'unprotected' borders. They do not have IDs; 'we do not know who they are' – as the American President Donald Trump repeatedly said. We do not even know which countries they are from. They are "stateless" people, as Bauman calls them (2008). And the fact that they are "stateless" is enough to make them suspicious. These once distant people are now among us. We share public transportation and public squares with them. We have seen their likes on television. The terrorist-like is our neighbour. We assume some of them may become dangerous at any moment. Even the fact that we are uncertain is frustrating. In one word, they are fearful; we feel insecure around them. From a psychoanalytic perspective, Paul Hoggett (1992) brilliantly summarizes the centrality of fear in the misrepresentation of the Other today.

> So what is it we fear? What is this catastrophe that stalks us like a crazy dog? We cannot say because we cannot name it. But it is there, right in our guts, and as soon as we find the means to do so we seek to represent it, despite the fact that it cannot be represented. We construct an endless series of misrepresentations all of which share one essential quality, the quality of *otherness of being not-me*.
>
> (Hoggett 1992, 346, italics added)

These others are a source of insecurity because they do not fit into one's rational sphere, following Bauman (1993). They are unassimilable to the modern *cognitive space*. They disturb the domestic societal order with their utmost difference and unassimilability. This is why "the ambient fears and securitarian obsessions have made the most spectacular career in recent years" (Bauman 2007, 55). Bauman argues that this situation reminds us of "just how insecure our security is, how feeble and vulnerable our comfort, how poorly safeguarded our peace and quiet" (2008, 38). The "stateless", Bauman adds, "represent every premonition and fear that haunts our sleepless nights" (ibid., 39). Translation, thus, can be, and has been a way, to pre-empt against the 'plotters.'

Translators are the agents that can decipher the presumable terrorists' whispering of the plotting in the dark nights and warn their people before the disaster happens. That is why they have to listen/watch carefully and transfer the message faithfully and accurately. But the translator may be frightened or frustrated, exactly like everyone else in the community – probably including some of the institutions employing them[9], and may be guided by distress in their decisions. The translator, like a journalist, having a pre-emptive responsibility toward their people and their employers may, thus, accentuate this fear and suspicion. Translation in its pragmatic type may also turn into a demonizing tool of the Other and a way of amplifying their dangers. For instance, the MEMRI, an organization devoted to "exploring the Middle East and South Asia through their media" in order "to inform the debate over U.S. policy in the Middle East,"[10] selectively translates from 'security' languages only certain text types and extracts of texts that feed the narrative of 'terror'. These texts, or usually extracts of texts[11], are a way of warning *Us* of the 'destructive' ideologies of the Others (see Baker 2006a, 2010; Boukhaffa 2017). Rafael writes: "translation [...] is in this sense a kind of *instrument of surveillance* with which to track and magnify the alienness of alien speech, *decoding dangers, containing threats, and planning for interventions*" (Rafael 2010, 386, italics added).

Thus, translation is barely an ideal encounter that concerns only the immediate agents directly involved in the transaction as the studied documents imply, but it may be used as an instrument that seeks to 'protect' the Self from the Other. In this regard, the American President George W. Bush emphasized the "dire need for translators to shore up national security" (Rafael 2010, 385). In 2006, he launched the National Security Language Initiative that aimed at the expansion of teaching critical languages such as Arabic, Farsi and Chinese (ibid.). Not only that, translation and interpreting can be "part of the *institution of war* and hence play a major role in the management of conflict – by all parties, from war mongers to peace activists" (Baker 2006a, 1–2, italics in original). Baker demonstrated how translation, for example, was an important tool, beside the military apparatus, in facilitating the invasion of Iraq. Ironically, translators/interpreters, who do not adhere to the principles of accuracy and faithfulness in contexts of war, may themselves become suspicious. They may be seen as traitors, especially if they belong to the invaded country/culture. Some of the NATO forces in Afghanistan, for example, looked at interpreters with a suspicious eye when they realized that they did not stick to 'faithfulness' in translating their messages. Jacques Follorou (2012) reports for the French daily, *Le Monde*, that

> [t]he military realized that, at times, interpreters took liberties with the translation of their statements. For the latter, this was in no way a betrayal but more of respect for cultural codes. There are things you don't ask an elderly man in Afghanistan. There are questions you don't ask a man in front of other people[12].
>
> (My translation)

Differences in the perception of the nature of interpreters' work caused the suspicion of the military forces. The interpreters' claim that shifts in interpreting were meant to respect certain cultural codes did not convince these fearful employers, who do not consider cultural sensitivity as part of the interpreter's job or ethical responsibility.

Overlooking otherness in codified ethics of associations from developed countries would have been relatively understandable four decades ago as the Other was still relatively distant and far. They were close only through literary translation. As such, they were not disturbing *Us* physically as they are now. They had not turned into "a crazy dog" yet – to borrow Hoggett's expression (1992, 346). They were rather still exotic and, therefore, a source of entertainment (see for example, Carbonell 2004, Faiq 2004, Boukhaffa 2021). In Bauman's terminology, they were within the *esthetic space*. The self would sometimes rejoice over their exoticism and strangeness while still maintaining a cognitive wall to keep them distant. This *esthetic self* would go back to their rational modernity once the spectacle ended (Bauman 1993). Designers of codes of ethics in developed countries have failed to adapt to the Other – once remote and undisturbing for the local domestic order and the immediate circle of translation – now too close and, therefore, disturbing the modern order or even presumably 'endangering' it. Some of these Others are now new kinds of vulnerable agents (e.g., immigrants, asylum seekers) who seem to disturb the classical modern interrelational order of the translation/interpreting transaction. They impose unprecedented translation/interpreting meanings and strategies beyond the myths of 'faithfulness,' 'completeness' and 'accuracy.' They also unveil the fragility of the discourse of modernity and its claimed universalism, homogeneity and order. No *equivalence* of their situation or of their stories, meanings, paths, tragedies and cultures exists within the domestic ways and categories of perception. They are not modern or 'civilized.' They are "*most* alien to European culture, the one most securely expelled from the name 'Man' ' ", if I can borrow Spivak's (2005, 115, italics in original) expression — hence the impossibility of their equivalent translation.

The new vulnerable 'client,' who is usually not the payer for the translation/interpreting services, is sometimes caught up in borders and zones of conflict, begging for survival. The rules of impartiality, faithfulness and objectivity in translation that codes of ethics preach may be the cause of their disastrous fate (see Inghilleri 2008, 2009, 2010, 2012 with respect to interpreting). These rules may result in putting them back in the hands of violent groups and, thus, in endangering their lives. The rules of codes of ethics and other legislative regulations of modernity are too rigid to allow any place for hospitality. They undermine any care for the vulnerable Other as they are too centred on the 'professional' and business interests of the immediate local agents. Following these rules and legislations, hospitality may be considered 'unprofessional' or even illegal. Derrida (1997) vehemently decries such laws that criminalize hospitality. Regarding one such law in France, he writes:

> it was a law allowing the prosecution, and even imprisonment, of those who shelter and help foreigners in a situation deemed illegal. This "offense of hospitality" (I still wonder who dared to associate these words) is punishable by imprisonment. What becomes of a country, one wonders, what becomes of a culture, what becomes of a language when one can speak of "offense of hospitality", when hospitality can become a crime, in the eyes of the law and its representatives?
> (Derrida 1997, n.p., my translation)

Hospitality – a crime in the eyes of law and potentially a misconduct from the perspective of the codes of ethics – is, however, at the heart of morality as it may save lives. In translation/interpreting, breaching the principles of 'objectivity,' 'faithfulness' and 'impartiality' in order to highlight or save the vulnerable or endangered Other transcends all codes or legislations. Inghilleri suggests that the decision to reject those prescribed codes and to be guided only by the ethical encounter is at the heart of ethics for interpreters, especially "in situations of considerable geo-political magnitude" (Inghilleri 2008, 222; see also Davis 2001).

Ethical translation in regard to otherness is a personal judgment that should also be oriented to those who are absent in the transaction and/or not paying for the 'ethical' service or too vulnerable to defend themselves. The translator's moral self may, in many instances, need to jump in and transgress codes of ethics to be moral. The translator may need to be 'unprofessional' or 'unethical' *to be moral*. To be able to be so, the translator's morality needs to be free and untainted by undue suspicion and constructed narratives that monger fear. It needs to pre-date all these narratives.

Following Bauman's thought, the establishment of rules and norms that follow the overarching precept of being *for* the other, are, in essence, "but a never-complete list of footnotes to that precept" (Bauman 2008, 33). The examined codes show little trace, if any, of those 'footnotes' of the principle of 'loving the neighbour or the other.' In contrast, they contain partial rules that highlight care for the powerful neighbour for their pay, because of fear or as a result of symbolic violence, and ignore the (vulnerable) Others, who have nothing to offer in return. According to these codes, translation is successful as far as the representation is coherent and embraceable by those who pay (clients/employers), and those who read the work. Worse, any translator's inclination toward others, which may conflict with the principles established in the codes of ethics, may be subject to disciplinary measures – exactly like the French law that criminalizes hospitality – as I discuss shortly.

As can be discerned from the foregoing analysis, the documents of the various studied organizations (regardless of their origin, nature or proclaimed function) yield similar results as far as the scope of the translator's morality is concerned, though there are some slight differences in their approaches. Importantly, codes of ethics of associations from developing countries (namely from Peru, India and South Africa) – but not the IAFET's code – adopt the same ethnocentric concept of *translation* as a 'faithful transfer of meaning.' These documents, thus, abandon their own (historical) local *translation* concepts, their country/history/culture's specificities and the specificities of their local relational interactions. They adopt Eurocentric ways wholesale. They copy the same Western modernist codification and structuring without successfully *translating* them into their local realities (see Rottenburg 1996, Sahlin-Andersson 1996 for Organizational Translation). Worse, some of them blatantly copy the associations from developed countries to the letter, as is the case of the ITAINDIA. Ethics in these codes are understood and codified in limited and vague principles that cater mostly to the dominant agents despite the claim of 'public protection.' The specificities of the different countries (cultural periphery/centrality, linguistic/cultural plurality, economic/political situation, colonial past – among other factors) are barely considered. All codes adopt the modernist "unitary ethics," in Bauman's (1993) terminology, which claims stability, certainty and universalism. Likewise, the studied associations' codes (regardless of whether they are unions, orders or voluntary associations) do not establish very different relations between the translator and the other agents involved in translation. They all adopt similar duties with limited scope and coverage, a fact which neutralizes the translator's moral self.

Notes

1 https://atio.on.ca/about/
2 We do not know what they mean by "the spread of civilization throughout the world," but this is a problematic statement as it is in a singular form.
3 It is important to keep in mind that the Nairobi Recommendation is not concerned with ethics. However, some of its statements may have effects on the translator's moral self, and this is the reason for its occasional inclusion in Part III for comparative purposes.
4 www.memri.org (Accessed on November 15, 2016).
5 The ATIO in Article 12 of the Discipline Committee Procedural Code – which clarifies the grounds on which disciplinary measures may be taken – excludes the disclosure of confidential information required or permitted by law.

6 Given the nature of the document, the Nairobi Recommendation makes no reference to virtues. Likewise, the FIT Translator's Charter barely touches on the issue of virtues.
7 Chesterman's (2001) comments were in fact on the ATA Code (old version) which was, strikingly, copied to the letter by the ITAINDIA.
8 The AUSIT shows relative awareness of the incompleteness of the code and highlights its guiding nature. Paradoxically, this awareness/flexibility is barely reflected in the discourse of the instructive articles. Most importantly, it does not completely exclude punitive action (which is, of course, based on the non-compliance with the established rules/principles), as I discuss shortly.
9 Of course, many institutions use 'fear' simply as a strategic/manipulative tool against their people.
10 www.memri.org/about
11 Studying MEMRI audio-visual translations of Moroccan political narratives, I have found that the organization translates only extracts of texts that feed the narrative of terror (Boukhaffa 2017). Although translations of the extracts are generally 'accurate' – as Baker (2010) has also shown – narrative (re)framing is identified at the paratextual level (e.g., addition of guiding introductions) and the decontextualization/recontextualization of the videos (ibid., 70).
12 www.lemonde.fr/a-la-une/article/2012/12/26/traducteur-pour-l-otan-un-metier-a-risques-en-afghanistan_1810352_3208.html (Accessed on February 12, 2018).

9 Postmodern Ethics

From Institutionally Restrained Morality of Codes of Ethics to Aporetic Social Responsibility

9.1 Moral Responsibility: An Institutional Concern in Modern Codified Ethics

All studied associations highlight, implicitly or explicitly, and to varying degrees, the act of *regularization*, *quality service*, *accountability*, *public protection* and *standardization of practice* in their objectives. The AUSIT, for instance, emphasizes in the very preamble of its code that the document is intended "to *regulate* the professional conduct of members of AUSIT" (italics added). Likewise, the ATIO emphasizes that its code of ethics "sets out ethical principles and *standards* of professional conduct, the objects of which are to ensure professional *accountability* and *quality* of service, protect members of the *public*, *promote the profession* and foster a spirit of solidarity and co-operation among members of the Association" (Object, italics added). To ensure that these objectives are achieved, translators are instructed to follow clear ethical and 'professional' principles designed by their associations. These principles spare the translator the responsibility of deciding and judging at their own discretion. The decisions are made for them as long as they follow the instructions of the codes to the letter. Decisions in practice as well as in interpersonal relations are not up to the individual translator's personal judgment. They are standardized and, hence, immune from any personal 'misjudgment' or 'misconduct.' It is the association of translators that is now responsible for the collective ethical conduct of all. The translator should follow the instructions because they do not represent themselves but the institution they belong to. Their conduct is not theirs; it is the institution's conduct, i.e., the association's. The collective standards and institutional regulations have, thus, redefined responsibility from being an individual matter pertaining to the individual translator to being an institutional concern. The moral authority has been officially proclaimed by the codifying associations and, thus, taken away from the individual translator. The latter is simply an executing agent of the institutional policy. They have no right or need for any (moral) decisions/interventions that run counter to the teachings of the association's code.

Morality as the individual's responsibility has, thus, been alienated in all studied documents in favour of the institutional ethics. These ethics, however, are economically driven and do not include the process of decision-making that caters to wider immaterial considerations and that may have repercussions on species outside the business network. They are more centred around translation as a business transaction that requires the preservation of the business agents' interests. Drawing on Max Weber, Bauman shows that with the birth of modern capitalism, "business ventured into a genuine frontier, a virtual no-man's land, free of all moral concerns and legal constraints and ready to be subordinated to the business's own code of behavior" (Bauman 2008, 74). This "unprecedented moral extraterritoriality" (or "secession") of business matters is an exemption from morality. It is a morality-free zone. Although modern nation states have reclaimed the 'no-man's land' of business by imposing some regulations, there is, however, another form of "secession" of business matters nowadays that is more global and larger in scale.

> Once more, business has acquired an 'extraterritorial territory', a space of its own where it can roam freely, sweeping aside minor hurdles erected by weak local powers and steering clear of the obstacles built by the strong ones. It can pursue its own ends and ignore or bypass all others as *economically irrelevant and therefore illegitimate*. And once more we observe social effects similar to those that met with moral outrage at the time of the first secession, only now (like the second secession itself) on an immensely greater, global scale.
> (Bauman 2008, 75, italics added)

The studied codes of ethics are, of course, located within this latter form of secession. These documents are based on economic relevance/calculations – like any other business codes – despite the specificities of the practice. They ignore the individual translator's social responsibilities to their world for being "economically irrelevant." The institution of the translator rather makes its own calculations based on economic considerations and provides the translator with relevant and profitable ethical guidelines. Koskinen affirms that such codes and their rules are not only a "marketing gimmick" but also "a convenient way of lulling one's conscience" (2000a, 121). The moral self of the translator is, thus, silenced or subordinated to the codes' collective morality; the translator's moral responsibility is, at best, substantially reduced.

Unfortunately, translators evading the institution's calculating ethics are liable to punitive actions. The institution deploys disciplinary measures to coerce their members to abandon the orientations influenced by their moral self. All associations (except the ATPP) follow expulsion policies for anyone not abiding by the codes of ethics, despite their differences regarding how strictly these are applied (as I showed in Part II). The ATIO, the SFT, the IAFET and the ITAINDIA have the strictest procedures of coercion[1]. The AUSIT and the SATI, on the other hand, rather stress their role as arbiters, without excluding disciplinary actions altogether (see AUSIT Board of Professional Conduct (BoPC), SATI Website[2], respectively). The inclusion of coercive measures in the case of the ATIO is not very surprising, given the nature of the association as an order that stresses the ideology of *public protection*. Such coercive measures are, however, less conceivable in the case of voluntary associations like the AUSIT, the ITAINDIA, the SATI or the IAFET. In the case of the SFT, they are even somewhat incoherent with a union's mission, whose main function is to defend the translator, first and foremost.

The awareness and explicit admission of the incompleteness of codes and of the transcendence of personal judgment by the AUSIT has not weakened the coercive authority of the institution, which ironically monitors and supervises 'exact' adherence to its *inexact* codes. The AUSIT has not abandoned its adjudication procedures – which are one of the major constraining means of modernity (see Bauman 1993), in cases where soft domination is not efficient (see Bourdieu 1990b). Translators who do not abide by the rules of 'faithfulness,' 'impartiality' and 'confidentiality,' for example, are subject to expulsion. One wonders how ethical it is to expel a translator who 'violates' these pre-determined rules to counter unethical, dangerous, polluting, gender-biased, discriminatory or xenophobic materials that are harmful to society or the planet. How can the association's disciplinary committee arbitrate on such a decision? Since some associations (like the AUSIT in this corpus) admit that the code is a guideline and that the translator makes decisions according to their ethical judgment of the situation at hand, I wonder how an ethical decision made by a translator following their moral self, devoid of mutuality or interest, would coincide with the decision of a calculating institution that focuses mostly on the business relations and the image of the network in the business milieu. I argue that in many cases the two positions/decisions will differ, given the difference in the forces driving them, i.e., the moral self and the business calculations, respectively. The two moralities (individual and institutional) are at odds; they cover two different spheres that may be conflicting in many cases. Besides, the individual moral decisions are never taken with certainty or in a completely satisfactory way. We know from Bauman (1993) how ambivalent and uncertain these decisions can be. There are many instances in which a translator may breach a duty or even a virtue to advance a more appropriate principle for the situation at hand (see Ricoeur 1990, 2000; MacIntyre 2007/1981). Some *a priori* duties like 'impartiality' or 'faithfulness' – if possible, at all – may result in immoral consequences, and the translator may need to decide to transgress them in many situations. Besides, interpretations of the same situation or the same principle guiding a certain decision may vary from one person to another, let alone from a person's moral judgment and an institution's calculating judgment. Thus, a translator's interpretation of a given situation may differ from that of a committee judging the former's decision, because they simply do not have the same considerations in mind. Importantly, even the same person may sometimes be torn between different decisions for the same situation. Moral decisions are the outcome of contradictory impulses, as we learn from Bauman (1993). All these questions and concerns show that disciplinary measures are unfounded as moral decisions are very complex and ambivalent.

As in all modern codified ethics, most designers of translator codes of ethics claim a clear cut between what is moral and what is immoral. They claim that morality is non-ambivalent, and, therefore, orderable. A code of ethics is, thus, imposed as "all-comprehensive, unitary ethics – that is, a cohesive code of moral rules which people could be taught and *forced to obey*" (Bauman 1993, 6, italics added). At best, some designers admit their codes' incomprehensiveness without questioning their faulty premises nor their coerciveness. Translators are, thus, constrained to follow these codes to reap the 'benefits' of their collaboration with the established system of the translation 'profession.' Modern translator associations, like the ones studied here – I reiterate – are calculative institutions. Their members are supposedly rational calculative translators who know that it is profitable to abide by their organization's calculative rules whereas non-abidance by these rules is economically self-destructive[3]. Drawing on Bauman's thought, translators as rational beings are exposed to "rationally designed external pressures which would assure that 'doing wrong does not pay' and so most individuals most of the time are discouraged from doing it" (ibid., 7). They, thus, obey the heteronomous codes to gain 'legitimacy' and financial 'rewards' because they know outlaws will taste the ordeals of exclusion and sanctions.

This state of affairs is not only a coercive control and an effacement of the translator's moral self but also, ironically, a relief from moral responsibility. The translator is freed from the ordeals of decision-making as moral responsibility shifts from their shoulders to their institution. Codes of ethics remove the frustrations and pains of the uncertainties they experience when they face ethical dilemmas. In short, the translator is saved from the inherent *aporia* of moral decision-making as the roadmap is already traced for them by the association. Translation, under the studied codes of ethics, is no longer the curse or "the debt one can no longer discharge," as Derrida puts it (1985, 174). It cannot be an "unavoidable failure," in Spivak's words (2005, 95). Once done following the codes' rules to the letter, the debt is paid in full and with complete success – if we believe the claims of translator associations. Codes of ethics purport to anticipate all misbehaviour and mistranslations. The translator is provided with the certainty of the consequences of their actions. Following the institutional rules surely guarantees the good and prevents the harm, in the institutions' claim (see Bauman 2003a/1995, 10). In short, like all modern enterprises, institutionalized codes of ethics ignore many ethical issues and ethical situations by applying their limited (but pretentious) regulations. Worse, they prevent the translator from responding to these unlimited issues/situations in the name of internal collective 'order.'

9.2 Universalism and Well Foundedness of Codes of Ethics

Translation codes of ethics that I examine in this work are all embedded in modernity. They are all both *universalist* and *well founded*, to borrow Bauman's terms. They adopt a deontological approach to ethics based on Kantian moral philosophy, which grounds morality in reason and foregrounds a priory duties, irrespective of consequences, or any other ends. In *Grounding for the Metaphysics of Morals*, Immanuel Kant says:

> [e]veryone must admit that if a law is to be morally valid, i.e., is to be valid as a ground of obligation, then it must carry with it absolute necessity. He must admit that the command, "Thou shalt not lie," does not hold only for men, as if other rational beings had no need to abide by it, and so with all the other moral laws properly so called. And he must concede that the ground of obligation here must therefore be sought not in the nature of man nor in the circumstances of the world in which man is placed, but must be sought a priori solely in the concepts of pure reason.
>
> (Kant 1993/1785, 2)

Following Kant's morals, the studied codes are *universalist* and thus non-contingent on any contextual variables. They claim – or at least do not relativize – the applicability of their *a priori* principles/rules, regardless of consequences or circumstances. They claim the objectivity, the consistency and the clarity of their rules/principles to any rational agent involved in the translation occupation, especially the translator. They reflect the concept of *translation* as a universal and objective act based on complete and impartial transportation of meaning without loss or addition. In addition, they dismiss any *other* (partial, contextual, local or particular) conceptualizations, which might unveil the fact that translation is beyond order, systematicity, objectivity and universalism. These studied codes are also presented as (near)complete[4]. They cater to the two main issues in the translation transaction, i.e., the meaning of *translation*, on the one hand, and the interpersonal (business) relations between the different agents involved in it, on the other hand. They explicitly instruct translators on how to deal with their clients/employers and give them a 'clear' blueprint on *how to translate*, i.e., to transfer meaning faithfully and impartially. Thus, in this modern order that the codes represent, they respond to virtually every issue touching the translator's occupation. Almost no residuals are left in this idealistic compartmentalization. But this order ignores particularities and exceptions – which definitely disturb and unveil the impossibility of this very order. To disguise these 'flaws,' the regulators/designers of code act as if nothing is left unaccounted for and hardly any newness can emerge unexpectedly. The least we can cite of the new developments ignored by these codes are the emerging technologies largely affecting the work of translators and their roles. In all studied codes, there is not a single instruction on how to deal with these technologies or even a reference to this rapidly evolving situation.

The studied codes are also '*well founded*' in the sense that they were established on the likeliness of their adoption by the modern rational agents they target. Modern translators and external agents are likely to embrace these rules because they are compatible with their view of what *translation* is and what relations it entails as a business transaction, as discussed in Part II. These codes seem plausible to modern rational agents who believe in the possibility of order and the efficiency and fairness of regularization. These agents are accustomed to the comfort of simple ready-made answers. They are confident in the way reality is compartmentalized for them. As such, they are likely to feel frustrated with complexity, uncertainties and questioning. That is why they are likely to blindly follow these external answers provided by the designers of codes. Also, translators would likely abide by these codes to preserve their membership within these large associations – many of which have the power to give them a legal title or a certificate. To follow the heteronomous ethical obligations of these organizations does not only guarantee 'professional recognition' of the translator member and, thus, the possibility to attract more business, but probably also a legal recognition – as in the case of the ATIO. A rational translator is not likely to reject these 'strong' foundations of codes of ethics (some conceptual and others pragmatic) or exchange them for the pursuit of a perplexing autonomous morality.

The claim that these codes of ethics are complete, ordered, objective and responsive to the major issues related to translation is, of course, fraught. These documents are never stable although they deny the possible contradictoriness, ambivalence, inefficiency, and even immorality of the principles and duties they espouse for certain translation situations. We occasionally witness cosmetic revisions within them – which is an indirect admission that translation and its ethics are uncontainable and unorderable in an exhaustive list of clear rules – no matter how long, or seemingly objective, that list is. In the studied corpus, the FIT, for example, adopted its Translator's Charter in 1963 and amended it in 1994. The ATIO also revised its code in 2009. The AUSIT's revised its codes in 2012 (first adopted in 1995).

The AUSIT revision enterprise remains the most remarkable endeavour by far among all the associations under study. The AUSIT declaratively admits the incompleteness of its code and highlights the role of the translator in making the appropriate "judgement and balanced decision-making in context" (Code of Ethics and Code of Conduct, Preamble). It acknowledges that "changes in the translation and interpreting industry mean the requirements of a code of ethics have also changed" (Introduction). Thus, a joint committee of scholars and AUSIT members, led by Uldis Ozolins, a scholar from Monash University, was established to review the association's Code of Ethics and Code of Conduct. Suggestions/recommendations were sought from the AUSIT members as well as from "representatives of all areas of the T & I [Translation and Interpretation] industry" (ibid.). One would expect newer academic insights to be included in the revised version as scholars/educators are an important part of this committee (a committee leader and two consultants). However, the industry's representatives seem to have had a major say. And some of the involved scholars' views are in line with the latter agents' and do not reflect the postpositivist views of *translation* now dominant in academia[5]. Those who tried to suggest somewhat reflexive ideas were not heard (see Ozolins 2014)[6]. The process of updating the AUSIT code has led to some of the following main decisions, among others:

- [...] The original principles were largely retained: Professional Conduct, Confidentiality, Impartiality, Competence, Accuracy, Professional Development and Professional Solidarity. One new principle was introduced *Clarity of Role Boundaries* – and the previous Employment principle was changed to *Maintaining Professional Relationships*. This ensures considerable continuity with the previous code.
  [...]
- On the issue of *advocacy*, while canvassing opinion and looking at possible formulations, the working group rejected advocacy as part of a T&I practitioner role.

- While the code is principally for practitioners, a formulation was found to link obligations of agencies or employers to aspects of the code [...].
- Issues of public comment and confidentiality were addressed to slightly lessen the very restrictive view encompassed in the original code.
- The wording was changed from an imperative "shall" to the RID-style [Registry of Interpreter of the Deaf style] descriptive wording, for example "Interpreters interpret in the first person."

(Ozolins 2014, 357–358, italics in original)

As is clear, the basic pillars that define the practice and its relational aspects, such as impartiality and accuracy, were all retained in the new version. The conduit model was preserved and intervention or "advocacy" rejected. Thus, responsibility remained limited to the immediate circle of translation, and larger societal or planetary issues were not addressed. Also, hardly any attention was paid to the new transformative types of translation or the technological aspects of translation despite the claim that this version of the code was written "in recognition of the significant development and diversification of the field in Australia" (Preamble). The last three points above, however, show dissatisfaction with some of the issues in the previous code, such as not addressing outside agents' obligations to provide adequate working conditions, restrictions on the translator disclosing information, as well as the authoritative tone of the articles. Also, reading through the AUSIT articles, one can occasionally discern some flexibility of tone, the inclusion of explanatory sections, and awareness of contextual ethics and peculiarities of certain situations:

> The AUSIT Code of Ethics defines the values and principles guiding the decisions interpreting and translating professionals make in practice. The related Code of Conduct and Conduct issues specific to translators and interpreters provide a framework for interpreting and translating professionals to use when exercising judgment in their practice. They are not intended to be exhaustive lists of the situations and circumstances that may comprise compliance and non-compliance with the Code of Ethics. Ethical interpreting and translating practice requires judgment and balanced decision-making in context. *Interpreters and translators who commit to practise in accordance with the Code of Ethics accept that they will be accountable for their conduct under AUSIT's processes for non-compliance.*
>
> (AUSIT Preamble, italics added)

There is here a clear admission of the incompleteness of the code of ethics and its summative and general nature. That is why the AUSIT encourages the establishment of specific codes for specialized translators/interpreters working in certain specific institutional settings. The AUSIT also makes it clear that the Code of Ethics and the Code of Conduct and their supplements contain guiding principles and are a framework for translators to draw on when making decisions and, in no way, comprise a complete list of all situations. However, in a striking turn, the last statement is utterly disappointing. By implementing a process of coercion, the AUSIT, paradoxically, undermines the fact that its guiding principles make possible different interpretations by different individuals in different situations (see Drugan 2011). It also ignores the fact that some conflicts may arise between these principles in some contexts. In sum, the AUSIT's flexibility of tone can be seen as a very timid response to the wind of postmodern thought that is blowing nearby (in some academic circles), although not an acknowledgement of the ill foundedness of the *translation* definition or of the very principle of codification as it exists today.

Following Bauman's (1993) analysis, translator institutions (i.e., translators' associations like the AUSIT and others) believe that they *can* contain morality in *non-ambivalent, non-aporetic, well founded* and *universal* code of ethics, and that they are only one small step away from perfection. For them, the perfect code "surely waits round the next corner. Or the corner after next" (1993, 9). Thus, minor revisions are made to fill in the small gaps, in the hope of achieving perfection. Although designers of codes of ethics, like all modern legislators/regulators and theorists, are aware of the 'very few' weaknesses in their projects, they never admit them as complex and real problems that are here to stay. These 'uninfluential' problems are always considered as small hurdles that are easy to quickly eliminate. The current codes are, thus, not perfect but very close to that, and they are developing in the right direction toward perfection. All they need is some improvement, an expansion or slight amendments. These (near)perfect codes do not require radical changes in their very underlying premises regarding *translation* and the interpersonal relations in the translation transaction. The cited associations claim that the foundations and basic pillars (i.e., rules/principles) are solid and true and, therefore, unshakeable, while the cosmetic changes are possible.

The universalism and well foundedness of the studied codes make them beyond any major upheavals. Their designers never engage in any substantive changes to their framing principles, nor do they question the ideas of codification and coercion in the first place. Although they may recognize the need to revise the codes to cater for the newest developments, they do not admit the fact that codes of ethics are inherently unable to cater for this disordered reality – more disordered than ever before, in today's world. They overlook the fact that these codes are not fit to address the proliferation of novel translation situations/contexts that require novel and innovative situated answers on the spot. The turn to postmodern ethics may give the translator the chance to face this ambivalence and disorder – although never with certainty.

9.3 The Translator's *Moral Self* in Postmodern Morality

The standardization of the translator's conduct in *a priori* and 'clear' rules in codes of ethics reduces translation to a simple unitary, containable and unambivalent work. The argument advanced by some is that untrained translators need clearly defined principles and applicable directives in codes of ethics (see Ozolins 2014). Ozolins (2014, 364), for instance, reports that the debate about the principle of 'accuracy' during the elaboration of the AUSIT code led to the explanation of the concept and the adoption of 'clear' criteria for accuracy. The adopted article reads:

> Interpreters and translators provide accurate renditions of the source utterance or text in the target language. Accurate is defined for this purpose as *optimal and complete, without distortion or omission and preserving the content and intent of the source message or text.* Interpreters and translators are able to provide an accurate and complete rendition of the source message using the skills and understanding they have acquired through training and education.
> (Code of Conduct, Article 5.1, italics added)

The committee rejected an earlier proposition that allowed for some adaptation to the context/situation as "being too unhelpful" (Ozolins 2014, 364). The rejected proposition reads:

> [i]nterpreters and translators shall endeavour to provide accurate and complete renditions of the original. It must be noted that *the meaning of accuracy depends on the context of the situation*; for example, the type of interpreting (conference or community), the translation brief, etc. The concept of accuracy is a *complex* one that is dealt with in detail in training. Interpreters and translators should strive to obtain formal training before practising.
> (Ozolins 2014, italics added)

This example shows that associations such as the AUSIT reject any open or uncertain proposition, like the latter, as they are "unhelpful." These associations rather claim the certainty and unitary nature of translation and the clarity of its boundaries, as well the clarity of its ethics and the unproblematic applicability of codes' rules to all situations. They adopt a totalitarian approach that claims to alleviate even the burden of interpretation for the translating agent.

These claims of translator associations are, of course, fraught. As we learn from Jacques Derrida (1985), uncertainty, confusion and the impossibility of universalization, or even of theorization, are post-Babelian phenomena that are here to stay. Uncertainty, incompleteness, partiality and complexity are part of the human condition since 'God' destroyed the Tower of Babel (a symbol of totalitarianism, completeness, trueness, standardization, regularization, structuring and universalization) and confused the tongues, Derrida tells us.

> The "tower of Babel" does not merely figure the irreducible multiplicity of tongues; it exhibits an incompletion, the impossibility of finishing, of totalizing, of saturating, of completing something on the order of edification, architectural construction, system, and architectonics. What the multiplicity of idioms actually limits is not only a "true" translation, a transparent and adequate interexpression, it is also a structural order, a coherence of construct. There is then (let us translate) something like an internal limit to formalization, an incompleteness of the constructure. It would be easy and up to a certain point justified to see there the translation of a system in deconstruction.
> (Derrida 1985, 165–166)

The deconstruction of the Tower of Babel symbolizes the confusion and instability that are characteristic of language and translation. It is also symbolic of partiality, irregularity, unevenness and disorder. Derrida has shown the flaws in principles like sameness, trueness, transparency and faithfulness in translation. He has highlighted the issue of untranslatability, i.e., the impossibility of completeness of any translation, in the image of a debt that can never be paid off. Drawing on Walter Benjamin (1923), Derrida affirms that because of these characteristics, translation is a complex task and a *problem* for the *translating subject*. "Benjamin does not say the task or the problem of translation. He names the subject of translation, as an indebted subject, obligated by a duty" (Derrida 1985, 179). Translation, according to both Benjamin and Derrida is an aporetic responsibility and a never discharged debt for the *translator* because it is an *uncertain* task, for which completeness is unattainable. Derrida argues that translation is a *transformative* process as it modifies the 'original.' He goes even further when he underlines that the 'original' is itself in constant transformation. Translation as a "debt" does not oblige the translator to faithfully transfer the ST because the latter is itself slippery, Derrida tells us. "Then the debt does not involve restitution of a copy or a good image, a *faithful* representation of the original: the latter, the survivor, is itself in the process of *transformation*. The original gives itself in *modifying* itself; this gift is not an object given; it lives and lives on in *mutation*" (ibid., 183, italics added). Benjamin in 'The Task of the Translator' (1923) – which Derrida analyzes – underlines the notion of text "survival" and affirms that the 'original' owes translation for the latter gives it a new life or an afterlife through transformation and renewal, thus helping it to reach maturity. "For in its afterlife – which could not be called that if it were not a *transformation* and a *renewal* of something living – the original undergoes a *change*. Even words with fixed meaning can undergo a maturing process" (2000/1923, 17, italics added). Following Derrida and Benjamin, the ordering and bordering of 'translation' as a systematic and measurable operation is untenable (see Davis 2001; Spivak 2000, 2005; Arrojo 2005, 2013; Wolf 2000). Not only translation is in a transformative and an inherently incomplete process, but also the so-called original is in a state of permanent modification, mutation and renewal as it survives. These philosophical insights raising the questions of transformation and change in translation – once abstract and seen as may be pertaining mainly to literary translation far from the daily practices of pragmatic translation – have now been empirically corroborated by many non-fiction transformative types of translation, as discussed in Part I.

The associations under study, however, still follow the Babelian myth. Exactly like the Semites who sought a universal language and structure (which is at the same time, a rational transparency and a colonial violence, as Derrida puts it (1985, 174)), the designers of these codes of ethics seek transparency and completeness via translation codified ethics. They compose and impose the universalist concept of *translation* as well as standard relational rules on all translating agents in all situations. But establishing a list of (ethical) rules and obliging the translator to live and work by them prevents the translator from carrying out the transformation and intervention that translation inevitably demands, and, therefore, from *performing their "task,"* which is, of course, a multifaceted responsibility that is at is at once linguistic, cultural, political, ecological, social and ethical. Not only is translation inherently uncertain as a textual/cultural operation, as we learn from the deconstruction scholars, but also as an ethical/social endeavour. And if morality in any field is characterized by uncertainty and ambivalence, as we learn from Bauman (1993), translation is a doubly daunting task to the translator, as it is a multidimensional, complex task. Thus, unlike what is proffered by contemporary codes of ethics, postmodern insights about ethics stress the *translator's* responsibility, visibility and agency. In postmodern morality, the translator is not armed with heteronomous rules they simply have to follow. They alone (and not any other institutions) are responsible for the translation outcome and its consequences.

If translators stop hiding their authorial role behind vague notions of ethical impartiality, they will have to learn how to face the consequences of their visibility and be responsible for the choices they make and the allegiances they choose to cultivate in their work. In fact, from this perspective, it would actually be unethical and irresponsible for translators to insist on hiding behind claims of neutrality or to wash their hands of the responsibilities involved in the highly complex and influential work they do.

(Arrojo 2013, 4)

The responsible translator may have to contravene their institution's pre-established codes to act responsibly. Blindly applying the decontextualized and calculative rules of codes of ethics can lead to the most unethical outcomes. Considering the rules of confidentiality, neutrality, faithfulness and impartiality as ethical principles, the translator is *not* responsible for the material content or for what their clients do or say (e.g., AUSIT Code of Ethics, Article 4). These rules shelter the translator from responsibility and cause their job to consist of simply following the patron/client's directives. These codes make translators themselves clients of patrons/clients.

Many writings about *translation* demonstrate a growing awareness of the contradictions of modernity and the implausibility of its claim to order. Theorists from TS and beyond have unveiled the impossibility of some of the framing principles that appear in modern codes of ethics. The insights from Derrida and his TS deconstructionist followers about 'translation' not only intersect with Bauman's ambivalent morality but also constitute an excellent case in point for his theorization. Translation, like morality, is beyond modern regularization or universalization. The ethical reality of translation consists of too much disorder to be contained, organized, or even assimilated. It is a beyond codification reality. Translation is "incurably *aporetic*," to use Bauman's term (1993, 11, italics in original). Translation decisions are made between contradictory "impulses" (Bauman 1993). To be a moral translator is to be able to select from a number of decisions, not one of which is certain or complete. These decisions cannot be established before the encounter with the translated material. Translation as such is an adventure through unknown alleys of discovery, from which the exit is never easy or clear. "[T]he translator must decide the undecidable, arrive at a translation without having passed through an open, already determined passage" (Davis 2001, 94). The translator is left to their fate to face the ambiguous and the uncertain in the moral encounter. They are disarmed of references and, thus, left with the incurable pain and frustration of uncertainty in their translation decisions[7]. They make their own disposable codes for every situation and instance. These self-made codes are in perpetual change and adaptation. They are never complete or satisfactory, nor applicable a second time. Translators have no guarantee that their moral self will always be guiding them toward making the right decisions – if there are any perfect decisions, at all.

Despite the frustration and pain associated with uncertainty and lack of references, translators are given an opportunity – *the opportunity to be moral*. Davis writes, "[t]o say that there is an impossible aspect to ethics is not to suggest that translation cannot be ethical. Rather, it suggests that ethical translation cannot follow a pre-formulated code of ethics, which [...] would ultimately be unethical" (2001, 49). The translator's uncertainty and ambivalence is a curse, but also an opportunity for the translator to be moral. "[T]he frustration of uncertainty is morality's gain," Bauman tells us (1993, 223). Postmodern ethics allow the translator to courageously face the unknown and the unpredictable – a fact which makes up the essence of the moral condition. Postmodern ethics is an opportunity – although an opportunity for which the results are *never* certain. It is the opportunity to be emancipated from the pre-ordained ethical regulations that incapacitate or paralyze the moral self. It is the opportunity for the moral self to restore and thrive as morality shifts back to the realm of personal autonomy from the power-assisted heteronomy that demobilizes it. Postmodern ethics allow the translator to respond to and care about one's world, which could not be the case under the calculative codes that are limited to caring to the powerful. Responsibility to one's world is, in the age of globalization, a more pressing task than ever for the translator.

9.4 The Translator's Ethical Challenges in the Age of Globalization

Bauman qualifies globalization as "an ethical challenge" (2008, 71; 2003b). People's lives and destinies are now more interconnected and interdependent than ever before. In today's globalized world, there is "mutual dependency" between people (2008, 26). What happens in one location may affect the lives of other species and people in remote places, as well as generations to come.

> [w]hatever else 'globalization' may mean, it means that we are all dependent on each other. Distances matter little now. Something that happens in one place may have global consequences. [...] However local their intentions might be, actors would be ill-advised to leave out of account global factors, since they could decide the success or failure of their actions. What we do (or abstain from doing) may influence the

conditions of life (or death) for people in places we will never visit and of generations we will never know.

(Bauman 2008, 71)

Because of the far-reaching consequences of our actions, we need to adapt our moral imagination to respond to the challenges of globalization; to think beyond the foreseeable, beyond the unseen to reach far distant locations/times. We need to stretch our morality of proximity into an unlimited moral coverage. For Hans Jonas, as reported by Bauman,

> although space and time no longer limit the effects of our actions, our moral imagination has not progressed much beyond the scope it had acquired in Adam-and-Eve times. The responsibilities we are ready to assume do not venture as far as the influence that our daily conduct exerts on the lives of ever more distant people.
>
> (Bauman 2008, 73)

Although translation is an intercultural task and has, therefore, always had far-reaching consequences on others in remote places, the fact that translation has become ubiquitous and the demand for it has skyrocketed in today's digital world makes its ethical challenges even more prolific and more complex. The increasing exchanges of goods and cultures as well as movements of people (resulting in increasingly hybrid cultures/ nations) increase indeed the need to communicate through translation, and therefore, increase its ethical impacts. Thus, the translator's decisions now have more wide-ranging effects on our world in the present and the future. And because of this enlarged scope of translation influence today, the moral burden on the translator is heavier than ever before. "[I]n our globalized world, ethical, socially aware translation has become a humanitarian necessity," as Gill and Guzmán put it (2011, 100).

In his *Translation and Globalization*, Cronin (2003) highlights the increasing demand for translation and discusses the interconnection of translation with culture, society, economics, politics and technologies in the age of globalization. He underlines the important role a reflexive translator can play in highlighting diversity and countering hegemony in today's world.

> In reflecting on the ends of translation, it might also be possible to see translation in a reflexive as opposed to a merely reflective mode [...]. That is, translators rather than being simple accessories to the fact of information inflation (reflective mode) might consider whether it would be more fruitful on the basis of identifiable ends to take a

selective approach to the information which circulates between cultures (reflexive mode).

(Cronin 2003, 66)

The role of the translator in today's "globotics transformation" – characterized by the "the convergence of globalisation and artificial intelligence" (Cronin 2021, 181) – is extremely important to cultural, social and ecological biodiversity – an ethical task *par excellence*. In order to be able to play this active role, the translator needs to be visible, selective and interventionist, rather than a conduit. "[I]t is by revealing, not disguising, their identity as translators that translators can make a legitimate bid to make more central interventions in culture, society and politics" (Cronin 2003, 67). In today's globalized world, empowered translators and TS scholars can play a crucial role in preserving cultural biodiversity by enlarging translation to include diverse practices that include and allow the translator's ethical agency. Tymoczko warns us that disempowered translators are vulnerable to alignment with the dominant, and translation to being a tool of hegemony and oppression in the age of globalization.

> Translators everywhere and at all times have been vulnerable to becoming mouthpieces for the dominant regimes of their cultures. At present new forms of this type of jeopardy are emerging along with the widespread networking of the world. A chief peril posed by globalization for translators – whether they are from Eurocentric contexts or not – is that they can become vehicles for the assertion of dominant Western values around the world, ideas that serve specific corporate and military interests and that are vehicles of neocolonialism. For translators and scholars from Europe, the Americas and other Western countries, this means colluding in Western exploitation; for scholars and translators elsewhere, it means becoming classic subalterns who buy into hegemonic thinking in the service of dominant global powers. Having the broadest possible conceptualization of translation helps translators keep ethical issues in focus; it reminds translators that translation methods themselves can serve ideology. The alternative to such awareness is that the profession of translation and the discipline of translation studies – both of which are purportedly dedicated to cultural exchange – will instead become vehicles of cultural homogenization and even oppression.
>
> (Cronin 2003, 414)

Unfortunately, the studied codes of ethics seek to curb the translator's agency from contributing reflexively to culture, society and politics. Instead, they prepare the translator to be a "vehicle" of cultural McDonaldization and domination.

These documents' rules are idealistic and decontextualized. They ignore the diverse exchanges in which translation is needed nowadays. Translation today can be a tool of war as it can be a tool of peace. In conflict zones, like Iraq, or more recently Syria, decisions to interpret/translate in the first place and/or the translation strategies adopted may have helped save lives or increase deaths in the immediate. In addition to the local atrocities, translators' decisions may have had repercussions on the global scene as these conflicts have generated unprecedented numbers of people in refuge/exile. Unfortunately, codes of ethics that highlight impartiality (and cater mostly to the client/patron) serve as translators/interpreters' shields from moral responsibility for the consequences of their decisions in conflict contexts (Inghilleri 2010, 2012). Worse, as Inghilleri (2010, 2012) shows, interpreters in conflict zones may come to share the same 'moral' codes as the military institution they serve. Inghilleri rightly affirms that conflict zones constitute a clear context that shows how implausible codes of ethics that try to conceal the practitioner's agency are. "What makes war an important context for the investigation of ethics is that codes of ethics, if they exist at all, largely lose their significance and their power to conceal the undeniability of interpreter agency" (2010, 192).

Unfortunately, the studied codes still lay claim to the idealism of the translational encounter and ignore all these global issues, which are becoming more pressing in the age of globalization. They limit the scope of responsibility to the agents in proximity. Worse, they deem the enlargement of one's ethical imagination and the reflexive approaches that Bauman and Cronin call for 'unprofessional' and sometimes unethical or even illegal, following many defining principles/rules stressed in these documents. Thus, the studied codes and any similar codes are anything but fit to face the challenges of globalization, in which local/current decisions/actions may have global/future consequences.

9.5 Conclusion

The nature, function and origin of the translator organizations do not tangibly affect their orientations regarding their members' ethical conduct, despite some uninfluential differences in their approaches. The Nairobi Recommendation and the FIT Translator's Charter, given their addressees (member States and member associations, respectively), are less concerned with the individual translator's moral issues, although they highlight many rules that negatively affect the translator's moral autonomy.

All studied codes of ethics stress *a priori* rules that assume the non-ambivalence of ethical encounters and underline obligations toward the immediate agents who are *economically relevant* to the translation transaction. Ethics in these documents are neither personal nor gratuitous.

They seek "external goods" to translation practice rather than "internal goods," in MacIntyre's terminology (2007/1981). The codes are exclusively oriented toward the powerful agents that influence them thanks to their economic and/or symbolic power, given the impoverished capital of the translator and their lack of autonomy and control over their occupation. "Freedom is the ontological condition of ethics," Foucault tells us (2001d/1984, 1531, my translation). A translator with low symbolic power and autonomy is easily alienable and can, therefore, hardly pursue ethical ends.

Many rules and principles in the codes of ethics are, in fact, technologies of alienation that cater to the dominant. Faithfulness, impartiality, confidentiality, quality and other virtue ethics that aim at 'protecting the public' are simple ideological shibboleths that, in fact, aim at being loyal to the powerful agents. As rigid as they are, these rules dangerously promote limited duty-based rules at the expense of unlimited and gratuitous moral responsibility toward our world: humans and their environment, current and future generations, and close and remote others. Thus, the underlying motivation for the elaboration of codes does not seem to be ethical *per se* but rather strategic[8]. These documents aim at regulating business relationships that can reassure powerful agents and dissipate their possible concerns regarding the 'quality' of translations, and probably also serve as an insurance policy against possible whistleblowing. They seek to align the individual translator's beliefs, attitudes and orientations with the collective institutional standards and guidelines of the association – which ultimately serve the powerful agents' interests. Besides facing this moral alienation, translators also face punitive measures, which purportedly establish order and prevent chaos. These measures complement the ideologies of subjugation. The translator who escapes alienation is tempted to remain a member of the association – submitting to and collaborating with the codes – in order to preserve their clientele or their title.

The studied associations' documents replicate codes of ethics of other professions and occupations that stress the limited business interactions within them. However, translation is a practice that involves multiple agents and variables. First and foremost, it involves many powerful beneficiary agents. Further, translation is not simply a service transaction but a complex cultural/social creation that influences agents beyond the immediate occupational circle and above the purely business considerations. Translators' and interpreters' responsibilities extend beyond their clients to include the wider community and world (Baker and Maier 2011b; see also Baker 2018, Boéri and de Manuel Jerez 2011, Gill and Guzmán 2011, Tymoczko 2007). This is because translation impacts on agents/others that may be thousands of miles away or generations to come. It impacts humans and non-humans. It impacts space and the earth. Its ethics are, thus, much more complex and ambivalent than ethics of most other occupations[9]. The effects of translation are wider, more diffuse, more ambivalent, more unpredictable, and more dissipated over time and space. Moral actions are contingent on diverse and sometimes contradictory principles, meanings of translation and uses of translations. What is a moral action in one type of translation with one type of client is probably *not* in others with a different type of client. Dealing with vulnerable clients or dominated cultures may necessitate different moral interventions/actions than dealing with dominant clients and/or dominant cultures. Also, moral action in an adaptation of a children's book may be different from a moral action in a media or political text. For these reasons, deontological approaches to translation ethics, based on *a priori* rules, are far from being appropriate for translation more than any other occupation. In this respect, Pier-Pascale Boulanger writes:

> we will say of translation that it is full of attitudes, ways of thinking and behaviors that suggest an ethics without however stating principles according to an a priori and peremptory logic. That is why we avoid talking about an ethics of translation, which is inherently predetermined, like a code of ethics. Now, translation, especially in its practice, but also in its theorization, occurs within the imponderable space of each new encounter of a textual material and a translating subject. When translation recognizes the value of imponderables (whether historical, political, social, institutional, linguistic or even psychoanalytic) and undertakes to reflect on them, as Translation Studies has been doing with ever-increasing vigor since the 1980s, it turns to open and renewable ethics. On the other hand, closed ethics, such as a predefined code or mode of action, causes translation to shift towards an annexionist writing tactic and a dogmatic way of thinking.
>
> (Boulanger 2004, 57, my translation)

Although some codes are open to revisions and updates – which is in fact an implicit acknowledgment of their incompleteness – they still claim universalism and well foundedness. The guiding principles (such as the definition of the practice itself) remain unshaken and the changes are usually cosmetic rather than radical.

Notes

1 See ATIO Code of Ethics, Articles 5.1.2., The Discipline Committee Procedural Code (2014); SFT Règlement intérieur [Internal Regulations] 2018, Article 3.2; IAFET Code of ethics, Article 1.1, Bylaws, Article 3, Section 6; ITAINDIA Membership Information/B, respectively.

2 www.translators.org.za/benefits-of-sati-membership/
3 Of course, this policy paradoxically impoverishes the translator economically and symbolically, as discussed in Part II.
4 As already discussed, although the AUSIT's code of ethics admits its incompleteness, it, paradoxically, stresses accountability for 'non-compliance' with the code's principles, thus, ignoring the conflict of these principles in some situations, their vagueness in application (see McDonough Dolmaya 2011), and differences in their personal interpretations (see Drugan 2011).
5 Ozolins (2014), one of the code designers, does not question the 'conduit' model embraced in the code and its "aversion to advocacy or cultural brokering" (2014, 355). The scholar also advances that "[i]n rewriting the AUSIT code, there were no submissions from employers, agencies or third parties that demanded interpreters play different roles" (ibid., 361).
6 For example, Ozolins (2014, 364) reports that one educator, who is a member of the committee, proposed a more open understanding of 'accuracy' but their proposition was rejected because the other members saw that the concept as such was "unhelpful" as it was "not explained."
7 Being disarmed of points of reference does not, however, mean not making judgments based on the calculation of risks and consequences – as Bauman's radical theory may appear to connote. What I mean is the disarmament from business and ideological Thirds (predominant in codes of ethics) that may guide the translator's decisions.
8 In Part II, we saw how these strategic calculations are, in fact, the powerful agents, who impose their views in these internal documents of translators.
9 Ironically, even some of these professions/occupations' codes show better awareness of larger environmental and societal issues as well as more self-care commitment than the translator's codes (see for example, Canada Medical Association Code of Ethics and Professionalism: https://policybase.cma.ca/documents/policypdf/PD19-03.pdf Accessed on January 7, 2020).

Part IV
Alternative Ethics

> Freedom is the ontological condition of ethics. But ethics is the form that freedom takes when it is informed by reflection.
> Foucault 2001d/1984, 1531, my translation

As argued in Part III, Bauman's postmodern morality represents an opportunity for the moral translator, especially in today's globalized and digital world. It frees them from pre-ordained codes and lets them face the uncertainty of the diverse translation situations. But although an outstanding approach from a critical perspective, Bauman's morality is not without its problems, as mentioned in the theoretical framework in Chapter 7. Although his concept of moral self is useful as a heuristic tool in analyzing and criticizing the codes embeddedness in purely economic and ideological considerations, I concede that Bauman gives very few answers as to the ways of recovering this moral self – which is inherently pre-modern and pre-social – or of how to adapt it to respond to diverse relational situations. I do not believe all types of calculation, which Bauman utterly refutes, are always undesirable. Cloaking the moral self in the robe of a *Resistant* calculator in an asymmetric relation, in relations of humiliation, hegemony or discrimination, is not only desirable but also morally required. The empowered translator, in such cases, becomes a calculative social subject that uses translation tactics and strategies to evade exploitation and cultural hegemony. Thus, while I reaffirm the plausibility of the notion of moral self as a generator of non-calculative gratuitous responses regardless of economic/ideological interests or Thirds, I, however, believe that denying all sorts of calculation in all circumstances is problematic. Beyond this reservation, however, one cannot not feel a gap in Bauman's thought regarding the restoration of one's moral self outside social settings – which are modern in essence. I rather argue that the moral self shapes and empowers itself in society. The translator's pre-social morality is too abstract to be conceivable or easily applicable as an alternative to codes of ethics.

DOI: 10.4324/9781032713557-14

222 *Alternative Ethics*

Being aware of the problems of Bauman's theorization, I do not abandon his notion of moral self as a non-calculative guide for an autonomous translator. What I do abandon is its instinctive nature. For this reason, I opt for Foucault's self-formative ethics in social settings – which are based on ancient ethics – as a complementary model that can compensate for this weakness. I refer to Foucault in order to complement Bauman's thought not only intellectually but also temporally, for while Bauman focuses on the modern era, Foucault starts at the roots. In this Part IV, I propose an alternative pathway for a translator's ethical empowerment and symbolic recognition. I draw on Foucault's notion of *epimeleia heautou* (self-care) as well as Transformative Learning theory to propose a critical pedagogical approach that can enable the learner-translator to intellectually self-transform and ethically self-constitute. I also propose a transitional charter for ethics that can accompany this work on the self.

10 Foucault's *Epimeleia Heautou* (Self-Care)

Michel Foucault presents most of his insights on ethics and morality in his later works, mainly *Histoire de la sexualité II: L'usage des plaisirs* [*The History of Sexuality II: The Use of Pleasure*] (1984a), *Histoire de la sexualité III: Le souci de soi* [*The History of Sexuality III: The Care of the Self*] (1984b) and *L'herméneutique du sujet* [*The Hermeneutics of the Subject*] (2001a/1982) – in addition to other shorter texts and interviews, in which he traces the genealogy of ethics in the Greek, Hellenistic and Roman traditions. In the introductory chapter of *The History of Sexuality II*, Foucault cautions his readers against the ambiguity of the term 'moral/morality,' which he defines as follows: "by 'morality,' one means a set of values and rules of action that are proposed to individuals and groups through various prescriptive apparatuses, such as the family, educational institutions, churches, etc." (1984a, 32, my translation). By morality, he also refers to the actual behaviour of individuals, i.e., how they abide by or resist the prescribed rules and values. Foucault calls this level "morality of behaviours" (ibid., 33, my translation). A third dimension of morality – and the most important in Foucault's work – is ethics. Ethics, for him, refers to the ethical constitution of the self as well as the personal and contingent responses to, or interpretations of, moral codes. In other words, it is the process of working on the self and caring for the self in order to transform oneself and respond to moral prescriptions contingently and differentially. Bob Robinson sums up Foucault's understanding of ethics as "a relation of self to itself in terms of its moral agency" (2011, n.p.). In one word, morality, for Foucault, consists of three dimensions: a moral code, actual acts of moral subjects and ethics[1].

Foucault concludes this section of differentiation between the three aspects of morality by asserting that morality is not to be reduced to abiding by the rules but should rather include the relational dimension to the self, i.e., the processes of subjectivation in order to shape one's ethical being. The ethical aspect of morality that involves the ethical constitution

DOI: 10.4324/9781032713557-15

of the self is the most important facet of ancient morality. The ethical constitution of the self, or self-care, is ethical in itself in Foucault's thought (1984a, 1984b). He writes:

> In short, for an action to be called 'moral,' it must not be reducible to an act or a series of acts that conform to a rule, a law, or a value. It is true that any moral action involves a relationship with the reality in which it is carried out, and a relationship with the code to which it refers; but it also implies a certain relation with the self. This relation with the self is not simply 'self-awareness' but it is the constitution of the self as an 'ethical subject'; it is a process in which the individual delimits that part of themselves that constitutes the object of their moral practice, defines their position with regard to the precept they follow, and establishes a certain mode of being that will serve as their moral accomplishment. And to do this, they act upon themself, undertake to know themself, control, test, improve, and transform themself.
> (Foucault 1984a, 35, my translation)

Foucault argues that in cases where the focus is on codes (their richness, comprehensibility, systematicity), and the institutions of power that enforce them and sanction the transgressors, little margin is left for self-constitution. "In these conditions, the subjectivation takes place mainly in a quasi-juridical form, where the ethical subject relates to a law, or set of laws, to which they must submit or else they face punishment" (ibid., 37, my translation). In other words, when the subjectivation is external and imposed, ethics fail to be contingent and personal. Therefore, self-constitution is possible and successful only when the subject is not coerced by institutions and rigorous legislation. This was the goal of ancient philosophy, he affirms, where the focus was on ethics, i.e., on the subject's self-constitution through ascetic work on the self, more than on codified morality.

> Moral thought in Greek or Greco-Roman antiquity was much more oriented toward the practices of the self and the question of *askesis* than toward the codifications of conducts and the strict definition of what is permitted and what is forbidden.
> (ibid., 37–38, my translation)

Although respect for law and conventions was usually highlighted, the content of the codes was not as important as the subject's self-constitution and their attitude toward them. Instead of codified morality, it is the self-mastery of the subject and their power over themselves that transform them into ethical subjects. In this relation to the self, the ethical subject "is called upon to take themself as an object of knowledge and a field of action, in order to transform, correct and purify themself, and achieve salvation" (Foucault 1984b, 56, my translation). Discussing sexual austerity in Greek thought, Foucault stresses the utterly personal and free nature of individuals' ethical responses to this issue. He reports that sexual austerity was not a coercive universal law for everyone, but rather a general precept from which some people may have wanted to derive their personal style. This choice of a moral style is singular and non-universalizable. Sexual austerity in the Greek tradition "belongs to a history that is more important for an understanding of the transformations of the moral experience than the history of codes: a history of 'ethics,' understood as the elaboration of a relationship with the self which allows the individual to constitute themself as the subject of moral conduct" (Foucault 1984a, 275, my translation).

Self-care, the heart of the predominant *culture of the self* in ancient traditions, had, thus, a purely individualistic and private nature irrespective of power/legislative institutions. In fact, it was the weakening of the socio-political framework (which may have been implemented to guard morality) that guaranteed self-care, and therefore, rigorous morality.

> Therefore, it was not the strengthening of public authority that could account for the development of this rigorous morality, but rather the weakening of the political and social framework in which the life of individuals used to unfold in the past,
> (Foucault 1984b, 55, my translation)

Personalized rules of behaviour and self-care are, thus, a sign of freedom, in the ancient traditions. Without freedom, one cannot exercise self-care and thus, cannot be moral. For the Greek Stoic philosopher, Epictetus, free humans are, by nature, devoted to self-care, which is at once a privilege and a duty, a gift and an obligation. This self-subjection is "a test of power and a guarantee of freedom" (Foucault 1984b, 81, my translation). The ascetic practices and technologies of the self reflect the subject's sovereignty and their freedom, but also test their proper handling of this endowed power and autonomy.

Besides the general emphasis on the ethical dimension of morality (i.e., self-constitution) and the subordination of codes, there is also a tacit recognition of the multifacedness of moral issues, or any other behavioural issues (like sexuality). Foucault affirms that "not only did the Greeks not seek to define a code of conduct that is binding on all, but they also did not seek to organize sexual behaviour as an area that is governed in all its aspects by a single set of principles" (Foucault 1984a, 275, my translation). The Greeks were, thus, aware that the complex question of morality

226 Alternative Ethics

cannot be responded to in an exhaustive and non-ambivalent code. Also, they were convinced that its multiple facets cannot be addressed by *one* and the *same* moral principle. Therefore, unlike modern philosophers of ethics, who prescribe and recommend the rational institutionalization and legislation of ethics in universal laws/codes, as Bauman demonstrates, ancient philosophers, aware of the complexity of moral issues, did not seek legislation for their thoughts about morality.

As Foucault (2001a/1982, 1984a, 1984b) reports in *The Hermeneutics of the Subject* and *The History of Sexuality* I and II, respectively, *epimeleia heautou* (self-care) is a central theme and aim in ancient morality, starting from Socrates's philosophy through Christian asceticism in the fifth century, reaching its climax during the first two centuries of Roman Imperial times. "In this practice of the self, such as it appears and is formulated in the last centuries of the so-called pagan era and the first centuries of the Christian era, the self basically appears as the aim; the end of an uncertain, and possibly circular, journey, which is the dangerous journey of life" (Foucault 2001a/1982, 239–240, my translation). Self-care was regarded as a general attitude, a manner of behaviour, of acting and of relating to oneself and to others. "The *epimeleia heautou* is an attitude toward the self, toward others and toward the world" (ibid., 12, my translation). In Foucault's terms, this implies "that one must convert one's gaze from the outside, from others, from the world, etc., toward 'oneself' " (ibid., my translation). Besides being an attitude, self-care constitutes a myriad of practices, activities and exercises (*askêsis*) that seek self-enhancement and self-(trans)formation. It is a real and practical endeavour, a labour on the self (see Foucault 2001a/1982, 1984b). This intensive work on the self is *not* a social withdrawal, however. Unlike Bauman's pre-social moral self, the ancient ethical subject is socially embedded. Self-care in ancient times "constituted, not an exercise in solitude, but a real social practice. And it did so in many ways. Indeed, it often took shape in more or less institutionalized structures" (Foucault 1984b, 67, my translation). Thus, self-care is an exchange, a reciprocal practice that privileges learning from one another. Institutions that advocate critical debate and involve symmetrical active exchange (rather than imposed knowledge) are not to be rejected but rather supported as being in the service of self-care. That being said, ethics is a personal matter and a self-constitution. It is a sort of "conversion" toward the self, in Foucault's terminology (2001a/1982). "It is toward oneself; it is toward the centre of oneself, it is in the centre of oneself that one must set one's aim" (ibid., 199, my translation). In short, although ethical learning takes social forms, it remains self-transformative, self-adjusting, self-corrective and a purely personal endeavour.

Another very important aspect of self-care is the development of critical reflection on one's representations and thoughts inculcated and reinforced through education in schools, family or other institutions (Foucault 2001a/1982). "In the *Alcibiades*, self-care was necessary because of the deficiencies of pedagogy; it was a matter of either supplementing it or replacing it" (ibid., 476, my translation). Self-care is a self-reflexive work that consists of permanent examination, purification, and filtering of one's ideas and opinions (Foucault 1984b, 79). Epictetus and the Hellenistic Plutarch warn that some people may be blinded and cannot see their own souls' ills. Worse, they may even perceive them as virtues. "The serious thing about diseases of the soul is that they pass unnoticed, or even that they can be mistaken for virtues" (Foucault 1984b, 74, my translation). Hence, constant self-examination of one's thoughts, judgments, and representations is an important aspect of self-control, self-knowledge, and thus, self-care. According to Foucault, Epictetus, in *Discourses*, suggests that "every representation should be subject to examination. We should be able to stop it and say, 'wait, let me see who you are and where you come from,' just like the night watchmen say, 'Show me your papers.' Do you get from nature the seal of approval that a representation must have?" (Foucault 1984b, 80, my translation). Self-care, thus, has a critical function. As Foucault reports, the ultimate aim of this reflection about one's thought is to undo bad habits, and eradicate false opinions, which may have been inculcated in us from the crowds, bad teachers, parents or surroundings. " 'To unlearn' (*de-discere*) is one of the important tasks of the culture of the self" (Foucault 2001a/1982, 477, my translation).

As already mentioned, self-constitution implies freedom and obligation. It is the ground for testing the judicious use of this freedom on oneself and *others*. Against critiques of selfishness, radical individualism and impracticality raised against Foucault's account on ethics[2], Nancy Luxon (2008, 397) argues that Foucault's turn to ancient ethics "reflects not a selfish interest in self-fashioning, but commitment to a set of ethical practices that would focus individuals squarely on their relations to others, and on their own words and deeds, as the necessary substance of ethical work." James Wong (2013), discussing Foucault's ontological priority of the care for the self, argues that self-care automatically requires an intensification of reciprocal social relations with others. He shows that the practice of self-care does not prevent involvement in collaborative political projects with others (see also Vintges 2001, Raaen 2011). Ethical subjects who take care of themselves and use their freedom appropriately are good not only to themselves but also to others. In Greek political thought, "the rationality of governing others is the same as the rationality of governing oneself" (Foucault 1984b, 110, my translation). Being in a position of power, the ethical subject who is successful in self-government and self-care has the potential to extend this success to the act of governing others. "It is the power over oneself that will regulate the power over others" (2001d/1984, 1535, my translation). Law is not enough; the governor is more important. Plutarch affirms, as reported by Foucault, that

> one cannot govern if one is not self-governed. But who, then, governs the governor? The law does, of course. However, the law must not be understood as the written law, but rather as reason, the *logos*, which lives in the soul of the governor and must never abandon them.
> (Foucault 1984b, 110, my translation)

The governor needs self-care, soul guidance and vigilance. Self-government and personal *ethos* are, thus, a crucial ethical nucleus that guarantees responsible stances regarding socio-political and civic issues (ibid., 116).

The ethical constitution of the self continued under the Christian tradition, according to Foucault, albeit with a radical conceptual and practical twist. In Christianity, subjection has taken the form of renunciation of the self – as a way of seeking the gratitude of the divine power. The 'Cartesian moment,' which upheld *evidence* as a nucleus for any philosophical thought, and thus, requalified *gnôthi seauton* (know oneself)] and disqualified *epimeleia heautou* (self-care) constitutes a moment of rupture with *morality* as a philosophical/knowledge form, and the moment it began to be conflated with mere spirituality (Foucault 2001a/1982)[3]. Since Descartes, scientific rationality, based on evidence, had become the only form of knowledge/philosophy. But with Emmanuel Kant, the concept of self-constitution was revived as part of knowledge. Foucault gives Kant the merit of reviving self-constitution as an ethical/philosophical attitude, by reconciling the ethical subject and the subject of knowledge (the former disqualified by Descartes) (Foucault 2001b/1983, 1230). Kant's 'emancipatory' project of Enlightenment (Aufklärung) moves people from a 'minority status' to a 'majority status,' i.e., from the state of 'obey, don't reason' to 'obey, and you can reason as much as you want' (Foucault 2001c/1984, 1383–1386). And in the move to a 'majority status,' individuals emancipate themselves from guardianship in order to constitute themselves. Foucault seems to credit Kant for the fact that he "reorders our very ways of thinking about things" (Allen 2003, 188). This does not mean, however, that he embraces Kant's modernist project, including his 'majority status' idea. Foucault does not adhere to Kant's universalist reason. Of course, the claim that morality consists of abiding by the 'Categorical Imperative' – the supreme universal principle and *a priori* standard of rational morality, which is compatible with rational beings' thinking (Kant 1997/1788) – would not convince the postmodern Foucault. Foucault writes: "the critical question, today, must be turned into a positive question: in what is given to us as universal, necessary, mandatory, what is the share of what is singular, contingent and subject to arbitrary constraints" (Foucault 2001c/1984, 1393, my translation).

Foucault's distance from the modern notion of self-constitution is not surprising to his readers[4]. Foucault had vehemently and lengthily argued against the modern constitution of the self reinforced through disciplinary modes of subjectivation and discourse (see for example, Foucault 1971, 1975). Interestingly, the shock that results from the purportedly paradoxical views in Foucault's thought regarding the two modes of subjectivation (i.e., ancient and modern) is alleviated once one discerns the nuances between them. To be concise, ancient self-constitution is self-reflexive, autonomous from power and carried out for its own sake, whereas its modern form reflects the power wish and its discursive practices. Modern subjectivation of individuals is rather the product of the technologies of power and may seek what Ziguras (2004, 128) calls "the professional-institutional level of social integration."

Although Foucault refrains from prescribing ancient ethics as a wholesale solution to all modernity's moral ills when he claims to stand outside the "histoire des solutions" [history of solutions] (Foucault 2001b/1983, 1205), he nevertheless argues that the moral issues that modern societies face are strikingly similar to those faced by ancient societies. Like the Greeks, many of us, nowadays, do not believe that morality should be imposed by coercive systems that interfere with personal beliefs and private lives, Foucault explains. We want a new morality but are unable to find one that is not founded in modern rationality. "Recent liberation movements suffer from not finding a principle on which to base the elaboration of a new morality," writes Foucault (2001b/1983, 1205, my translation). In view of this impasse, some of Foucault's followers and other postmodern perspectives on ethics, in general, plead for a return to ancient ethics or at least inspiration from them (see, for example, Meijl 2000; Kelemen and Peltonen 2001; Vintges 2001; MacIntyre 2007/1981, 1988; Annas 2006; Luxon 2008; Raaen 2011, Wong 2013). And this is the perspective that the current project espouses.

Similarly to Bauman, Foucault evokes ethics that do not reside in modernity. But unlike Bauman's *morality* that is quite a primitive instinct and pre-social, Foucault's *ethics* reside in ancient traditions and are embedded in society. In addition, the former highlights the morality of otherness assuming that the primitive moral self is able to cater to it, whereas Foucault underscores ethics of the self as a pre-condition for ethics of otherness. Bauman's aim is the emancipation from ethical codes of modernity and the return to the morality of proximity, and of distance, adapted to the digital era, while Foucault stresses the fact that the ethical subject is freely self-constituted through *akêsis*, i.e., labour on the self to transform, correct and purify it. I argue that this self-care and work on the self of Foucault is what is missing in the morality of Bauman, who takes it for granted that morality is out there in everyone and just needs to be revived. As Kelemen and Peltonen (2001, 161) argue, "the individual cannot count on moral

230 Alternative Ethics

impulses, since our experiences are often already shaped by institutional discourses such as pedagogy or psychology." The merit of Foucault's notion of self-care over Bauman's moral self is that it is socially embedded, and co-habitable with institutions – an insurmountable modern phenomenon. Also, while Bauman stresses the ambivalence of moral decisions, which is very characteristic of translation practice, Foucault underlines preparation for this ambivalence, i.e., self-formation/training to face it. Besides, Foucault's philosophy – unlike Bauman who is radical in his rejection of codes – allows some space for codes on the condition that they be stripped of their judicial trappings – an important factor for those who seek judicial and gradual change, as is the case of the current project.

In this project, Foucault's self-care complements Bauman's critical theory that I used to analyze the role of the translator's morality in these codes. I draw on Foucault's framework to propose alternative ethics to the current translator codes of ethics. I propose ethical undertakings that may enhance the translator's self-constitution in socio-institutional spheres. Foucault's self-care is a powerful concept as it may not only enhance the translator's ethics but also their capital.

Following Foucault, only the institutions that support the *culture of the self* are fit to enhance self-care ethics. That is why there is a pressing need to foster this culture in the institutions concerned with translation if we want to promote the translator's self-care. This culture should be enhanced in the educational institution, the translator organization and TS. Most importantly, it should include a critical pedagogical approach that can put into practice self-care ethics. In the meantime, non-coercive guiding charters for ethics that do not impede self-care ethics can still exist within this framework of the culture of the self.

Notes

1 At this stage, it is worth highlighting some differences between Foucault's 'morality/moral codes' and 'ethics,' on the one hand, and Bauman's understanding of '(codes of) ethics' and 'morality,' on the other hand. 'Morality' is a general term in Foucault's thought that includes the three components mentioned above. Moral codes, one of these components, do not necessarily refer to coerced regulations, while (code of) ethics, in Bauman's analysis, refer to universalized rules that are enforced through guarding/legislative institutions. On the other hand, ethics in Foucault's analysis is close to Bauman's morality, but with some differences. Bauman's morality is pre-social and impulsive (i.e., within us) whereas Foucault's ethics refer to the ethical constitution of the self. I use the same respective terminology of the two thinkers when referring to their respective frameworks. However, in my general discussions, I use the terms 'moral' and 'ethical' interchangeably to refer to personal ethics or

autonomous personal responses, and 'codes of ethics' to refer to legislated/imposed ethics.
2 For example, Ella Myers (2008) argues that care for the self as a strategy to reshuffle power relations in order to make them more equitable is limited, and that self-care further fosters individualism. Amy Allen (2004) refutes Foucault's claim that the relationship with oneself is ontologically prior to relationships with others. Nancy Fraser (1994) and Charles Taylor (1989, 1991) take Foucault for a moral nihilist.
3 It is noteworthy, however, that in ancient traditions, there was no exclusionary opposition between self-knowledge and self-care. As Gros explains this, "the opposition between self-care and self-knowledge is not exclusive; rather, it is a question of establishing relations of subordination and structures of predominance" (Gros 2002, 235, my translation).
4 It is noteworthy that this late reading of Kant and admiration for his project perplexed many. Habermas (1994), for example, accused Foucault of contradiction in his thought or of having two Kants. Allen rather argues that "Foucault does not reject the Kantian critical framework; instead, he takes it up in a radically *transformative* way" (Allen 2003, 190, italics added).

11 Alternative Ethics in Institutions

11.1 Enhancing the Culture of the Self in Translation Studies, Translation Education and the Translation Occupation

Following Foucault (1984b), self-care is not a solitary endeavour but a labour on the self within society and, often times, within institutions. The translator can work on the self in their institutions, namely the educational institution and the self-governing institution, i.e., the association. However, these institutions need to be flexible enough to accommodate such self-transformative work. The translator's ethical self-constitution develops by abandoning the coerciveness of institutionalized rules and enhancing the *culture of the self* in TS, translator education and the translation occupation.

11.1.1 Enhancing the Culture of the Self in Translation Studies

Baker and Maier (2011b, 7) argue that "[t]he literature on ethics, like most of the literature on translation and interpreting, has traditionally assumed that translators and interpreters are primarily responsible to their clients, or the author of the source text in the case of literary translation in particular." Things have, however, considerably changed since the cultural turn and the hermeneutic writings, as reported in Part I. More attention has been drawn to Otherness, social responsibility, as well as power issues in translation. The recent orientation in TS seems to be influenced by the emphasis put by some contemporary ethicists on ethics of Otherness, as a way to distance themselves from ancient ethics that may be perceived as egocentric practices. Regarded as an unequivocal ethical stance that needs to be fostered in TS, this move has, thus, rarely been questioned. I argue that TS literature about ethics has, however, overemphasized Otherness and social responsibility at the expense of the translator's *self-empowerment*. It has ignored the fact that the neglected and subjugated *self* may be unable to care for the *Other* gratuitously. I believe that responsibility toward otherness and social responsibility are not principles that translators need to be reminded of outside the realm of self-care. Care for the self has ontological precedence over care for the others. Self-care is a precondition for any intellectual, ethical or political emancipation and is itself a political and ethical act as it liberates the self from subjectivation by an external power. As Foucault (2001d/1984, 1533) tells us, self-care in ancient ethics is the nucleus of all ethics, including ethics toward otherness. "For the Greeks, it is not because it involves care for others that it is ethical. Self-care is ethical in itself; but it involves complex relationships with others, insofar as this ethos of freedom is also a way of caring for others" (ibid., my translation).

This book challenges the dominant TS discourse about, and approaches to, ethics. While my aims are not very different from the scholars who advocate ethics of otherness and social responsibility, our means are quite different. My current project aims at reorienting ethics of otherness to have self-care as its nucleus and point of departure. I believe that ethics of otherness and social responsibility has made a wrong departure and pointed in the wrong direction as it has neglected the subject, the source of the care that might be expended toward others. These approaches have overlooked the fact that the translator does not have enough power to impose their ethical choices and, therefore care for others. In order to care for others, one needs to care about oneself, for *nemo dat quod non habet*. A disempowered translator, who does not take care of themself, may never know how or why to care for others. A translator cannot take virtuous actions toward others if they are not themselves virtuous and empowered. Responsibility for others requires a reflective, autonomous and empowered translator, who is equipped with personalized ethical tools that allow them to deal with this complex and ambivalent task. Thus, my project calls for a return to the ethics of the *self* in TS.

Some recent publications have started to tackle the question of prioritizing the self from financial or mental perspectives, i.e., how the translator/interpreter needs to be financially secure and mentally stress-free to exercise their agency. Costa et al.'s (2020) paper, for instance, is one of the rare publications in the field of interpreting that posits that self-care is an ethical responsibility for interpreters working in sensitive contexts. The article argues that interpreters working in challenging situations, such as refugee detention centres, need support and self-care to alleviate stress and trauma, with the aim "to keep oneself fit and well prepared to perform interpreting assignments to the highest standards" (2020, 36). Lambert (2023), in brief remarks, takes a relatively different stance, as he advances "enlightened egoism" that is "made up of a complex network of competing elements that require careful and sensitive appraisal, as opposed to being understood as a one-dimensional pursuit of immediate, selfish goals" (165–166). By this, Lambert mostly emphasizes the overlap between the interests of the self and the other, therefore, getting closer to Pym's ideal of 'cooperation.' The idea of self-care in Lambert's work and in that of Costa et al. is encouraging but needs to be taken further than the issues associated with the working conditions and wellbeing of translators/interpreters.

TS needs to support the art of critical self-reflection and the work on the self that allow a translator/interpreter to find their path autonomously and without a supreme guide. Foucault's notion of *epimeleia heautou*, employed in this work – and its more global aims, far from calls for egoism or self-interest – is a call for an ethical empowerment that allows the translator to practise virtuous actions toward others. The ultimate aim of this self-empowerment is to afford some space for others from within the (cultural) self (see Iser 1995).

11.1.2 Enhancing the Culture of the Self in Translation Education

As discussed in Part II, the translator's embodied cultural capital is the main supply for their symbolic capital. But the translator's cultural capital does not involve only technical skills and theoretical knowledge but includes ethical enhancement as well. Translation is not a simple technical endeavour but a moral task, *par excellence* (Baker and Maier 2011b, Goodwin 2010, Baker 2018/1992). "[E]thics is not extrinsic to translation (and interpreting), an activity that in itself is intrinsically ethical" (Baker and Maier 2011b, 3). Most importantly, the very conceptualization of *translation* is an ethical task, and so are the issuing practices from this conceptualization. Translator/translation ethics, thus, should be at the heart of the translator's education and, therefore, an important component of their embodied cultural capital.

As translation education is supposedly linked to TS research, ethics of otherness and social responsibility would be prevalent in translation classrooms since the cultural turn. However, ethics have had a minor position within translation curricula in many education institutions around the world (Baker and Maier 2011b, Drugan and Megone 2011, Drugan 2017). The traditional ethos of *neutrality* and *fidelity* are still prevalent in today's classrooms in conformity with the business-oriented codes of ethics. Unfortunately, many university educators still instruct their students to follow 'professional' codes of ethics unquestioningly (Baker and Maier 2011b). Translation didactics has been working to respond to the 'practical' demands of the market and employers, thus often neglecting research about ethics in TS itself. They have been more market-centred than discipline-centred. Hence, instead of educating student-translators on how to improve their conditions, their work and their societies, and empowering them ethically (which many TS scholars advocate), some translation classrooms seem to be guided by the market's internal logic, as I explained in Part II. The question, therefore, is: how ethical and how proactive is a pedagogy influenced by market orientations rather than larger social and ethical considerations?

> [I]f the goals are set by the employers and officials alone, and academics react only to the existing (technology- and economy-driven) demands set by the field, then the training institution fails in its most fundamental task of educating new generations to not only adapt to existing conditions, but also to research, develop and improve them.
> (Koskinen 2012, 7)

Of course, universities cannot be completely isolated from the translation market realities. However, they need to remain immune to external impositions that seek corporate profit against ethical considerations, social/planetary concerns or the dignity of translators (see Kearns 2008).

Against this backdrop, many TS scholars have recently called for the integration of ethics into translation curricula. The special issue of *Ethics* in *Interpreter & Translator Training* (2011) is a case in point. The guest editors call on educators

> to engage far more directly and explicitly with the issue of ethics and build it into the curriculum. They need to offer trainee translators and interpreters the conceptual means to reflect on various issues and situations that they may be confronted with in professional life, and which they may find morally taxing, without having to fall back unthinkingly on rigid, abstract codes of practice.
> (Baker and Maier 2011b, 3)

Koskinen (2012) responded to this call for a more engaged classroom by proposing a framework of critical pedagogy that counters the marketization and commodification of education. Another interesting call comes from Moorkens and Rocchi (2021, 328) who argue that "ethical training for translators and the need for transformative change in the way that ethics is perceived across this industry" is needed. Ethical training should "provide translators with the intellectual tools to understand how developing the virtues of a good translator will also contribute to their own personal flourishing" (ibid.). While these calls and projects are encouraging, I believe the culture of the self has to be further emphasized in translation pedagogy – knowing that it has long been adopted by many education theorists (see for example, Ball 1990, Marshall 1996, Popkewitz and Brennan 1998, Olssen 1999, Raaen 2011). I argue that Foucault's notion of self-care present an opportunity to translation scholars, educators and translators to help concretize the ambitious project of ethical and cultural empowerment that many TS scholars have sought.

Such a self-based pedagogy should not only seek to train competent practitioners but also to educate critical and empowered translators. Drawing on Freire (1998), Koskinen rightly argues that "education is fundamentally a matter of the formation of the self and of creating a historical and ethical understanding of both society and our own position(s) within it" (Koskinen 2012, 8). Translation pedagogy that is centred on the self should aim to transform the translator and make them able to think critically and to examine all assumptions they adhere to unknowingly or uncritically, such as the teachings of codes of ethics of associations – which are found to unethically disempower their capital and neutralize their moral self.

11.1.3 Enhancing the Culture of the Self in the Translation Occupation

As shown in Part II, translator organizations instruct members to follow codes of ethics unconditionally, and, thus, neutralize the personal responsibility of the translator. At best, they admit their incompleteness (e.g., AUSIT) and/or organize workshops/training sessions to explain their rules (e.g., l'Ordre des traducteurs, terminologues et interprètes agréés du Québec [Québec Certified Translators, Terminologists and Interpreters Association] (OTTIAQ)[1]). At worst, they adopt disciplinary measures in order to enforce them. Yet, a virtuous translator takes responsibility for their personal decisions and choices, independently of codified ethics, which are mainly influenced by employers or clients' aspirations and suggestions. Thus, the precondition for the promotion of the culture of the self in the translation occupation is the elimination of the disciplinary adjudications related to codes of ethics. "Freedom is the ontological condition of ethics," as we learn from Foucault (2001d/1984, 1531, my translation). The dismantling of disciplinary committees and coercive measures of associations is the first step for the translator to (re)gain their *ethical sovereignty and autonomy*[2]. This is because the current codes of ethics, established as part of the process of professionalization – which supposedly implies self-control of the translation occupation – not only ignore the complexity of the ethical encounters but also negatively affect the translator's symbolic recognition.

This culture of the self needs to be reflected not only in documents revolving around ethics but also in all translators' internal discourses and actions. Translator associations need to be transformed into a space that promotes self-care discourse and self-enhancement actions. This includes the promotion of self-worth through raising the translator's awareness about the real value of their practice. The organizations' main mission should consist of making its members take pride in being translators and in belonging to the network. Members also need to find associations as a space where they intensify social networking with equal peers in order to exchange experience and information and learn from one another. Translator organizations need to be a space for debate and interaction, rather than a body of imposition/coercion. Associations also need to encourage forum platforms, workshops, seminars and webinars that not only debate ethical issues *per se* but also reflect on the different linguistic, cultural, political, social and economic issues (in)directly related to the translation practice. Translators in these learning encounters should be given a voice to express themselves freely among peers, reflect about themselves and build their own personal learning path, following their learning style, needs and preferences.

To pave the way for self-care ethics, institutions (both formal educational institutions and associations of translators) need to be reformed and transformed in a way to advocate critical debate and foster symmetrical active exchange (rather than impose knowledge). In other words, these institutions need to be at the *service* of self-care. Morality is a personal matter and a personal constitution. "Each one is the architect of their own morality," as Seneca put it (Foucault 1984b, 115, my translation). These institutions' roles need to be understood as facilitating and enhancing self-learning and critical thinking rather than transferring/transmitting information or imposing rules. The translator should be the active one who selects and adapts the elements that are beneficial for their self-constitution. Most importantly, translator organizations and educational institutions need to embrace plurality as an inherent aspect of translation and accept *translation* as an open concept and translators as emancipated active agents.

That said, fostering the culture of the self in these institutions may not be without hurdles. Some translators themselves may resist engaging in promoting such change. We know that the pressures from the powerful agents are enormous, and some translators may not be (intellectually/ethically) ready to take on the challenge of resisting those external impositions. Likewise, not all educators endorse this culture that seeks the empowerment of the translator in translation programs. We know that not all scholars – who are part of the field of power – align with translators, as discussed in Part II. However, there are many other influential TS scholars who support the translator's recognition and ethical autonomy, as discussed earlier in the book. The challenge is to recruit more of these TS scholars/educators who assume "ethical positions that are not indebted to or controlled by special interests" (Tymoczko 2009, 418), and who are able to introduce these translator-centered ethics not only in their writings

238 *Alternative Ethics*

but also in their classrooms. There remain two important questions: what is the fate of codes of ethics in such a culture of the self within translator associations? and what pedagogical approach is best suited to apply self-care ethics within educational institutions? These are the questions I try to answer in what remains of this book.

11.2 An Alternative Charter *for* Ethics

In postmodern thought, as in ancient ethics, there is a deep conviction that "a foolproof, non-ambivalent, universal and objectively founded ethical code will never be found," as Meijl (2000, 70) rightly argues in his account of codes of ethics of anthropological associations (see a similar account of 'professional' communication codes of ethics by Holtzhausen 2015). Thus, a radical approach would seek to abolish such codes as their defects are inherent in their nature, and, therefore, unsurmountable through reviews and updates. I share the conviction that codes can never be perfect. However, as someone who has a modest ambition and seeks incremental change, I rather seek to strip codes of their judicial robes as well as make a deep change in their nature/approach and discursive tone, as a first step in the process of boosting postmodern subjective ethics. Thus, I believe that a charter for non-coercive ethics, similar to those in Foucault's account[3], is desirable – although not necessary for all translators. It can be a judicious transition from heteronomous absolutist codification to postmodern relativism. Such a charter needs, however, to be at the service of the culture of the self and compatible with its framework. The translator needs to be autonomous in determining the *ethical substance* and the contingent ethical responses to the ethical principles highlighted. This is what Foucault (1984a, 33) calls "morality of behaviours."[4]

In what follows, I propose a draft of a charter for ethics, which does not claim to be exhaustive or perfect. It is an open and lateral platform, a trigger for symmetrical dialogue and debate among translators. It may be a transitional document that could lead to another more advanced platform coming from translators themselves. This charter, I argue, is viable and probably desirable within the culture of the self, for two main reasons. First, one of the guiding principles of this charter is an inclusive definition of *translation* as a complex cluster concept and a self-concept of the translator as an autonomous *creator* of materials that are related to other materials, beyond the traditional roles assigned to them as a mere transferor of others' (authors') meanings. Second, the draft stresses the translator's self-care, and by extension, seeks to expand ethical responsibility beyond responsibility to those who are able to pay for it or those who have the power to seize it. The current draft seeks to "stretch" the translator's ethical imagination to go beyond catering only to those within sight (see Bauman 1993), especially in today's "translation age" – as Cronin (2012) has termed it – in which translation has become ubiquitous. Thus, what is generally neglected in codes of ethics – the acting agent (i.e., the translator), their dignity and rights, as well as the absent and invisible others – is compensated for in this proposed draft. Ultimately, the proposed draft will be one component of a global approach to the culture of the self that seeks to enhance the translator's capital (by assuring the respect of their economic rights, their dignity, their autonomy and their value as cultural creators and disseminators of knowledge), and ethical agency.

In sum, the interpersonal aspects of the charter seek to foster more balanced relations between all agents. Its guidelines apply to three circles: the circle of *translators* themselves, the circle of the *other agents* directly involved in translation, and the *world-wide* circle, with self-care being, of course, the nucleus of responsibility to all circles. Below is the proposed draft of a translator's charter for ethics.

The Translator's Charter for *Ethics*

Preamble

Because *translation* is a complex activity, very diverse practices may fall under the umbrella term 'translation.' It follows that ethical responsibility requires awareness of the context, the situation, the text type and the performative/discursive dimensions, outcomes, and repercussions of the translated text, among other factors, on the immediate receivers as well as the (in)directly impacted others in the present and the future. The proposed charter consists of general guidelines rather than ready-to-implement responses to ethical matters. Translators use their ethical judgment in responding to diverse ethical dilemmas contingently.

This charter revolves around the ethics of *responsibility* to three circles within the realm of translation ethics: 1) the circle of the translators themselves, their relation to themselves, their work and their colleagues; 2) the circle of the other agents directly involved in translation transactions, mainly clients, employers and authors; 3) the circle of the wider society and planet that may be impacted by the disseminated discourse through translation. It is noteworthy that some statements can apply to more than one circle or to all three circles at once.

The Overarching Societal and Planetary Circle

Translators undertake their work *responsibly* and thoroughly.

240 *Alternative Ethics*

1. Translators are gratuitously responsible agents and autonomous experts in their exercise of judgement during diverse translation practices and situations. (Ethical/cultural/symbolic capital)
2. Translators are aware of the complexity and inherent ambivalence of ethical issues in texts, paratexts, and beyond (in interpersonal relations). (Ethical imagination)
3. Translators are aware of the far-reaching consequences of their decisions and choices for others (present and future generations, humans and non-humans). (Ethical imagination)
4. Translators are aware of cultural differences and sensitivities, and adopt an *inclusive*, rather than an appropriating, or excluding, mindset. (Ethical/cultural empowerment)

The Circle of Translators

1. Translators practise and commit to self-care, excellence and well-being. (Cultural/ethical/mental empowerment)
2. Translators engage in a life-long learning process. They continuously and reflectively question their inherited assumptions/presuppositions in order to transform and purify themselves. (Cultural/ethical empowerment)
3. Translators engage in knowledge/expertise sharing with their colleagues. (Cultural/social capital)
4. Translators are respectful, courteous and supportive of their colleagues. (Social/ethical empowerment)
5. Translators claim due recognition and respect both symbolically and economically. (Cultural/economic/symbolic capital)

   - Translators do not accept work that is demeaning to them as creative cultural producers.
   - Translators do not accept low fees for their work.
   - Translators do an important work of post-editing and revision of MT and TM outputs, which include important intellectual/ethical decisions, and therefore do not accept low fees for 'only the translated words.' (Economic/symbolic capital)
   - Translators do not accept work that is unreasonable in terms of deadline or working conditions. (Cultural/symbolic capital)
   - Translators do not accept any changes made to their translations without their approval. (Symbolic capital)
   - Translators do not accept added paratexts without their approval. (Symbolic capital)

- Translators are creators of cultural products and should have the same recognition as their counterparts in the field of cultural production.
- Translators strive for all the same advantages granted to cultural producers, mainly, all social insurance/benefit schemes.
- Translators are entitled to remuneration for any subsequent use/success of their translations.

6. Translators do not compromise their ethical judgements and do not adopt any agents' (un)ethical orientations. (Ethical/symbolic empowerment)
7. Translators are aware of the advantages, limitations and undesirable consequences of Computer Aided Translation (CAT) or AI tools, and, therefore, use them judiciously and autonomously. (Ethical/cultural empowerment)

The Circle of the Other Business Agents

1. Translators foster mutually respectful relations with all agents involved in translation. Each agent has rights and responsibilities toward the other agents. (Symbolic empowerment)
2. Translators advise their clients/employers/authors about the appropriate methods to carry out tasks at hand. (Cultural/symbolic capital)
3. Translators strive to raise public awareness (including their clients'/employers') to the complexity/specificities of their work. (Symbolic recognition)
4. Translators act with integrity, honesty, transparency and respect with all agents. (Ethical empowerment)
5. Translators keep information confidential unless it contains dangerous/unethical components that may harm others or the planet. This includes the consensual use of Machine Translation for protected/classified information. (Ethical imagination)
6. **Quality**: quality is a relative standard. Standards differ depending on the type of translation, the purpose, function and context of the translated text. The translator strives to achieve the best quality possible required for every specific assignment. (Cultural empowerment)
7. Translators do not accept work that is beyond their competence. (Ethical empowerment)

This draft of a charter allows the translator autonomy in their ethical decisions and their work. It frees the translator from the coercive rules that restrain their responsibility and limit it to some agents at the expense of others, including themselves. On the other hand, this charter leaves the

242 *Alternative Ethics*

translator unarmed with any heteronomous rules in facing the frustration and ambivalence of moral decisions (see Bauman 1993). It puts on them the burden of relying on their own judgment.

This input may sound too general for those who seek exact and easy answers to specific issues. But every ethical situation is unique, and, therefore, escapes any *a priori* prescriptions. A charter like this rather aims at encouraging translators to be reflective and critical when facing charged ethical dilemmas. Thus, this document or any similar one requires empowered translators, or translators in the process of being empowered, who are able to accommodate, adapt and implement their general principles contingently. The current document will remain void unless it is accompanied with work on the self and a prevalent culture of the self within institutions related to translation/translators. As we learned from Foucault, such a charter could be only one dimension of morality. And it could be meaningful only if it is accompanied by the nucleus of morality, i.e., self-care. Thus, self-care needs to be fostered in educational institutions as well as translators' representative bodies in order to self-empower translators not only ethically but also culturally and symbolically. This is what I turn to in the next chapter where I propose Transformative Learning (TL) theory, which I believe complements ethical self-constitution and helps implement it at the practical level in translation classrooms.

Notes

1 https://ottiaq.org/en/future-member/training-on-ethics-professional-conduct-and-professional-practice (Accessed on December 30, 2020).
2 For example, the American Anthropological Association, engaged in a practice close to translation, has taken a step forward by eliminating the adjudication processes and adopting a more education-centred code of ethics in its version published in *Anthropology Newsletter* of March 1998 (Meijl 2000). This can be an experience for translator associations to look into.
3 It is worth reminding readers that non-coercive codes in ancient ethics constituted one of the dimensions of morality, as reported by Foucault (1984a).
4 It is worth reminding readers that this is a second level of morality, in Foucault's account. And the third and most important dimension of the translator's morality is 'self-care,' which will be discussed in the last chapter.

12 Transformative Learning Theory for Adult Education in the Service of Ethics of Self-Care

Self-care is not an abstract attitude but a range of activities and tasks that involve practical life-long *labour* on the self. Foucault reports on a myriad of activities that ancient people undertook as part of their self-constitution (1984b). However, he does not provide a precise or practical methodological path on how to undertake them and, thus, achieve the best self-subjectivation outcomes in modern institutions – which may be resistant to such a very participant-centred orientation. Thus, Foucault's remarks about practical activities in ancient traditions that enhance the self are not ready-to-implement exercises in modern times/institutions. The procedural question of *how* this self-constitution and self-care and the activities related to them can be pedagogically framed, approached, instantiated and implemented in tangible forms in today's institutions is not, of course, Foucault's focus. This is quite understandable since Foucault was rather descriptive and did not seek to propose – or at least did not admit proposing these ancient ethical endeavours as an answer to modern ethical issues.

For this self-care work to be viable, it needs to be embodied pedagogically through an approach(es) that is/are conceptually consistent with its essence and aims, and applicable in modern institutions. For this purpose, I resort to Transformative Learning (TL) theory for adult education, which, I believe, complements Foucault's work on ethical self-constitution, and is conceptually compatible with it. It complements it in the sense that it can frame it pedagogically and translate it into a critical approach in today's educational institutions, as I demonstrate shortly. But first, let me present the main core elements and fundamental components of transformative theory as presented by Jack Mezirow and enriched later by his followers and critics.

12.1 Transformative Learning and Ethical Growth

Transformative Learning (TL) for adult education was first introduced by Jack Mezirow in the late 1970s. His theory has been critiqued, taken up and developed over the years by himself and many other researchers in the field of adult education. Mezirow defines transformative learning as

> the process by which we transform our taken-for-granted frames of reference (meaning perspectives, habits of mind, mind-sets) to make them more inclusive, discriminating, open, emotionally capable of change, and *reflective* so that they may generate beliefs and opinions that will prove more true or justified to guide action. Transformative learning involves participation in constructive *discourse* to use the experience of others to assess *reasons* justifying these assumptions, and making an action decision based on the resulting insight.
> (Mezirow 2000, 7–8, italics added)

Central to Mezirow's TL is critical reflection on one's experience as well as dialogue with others – the two aspects mostly stressed in self-care ethics. These core components lead to the transformation of one's frames of reference. "It is the revision of a frame of reference in concert with reflection on experience that is addressed by the theory of perspective transformation – a paradigmatic shift" (Taylor 2008, 5). This may happen following a major triggering event, a "disorienting dilemma," in Mezirow's (2000) terminology, or it may happen slowly and incrementally (Taylor 2008). Brock (2015) recently advanced a more straightforward definition of TL: "transformative learning is when a learner is struck by a new concept or way of thinking and then follows through to make a life change" (2015, 234).

According to TL theory, adults' learning process consists of critically reflecting on, and understanding, the origin of one's experience and its contextual frames. It is about understanding one's values and beliefs in relation with their historical, cultural and social underpinnings. Transformation theory asserts that making meaning includes "becoming critically aware of one's own tacit assumptions and expectations and those of others and assessing their relevance for making an interpretation" (Mezirow 2000, 4). It is about putting this experience under permanent "critical scrutiny," according to Edward Taylor (2008, 6). This involves questioning "instrumental learning" and challenging one's assumptions by exposing them to dialogue with others, or what Mezirow (2000) calls "rational discourse" – following Habermas's thought. This dialogue is twofold. It is a dialogue with the self and with the others (Taylor 2009, 9). The ultimate aim is to arrive at a better-informed judgment (ibid., 10). This involves not only a "critical reflection on the validity of [one's] assumptions or premises" (ibid., 7), and awareness of the existence of more than one perspective, but also openness to newer perspectives and categories. This is what Mezirow calls "mindfulness," as opposed to "mindlessness," which unreflectively "involves relying on past forms of action or previously established distinctions and categories" (ibid.). In one word, TL is a reflection about what made us think the way we think – a meta-reflection. Adults' reflections may lead them to discover that their old assumptions are not justifiable or valid.

Individual experience, critical reflection and dialogue as interdependent core elements of Mezirow's initial theorizing have been supplemented by three other elements, which are no less important. These are holistic orientation, awareness of context and authentic practice (Taylor 2009). Holistic orientation tries to overcome Mezirow's view that regards critical reflection as a purely rational process, neglecting other learning dimensions, such as the affective and the relational, which also trigger reflection about held assumptions (ibid.).

Awareness of context implies that contextual, personal and background factors (prior histories and experiences, and (socio)cultural differences) all play a crucial role in the transformative process and the readiness for transformation, as well as the immediacy of responding to a triggering event that may lead to *a perspective transformation*. The same triggering events for the same people may not all lead to (the same) perspective transformation. A simple lecture can lead to a transformation for some students, while only a remarkable or shocking incident may do so for others.

The last core element in transformative learning is *authentic relationships*. Establishing positive and productive relations of trust and respect with the educator and peers is more likely to enhance the transformative process, as learners may perceive transformation as "threatening and an emotionally charged experience" (ibid., 13). Healthy and genuine relationships ensure that emotions and feelings can be safely managed during the transformative process (Taylor 2000, 308).

Besides enriching Mezirow's original theory by including more factors that affect perspective transformation, later input to this theory has emphasized the social repercussions of transformative learning, beyond the individual epistemic transformation. The newer approaches to transformative theory consider that transformation is not only an epistemic shift but a "multifaceted phenomenon" that includes an inextricable link between individual transformation and social change (Hoggan 2016, 66). "Critical reflection in this orientation is more about *ideological critique*, where learners develop an *awareness of power and greater agency* (political consciousness) to *transform society and their own reality*" (Taylor 2009, 5, italics added).

This social perspective includes different views that underline the cultural and social context of transformation and its social aims. The most influential and encompassing of larger contextual factors are the *emancipatory*

246 *Alternative Ethics*

and the *planetary* perspectives (see Taylor 2008 for a full review of the different approaches). According to Taylor, the *emancipatory* view is

> a theory of existence that views people as subjects, not objects, who are constantly reflecting and acting on the transformation of their world so it can become a more equitable place for all to live. Its goal is social transformation by demythicizing reality, where the oppressed develop a critical consciousness (that is, conscientization).
>
> (Taylor 2008, 8)

Brookfield (2000, 2009), one of the proponents of conceptualizing "critical reflection" in transformative learning from a *critical theory* perspective, argues that the primary goal of transformative learning is to counter hegemonic discourses and practices. The aim is to question the apparent "commonsense wisdom," which is in fact driven by hegemonic assumptions (Brookfield 2000, 137). "The subtlety of hegemony is that over time it becomes deeply embedded, part of the cultural air we breathe [...] if there is a conspiracy here, it is the conspiracy of the normal" (ibid., 138). Critical reflection, in this view, centres around questioning the natural, the taken-for-granted, and the 'true' knowledge.

> It has as its specific purpose a focus on two main processes: power and hegemony. Critical reflection calls into question the power relationships that allow, or promote, one set of practices considered to be technically effective. It assumes that the minutiae of practice have embedded within them the struggles between unequal interests and groups that exist in the wider world... . For reflection to be considered critical, then, it must have as its explicit focus uncovering, and challenging, the power dynamics that frame practice. Critical reflection also focuses on uncovering and challenging hegemonic assumptions, those assumptions we embrace as being in our best interests when in fact they are working against us. It endeavors to make people aware of how practices that are viewed as natural, common sense, and desirable [...] are in fact constructed and transmitted by powerful minority interests to protect the status quo that serves these interests so well.
>
> (Brookfield 2009, 126)

The ideas of "ideology critique," for Brookfield, should be central to critical reflection and, by extension, to transformative learning (ibid., 128). This includes identifying and challenging dominant and held dear assumptions "that are actually destroying [one's] sense of well-being and serving the interests of others" (ibid. 127). Most importantly for this analysis, critical reflection, when seen from Brookfield's critical theory perspective "focuses not on how to work more effectively or productively within an existing system, but on calling the foundations and imperatives of the system itself into question, assessing their *morality*, and considering *alternatives*" (ibid., 127, italics added).

Similar to the emancipatory approach, the *planetary* approach is concerned with the larger context of transformative learning and its global aims of socio-political change. But unlike the former, the ecological change becomes central to transformative learning.

> The goal of transformative education from this perspective is reorganization of the whole system (political, social, educational). It is creating a new story from one that is dysfunctional and rooted in technical-industrial values of Western Eurocentric culture, which gives little appreciation to the natural, or to an integral worldview. This view recognizes the interconnectedness among universe, planet, natural environment, human community, and personal world. Most significant is recognizing the individual not just from a social-political dimension but also from an ecological and planetary one. Transformation is not only about how we view our human counterparts; it explores how we, as humans, relate with the physical world.
>
> (Taylor 2008, 9–10)

The planetary approach is, thus, more encompassing than the emancipatory approach as it extends the aims of transformative learning to include ecological consciousness and reflection on one's relations to the physical environment – and this reminds us of Cronin's (2017) similar ideas of interconnectedness and the stretching of the translator ethics to include the ecological dimension.

Besides the cited critiques of Mezirow's original theory for being limited to personal epistemic transformation, i.e., self-actualization, to use Taylor's term (2008, 10), his theory is also criticized for neglecting cultural and social differences in learning (ibid.). The social and emancipatory transformation perspectives, on the other hand, recognize these differences and highlight the importance of considering the learner's positionality in regard to race, class, gender, sexual orientation, and how these factors affect the process and the practice of transformative learning (ibid.).

Mezirow's epistemic self-transformation has been criticized for the same reasons as Foucault's ethical self-constitution, as they both focus more on personal enhancement than on social change or the changing of one's surroundings. In transformative learning theory, the latest developments have certainly enlightened us about broader perspectives in terms of the aims and prospects of transformative learning. However, one cannot help but recognize the merits of Mezirow's original theory. Social/planetary

248 *Alternative Ethics*

change advocated in later writings cannot happen without epistemic change and personal enhancement. As Foucault (2001d/1984, 1533) convincingly argues, self-transformation is a way of caring for one's surroundings – if not the only way. Thus, even if one posits that Mezirow's theory has its limitations, one cannot invalidate it. And I believe this is what his critics have done. They have not dismissed his work; they rather enriched it. My analysis is undertaken within this latter framework, which reconciles Mezirow's/Foucault's theories of self-transformation with social/emancipatory/planetary perspectives. Transformative learning, although self-centred, has larger social, ethical and planetary implications.

Since the aim of this work is to propose an ethical alternative based on the self-care concept to the current codes of ethics, I believe that transformative learning is a solid approach that can enhance self-care, and by implication, contribute to both the ethical and intellectual (or cultural) empowerment of the translator. I have previously pointed out that the ethical and the intellectual/cultural are generally inextricably linked. The ethical question is a question of thought in essence, although these two components – i.e., ethics and thought – do not *always* or inevitably proceed hand in hand (see Gilligan 1981). Culture is not always moral (Gilligan 1981, 139). Examples from history are numerous; the most obvious from recent history is the cultured fascists, as Carol Gilligan reminds us. To be cultured, one does not necessarily need to be moral. However, to be moral, one needs to work on one's *thought* about oneself and others in order to enhance it, purify it and transform it.

William Perry (1970, 1981) presents the cultural and ethical growth scheme, which shows the transformative process that learners can go through. According to Perry, there are four stages or "developments" in the intellectual and ethical growth of an individual. The first stage is *dualism*. In this phase, meaning for the learner is divided into "two realms – Good versus Bad, Right versus Wrong, We versus They, All that is not success is Failure, and the like. Right Answers exist *somewhere* for every problem, and authorities know them" (Perry 1981, 79, italics in original). At this stage, the learner is ready to get instrumental teaching, i.e., 'true' quantitative information from the source of knowledge (teacher), who knows what is right and what is wrong. Students and much of their environment conspire "to maintain the illusion that meaning existed 'out there,' along with rightness, power, and sound advice" (ibid., 90). Uncertainty and confusion at this stage are easily overcome by resorting to "external authority, secure in the expectation of an answer" (ibid.). The student is a mere empty vessel that needs to be filled with 'true' knowledge and clear ethical principles that need to be obeyed. They are responsible for following the Authorities' instructions and the principles the latter *know* are ethical. "Agency is experienced as 'out there' in Authority" (ibid.). Any hesitancy from these Authorities may be confusing or seen as a weakness. This stage is excessively teacher-centred (Garrison 1991, 297).

The second stage is *multiplicity*. "Diversity of opinion and values is recognized as legitimate in areas where right answers are not yet known" (Perry 1981, 90), although these opinions are seen as not very systematic or coherent ideas; they are seen as simple opinions. The learner, at this stage, recognizes that acute judgment is not appropriate. They become aware that "everyone has a right to his [sic] own opinion" (ibid., 80). In the middle of this stage, uncertainty is felt, but seen as temporary. At later phases in this stage, uncertainty is completely legitimate and "unavoidable, even in physics" (ibid., 82–83). The learner-authority relationship shifts. The teacher as the only source of knowledge is no longer a valid assumption. This later phase of 'multiplicity" is characterized by freedom from the tyranny of Authority, and the orientation toward embracing the idea of "uncertainty of a legitimized Multiplicity" (ibid., 83). Uncertainty may be emotionally threatening and tense, especially at its beginnings, as students are pulled out of their zone of "safety in dualism" (Clarkeburn et al. 2003, 445–446), and their learning is more subject-centred (Garrison 1991, 297).

The third stage is *relativism*. Knowledge itself becomes relative and diverse, a fact which keeps discussions, debates and disagreements open and ongoing (Perry 1981, 90). "Knowledge is qualitative, dependent on contexts" (Perry 1981, 90). The introduction of thinking about one's thinking (i.e., meta-thinking) and irreducible uncertainty are the main features of later phases in this stage. Learners settle with the bane of uncertainty being here to stay, as Bauman (1993) would have put it. The experienced uncertainty becomes acute and even more threatening. Learners, thus, experience "distress in relativism" (Clarkeburn et al. 2003, 446). This stage is experience-centred (Garrison 1991, 297).

The last stage in the ethical/intellectual development is *Commitment*. At this stage, "An affirmation, choice, or decision (career, values, politics, personal relationship) [is] made" and "[a]gency is experienced as within the individual" (Perry 1981, 80). This "Commitment" is distinct from unquestioned "*c*ommitment" to beliefs in certainty, in the sense that it is conscious and questioned, and also because it issues from an awareness of *relativism*, characterized by uncertainty and ambivalence (Perry 1981). In other words, learners self-transform and embrace their ethical/intellectual values following questioning and uncertainty. At this stage, the intellectual, the epistemological, and the ethical coincide. "It is in the affirmation of Commitments that the themes of epistemology, intellectual development, ethics, and identity merge" (ibid., 97). The embraced values, however, are never constant, and the research is never accomplished. It remains an open and ongoing inquiry. Perry argues that in the midst of Commitment,

250 *Alternative Ethics*

there is still pain in the orderings of priorities in respect of time, energy and action, but there are "periodic experiences of serenity and well-being in the midst of complexity and paradoxes – moments of 'getting it all together'" (ibid., 95). This stage is inquiry-centred as it involves active reasoning (Garrison 1991, 297).

Perry's scheme may be very useful for transformative learning approaches that centre on ethical self-transformation (or self-care ethics). It can be used as a guide for educators when designing the appropriate material content for the appropriate level of intellectual and ethical growth/constitution of their students. This is because "[a] misguided understanding of student meta-ethical development can obstruct successful ethics teaching efforts, because this understanding is a prerequisite for higher levels of moral reasoning skills and even moral sensitivity" (Clarkeburn et al. 2003, 444). The merit of Perry's scheme in identifying the stage of ethical development of learners for transformative learning approaches centred on ethical self-constitution lies in the conceptual convergence of the two approaches and the similarity of their overall aims. They both promote self-inquiry, are critically based, and open to and inclusive of other perspectives, in addition to having a focus on the individual's agency and their emancipatory aims, not to mention a focus on the personal ethics constitution. Now let's see how TL and Perry's scheme can help enhance self-care ethics in the translator's classroom.

12.2 The Translator's *Self-Care* through Transformative Learning in a Translation Classroom

Both self-care and TL seek *self-transformation* through *critical reflection, labour on the self* and *dialogue with others*. The core elements of self-care, like the principles of transformative learning theory, include dialogue, reciprocity and learning from others – without, however, uncritically adopting their ideas or blindly following their paths. Both approaches stress the importance of the individual's active involvement in their learning process and their responsibility for their self-enhancement. They also both reject instrumentalist approaches that prescribe specific courses of action, as well as hierarchical transmissionist methods that reinforce the learner's dependence and passivity. Both models promote participant and inquiry-centred approaches and underline self-directed learning, making it a personal craft. Every learner is unique and, therefore, every learner follows a unique learning path at a different pace, independently of the teacher/teaching (institution's) objectives/aims. The educator is a facilitator, a guide and a counsellor, rather than the source of knowledge or the model to follow. Self-care and TL foster critical reflection on oneself and permanent examination, filtering and purging of one's representations and thought. They both underline undoing bad habits and cleansing unjustified opinions and folk concepts inherited from the crowd, inculcated by some educators, parents, books or one's milieu, at large. Thus, *unlearning* is one of the main tasks of the two approaches. As far as their ultimate aims, TL and self-care converge in similar ways. They both seek the empowerment of the individual for the ultimate aim of emancipatory/social change. As for their implementation, the approaches can be implemented only in education atmospheres that advocate critical reflection and encourage symmetrical active exchange. Further, they can be implemented autonomously or in other (in)formal settings. They also can start in institutions and be continued individually as a life-long work on the self.

Self-care through TL has never been evoked in translation/interpreting pedagogy. To my knowledge, TL made an appearance in an article by Rosario Martín Ruano (2015). In this publication, the author advocates a transformative approach to the training of legal translators and interpreters in order to problematize the established normative discourses of 'equivalence' and 'neutrality,' prevalent in the field. The introduction of transformative theory in this text, however, lacks an in-depth analysis of the theoretical underpinnings and different core components that make up this theory as well as its evolution. Besides, although problematizing the issues of 'neutrality' and 'equivalence,' the author is not ready to renounce these strong social myths altogether.

> [r]elying on these critical approaches does not necessarily imply renouncing neutrality as it is socially understood, but helps to understand the very complex, many-sided and multi-level conflicting demands LITs [legal interpreters and translators] need to conciliate in order to adhere to it.
>
> (2015, 150)

The current proposal questions the very way translation is socially understood as a neutral activity. Most importantly, it stresses the role of this approach in enhancing the practitioner's self-care as presented by Foucault.

Self-care through TL can be adapted in different ways according to one's objectives, students' needs, motivations and learning styles. In what follows, I do not present static methodological procedures but a guiding framework and suggestions that can be applied in various ways at the discretion of the educators and their learners. As an educator for 14 years, I always believed the procedural elements as well as the suitable material are to be co-decided by the involved actors themselves (i.e., learners with the guidance of the educator), depending on their needs, preferences, settings and prior experiences as well as individual positionalities in regard

252 Alternative Ethics

to different issues, such as race, class, culture, environment and so forth – as advocated by the emancipatory/planetary approaches to TL.

The translator's self-care through TL requires work on the self on one primary level that includes two interrelated elements; the *translation* concept and the translator's *self-concept*. The first ethical and intellectual task of all translators and academics is to work on the transformation of the taken-for-granted definition of *translation* – reiterated in many contemporary codes of ethics and reinforced by some education institutions. Of course, this work, by definition, includes work on the transformation of the translator's self-concept. The second dimension of self-care ethics – or more precisely, the extension or result of self-care that follows from the first endeavour – is how to engage in the social dissemination of one's newly embraced ideas about oneself and one's practice, and how to apply them in one's practice to provoke social/planetary change. This is very important because the personal epistemic change may not always trigger action or social change, or even be reflected in personal practice, as argued by Mezirow's critics (Taylor 2008, Brookfield 2000, Biasin 2018). And if the epistemic change does not lead to action and social change, it remains valueless. This level of engagement involves awareness of the role of translation/translator in shaping one's world relations at the cultural, social, geopolitical, economic and ecological levels. These latter dimensions of the translated material at hand go under scrutiny by the empowered translator in order to produce an ethical translation outcome in *action*.

12.2.1 The Translator's Liberation from the Reductive Conceptualization of Translation *and from their Demeaning Self-Concept*

As we learn from Perry's (1981) scheme, cultural and ethical growth may happen simultaneously. The two processes follow the same stages and may even overlap and coincide. What may appear as non-moral educational content can make an important contribution to the ethical enhancement of the learner when exposed to other ways of seeing and doing things. Carol Gilligan (1981, 156) argues that "the educational experiences that foster moral development will be those that enhance the capacity to shift perspectives." The study of literature and history, for example, "take on central importance in moral education, not by virtue of the moral dilemmas that can be extracted from their texts, but because of their potential for extending experience through the study of other lives, both past and present" (ibid.). James Gibbs (1981), discussing the interplay between the intellectual and the moral in our neighbouring discipline of anthropology, argues that "[t]he same material that anthropologists use to foster the student's intellectual development – by speeding and guiding the shift from absolutistic thinking – and ego development [sic] also can be used to foster the student's moral development" (1981, 428). Thus, several developmental objectives can be targeted simultaneously (ibid.). This is especially true in the case of translators whose practice is both an ethical and intellectual endeavour (see Goodwin 2010, Baker and Maier 2011b, Baker 2018), as is their shaking of its dominant understanding (see Tymoczko 2007).

The main task for the translator's self-care enhancement as an autonomous ethical agent includes a critical examination of the deeply held concept of *translation* and the *self-concept* of the translator. By now, we know that the widely held concept of *translation* as an equivalent, faithful, neutral or subservient transfer of meaning (and the like) is problematic. This ethnocentric conceptualization involves the exclusion of others' concepts (cultural and historical), which is *ipso facto* unethical. At the practical level, it neutralizes the translator's moral agency, fosters their passivity and may reinforce their submission to other agents' (author, client/patron) wishes. On a more personal level, it fosters their self-neglect and undermines their self-esteem. This is not to mention the fact that it ultimately inhibits their symbolic recognition. As Tymoczko (2007, 2009) suggests, intellectually questioning this concept is, therefore, the heart of all ethical questions in translation.

The work on the self involves mainly foregrounding the multifacetedness of the translation concept (Tymoczko 2007, 2009, 2010) and the complex roles the translator plays. Tymoczko's remarks are extremely encouraging for a move in this direction. By now, we have started to accumulate at least a rough knowledge about other practices and concepts in other times and cultures (see, for instance, Trivedi 2006, Raihani 2024). And most importantly, we have clear evidence from contemporary practices that the *one* concept is fraught and that *translation* is plural. Work on the openness of *translation* to make it more inclusive will most likely reveal the ideological underpinnings of the current dominant conceptualization and help translators "develop self-reflexivity, which is essential for empowerment and the exercise of ethical agency" (Tymoczko 2009, 414). Openness to, and inclusion of, other practices and concepts can be useful to resist exclusion, hegemony and exploitation as well as to enhance the translator's intellectual, symbolic and ethical agency. These other practices "underscore and legitimate the *initiative*, *authority* and *agency* of the individual translator" (Tymoczko 2009, 410, italics added), and "suggest a new ethical positioning for translators" (ibid., 405). Translators will be able to interfere (following other models, beyond the conduit model) to counter content they judge irresponsible/unethical. Openness to other concepts broadens and multiplies their choices and chances to cater to different and complex (ethical) situations. In one word, "[t]he world's ideational reserves about *translation* can help translators to act creatively and powerfully and to become effective *intellectual* and *ethical* agents" (ibid., 417, italics

254 Alternative Ethics

added). At the practical level, the "cluster concept" of *translation* would equip the translator with diverse sources, tools and strategies to face the practical challenges of today's globalized era, which require innovation, creativity and, especially, swift and easier adaptation to constant shifts in a wide range of practices. This will, potentially, elevate translators to being authentic cultural producers, and not copiers as they are seen today.

> Many image schemas for *translation* worldwide release translators from the constraints of semantic transfer and a problematic quest for equivalence, offering them a great deal more freedom to create texts, to make meaning, *to be active cultural agents*. This freedom is particularly important at present in adapting to the challenges of globalization and the new demands currently being made on translators.
> (Tymoczko 2009, 413, italics added)

In sum, adopting the cluster concept enhances both the translator's cultural capital and their ethical agency.

Activities in translation classrooms need to revolve not only around these different conceptualizations and practices of translation but also around the historical, ideological, political, economic, religious and cultural underpinnings of the dominant concept. Learners need to know how this concept has been disseminated and passed down from one generation to another, and from one culture to another, i.e., how it has been universalized and accepted as a common sense discourse – and especially what the consequences of such a discourse have been. Learners need to know how this definition has transcended other competing definitions throughout history and, thus, became the only acceptable myth; what powers and conditions have helped its exclusive triumph. They need to know why this definition has been embraced by modern education institutions and translator associations as the only legitimate one, despite the clear evidence of its faultiness, as nowadays practices have revealed. Learners need to know who has had an interest in such a definition and such a role/identity ascribed to the translator, and thus, *who* may have worked to reinforce it as the only legitimate social discourse and practice as it still stands and *why*. They need to know who has given it the current legal status of a derivative creation, differently from other forms of literary/artistic creations – which deny dependence on previous texts – and why. Educational activities should reveal who has benefited from the dissemination of this discourse, how this discourse has been embedded in power asymmetries and how it has been used to exploit translators and harness other vulnerable and dominated users/people/countries involved in translation. They should also uncover how this concept may be leading to unethical practices nowadays. In one word, classroom activities should allow the study of this hegemonic concept from all perspectives. Like social scientists, learners-translators need to know how the contingency of the situation has been obliterated, and how this discourse around translation/translators has become the only legitimate and acceptable law/discourse.

Self-care through TL allows the learner to not only unpack all the above questions and others surrounding *translation* but to understand the frame of reference or habit of mind that is at the root of their own adoption of the dominant concept. It allows the learner to reflect on the self to reveal what there is in their surroundings, society, culture, politics, education and religion that inhibits them from seeing beyond what is presented to them about *translation* and other issues. This work on the self ultimately

> exposes the social and cultural embeddedness and taken-for-granted assumptions in which the *self* is located; explore[s] the interests served by the continuation of the *self thus positioned;* incite[s] a refusal to be positioned in this way when the interests served are those of domination and oppression; and encourage[s] *alternative* readings of the text of experience.
> (Tennant 1998, 374, italics added)

Self-care through TL allows translators to engage critically with their own past experiences to find out how their frames of thought constrain their views about *translation,* about themselves and about their world, in order to achieve "perspective transformation," and reformulate these views "to permit a more inclusive, discriminating, permeable, and integrative perspective; and of making decisions or otherwise acting upon these new understandings" (Mezirow 1990, 14). This self-questioning process ultimately allows the translator to purify themselves from (self)hegemonic views/representations and substitute the current views of oneself and one's work/world with more intellectually and ethically justified answers. Foucault argues that the ethical subject "is called upon to take themselves as an object of knowledge and a field of action, in order to transform, correct and purify themselves, and achieve salvation" (Foucault 1984b, 56, my translation). Self-care through TL processes are likely to liberate the learner-translator from the safety of 'dualism' offered in the current dominant definition of *translation* – which is reductive and exclusionist, by definition – to engage with a multiplicity of definitions, embrace relativism and, then, commit to a certain course of action for social change (see Perry 1981).

Self-liberation from the reductive concept of *translation* results in the transformation of the translator's *self-concept*. It awakens the translator to their value in society, and may, by extension, drive others to recognize them as valuable contributors to their lives. As Chesterman rightly argues,

> [t]he more we understand about translation, and the more we can transmit and develop this understanding in translator training, the more it should be possible for translators to feel masters of their craft, masters of the various conceptual and technical tools that they use. It is surely this feeling of expertise – of knowing what one is doing, how to do it, and why one is doing it in that way – that brings a sense of professional dignity and human value.
>
> (Chesterman 2005, 208)

The learner-translator, thus, moves from perceiving the self as a mechanical transferor of ready-made meanings to perceiving it as an intellectual creator who performs complex functions, including complex critical skills. Self-care ethics through TL opens the learner-translator's eyes to their mobile and constantly changing roles. They become aware that in their work, every situation is different and always anew, requiring newer decisions and, therefore, newer roles. Also, they become aware that the results of the decisions they make are never guaranteed; they are always a wait-and-see, and probably never completely satisfying. The new self-concept includes ambivalence as part and parcel of the translator's work. Most importantly, the new self-concept opens the translator's eyes to the immensity and complexity of their responsibility toward many people and species, some of which they never see, know, or even think they may impact by their everyday translation choices, or decisions to translate or not.

In sum, the new self-concept includes mainly self-awareness of the complexity of the translator's cultural capital. Besides being an ethical undertaking, self-enhancement and the perception of one's cultural capital as complex is also a first step to convincing the other agents of this complexity. True, other work is needed (like lobbying, highlighting institutionalized cultural capital as well as external support), and this self-transformation of the translator is only one first step in the process of empowerment and liberation from their dominated positioning. But it is a crucial and a prerequired step. Ultimately, the translator's new self-concept would be reflected in their everyday practice, taking unique (ethical) positions in their actual choices/decisions, and this includes, of course, social action that reflects the new perception of their practice, themselves and the world.

12.2.2 The Practical Implications of Self-Care Through TL on the Translator's Ethical/Intellectual Imagination

Self-care through TL – which may be conceived of as only an epistemic/cultural enhancement, at the outset – is in fact threefold. First, it empowers the translator's embodied cultural capital by widening their perspectives and enlarging their potentials and cultural resources, thanks to their awareness of the plurality of the concept of *translation*. Second, it liberates the translator from their demeaning self-concept as a subservient conduit of other authors' meanings – which is the nucleus of all ethics. Third, this cultural empowerment of translators is, at the same time, a liberation of otherness from cultural domination as it helps other concepts (from other cultures, times and perspectives) to re-emerge from oppression and domination/oblivion. The translator, thus, becomes the ethical and cultural agent who makes this Otherness visible, who gives it a space within the self's space, and therefore, promotes "cultural biodiversity" (Tymoczko 2007, Cronin's 2017, Hutchings 2021). As importantly, self-care through TL enables the translator to extend the boundaries of their responsibility in their practice to include their world. A self-cared translator is more susceptible to extend this care to others. Embracing the newer self-image of an important disseminator of knowledge ultimately makes the translator aware of the important social role they play in shaping their world.

We know that translation is a socially engaging work – regardless of specialization – and unlike many other occupations/'professions,' it involves many other people beyond the immediate agents involved in it. It involves people from at least two cultures, and sometimes people from different generations if the translated text survives or affects the world for a certain time to come. It also concerns other species and the planet at large. It reinforces practices that harm other species and the environment or resist them. Translation, if misused – like the act of polluting – may affect the future of our planet. This is because a translation does not only tell us about how others do things, live or think but may also make people do things, live and think in certain ways and not others. Translation, as discourse, helps shape social practices and social relations, as we learn from critical discourse analysts (e.g. Fairclough 2003, 2010; van Dijk 1993). What is translated is a discourse that reflects and is reflected in social actions. This discourse helps reinforce or subvert relational hierarchies, blinds or opens our eyes to animal sufferings and downplays or raises our awareness of the challenges to our mere future survival on earth. Translation reflects and orients our life at large. Thus, translation ethics is way more complex, way more encompassing and consequentially far reaching. This is especially true as translation makes up a large part of the globally disseminated discourse today.

A translation classroom needs to take account of all these socio-political, economic, cultural and ecological dimensions of translation. It needs to raise learners-translators' awareness of the strong link that exists between their choices at the micro-level and these complex global issues.

> Translation pedagogy should strive for a translator (whether the subject is thought about as a 'profile' or as an 'image') who is self-aware as well

as skilled and competent, and one who translates with her or his "eyes open" (Barsky 2005) – i.e., able to see the context of the translation event and its historicity and be aware of the social implications of the language negotiation in which they participate.

(Gill and Guzmán 2011, 99)

Self-care ethics through TL pedagogy aims at empowering the translator in a way that they become aware of the socio-planetary effects of the discourse dynamics they are involved in and the relationships their translations are fostering as well as the future these translations are helping to shape.

A classroom of self-care through TL is also about making the translator conscious of their own narratives/ideologies, their sources, their consequences, their reliability and justifiability, as well as the narratives/ideologies of the author of the translated materials and those of the agents involved in the translation operation (especially the commissioners). This is because "[c]ultural canon, socioeconomic structures, ideologies and beliefs about ourselves, and the practices they support often conspire to foster conformity and impede development of a sense of responsible agency" (Mezirow 2000, 8). Questioning the mental structures that inhibit one from seeing the problems within one's representations is at the heart of Self-care through TL.

For students to accomplish locating the 'truth' of a translation, they must become keen observers of their own understanding of relations and narratives in the world, or to use an ecological term, their own 'connectedness' to the material at hand. Reflective consciousness is central to the learning. Students are encouraged to expose fully the narratives they perceive and how they proceed with their translation choices to re-construct narratives.

(Gill and Guzmán 2011, 102)

The learner-translator's self-reflexive decisions that link the instant, local verbal choices in a translation to global considerations need to be part and parcel of self-transformative classrooms. In other words, learners should be aware of *why they do what they do* and of *what their decisions do to their world*.

In a self-care through TL classroom, learners-translators can be social scientists and critical discourse analysts, who are aware of the possible repercussions of their translated materials – and in particular their strategies of translation – on power relations, social practices, social relations and potentially environmental issues.

In the context of teaching translation, a productive translation zone would be one of a geopolitical critique in and through language and communication. Translators formed in this critical space can also be social theorists, aware of the fluidity of the social fabric that surrounds them and of which they themselves are part and product.

(Gill and Guzmán 2011, 97)

Self-care through TL pedagogy empowers learners to see translation as a situational practice that entails and engage different facets of morality in different instances. It allows them to see themselves as playing an important role in knowledge dissemination and, therefore, their world dynamics. Learners-translators eventually realize the impossibility to follow a pre-determined list of stable principles/rules or strategies that may lead to infringe upon more global planetary/human principles. The principle of 'fidelity' pertaining to translation as a linguistic/cultural transference may contradict more overarching principles, like responsibility to humans and species, as they may contradict the principle of respecting others' differences and uniqueness. 'Detachment' in translation may imply letting dangerous/harmful material circulate. The translator becomes aware that even notions advocated as ethical strategies to highlight Otherness may sometimes lead to unethical outcomes. For example, *foreignization* may not always be ethical, in contrast to Venuti's generalized claim; it was adopted in some contexts to represent the other as primitive (see Faiq 2004). Self-care ethics means autonomy from these *a priori* principles and *a priori* codes and freedom to choose, adapt to situations and make difficult decisions, which are constantly shifting and always uncertain.

Self-care through TL broadens the translator's ethical scope. The ethical concern becomes limitless and beyond restriction to certain agents, at the expense of others. It fosters complex thinking that enables the practitioner to see far beyond their immediate circle, i.e., to extend their vision to see the unforeseeable, to think about the unthinkable, and to expect the unexpected. The complexity and far-reaching consequences of translation (Cronin 2017), in addition to the multifaceted nature of the practice (Tymoczko 2007), position the translator, as a social agent, in the midst of an overwhelming and burdensome responsibility. Their work becomes highly demanding, both intellectually and ethically, as their practice requires not only high skills and knowledge in many different domains but also high socio-political, economic, cultural, social and planetary awareness or "conscientization," to use Mezirow's term (1990).

Self-care through TL is liable to unveil to the learner not only the narrow vision of the established rules but also the ideological and manipulative implications of some of them as they may simply be tools to protect the powerful agents. It self-liberates the learner-translator from "moral ideology" to embrace "ethical responsibility" (Gilligan 1981, 155). Critical reflection in self-care through TL will lead to a process of cleansing

260 Alternative Ethics

the self from inherited concepts and rules that some translators may have adopted unreflectively. This, in some cases, may imply the relativization of the business responsibility or even its annulment when it conflicts with wider and more global responsibility to the wider community or the planet. Loyalty to the 'ethical' orientations of the patron/client as opposed to one's convictions is a ground for work, in this regard. Self-care through TL enlarges the scope of the translator's work and responsibility to include *everyone*. The self-cared translator does their work as an engaged world *citizen* and not only as a simple practitioner guided by limited business regulations (see Baker and Maier 2011b). *Action* is the most important phase in the self-care process. The translator educated in self-care through TL moves away from the Kantian 'minority and majority statuses' alike (i.e., from 'obey, don't reason'; and 'obey and you can reason as much as you want') (Foucault 2001c/1984) to the new autonomous practitioner who reflects and *does not obey*; a practitioner who reflects and *acts* accordingly.

In sum, there are two main levels in the work on oneself: meta-level (theorizing/thinking) about *translation* and the translator's self-concept (in relation with other agents and the world), on the one hand, and practical theorizing about the cultural, political, economic, social and ecological dimensions of the material at hand, on the other hand. These two levels are inextricable; they can be worked on simultaneously with the same material as they inform each other. However, the latter level cannot be fully translated into one's *actual* practice unless the former work is achieved. In other words, translators cannot be alert to the extra-textual aspects of their work unless they are self-cared.

12.2.3 *The Learner's Self-Transformative Process*

Following Mezirow's model, the learner goes through many stages in their self-transformation process. This process involves a *Disorienting Dilemma*, to start with. In the case of translators, this includes shaking off 'dualist' assumptions – in Perry's (1981) scheme of ethical/intellectual development – about *translation* as merely equivalence, faithfulness and the like, as well as their *self-concept* as faithful carriers/transporters of meaning. At this stage, which is the most important in the transformative journey, the learner-translator becomes aware that the views or representations they have had are not plausible or justifiable, and the frames of reference behind them are fraught. This usually happens when they face a triggering event that shows the sharp internal contradictions within the views they may hold. For example, a dissonance occurs in the learner-translator's mind when they become aware of other concepts of *translation* in other cultures and times; when they reflect on the transformations and adaptations translators actually perform in their translations, especially nowadays; when they discover the ideological underpinnings of the dominant concept; when they discover the atrocities that have been committed in the name of the concept they adopt; when they find out how this concept undermines the value of their work; when they discover the repercussions of this limited understanding on different ethical/societal/planetary issues.

Any pedagogical material that can unveil the implausibility of the concept students may have can serve as a triggering event for a self-transformation process. Activities in a self-care through TL classroom may range from historical texts that show the religious/ideological, political or cultural underpinnings of the mainstream concept or extracts from translators' autobiographies/interviews, to exposure to authentic translations that include tangible/noticeable traces of change and, therefore, demonstrate the transformative nature of translation. Watching a simple extract of a movie or examining a localized product can serve well the purpose. For instance, in an undergraduate audiovisual translation (AVT) course – which did not have any specific theoretical aims, nor did it aim only to enable students to question the mainstream *translation* definition – I introduced the students to the French subtitles of the movie "Matilda,"[1] which is far from having any obvious ideological or political implications that can justify politically-driven transformations in its subtitling – apart from the space/time constraints. As a class warm-up, I elicited some definitions students have of *translation*. Of course, the students and I went through the procedure, discussing first the importance of subtitling and its characteristics as well as its extra-linguistics dimensions, among other steps. Students worked to identify some transformations and classify them into interventions due to technical constraints and changes due to political/ideological or cultural considerations. They, for example, found that the subtitle in French did not translate 'federal prison' faithfully, as the term 'federal' was removed, among many other adaptations/manipulations due to technical (space/time) and cultural considerations. Of course, they discussed the reason behind the change and agreed that the intervention is because some major Francophone countries, mainly France, do not have a federal system of government, but are rather central systems. At the end, I asked students to revisit their initial definitions to make it inclusive of the transformations they have found in the movie subtitles, which were mainly due to cultural, political and technical reasons. They wrote their redefinitions individually, discussed them in pairs, and then with the whole class. The proposed definitions were compared to their initial definitions. Interestingly, the discussions went beyond the revised definitions, and included the students' general perception/feeling, as well as their skepticism and doubts. The objective was not, of course, to reach a definite answer, but to trigger questions and a sense of unsafety with folk

262 Alternative Ethics

assumptions about *translation*. Importantly, students started to discuss the kind of knowledge and expertise the translator needs, apart from linguistic expertise, and how complex and multidimensional this knowledge/expertise should be to solve some of the issues encountered in subtitling. Some other issues that could be discussed – probably at a later stage – are the negotiations of the translator's choices with the other involved agents, among others.

Although the class objective was to enable students to identify some of the characteristics and extra-linguistic dimensions of AVT (precisely, subtitling), I implicitly integrated the redefinition of *translation*. This shows that we do not need to have a theoretically-oriented curriculum or one that revolves around the questioning of the mainstream definition of *translation* to integrate such ideas in our everyday classes. We can always find ways to integrate them in already established practice-oriented curricula. There are always ways to evade institutional directives/constraints and powerful agents' impositions! An activity like this can be introduced in undergraduate classes. Generally, students at this level are able to easily notice these transformations and start questioning early in their undergraduate level their taken-for-granted and inherited assumptions about *translation*. I am quite certain there is always a way to integrate self-transformation triggering ideas/events in other technical texts – of course to different extents, as some types of texts show transformations more clearly than others.

Other activities may include reading (extracts from) texts that show the colonialist embeddedness of the dominant concept of *translation*, or (extracts from) texts that show other conceptualizations in other cultures or times, or simply texts or translator interviews/autobiographies that advocate transformation. Questions that challenge the mainstream assumptions may accompany the readings. The questions should not aim at reaching definite answers but at creating debate and provoking some uneasiness about the taken-for-granted assumptions. Triggering/stimulating questions could, for example, revolve around the difference between the principles propounded by codes of ethics and the principles highlighted in the reading materials; where they intersect or diverge and what implications each principle has for practice; which principle(s) sounds more plausible and why. Questions could also trigger an examination of the marketing dimensions or the alienating nature of some rules/principles, and how they may undermine the translator's capital and ethical agency. This stage of critical observation/analysis can be followed up by open discussions, debates, critical essays, personal stories/anecdotes, and revisiting prior knowledge/understandings. Scenarios such as those proposed by Baker and Maier (2011b) can also be interesting follow-up activities.

More practice-oriented assignments in a self-care through TL classroom may include the review of existing translations of polemical/problematic texts (such as illegal, polluting, controversial, discriminatory or resisting extracts). An example could be translations embedded in certain political narratives that use subtle discursive elements to highlight certain views and undermine others, like the use of passive voice/nominalization (Hatim and Mason 1997, Munday 2012), or the use of extra-textual strategies in news reports/political discourses (see Baker 2006a, 2010; Boukhaffa 2017, 2018). Another practice-oriented activity can be the translation of new texts, in which faithfulness may clearly equate irresponsibility (see Gill and Guzman 2011). The work on these kinds of texts or translations can be followed by an individual commentary that explains and justifies one's choices, followed by group or class debate.

After triggering activities or *disorienting dilemmas* have allowed learners-translators to recognize how unjustifiable conventional representations or opinions can be, the phase of *self-examination* sets in. This stage may be characterized by anger, guilt, or shame or a mix of these feelings. The learner may question the self for being part of the conspiracy and for disseminating an unjustified discourse. They may also feel guilty for having unknowingly fostered hegemony and done wrong to others by following the dictates of an unjustified concept in their practice. They may feel ashamed that they have been blind to these incoherencies for all this time. Finally, they may feel angry that they have helped in their self-demeaning. At this stage, the facilitator's role is very important in creating an anxiety-free atmosphere and providing counselling in order to boost the learner's self-confidence and alleviate feelings of guilt, shame and self-reproof, as later developments of TL have emphasized (see Taylor 2008). Learners need to get the assurance that they are not the only ones who embrace such reductive concepts unreflectively nor are they the only ones who adopt many other unjustified discourses in different areas of life.

The next stage is the *critical assessment of assumptions*. Now, the learner-translator reflects critically on their previous presuppositions about *translation/themselves* and assesses them. They try to understand the roots of these assumptions. They probably re-examine their cultural background and their previous educational experiences in the translation field and beyond. But most importantly, they may question the very frame of reference or habit of mind that led them to adopt such conceptions from an early age, like anyone in their community. They may, thus, examine their (cultural, religious, geographic, political, historical) background that helped shape their way of thinking and the consequences of such thinking. They may also examine the modern and capitalist business narratives, as well as the geopolitics of today that helped shape their way of thinking in general and their thought about translation and translators, in particular.

The *recognition that one's discontent and the process of transformation are shared* is the stage where the learner understands that their discontent with their old assumptions and representations of *translation/themselves* is the same for many others, especially peers – and even their previous educators. This, of course, reassures them that they are not alone in this. There are many others like them who have unreflectively adopted unjustified conceptualizations and have undergone or are undergoing the same process of transformation. Peer support and sharing is important, at this stage. Learners share their experiences with peers, talk about the possible reasons behind such understandings. This way, they raise each other's awareness of common issues, especially if they come from the same culture. If they have different cultural backgrounds, on the other hand, they together reflect on how this understanding has been universalized and why. Each one of them may bring in, or at least speculate on, how and why their respective communities/regions/countries have adopted such a conceptualization even though it does not historically or culturally belong to them. Also, they may reflect on how and why their communities have abandoned their own historical concepts.

After the invalidation of the old assumptions comes the *exploration of options for new roles, relationships and actions*. At this stage, the learner tries to understand the implications of each option for themselves and others, and, therefore, embrace the most justifiable, reliable and inclusive option. The learner at this stage becomes aware of the diverse and shifting roles of the translator. Hence, they explore newer roles and actions. They may explore newer relations with others, and especially the other agents directly involved in the translation transaction. That being said, learners are the ones who decide which new meaning(s) they want to embrace. Educators should remind themselves that self-care through TL is not about providing answers or even finding one's ultimate answers but mainly about raising questions and opening up new horizons for one's thought and releasing oneself from stagnant/static ways of thinking. In one word, self-care through TL is about *explorative, active* and *constant reflective creation of thought and newer roles/positions*.

After exploration comes the *planning of a course of action*. The learner, at this stage, decides on the path they want to follow, considering all the available options. They plan how to enact what they have learned and decided. This includes the new relations as well as the representation of the self that the new thought entails. If, for example, *translation* as a cluster concept is adopted as an option, then the course of action may be a more active role (agency) and autonomy in the translation process itself. This may include the decision to be more responsible for the content being translated. Thus, they may start considering using the repertoire of strategies of translation available in other cultures and times, or any other intervention strategies. Most importantly, they start to justify their translation choices. The course of action may also include the relational aspects with clients/patrons, authors and others. The translator may plan a better representation of themselves. They may also plan to have a say on what they do, or negotiate more favourable conditions for their work (including their remuneration). Also, this may entail questioning current copyright law.

Having planned their course of action, the learner-translator then *acquires knowledge and skills for implementing their plans*, which is an important stage in the self-care process. As translation at this stage may no longer be seen as simple linguistic transfer skills, but complex skills and knowledge of various issues (social, political, historical, ecological), the learner-translator may need to self-cultivate in different fields as well as dig into the repertoire of strategies that may be available in other cultures and in the different temporary types of translation. And the new knowledge to be acquired in order to implement one's plans will doubtless include an in-depth knowledge of geopolitics and the social, economic and ecological fields.

Provisional trying of new roles follows the acquisition of newer knowledge and skills necessary for the implementation of one's course of action. In self-care through TL pedagogy, learners should be provided with opportunities to simulate the new roles, at this stage, in order to see how well prepared they are and identify any possible gaps. They can be given different scenarios/contexts to see how they will implement their new beliefs and respond to ethical challenges in light of their transformed beliefs about *translation* and about themselves and the world in which they operate. Learners-translators at this stage try other roles beyond the traditionally assigned ones of transmitters of meaning. It is noteworthy that different learners will likely try different roles and focus on different aspects of translation. Some of them may focus on the translation process itself (for example, they may try to be more visible), while some others may focus on the relational aspects (for example, they may try to oppose some briefs and propose alternatives), and some others may focus on both aspects depending on the level of reflection and self-transformation they have achieved as well as on their newer orientations.

After some time of practice with the new roles adopted comes the *building of competence and self-confidence in these roles and relationships*. The learner-translator becomes more competent and confident in applying their new assumptions about *translation* and themselves and in responding to wider and ambivalent ethical issues/situations. They also acquire practice in asserting themselves in their relationships with the other agents. At this stage, they are able to present themselves as experts in the field. However, some learners-translators who fail to build enough self-confidence or to accumulate enough knowledge may become reluctant to move forward as they may still lack the tools to do so. Some may even go back to square one if they feel that the newer role they are about to take on is socially and institutionally objectionable. Learners-translators build confidence only if they are encouraged that their new roles and relationships are viable and justified – hence, the importance of a guiding counsellor/educator in supporting the learners who show such reluctance to move on.

The last stage of this self-transformative process is the *reintegration into one's life on the basis of conditions dictated by one's new perspective*. The learner-translator at this stage has completely self-transformed and the newer assumptions have become part of their being. New behaviour, occupational habits and practices, based on the new self, have taken over. Ethical/occupational challenges are responded to according to the new beliefs in a quasi-spontaneous manner. It is important, however, that the new frame of reference and the new perception of one's work and oneself do not turn into another set of stagnant perspectives and assumptions. They should rather remain active, mutative, flexible and open to change again. This new perspective should not be a definitive answer but rather a permanently questioning perspective that is always uneasy with itself.

It is noteworthy that the stages described above do not (always) occur in this linear manner, nor do they happen as one stage at each class/course in the same way/pace for all learners. Self-transformation is rather recursive and more complex than it may seem. Regressions or deflections are always possible. Some learners, experiencing acute distress, may react with "postponement, apathy, or rage," as we learn from Perry (1981, 90). Perry discusses three types of deflection from intellectual and ethical growth. The first is *Temporizing*, which implies that some learners put off decision-making and reconsign "the agency for decision to some event that might turn up" (ibid.). Learners experiencing temporizing feel they are not ready or not yet able to be responsible for their decisions. Thus, they often experience a sense of fear, shame or guilt (Perry 1981, 91). In a translation classroom, some learners may feel they are not able to face the social/institutional reaction, or the economic repercussions of their choices. Another type of deflection is *Escape*, which is characterized by "alienation" and "abandonment of responsibility" altogether (ibid., 80). It is a sort of un-commitment or 'detachment,' which "can become a settled condition" (ibid., 92). The third type of deflection is *Retreat*. It is characterized by regression to the safe zone of *dualism* – which is coloured by "moralistic righteousness and righteous hatred of Otherness" (ibid., 91) – in order to avoid complexity and ambivalence (ibid., 80, 91). In addition to these possible deflections, a learner may take longer in a certain phase than their peers while others may skip a certain stage(s). Individual learners do not all go through all stages in the same manner, nor do they experience them in the same way. These stages may take from

Transformative Learning in the Service of Ethics of Self-Care

a few months to a few years depending on individuals' learning styles, histories, needs, motivations and personalities. That is why they need to be catered to by teachers/counsellors varying activities/materials depending on learners' needs at certain stages because learners respond differently to different stimuli/materials. The educator designs their lessons following an assessment of the situation/stage of every learner and individualizes their teaching.

In sum, the prospective transformation of the *translation* concept and the translator's self-concept is the main focus of self-care through TL. It purges the self of implausible, self-denigrating and hegemonic presuppositions. It also raises self-value for oneself and others. Ultimately, this has implications for the translator's choices – which are informed by the socio-political, ideological, ecological and economic dimensions of the task at hand.

12.2.4 The Educator's and Learner's Respective Roles in Self-Care Through TL

Self-care ethics is a work on the self to self-transform. The social work of exchange with others that it involves is only a means to opening up to newer perspectives and experimenting and testing the relevance of one's representations. In self-care through TL pedagogy, the learner does not passively receive knowledge from authorities (the authority of the educator, the authority of the association or the authority of some sacred dogma) but rather self-manages and self-directs their learning processes (see Hammond and Collins 2004/1991). Self-care through TL is a learner-centred approach, by definition, i.e., it foregrounds learning/learner over teaching/teacher. This is important for two main reasons. First, learners tend to remember what they have *learned* and forget what they have *been taught* – which means active learning is more efficient than passive learning (i.e., teaching)[2]. Second, this approach helps foster life-long learning and autonomy of learners and future practitioners.

Learning via this approach not only requires and promotes an examination of one's practical tactics in one's (future) practice but also an examination of one's inner self and how this interacts with the world around oneself. Learners-translators autonomously self-reflect on their habits of mind when encountering disorienting dilemmas or triggering events and, therefore, become aware of the contexts and the grounds of their taken-for-granted assumptions, and ultimately embrace ideas that are more justified. Self-care through TL allows the learner-translator to experiment with a myriad ethical situations and to critically assess the pros and cons of different ethical responses. While the learner-translator opens up to diverse views (peers', scholars' and educators') in order to see what others see and open their eyes to other ethical horizons, they do not embrace them wholesale and unreflectively but construct their own views. In other words, they actively and autonomously produce their ideas and knowledge. Self-care through TL fosters the idea of *learning to learn*. Its aims to develop life-long autonomous thinkers and practitioners. "Fostering greater autonomy in thinking is both a goal and a method for adult educators," as Mezirow puts it (2000, 29). The ultimate goal is to guide learners toward becoming liberated and responsible translators for themselves and others, "that is, to make more informed choices by becoming more critically reflective as 'dialogic thinkers' (Basseches, 1984) in their engagement in a given social context" (ibid., 30).

On the other hand, the translation educator in self-care through TL takes the role of a counsellor and facilitator, as well as a self-learner. Foucault's self-care ethics is as relevant to the teacher's self-reflexivity, autonomy and empowerment as it is to their students' (see Raaen 2011). Teachers should also be open to learning and self-transformation regarding their teaching, their view of learning processes and learners, as well as their positions about other life issues. In self-care through TL classrooms, the teacher turns into "a collaborative learner" (Mezirow 2000, 15), with a guiding, rather than a teaching, role. Their main and only task is *letting learning take place,* in Heidegger's words:

> Teaching is more difficult than learning because what teaching calls for is this: *to let learn*. The real teacher, in fact, lets nothing else be learned than – learning. His conduct, therefore, often produces the impression that we properly learn nothing from him, if by "learning" we suddenly understand merely the procurement of useful information. The teacher is ahead of his apprentices in this alone, that he has still far more to learn than they – *he has to learn to let them learn*. [...] If the relation between the teacher and the taught is genuine, therefore, there is never a place in it for the authority of the know-it-all or the authoritative sway of the official.
>
> (Heidegger 1968, 15, italics added)

In self-care through TL classes, the educator abandons the know-it-all mantle. They rather *learn* to let learners learn. They also reduce their institutional voice, the voice of power. They are, of course, initiators – sometimes sources/provokers of controversial debates – but they do not have the final say nor the 'best' answer. Translation educators who adopt self-transformative approaches do not aim at indoctrination. They rather create a democratic atmosphere of free debate and autonomous self-enhancement for themselves and others. "This involves blocking out power relationships engendered in the structure of communication, including those traditionally existing between teachers and learners" (Mezirow 2000, 31). Raaen, drawing on Foucault's notions of *parrhesia* (frankness) and self-care, affirms that

> teachers can assure their students that they can critically reflect on their teachers' activities in public. An indication that *parrhesia* is present in the teaching context occurs when both experts and non-experts (in this context, both teachers and students) are given the opportunity to develop and practise their autonomy within a frank, argumentative conversation.
>
> (Raaen 2011, 636)

The teacher, thus, not only provide learners with the opportunity to reflect on, and co-build, their education activities, but also gives themselves the chance to move away from teaching according to the policies of an authority that may favour (commercial, political) agendas over ethical/social considerations. The educator who adopts self-care through TL does not claim to be neutral, as they clearly position themselves as resistant to dictations of some agents in the field of power and take the side of the dominated, including the dominated translator. The very adoption of this critical approach instead of another approach is already a sort of socio-political positioning. Adopting TL, educators position themselves as "cultural activists," who are committed to social reform and "a greater realization of agency for all learners" (Mezirow 2000, 30).

This position is, however, not without risk for both the educator and the learner. The educator should be aware of the social conflict in which their teaching/learning approach is embedded and should share its risks as well as its potential opportunities with their learners-translators. The educator and the learner should together decide on the tactical approaches on how to face the challenges and handle this complex and risky endeavour. It is through negotiation, rather than imposition, that the educator should convince their learners to engage in their self-transformative project – which is, by default, a social, political, activist and ethical endeavour.

Because of the feeling of insecurity that self-transformation may induce, the educator in self-care through TL pedagogy provides a supportive environment that can ensure self-confidence, trust and emotional security. They support learners in order to allow them to liberate themselves from self-constraining beliefs about their abilities to take charge of their learning and their lives. The goal of self-care through TL is the empowerment of individual learners so that they are, first and foremost, aware of their strengths and able to mobilize and make full use of their abilities in order to transform their frames of reference. In short, in order to handle the affective dimension of constructive learning, the translation educator needs to establish positive and *authentic relationships* with the learners and among learners (see Taylor 2000, 2009).

Although self-care through TL is, by definition, learner-centred, the educator may occasionally need to give some background lectures adopting interactive methods. "In order to develop, critical thinking requires wide knowledge and an understanding of what others have already discovered and thought" (Koskinen 2012, 11). A little transmissionist work done in an interactive way may serve as a background for self-centred work but should cease to dominate and leave space for critical reflection work at very early stages of learning. Transmissionist work is necessary to acquire information background; transformative work is to build reflective views/knowledge.

Another very important aspect of the educator's role is the introduction of material that is appropriate to the students' levels of intellectual and ethical growth, taking into account their individual differences. The individualization of teaching/learning through a variety of activities is key to responding to the diversity of styles, experiences, needs, preferences as well as individual positionalities in regard to social issues such as race, class, gender and sexual orientation. I believe Perry's scheme of development can serve to identify whether the learner has moved beyond the dualist stage regarding these issues and others and is, therefore, ready to engage with controversial materials that challenge the mainstream social discourse/knowledge some of them may have brought to the classroom. Or they still need triggering materials that will question their dualist thinking. In short, the self-care through TL course should be designed judiciously in a way that provokes gradual engagement with the new approach, taking all the discussed variables into account.

12.3 Conclusion

Self-care through TL has the potential to empower translators intellectually, ethically and symbolically to face the uncertainties of ethical encounters and build awareness of the power asymmetries in which their work is embedded. With the support of the scholar (an agent from the field of power), self-care through TL ultimately allows the translator to *gradually* "crack[ing] the conduit model," to use Inghilleri terms (2012, 97), and act ethically and autonomously. At the centre of this work on the self is the transformation of one's self-concept through a more justified understanding of one's practice – which, by extension, enlarges ethical perspectives, and makes a translator more critical as to the extratextual dimensions of their everyday work, and, therefore, exercise their full agency. The translator's active involvement in different institutions – including one's institutions – to gradually change the *status quo* is most important; it is not only about changing one's perspective about one's practice and oneself but mainly about engaging in gradually implementing that change, voicing it and, most importantly, changing outsiders' views of *translation* and translators.

Symbolic empowerment through self-care is interlinked with ethical empowerment and is its prior condition, and they both require intellectual empowerment and self-awareness. Collectively emphasizing one's significant knowledge/expertise and the different roles translators play may lead to a recognition that is relatively proportionate with this complex cultural endeavour. The recognition of one's cultural capital and ethical responsibility is then likely to convert into some form of external recognition of the translator as a cultural producer and/or a partitioning expert should translators have a better external support from one of the agents in the field of power and more internal unity.

It remains to be seen how this proposed pedagogy of self-care through TL will find a way into translation classrooms and how it may affect the translator of tomorrow. I am well aware, as I argued on a few occasions earlier, that this approach, like any critical pedagogical approach, may not be embraced by all educators – many of whom align with the dominant agents and are constrained by the market forces. However, the initiatives taken in translation classrooms regarding ethics and empowerment through critical pedagogies (as we know from the publications cited earlier) remain encouraging signs of a gradual change that is taking place in many parts of the world.

Notes

1 https://en.wikipedia.org/wiki/Matilda_(1996_film)
2 The Australian novelist, Patrick White in his novel, *The Solid Mandala* (1966), puts this statement in the mouth of one of his characters: "I forget what I was taught. I only remember what I have learnt."

Conclusions
Challenges and Project Ethicality

This book has argued that the process of regularization underlying the creation of codes of ethics, in fact, reflects and reinforces an external control of the occupation by the powerful agents who benefit from/consume translations, despite the codes' public statements of professionalization that supposedly imply self-control and external recognition. The discourse in codes of ethics is, indeed, an internal expression of this *patronage* mode of occupational control that reinforces the translator's low capital and lack of autonomy. This mode is manifest in the *translation* view and the interrelation instructions that assign translators a low status in the eyes of the other agents involved in translation, namely large clients, employers, authors and publishers, and the public at large. Drawing on the sociology of professions, the book showed that the translator's lack of recognition is due to three main factors: the fragmentation of translators, the power and concentration of the agents who need translations, and the scarcity of external support.

As a result of this low status, the individual translator's moral self is generally neutralized, in the name of 'faithfulness' and 'professionalism,' and this may result in a limited responsibility and loyalty to the immediate 'professional' context and the powerful agents involved in the translation circle. The book has argued that the external patronage view of translators/translation, reinforced internally through codes of ethics and other internal documents, does not allow translators to be equipped with substantial ethical background/tools to exercise their ethical agency and fulfill their social/planetary responsibilities. The translator cannot be ethically autonomous and responsible if they are not autonomous in their choices/decisions; if they do not have control over their occupation. The translator's neutralized moral self reflects their undermined capital. This is why I have argued throughout this book, following Foucault, that ethical responsibility is dependent and posterior to symbolic empowerment and autonomy. And the key for symbolic empowerment and autonomy is self-awareness and (self)-education.

DOI: 10.4324/9781032713557-18

Because of the translator's lack of symbolic recognition as professionals and/or authors and their ethical neutrality, manifest in their internal documents, the book questioned the very principle of ethics codification as a coercive project based on pre-determined duties for an occupation that is intrinsically ambivalent and for practitioners who have a low status and little external support. Importantly, it revealed the overarching ideologies behind this modern project and behind the dominant views of *translation/ translators*, their main beneficiaries, their underlying sources, the contexts in which they have flourished and become 'solid' and unshakeable, and especially how these narratives and their contexts reinforce the dominated status of translators, and therefore, neutralize them ethically.

In Part IV, I presented alternative ethical pathways that are likely to enhance the translator's symbolic capital and ethical autonomy, with some external support from the field of power, manifest in academics/scholars. Drawing on Foucault's dimensions of morality, I drafted a transitional noncoercive charter for ethics – to make the transition to ethics of self-care viable – and presented a critical pedagogy to self-care. As part of a holistic approach, I recommended that these two elements be nurtured within a culture of the self that is enhanced within the institutions concerned with the translation practice, namely TS, the translation occupation and translation pedagogy. Concerning TS, I called for a shift in focus from otherness and social responsibility to self-care, for one cannot care and be responsible for others if one does not enact self-care. For the translation occupation, I argued that translator organizations need to be transformed in a way to give voice and choice to the individual member. And regarding translation programs, I advocated a critical pedagogy that is centred on the self and that is self-transformative and reflexive.

More specifically, I drew on transformative learning theory to instantiate ethics of self-care in modern educational institutions. The proposed approach seeks two ultimate aims: the enhancement of the translator's capital (respect for their economic rights, their dignity, their autonomy and their value as cultural creators and disseminators of knowledge), and the empowerment of their ethical self. I showed that that the translator's symbolic empowerment through self-care is interlinked with their ethical empowerment but emphasized that the former has ontological priority (Foucault 2001d/1984, 1531). I argued that the epistemic enhancement and its emancipatory and planetary components complement each other in a way that self-transformation most likely leads to responsible ecological/ social action.

The effective implementation and success of the approach proposed in this work is, of course, not without challenges. The powerful agents benefitting from translation would resist it because of the change it is likely to bring about that would undermine their interests. The approach is viable only with more engagement and support from scholars/educators, one of the agents in the field of power. The situation of this source of power is, however, complicated due to the scholars' internal fragmentation and their low positioning in the field of power, compared to the other agents with whom the translator struggles for recognition. Yet, I argued that this source of power (i.e., scholars/educators) still has some room for manoeuvres to include empowering views in their teaching programs and research projects. Since the cultural turn, we have seen encouraging signs in this respect, as more scholars line up with translators and support their empowerment, despite the fierce resistance of others, who line up with the dominant agents in the field of power. The stake is to recruit more scholars who line up with translators and are able to focus on self-care and the elevation of the translator's self-concept. Most importantly, there must be a focus on the translation of these scholars' emancipatory concepts and pronouncements into tangible work in translation classrooms and into their (external) discourse with the other agents (especially the ones in the field of power), whenever and wherever those opportunities of communication with these agents arise. The aim, of course, is to shake their categories of perception of translation/translators.

Central to the approach suggested in this work is the translator self-transformation to enhance one's capital and moral self. Imposing symbolic recognition through self-care ethics may, however, seem problematic. Should professional translators become more powerful than the other agents involved in translation, they may exercise hegemony and enforce relations of exploitation over them, a fact which may reproduce similar problems and give rise to unethical practices that are not less problematic. This raises the question: how ethical is a project like this, in the first place? Is the proposed ethical endeavour not a search for egocentric goals, demanding and imposing translators' symbolic power, rather than seeking ethical behaviours/practices *per se*? Is that not simply going to reverse the power relations and have new agents at the bottom of the social order? To respond to these legitimate potential questions, I first reiterate that this project is a modest one and is far from an idealistic approach that seeks unachievable subversion. My approach rather seeks a gradual change and *minimization* of relations of dominance and ethical alienation. And to reassure those who may claim that a project like this simply seeks to reshuffle power relations in a way that translators take a dominant position, I argue that even if the relations are reshuffled – which is far from possible anyway as the dominant agents remain concentrated and powerful in today's world – an empowered translator who is self-caring cannot exercise the harshest types of hegemony or exploitation. As Foucault affirms, power relations are irradicable and, in some cases, are not even so harmful. Hence, an *ethical* project like this does not seek to impose other relations of exploitation but – in Foucault's words – "to give oneself the rules of law, the techniques of management and also the morals, the ethos, the practice of the self, which will allow, in these games of power, to play with the least possible domination" (2001d/1984, 1546, my translation). Self-care would lead to self-government of the empowered translators and would, therefore, be a regulator of their conduct toward others (see Foucault 1984b). The approach of self-care adopted in this project is important because not many other forms of empowerment may lead to a powerful agent who acts ethically. "Self-care appears to be a pedagogical, ethical and also ontological condition for the constitution of the good ruler" (Foucault 1540–1541, my translation). In sum, what makes a project like this ethical is that its ultimate goal – in an ideal situation – would be to make the translator able to cater for their world with minimum domination. But adopting a realistic vision, this project simply seeks to minimize the translator's symbolic domination and ethical alienation.

References

ABDALLAH, Kristiina. 2013. 'Anthony Pym 2012. On Translator Ethics. Translated by Heike Walker. Revised by the Author. Amsterdam/Philadelphia: John Benjamins Translation Library.' *HERMES* 26 (51): 113–115.

ABDALLAH, Kristiina and Kaisa KOSKINEN. 2007. 'Managing Trust: Translating and the Network Economy.' *Meta* 52 (4): 673–687.

ACKRILL, J. L. 1973. *Aristotle's Ethics*. London: Faber & Faber.

ALLEN, Amy. 2003. 'Foucault and Enlightenment: A Critical Reappraisal.' *Constellations* 10 (2): 180–198.

———. 2004. 'Foucault, Feminism, and the Self: The Politics of Personal Transformation.' In *Feminism and the Final Foucault*, edited by Dianna TAYLOR and Karen VINTGES, 235–257. Urbana & Chicago: University of Illinois Press.

ALSANEA, Rajaa. 2007. *Girls of Riyadh*. Translated by Rajaa ALSANEA and Marilyn BOOTH. New York: The Penguin Press/ London: Fig Tree.

ALTHUSSER, Louis. 1971. *Lenin and Philosophy and Other Essays*. Translated by Ben BREWSTER. New York: Monthly Review Press.

ANGELELLI, Claudia. 2004. *Revisiting the Interpreter's Role: A Study of Conference, Court, And Medial Interpreters in Canada, Mexico, and the United States*. Amsterdam & Philadelphia: Benjamins.

ANNAS, Julia. 2006. 'Virtue Ethics.' In *The Oxford Handbook of Ethical Theory*, edited by David COPP, 515–536. Oxford & New York: Oxford University Press.

APPIAH, Kwame Anthony. 2000/1993. 'Thick Translation.' In The *Translation Studies Reader*, edited by Lawrence VENUTI, 417–429. London & New York: Routledge.

ARISTOTLE. 1973. 'The Nicomachean Ethics.' In *Aristotle's Ethics*, edited by J. L. ACKRILL, 41–181. London: Faber & Faber.

ARROJO, Rosemary. 2005. 'The Ethics of Translation in Contemporary Approaches to Translator Training.' In *Training for the New Millennium: Pedagogies for Translation and Interpreting*, edited by Martha TENNENT, 225–245. Amsterdam & Philadelphia: Benjamins.

———. 2013. '"Translators" Code of Ethics.' In *The Encyclopedia of Applied Linguistics*, edited by Carol A. CHAPELLE, 1–5. Oxford: Blackwell Publishing.

ASAD, Talal. 1986/2010. 'The Concept of Cultural Translation in British Social Anthropology.' In *Critical Readings in Translation Studies*, edited by Mona BAKER, 7–27. London & New York: Routledge.

BACHMANN-MEDICK, Doris. 2006. 'Meanings of Translation in Cultural Anthropology.' In *Translating Others*. Vol. 1, edited by Theo HERMANS, 33–42. Manchester: St Jerome.

———. 2009. 'Introduction: The Translational Turn.' *Translation Studies* 2 (1): 2–16.

BAIXAULI-OLMOS, Lluís. 2013. 'A Description of Interpreting in Prisons: Mapping the Setting through an Ethical Lens.' In *Interpreting in a Changing Landscape*, edited by Christina SCHÄFFNER, Krzysztof KREDENS and Yvonne FOWLER, 45–60. Amsterdam & Philadelphia: Benjamins.

———. 2017. 'Ethics Codes as Tools for Social Change in Public Service Interpreting: Symbolic, Social and Cultural Dimensions.' *JoSTrans* 28: 250–272.

———. 2021. 'Ethics Codes for Interpreters and Translators.' In *The Routledge Handbook of Translation and Ethics*, edited by Kaisa KOSKINEN and Nike K. POKORN, 297–319. London & New York: Routledge.

BAKER, Mona. 2005. 'Narratives in and of Translation.' www.academia.edu/218861/Narratives_in_and_of_Translation (Accessed on February 17, 2015).

———. 2006a. *Translation and Conflict. A Narrative Account*. London & New York: Routledge.

———. 2006b. 'Translation and Activism: Emerging Patterns of Narrative Community.' *The Massachusetts Review* 47 (3): 462–484.

———. 2007. 'Reframing Conflict in Translation.' *Social Semiotics* 17 (2): 151–169.

———. 2008. 'Ethics of Renarration: Mona Baker is Interviewed by Andrew Chesterman.' *Cultus* 1 (1): 10–33.

———. 2010. 'Narratives of Terrorism and Security: "Accurate" Translations, Suspicious Frames.' *Critical Studies on Terrorism* 3 (3): 347–364.

———. 2018/1992. *In Other Words. A Coursebook on Translation*. 2nd ed. London & New York: Routledge.

BAKER, Mona and Carol MAIER (eds). 2011a. 'Ethics and the Curriculum' [Special Issue].' *The Interpreter and Translator Trainer* 5 (1).

———. 2011b. 'Ethics in Interpreter & Translator Training.' *The Interpreter and Translator Trainer* 5 (1): 1–14.

BAKHTIN, M. Mikhail. 1981. *The Dialogic Imagination: Four Essays*. Edited by Michael HOLQUIST. Translated by Caryl EMERSON and Michael HOLQUIST. Austin & London: University of Texas Press.

BALL, Stephen. 1990. *Foucault and Education: Disciplines and Knowledge*. London: Routledge.

BANCROFT, Marjorie. 2005. *The Interpreter's World Tour. An Environmental Scan of Standards of Practice for Interpreters*. Woodland Hills: The California Endowment.

BANDIA, Paul. 2005. 'Esquisse d'une Histoire de la Traduction en Afrique.' *Meta* 50 (3): 957–971.

BARBER, Bernard. 1963. 'Some Problems in the Sociology of the Professions.' *Daedalus* 92 (4): 669–688.

BARSKY, Robert. 2005. 'Translating into Fifteen Years of Prison or When Not to Say "You May, Officer".' Translation and Social Activism Conference, York University.

BARTHES, Roland. 1984/1968. 'La mort de l'auteur.' In *Le Bruissement de la langue: Essais critiques IV*, 63–69. Paris: Editions du Seuil.
―――― 1989/1957. *Mythologies*. Paris: Editions du Seuil.
BASALAMAH, Salah. 2004. 'Du droit à l'éthique du traducteur.' *TTR* 17 (2): 67–88.
――――. 2007. 'Translation Rights and the Philosophy of Translation.' In *In Translation—Reflections, Refractions, Transformations*, edited by Paul ST-PIERRE and Prafulla KAR, 117–132. Amsterdam & Philadelphia: Benjamins.
――――. 2009. *Le droit de traduire, Une politique culturelle de la mondialisation*. Ottawa: Les Presses de l'Université d'Ottawa.
BASALAMAH, Salah and Gaafar SADEK. 2014. 'Copyright Law and Translation: Crossing Epistemologies.' *The Translator* 20 (3): 396–410.
BASSECHES, Michael. 1984. *Dialectical Thinking and Adult Development*. Norwood: Ablex.
BASSNETT, Susan and André LEFEVRE. 1990. *Translation, History and Culture*. London: Pinter.
BASSNETT, Susan and Harish TRIVEDI. 1999. 'Introduction: Of Colonies, Cannibals and Vernaculars.' In *Post-Colonial Translation: Theory and Practice*, edited by Susan BASSNETT and Harish TRIVEDI, 1–18. London & New York: Routledge.
BAUDRILLARD, Jean. 2005. 'A la recherché du mal absolu.' *Libération*, February 17. www.liberation.fr/tribune/2005/02/17/a-la-recherche-du-mal-absolu_509985/?xtor=rss-450 (Accessed on March 21, 2016).
BAUMAN, Zygmunt. 1993. *Postmodern Ethics*. Malden: Blackwell.
――――. 1994. 'Morality without Ethics.' *Theory, Culture & Society* 11: 1–34.
――――. 2003a/1995. *La vie en miettes: Expérience postmoderne et moralité*. Translated by Christophe Rosson. Rodez: Le Rouergue/Chambon.
――――. 2003b. 'Globalisation as Ethical Challenge.' *Polish Sociological Review* 143: 247–258.
――――. 2007. *Liquid Times: Living in an Age of Uncertainty*. Cambridge/Malden: Polity Press.
――――. 2008. *Does Ethics Have a Chance in a World of Consumers?* Cambridge & London: Harvard University Press.
BECKER, Gerhold (ed). 1996. *Ethics in Business and Society*. Berlin: Springer.
BÉNICHOU, Paul. 1973. *Le sacre de l'écrivain (1750–1830). Essai sur l'avènement d'un pouvoir spirituel laïque en France*. Paris: J. Corti.
BENJAMIN, Walter. 2000/1923. 'The Task of the Translator.' In *Translation Studies Reader*, edited by Lawrence VENUTI, Translated by Harry ZOHN, 75–85. London & New York: Routledge.
BENTHAM, Jeremy. 2000/1781. *An Introduction to the Principles of Morals and Legislation*. Kitchener: Batoche Books.
BERMAN, Antoine. 1984. *L'épreuve de l'étranger: Culture et traduction dans l'Allemagne romantique*. Paris: Gallimard.
――――. 1999/1985. *La Traduction et la lettre ou l'auberge du lointain*. Paris: Editions du Seuil.
――――. 1999/1995. 'Le projet d'une critique « productive ».' In *Pour une critique des traductions*, edited by John Donne, 35–97. Paris: Gallimard.

BHABHA, K. Homi. 1990. 'The Third Space. Interview with Homi Bhabha.' In *Identity, Community, Culture, Difference*, edited by J. RUTHERFORD, 207–221. London: Lawrence and Winhart.

———. 1994. *The Location of Culture*. London and New York: Routledge.

BIASIN, Chiara. 2018. 'Transformative Learning: Evolutions of the Adult Learning Theory.' *Phronesis* 7 (3): 5–17.

BOÉRI Julie and Jesús DE MANUEL JEREZ. 2011. 'From Training Skilled Conference Interpreters to Educating Reflective Citizens.' *The Interpreter and Translator Trainer* 5 (1): 41–64.

BOORSTIN, Daniel J. 1983. *The Discoverers: A History of Man's Search to Know his World and Himself*. New York: Random House.

BOOTH, Marilyn. 2008. 'Translator v. author (2007) Girls of Riyadh go to New York.' *Translation Studies* 1 (2): 197–211.

BOS, R. ten and Hugh WILLMOTT. 2001. 'Towards a Post-dualistic Business Ethics: Interweaving Reason and Emotion in Working Life.' *Journal of Management Studies* 38(6): 769–793.

BOUKHAFFA, Abderrahman. 2017. 'Audiovisual Translation and Narrative (Re)framing: MEMRI's Subtitling of Moroccan Political Narratives.' *The Journal of International Social Research* 10 (50): 63–71.

———. 2018. 'Narrative (Re)framing in Translating Modern Orientalism: A Study of the Arabic Translation of Lewis's *The Crisis of Islam: Holy War and Unholy Terror*.' *The Translator* 24 (2): 166–182.

———. 2021. 'Translating the Middle East: From the Exotic to the Crazy Dog.' In *Translating Feat – Translated Fears: Understanding Fear across Languages and Cultures*, edited by Teresa SERUYA, Maria Lin MONIZ and Alexandra LOPES, 19–38. Berlin: Peter Lang.

BOULANGER, Pier-Pascale. 2004. 'L'épistémologie cinétique de la traduction: catalyseur d'éthique.' *TTR* 17 (2): 57–66.

BOURDIEU, Pierre. 1986. 'The Forms of Capital.' In *Handbook of Theory and Research for the Sociology of Education*, edited by John G. RICHARDSON, 241–258. New York: Greenwood Press.

———. 1990a. *In Other Words: Essays towards a Reflexive Sociology*. Translated by Mathew ADAMSON. Stanford: Stanford University Press.

———. 1990b. *The Logic of Practice*. Translated by Richard NICE. Cambridge: Polity Press.

———. 1991. *Language and Symbolic Power*. Translated by Gino RAYMOND and Matthew ADAMSON. Cambridge: Polity Press.

———. 1993. *The Field of Cultural Production: Essays on Art and Literature*. Edited and introduced by Randal JOHNSON. Cambridge: Polity Press.

———. 1996. *The State Nobility: Elite Schools in the Field of Power*. Translated by Lauretta CLOUGH. Cambridge: Polity Press.

———. 1998a. *Practical Reason: On the Theory of Action*. Stanford: Stanford University Press.

———. 1998b. *Acts of Resistance Against the New Myths of our Time*. Translated by Richard NICE. Cambridge: Polity Press.

BOURDIEU, Pierre and Loïc, J. D., WACQUANT. 1992. *An Invitation to Reflexive Sociology*. Chicago: University of Chicago Press.

BOWKER, Lynne. 2005. 'Professional Recognition in the Canadian Translation Industry: How is it Perceived by Translators and Employers?' *Translation Quality Watch* 1 (1): 19–32.

———. 2021. 'Translation Technology and Ethics.' In *The Routledge Handbook of Translation and Ethics*, edited by Kaisa KOSKINEN and Nike K. POKORN, 262–278. London & New York: Routledge.

BRENNAN, David. 2019. 'Historians and Journalists Defend Donald Trump After President Is Mocked on Ancient Rome Comments.' *Newsweek*, October 17. www.newsweek.com/historians-journalists-defend-donald-trump-president-mocked-ancient-rome-comments-italy-1465879

BRISSET, Annie. 2008. 'Formation des traducteurs: les critères du Bureau canadien de la traduction sont-ils judicieux?' *TTR* 21 (2): 131–162.

BROCK, Sabra. 2015. 'Learning and Transformation.' In *Exploring Learning & Teaching in Higher Education*, edited by Mang LI and Yong ZHAO, 233–250. Verlag & Berlin: Springer.

BROOKFIELD, Stephen. 2000. 'Transformative Learning as Ideology Critique.' In *Learning as Transformation*, edited by Jack MEZIROW and Associates, 125–148. San Francisco: Jossey-Bass.

———. 2009. 'Engaging Critical Reflection in Corporate America.' In *Transformative Learning in Practice: Insights from Community, Workplace, and Higher Education*, edited by Jack MEZIROW, Edward W. TAYLOR and Associates, 125–135. San Francisco: Jossey-Bass.

BROWN, Richard. 2013/1905. *History of Accounting and Accountants*. London & New York: Routledge.

BUZELIN, Hélène. 2005. 'Unexpected Allies. How Latour's Network Theory could Complement Bourdieusian Analyses in Translation Studies.' *The Translator*, 11 (2): 193–218.

———. 2014. 'How Devoted Can Translators Be? Revisiting the Subservience Hypothesis.' *Target* 26 (1): 63–97.

CALINESCU, Matei. 1991. 'From the One to the Many. Pluralism in Today's Thought.' In *Zeitgeist in Babel*, edited by Ingeborg HOESTEREY, 156–174. Bloomington & Indianapolis: Indiana University Press.

CARBONELL, Ovidi. 2004. 'Exoticism, Identity and Representation in Western Translationfrom Arabic.' In *Cultural Encounters in Translation from Arabic*, edited by Said FAIQ, 26–39. Clevedon & Buffalo: Multilingual Matters.

CAZDYN, Eric. 2010/2004. 'A New Line in the Geometry.' In *Critical Readings in Translation Studies*, edited by Mona BAKER, 449–459. London & New York: Routledge.

CHAMBERLAIN, Lori. 2012/1988. 'Gender and the Metaphorics of Translation.' In *Translation Studies Reader*, 3rd ed., edited by Lawrence VENUTI, 254–268. London & New York: Routledge.

CHESTERMAN, Andrew. 2001.'Proposal for a Hieronymic Oath.' *The Translator* 7 (2): 139–154.

———. 2005. 'Causality in Translator Training.' In *Training for the New Millennium: Pedagogies for Translation and Interpreting*, edited by Martha TENNENT, 191–208. Amsterdam & Philadelphia: Benjamins Translation Library.

———. 2009a/1997. 'Ethics of Translation.' In *Translation as Intercultural Communication*, edited by Mary SNELL-HORNY, Zuzana JETTMAROVÁ and Klaus KAINDL, 147–57. Amsterdam & Philadelphia: Benjamins.

———. 2009b. "The Name and Nature of Translator Studies." *Hermes – Journal of Language and Communication Studies*, 42: 13–22.

———. 2016/1997. *Memes of Translation. The Spread of Ideas in Translation Theory*. Amsterdam & Philadelphia: Benjamins.

———. 2019. 'Post Errorem.' *Perspectives*, 27 (5): 664–674. DOI: 10.1080/0907676X.2018.1450884

———. 2021. 'Virtue Ethics in Translation.' In *The Routledge Handbook of Translation and Ethics*, edited by Kaisa KOSKINEN and Nike K. POKORN, 13–24. London & New York: Routledge.

CHEYFITZ, Eric. 1991. *The Poetics of Imperialism: Translation and Colonization from the Tempest to Tarzan*. New York: Oxford University Press.

CLARKEBURN, Henriikka, Roger DOWNIE, Craig GRAY and Robert MATTHEW. 2003. 'Measuring Ethical Development in Life Sciences Students: A Study Using Perry's Developmental Model.' *Studies in Higher Education* 28 (4): 443–456.

CLIFFORD, Andrew. 2004. 'Is Fidelity Ethical? The Social Role of the Healthcare Interpreter.' *TTR* 17 (2): 89–114.

CLIFFORD, James and George E. MARCUS. 1986. *Writing Culture: The Poetics and Politics of Ethnography: A School of American Research Advanced Seminar*. Berkley: University of California Press.

COKELY, Dennis. 2000. 'Exploring Ethics: A Case for Revising the Code of Ethics.' *National Consortium of Interpreter Education Centers*: 1–24.

COSTA, Beverley, Raquel Lázaro GUTIÉRREZ and Tom RAUSCH. 2020. 'Self-care as an Ethical Responsibility: A Pilot Study on Support Provision for Interpreters in Human Crises.' *Translation and Interpreting Studies* 15 (1): 36–56.

CRAGG, Wesley (ed). 2005. *Ethics Codes, Corporations and the Challenge of Globalization*. Cheltenham & Northampton: Edward Elgar.

CRONIN, Michael. 2003. *Translation and Globalization*. London: Routledge.

———. 2006. *Translation and Identity*. Oxford & New York: Routledge.

———. 2010/1998. 'The Cracked Looking Glass of Servants.' In *Critical Readings in Translation Studies*, edited by Mona BAKER, 247–262. London & New York: Routledge.

———. 2012. *Translation in the Digital Age*. New York: Routledge

———. 2013. 'Mind the Gap: Translation Automation and the Lure of the Universal.' *TTT* 26 (2): 193–218.

———. 2017. *Eco-Translation: Translation and Ecology in the Age of the Anthropocene*. London & New York: Routledge.

———. 2021. 'Translation and Posthumanism.' In *The Routledge Handbook of Translation and Ethics*, edited by Kaisa KOSKINEN and Nike K. POKORN, 279–293. London & New York: Routledge.

DALOZ, Laurent. 1986. *Effective Teaching and Mentoring: Realizing the Transformational Power of Adult Learning Experiences*. San Francisco: Jossey-Bass.

DAM, Helle V. and Kaisa KOSKINEN (eds). 2016. 'The Translation Profession: Centres and Peripheries' [Special Issue]. *Journal of Specialised Translation* 25: 1–4.

DAM, Helle V. and Karen Korning ZETHSEN. 2008. 'Translator Status: A Study of Danish Company Translators.' *The Translator* 14 (1): 71–96.

———. 2010. 'Translator Status: Helpers and Opponents in the Ongoing Battle of an Emerging Profession.' *Target* 22 (2): 194–211.

———. 2011. 'The Status of Professional Business Translators on the Danish Market: A Comparative Study of Company, Agency and Freelance Translators.' *Meta* LVI 4: 976–997.

DAVIS, Kathleen. 2001. *Deconstruction and Translation*. Manchester: St. Jerome.

DE KOCK, Leon. 1992. 'Interview with Gayatri Chakravorty Spivak: New Nation Writers Conference in South Africa.' *ARIEL: A Review of International English Literature* 23 (3): 29–47.

DERRIDA, Jacques. 1985. 'Des Tours de Babel.' In *Difference in Translation*, translated and edited by Joseph GRAHAM, 165–248. Ithaca and London: Cornell University Press.

———. 1997. 'Quand j'ai entendu l'expression "délit d'hospitalité"…' *Plein droit* 34. www.gisti.org/spip.php?article2851

DÍAZ CINTAS, Jorge. 2012. 'Clearing the Smoke to See the Screen: Ideological Manipulation in Audiovisual Translation.' *Meta* 57 (2): 279–293.

DROIT, Roger-Pol. 2009. *L'éthique expliquée à tout le monde*. Paris: Editions du Seuil.

DRUGAN, Joanna. 2011. 'Translation Ethics Wikified: How Far Do Professional Codes of Ethics and Practice Apply to Non-professionally Produced Translation?' *Linguistica Antverpiensia* 10: 111–131.

———. 2017. 'Ethics and Social Responsibility in Practice: Interpreters and Translators Engaging with and beyond the Professions.' *The Translator*, 23 (2): 1126–142.

———. 2019. 'Ethics.' In *The Routledge Handbook of Translation and Philosophy*, edited by Piers RAWLING and Philip WILSON, 243–255. London: Routledge.

DRUGAN, Joanna and Chris MEGONE. 2011. 'Bringing Ethics into Translator Training. An Integrated, Inter-Disciplinary Approach.' *The Interpreter and Translator Trainer* 5 (1): 183–211.

DRUGAN, Joanna and Rebecca TIPTON (eds). 2017. 'Special Issue: Translation, Ethics and Social Responsibility.' *The Translator* 23 (2).

———. 2017. 'Introduction: Translation, Ethics and Social Responsibility.' *The Translator* 23 (2): 119–125.

EAGLESTONE, Robert. 2005. 'Levinas, Translations and Ethics.' In *Nation, Language and the Ethics of Translation*, edited by Sandra BERMANN and Michael WOOD, 127–138. Princeton & Oxford: Princeton University Press.

EAGLETON, Terry. Anniversary Edition. 2008. *Literary Theory: An Introduction*. Minnesota: University of Minnesota Press.

ERMARTH, Elizabeth Deeds. 1991. *Sequel to History Postmodernism and the Crisis of Representational Time*. Princeton: Princeton University Press.

———. 2001. 'Beyond History.' *Rethinking History* 5 (2): 195–215.

FAIQ, Said. 2004. 'Cultural encounters in translating from Arabic.' In *Cultural Encounters in Translation from Arabic*, edited by Said Faiq, 1–13. Clevedon & Buffalo: Multilingual Matters.

FAIRCLOUGH, Norman. 2003. *Analyzing Discourse – Textual Analysis for Social Research*. New York: Routledge.

———. 2010. *Critical Discourse Analysis: The Critical Study of Language*. 2nd ed. London & New York: Routledge.

FIOLA, Marco (ed). 2004. 'Présentation: Traduction, éthique et société [Translation, Ethics and Society]' [Special Issue]. *TTR* 17 (2).

FLEXNER, Abraham. 1915. *Is Social Work a Profession?* New York: New York School of Philanthropy.

FLOTOW, Luise von. 1997. *Translation and Gender. Translating in the 'Era of Feminism'*. Manchester: St Jerome/ Ottawa: Ottawa University Press.

———. 2007. 'Gender and Translation.' In *A Companion to Translation Studies*, edited by Piotr KUHIWCZAK and Karin LITTAU, 92–105. Clevedon: Multilingual Matters.

———. (ed). 2011 *Translating Women*. Ottawa: University of Ottawa Press.

FOLARON, Deborah and Hélène BUZELIN. 2007. 'Introduction: Connecting Translation and Network Studies.' *Meta* 52 (4): 605–642.

FOLKART, Barbara. 2007. *Second Finding. A Poetics of Translation*. Ottawa: University of Ottawa Press.

FOLLOROU, Jacques. 2012. 'Traducteur pour l'OTAN, un métier à risques en Afghanistan.' *Le Monde*, December 26. www.lemonde.fr/a-la-une/article/2012/12/26/traducteur-pour-l-otan-un-metier-a-risques-en-afghanistan_1810352_3208.html (Accessed on February 12, 2018).

FOUCAULT, Michel. 1975. *Surveiller et punir*. Paris: Gallimard.

———. 1984a. *Histoire de la sexualité II. L'usage des plaisirs*. Paris: Gallimard.

———. 1984b. *Histoire de la sexualité III. Le souci de soi*. Paris: Gallimard.

———. 2001a/1982. *L'herméneutique du sujet, cours au collège de France 1981–1982*. Paris: Hautes Études/Gallimard/Seuil.

———. 2001b/1983. 'A propos de la généalogie de l'éthique: Un aperçu du travail en cours.' In *Dits et écrits II, 1976–1988*, edited by Daniel DEFERT and François EWALD, 1202–1230. Paris: Gallimard.

———. 2001c/1984. 'Qu'est-ce que les Lumières?' In *Dits et écrits II, 1976–1988*, edited by Daniel DEFERT and François EWALD, 1381–1397. Paris: Gallimard.

———. 2001d/1984. 'L'éthique du souci de soi comme pratique de la liberté.' In *Dits et écrits II, 1976–1988*, edited by Daniel DEFERT and François EWALD, 1527–1548. Paris: Gallimard.

———. 2001e/1988. 'Les techniques de soi.' In *Dits et écrits II, 1976–1988*, edited by Daniel DEFERT and François EWALD, 1602–1632. Paris: Gallimard.

FRASER, Nancy. 1994 'Michel Foucault: A Young Conservative?' In *Critique and Power: Recasting the Foucault/Habermas Debate*, edited by Michael KELLY, 185–210. Cambridge: MIT Press.

FREIDSON, Eliot. 1970. *Profession of Medicine: A Study in the Sociology of Applied Knowledge*. New York: Dodd, Mead &Co.

———. 1984. 'The Changing Nature of Professional Control.' *Annual Review of Sociology* 10:1–20.

———. 1986. *Professional Powers: A Study of the Institutionalization of Formal Knowledge*. Chicago: University of Chicago Press.

———. 1994. *Professionalism Reborn: Theory, Prophecy and Policy*. Cambridge & Oxford: Polity Press & Blackwell Publishers.

FREIRE, Paolo. 1998. *Pedagogy of Freedom. Ethics, Democracy and Civic Courage*. Lanham: Rowman & Littlefield.

GAGNON, Chantal. 2006. 'Ideologies in the History of Translation: A Case Study of Canadian Political Speeches.' In *Charting the Future of Translation History*, edited by Georges L. BASTIN and Paul F. BANDIA, 201–223. Ottawa: University of Ottawa Press.

GAGNON, Chantal and Esmaeil KALANTARI. 2017. 'Canadian Translated Politics at the Economic Club of New York.' *The Translator* 23 (1): 17–30.

GARRISON, Randy. 1991. 'Critical Thinking and Adult Education: A Conceptual Model for Developing Critical Thinking in Adult Learners.' *International Journal of Lifelong Education* 10 (4): 287–303.

GIBBS, James Lowell. 1981. 'Anthropology.' In *The Modern American College: Responding to the New Realities of Diverse Students and a Changing Society*, edited by Arthur W. CHICKERING and Associates, 417–439. San Francisco: Jossey-Bass.

GIDDENS, Anthony. 1991. *Modernity and Self Identity: Self and Society in the Late Modern Age*. Cambridge: Polity Press.

GILL, Rosalind and María Constanza GUZMÁN. 2011. 'Teaching Translation for Social Awareness in Toronto.' *The Interpreter and Translator Trainer* 5 (1): 93–108.

GILLIGAN, Carol. 1981. 'Moral Development.' In *The Modern American College: Responding to the New Realities of Diverse Students and a Changing Society*, edited by Arthur W. CHICKERING and Associates, 139–157. San Francisco: Jossey-Bass.

GIUSTINI, Deborah. 2019. 'Donald Trump's Perplexed Italian Translator Reminded us Why Some Jobs are Best Kept Invisible.' *National Post*, October 23.

GODARD, Barbara. 1990. 'Theorizing Feminist Discourse/Translation.' In *Translation, History and Culture*, edited by Susan BASSNETT and André LEFEVERE, 87–96. London & New York: Printer.

GODBOUT, Marielle. 2012. 'Looking to Sociology to Trace a More Successful Path towards the Professionalization of Translation.' *Eighth Symposium on Translation, Interpretation and Terminology*, December 11, 12 and 13, 2012. Havana, Cuba.

———. 2016. 'Lack of Status – Are Translators the Authors of their Own Misfortune?' *Circuit* 131. www.circuitmagazine.org/dossier-131/lack-of-status-are-translators-the-authors-of-their-own-misfortune (Accessed on September 1, 2019).

GOFFMAN, Erving. 1981. *Forms of Talk*. Philadelphia: University of Pennsylvania Press.

GOLDMAN, Alan H. 1980. *The Moral Foundations of Professional Ethics*. Totowa: Rowman & Littlefield.

GOODE, William. J. 1960. 'Encroachment, Charlatanism, and the Emerging Profession: Psychology, Sociology and Medicine.' *American Sociological Review* 25: 902–914.

GOODWIN, Phil. 2010. 'Ethical Problems in Translation: Why We Might Need Steiner After All.' *The Translator* 16 (1): 19–42.

GOUADEC, Daniel. 2007. *Translation as a Profession*. Amsterdam & Philadelphia: Benjamins.

GOUANVIC, Jean-Marc. 2001. 'Ethos, Ethics and Translation.' *The Translator* 7 (2): 203–212.

———. 2005. 'A Bourdieusian Theory of Translation, or The Coincidence of Practical Instances: Field, Habitus, Capital and Illusio.' *The Translator. Bourdieu and the Sociology of Translation* 11 (2): 147–166.

GREENWOOD, Ernest. 1957. 'Attributes of a Profession.' *Social Work* 2 (3): 45–55.

GROS, Frédéric. 2002. 'Sujet moral et soi éthique chez Foucault.' *Archives de Philosophie* 65 (2): 229–237.

GULDIN, Rainer. 2016. *Translation as Metaphor*. Oxon/New York: Routledge.

HABERMAS, Jurgen. 1994. 'Taking Aim at the Heart of the Present." In *Critique and Power: Recasting the Foucault/Habermas Debate*, edited by Michael KELLY, 149–156. Cambridge: MIT Press.

HALE, Sandra. 2007. *Community Interpreting*. Basingstoke: Palgrave Macmillan.

HALL, Stuart. 1980. 'Encoding/decoding.' In *Culture, Media, Language—Working Papers in Cultural Studies*, edited by S. HALL, D. HOBSON, A. LOWE and P. WILLIS, 117–127. London: Routledge.

HAMMOND, Merryl and Rob COLLINS. 2004/1991. *Self-Directed Learning: Critical Practice*. London & New York: Routledge Falmer.

HARDING and Monwabisi K. RALARALA. 2017. 'Tell Me the Story is and Do Not Leave out Anything.' Social Responsibility and Ethical Practices in the Translation of Complainants' Narratives: The Potential for Change.' *The Translator* 23 (2): 158–176.

HATIM, Basil and Ian MASON. 1997. *The Translator as Communicator*. London & New York: Routledge.

HEIDEGGER, Martin. 1968. *What is called Thinking?* Translated by J. Glenn GRAY. New York, Evanston & London: Harper and Row.

HEILBRON, Johan and Gisèle SAPIRO. 2007. 'Outline for a Sociology of Translation: Current Issues and Future Prospects.' In *Constructing a Sociology of Translation*, edited by Michaela WOLF and Alexandra FUKARI, 93–107. Amsterdam: John Benjamins.

HERMANS, Theo. 2008. *The Conference of the Tongues*. Manchester: St. Jerome.

———. 2009. 'Translation, Ethics, Politics.' In *The Routledge Companion to Translation Studies*, edited by Jeremy MUNDAY, 93–105. New York: Routledge.

———. 2010/1996. 'The Translator's Voice in Translated Narrative.' In *Critical Readings in Translation Studies*, edited by Mona BAKER, 193–212. London & New York: Routledge.

HERMANS, Theo and Ubaldo STECCONI. 2002. 'Translators as Hostages of History.' Luxembourg and Brussels Conferences on January 17–18, 2002: 1–17.

https://fdocuments.net/document/translators-as-hostages-of-history-upweb-translators-as-hostages-of-history.html (Accessed on March 15, 2019).

HOGGAN, Chad. 2016. 'A Typology of Transformation: Reviewing the Transformative Learning Literature.' *Studies in the Education of Adults* 48 (1): 65–82.

HOGGETT, Paul. 1992. 'A Place for Experience: A Psychoanalytic Perspective on Boundary, Identity and Culture.' *Environment and Planning D: Society and Space* 10 (3): 345–356.

HOLTZHAUSEN, Derina. 2015. 'The Unethical Consequences of Professional Communication Codes of Ethics: A Postmodern Analysis of Ethical Decision-making in Communication Practice.' *Public Relations Review* 41: 769–776.

HUBSCHER-DAVIDSON, Séverine. 2021. 'Ethical Stress in Translation and Interpreting.' In *The Routledge Handbook of Translation and Ethics*, edited by Kaisa KOSKINEN and Nike K. POKORN, 415–430. London & New York: Routledge.

HUTCHINGS, Stephen (ed). 2021. 'Translation and the ethics of diversity' [Special Issue]. *The Translator* 27 (4).

IGNACIO Garcia. 2009. 'Beyond Translation Memory: Computers and the Professional Translator.' *The Journal of Specialised Translation* 12: 199–214.

INGHILLERI, Moira. 2003. 'Habitus, Field and Discourse: Interpreting as a Socially Situated Activity.' *Target* 15 (2): 243–68.

———. 2005a. 'Mediating Zones of Uncertainty: Interpreter Agency, the Interpreting Habitus and Political Asylum Adjudication.' *The Translator* 11 (1): 69–85.

———. 2005b. 'The Sociology of Bourdieu and the Construction of the 'Object' in Translation and Interpreting Studies.' *The Translator* 11 (2): 125–145.

———. 2008. 'The Ethical Task of the Translator in the Geo-Political Arena: From Iraq to Guantanamo Bay.' *Translation Studies* 1 (2): 212–223.

———. 2009. 'Translators in War Zones: Ethics under Fire in Iraq.' In *Globalization, Political Violence and Translation*, edited by Esperanza BIELSA & Christopher W. HUGHES, 207–221. New York: Palgrave Macmillan.

———. 2010. '"You Don't Make War Without Knowing Why": The Decision to Interpret in Iraq.' *The Translator* 16 (2): 175–196.

———. 2012. *Interpreting Justice. Ethics, Politics and Language*. New York: Routledge.

INGHILLERI, Moira and Sue-Ann HARDING (eds). 2010. 'Translation and Violent Conflict' [Special Issue]. *The Translator* 16 (2).

ISER, Wolfgang. 1978. *The Act of Reading: A Theory of Aesthetic Response*. Baltimore: Johns Hopkins University Press.

———. 1995. 'On Translatability: Variables of Interpretation.' *The European English Messenger* IV (1): 30–38.

JACKSON, Jen. 2017. 'Beyond the Piece of Paper: A Bourdieuian Perspective on Raising Qualifications in the Australian Early Childhood Workforce.' *European Early Childhood Education Research Journal* 25 (5): 796–805.

JACQUEMOND, Richard. 1992. 'Translation and Cultural Hegemony: The Case of French-Arabic Translation.' In *Rethinking Translation: Discourse, Subjectivity, Ideology*, edited by Lawrence VENUTI, 139–158. London: Routledge.

JAFFRO, Laurent. 2006. 'Foucault et le problème de l'éducation morale.' *Le Télémaque* 29 (1): 111–124.

JOHNSON, Terence. 2015/1977. 'The Professions in the Class Structure.' In *Industrial Society: Class, Cleavage and Control*, edited by Richard SCASE, 93–110. Abingdon & New York: Routledge.

———. 2016/1972. *Professions and Power*. Abingdon & New York: Routledge.

KAFI, Mohsen, Masood KHOSHSALIGHEH and Mohammad Reza HASHEMI. 2018. 'Translation Profession in Iran: Current Challenges and Future Prospects.' *The Translator* 24 (1): 89–103.

KANT, Emmanuel. 1993/1785. *Grounding for the Metaphysics of Morals*. Translated by James W. ELLINGTON. Indianapolis & Cambridge: Hackett Publishing.

———. 1997/1788. *Critique of Practical Reason*. Edited by Mary J. GREGOR. Cambridge: Cambridge University Press.

KATAN, David. 2011. 'Occupation or Profession: A Survey of the Translators' World.' In *Identity and Status in the Translational Professions*, edited by Rakefet SELA-SHEFFY and Miriam SHLESINGER, 65–88. Amsterdam & Philadelphia: Benjamins.

KAVALIAUSKAS, Tomas. 2011. *The Individual in Business Ethics: An American Cultural Perspective*. Hampshire: Palgrave Macmillan.

KEARNS, John. 2008. 'The Academic and the Vocational in Translator Education.' In *Translator and Interpreter Training. Issues, Methods and Debates*, edited by John KEARNS, 184–214. London: Continuum.

KEGAN, Robert. 1994. *In Over Our Heads: The Mental Demands of Modern Life*. Cambridge: Harvard University Press.

KELEMEN, Mihaela and Tuomo PELTONEN. 2001. 'Ethics, Morality and the Subject: The Contribution of Zygmunt Bauman and Michel Foucault to `Postmodern' Business Ethics.' *Scandinavian Journal of Management* 17 (2): 151–166.

KENNY, Dorothy. 2011. 'The Ethics of Machine Translation.' *Proceedings of the XI NZSTI National Conference*, Auckland, New Zealand. http://doras.dcu.ie/17606/

———. 2019. 'Machine Translation.' In *The Routledge Handbook of Translation and Philosophy*, edited by Piers RAWLING and Philip WILSON, 428–45. London: Routledge.

KENNY, Dorothy, and Stephen DOHERTY. 2014. 'Statistical Machine Translation in the Translation Curriculum: Overcoming Obstacles and Empowering Translators.' *The Interpreter and Translator Trainer* 8 (2): 276–94.

KIRALY, Don. 2000. *A Social Constructivist Approach to Translator Education: Empowerment from Theory to Practice*. Manchester & Northampton: St. Jerome.

KO, Leong. 2006. 'Fine-Tuning the Code of Ethics for Interpreters and Translators.' *Translation Quality Watch* 2 (3): 45–57.

KOSKINEN, Kaisa. 2000a. *Beyond Ambivalence: Postmodernity and the Ethics of Translation*. Tampere: University of Tampere.

———. 2000b. 'Institutional Illusions.' *The Translator* 6 (1): 49–65.

———. 2012. 'Public Translation Studies in the Classroom.' *The Interpreter and Translator Trainer* 6 (1): 1–20.
———. 2020. *Translation and Affect*. Amsterdam & Philadelphia: Benjamins.
KOSKINEN, Kaisa and Nike K. POKORN. 2021. 'Ethics and Translation: An Introduction.' In *The Routledge Handbook of Translation and Ethics*, edited by Kaisa KOSKINEN and Nike K. POKORN, 1–10. London & New York: Routledge.
KRISTEVA, Julia. 1969. *Séméiôtiké: recherches pour une sémanalyse*. Paris: Edition du Seuil.
KRUGER, Haidee and Elizabeth CROTS. 2014. 'Professional and Personal Ethics in Translation: A Survey of South African Translators' Strategies and Motivations.' *Stellenbosch Papers in Linguistics* 43: 147–181.
LAMBERT, Joseph. 2018. 'How Ethical are Codes of Ethics? Using Illusions of Neutrality to Sell Translations.' *The Journal of Specialised Translation* 30: 269–290.
———. 2021. 'Professional Translator Ethics.' In *The Routledge Handbook of Translation and Ethics*, edited by Kaisa KOSKINEN and Nike K. POKORN, 165–179. London & New York: Routledge.
———. 2023. *Translation Ethics*. London & New York: Routledge.
LARKOSH, Christopher. 2004. 'Levinas, Latin American Thought and the Futures of Translational Ethics.' *TTR* 17 (2): 27–44.
LAYGUES, Arnaud. 2004. 'Le traducteur semeur d'éthique: pour une application de la pensée d'Emmanuel Lévinas à la traduction.' *TTR* 17 (2): 45–56.
LEE, Hyang and Seong Woo YUN. 2020. 'How Can We Improve the Codes of Ethics for Translators?' *Babel* 66 (4–5): 706–718.
LEFEVERE, André. 1990. 'Translation: Its Genealogy in the West.' In *Translation, History & Culture*, edited by Susan BASSNETT and André LEFEVERE, 14–28. London & New York: Pinter Publishers.
———. 1992. *Translation, Rewriting, and the Manipulation of Literary Fame*. London & New York: Routledge.
LEVINAS, Emmanuel. 1991. *Entre nous: Essais sur le penser-à-l'autre*. Paris: Grasset & Fasquelle.
———. 1995. *Altérité et transcendance*. France: Fata Morgana.
LITTAU, Karin. 2010/1997. 'Translation in the Age of Postmodern Production: From Text to Intertext to Hypertext.' In *Critical Readings in Translation Studies*, edited by Mona BAKER, 435—448. London & New York: Routledge.
LIU, Fung-Ming. 2013. 'Revisiting the Translator's Visibility: Does Visibility Bring Rewards?' *Meta* 58 (1): 25–57.
LUHMANN, Niklas. 1992. 'Operational Closure and Structural Coupling: The Differentiation of the Legal System.' *Cardozo Law Review* 13: 1419–1441.
LUXON, Nancy. 2008. 'Ethics and Subjectivity: Practices of Self-Governance in the Late Lectures of Michel Foucault.' *Political Theory* 36 (3): 377–402.
LYOTARD, Jean-François. 1979. *La condition postmoderne. Rapport sur le savoir*. Paris: Minuit.
MACINTYRE, Alasdair. 1977. 'Epistemological Crises, Dramatic Narrative and the Philosophy of Science.' *The Monist* 60 (4): 453–472.

———. 1988. *Whose Justice? Which Rationality?* Indiana: University of Notre Dame Press.
———. 2007/1981. *After Virtue: A Study in Moral Theory*. Indiana: University of Notre Dame Press.
MARAIS, Kobus. 2014. *Translation Theory and Development Studies: A Complexity Theory Approach*. New York: Routledge.
MARSHALL, James. 1996. *Michel Foucault: Personal Autonomy and Education*. Dordrecht: Kluwer Academic Publishers.
MARTÍN RUANO, Rosario. 2015. '(Trans)formative Theorising in Legal Translation and/or Interpreting: A Critical Approach to Deontological Principles.' *The Interpreter and Translator Trainer* 9 (2): 141–155.
———. 2017. 'Developing Public Service Translation and Interpreting Under the Paradigm of Recognition: Towards Diversity-Sensitive Discourses on Ethics in PSIT.' In *Ideology, Ethics and Policy Development in Public Service Interpreting and Translation*, edited by Carmen Valero-Garcés and Rebecca Tipton, 21–37. Bristol & Blue Ridge Summit: Multilingual Matters.
MCDONOUGH Dolmaya, Julie. 2011. 'Moral Ambiguity: Some Shortcomings of Professional Codes of Ethics for Translators.' *The Journal of Specialised Translation* 15: 28–49.
MEHREZ, Samia. 1992. 'Translation and the Poscolonial Experience: The Francophone North African Text.' In *Rethinking Translation*, edited by Lawrence VENUTI, 120–138. London & New York: Routledge.
MEIJL, Toon van. 2000. 'Modern Morals in Postmodernity: A Critical Reflection on Professional Codes of Ethics.' *Cultural Dynamics* 12 (1): 65–81.
MELBY, Alan. 1997. 'Some Notes on The Proper Place of Men and Machines in Language Translation.' *Machine Translation* 12: 29–34.
MESCHONNIC, Henri. 1999. *Poétique du traduire*. Lagrasse: Verdier
MEZIROW, Jack. 1990. 'How Critical Reflection Triggers Transformative Learning.' In *Fostering Critical Reflection in Adulthood: A Guide to Transformative and Emancipatory Learning*, edited by Jack MEZIROW and Associates, 1–21. San Francisco: Jossey-Bass.
———. 1998. 'On Critical Reflection.' *Adult Education Quarterly* 48 (3): 185–198.
———. 2000. 'Learning to Think Like an Adult. Core Concepts of Transformation Theory.' In *Learning as Transformation*, edited by Jack Mezirow and Associates, 3–33. San Francisco: Jossey-Bass.
———. 2009. 'Transformative Learning Theory.' In *Transformative Learning in Practice: Insights from Community, Workplace, and Higher Education*, edited by Jack MEZIROW, Edward W. TAYLOR and Associates, 18–31. San Francisco: Jossey-Bass.
MIKKELSON, Holly. 2000. 'Interpreter Ethics. A Review of the Traditional and Electronic Literature.' *Interpreting* 5 (1): 49–56.
MILL, John Stuart. 1969/1861. 'Utilitarianism.' In *Essays on Ethics, Religion and Society*, edited by J. M. ROBSON, 203–259. Toronto: University of Toronto Press/ London: Routledge & Kegan Paul.

MONZÓ-NEBOT, Esther and Melissa WALLACE. 2020. 'Ethics of Non-Professional Translation and Interpreting' [Special Issue]. *Translation and Interpreting Studies* 15 (1).

MOORKENS, Joss and Marta ROCCHI. 2021. 'Ethics in the Translation Industry.' In *The Routledge Handbook of Translation and Ethics*, edited by Kaisa KOSKINEN and Nike K. POKORN, 320–337. London & New York: Routledge.

MUNDAY, Jeremy. 2012. *Evaluation in Translation: Critical Points of Translator Decision-Making*. London & New York: Routledge.

MYERS, Ella. 2008. 'Resisting Foucauldian Ethics: Associative Politics and the Limits of the Care of the Self.' *Contemporary Political Theory* 7: 125–146.

NIDA, Eugene. 1964. *Towards a Science of Translating: With Special Reference to Principles and Procedures Involved in Bible Translating*. Leiden: E. J. Brill.

NIRANJANA, Tejaswini. 1992. *Siting Translation: History, Post-structuralism, and the Colonial Context*. Berkeley: University of California Press.

NORD, Christiane. 2005/1988. *Text Analysis in Translation: Theory, Methodology, and Didactic Application of a Model for Translation-Oriented Text Analysis*. Translated by Christiane Nord and Penelope Sparrow. Amsterdam & New York: Rodopi.

———. 1991. 'Scopos, Loyalty, and Translational Conventions.' *Target* 3 (1): 91–109.

———. 1997. *Translating as a Purposeful Activity. Functionalist Approaches Explained*. Manchester: St Jerome.

O'BRIEN, Sharon. 2012. 'Translation as Human–Computer Interaction.' *Translation Spaces* 1: 101–122.

OLSSEN, Mark. 1999. *Michel Foucault: Materialism and Education*. Westport & London: Bergin & Garvey.

OZOLINS, Uldis. 2014. 'Rewriting the AUSIT Code of Ethics – Principles, Practice, Dispute.' *Babel* 60 (3): 347–370.

PARKS, Tim. 2010. 'Why Translators Deserve Some Credit.' The *Guardian*, April 25.

PARSONS, Talcott. 1954. *Essays in Sociological Theory*. Glencoe: Free Press.

———. 1968. 'Professions.' In *The International Encyclopedia of the Social Sciences 12*, edited by David L. SILLS, 536–547. New York: MacMillan.

———. 1991/1951. *The Social System*. London: Routledge.

PERRY, William G., Jr. 1970. *Forms of Intellectual and Ethical Development in the College Years*. New York: Holt, Rinehart and Winston.

———. 1981. 'Cognitive and Ethical Growth: The Making of Meaning.' In *The Modern American College: Responding to the New Realities of Diverse Students and a Changing Society*, edited by Arthur W. CHICKERING and Associates, 76–116. San Francisco: Jossey-Bass.

PHELAN, Mary, Mette RUDVIN, Hanne SKAADEN, and Patrick KERMIT. 2020. *Ethics in Public Service Interpreting*. London & New York: Routledge.

POLIZZOTI, Mark. 2018a. *Sympathy for the Traitor: A Translation Manifesto*. Cambridge/Massachusetts/London: MIT Press.

———. 2018b. 'L'art de la traduction.' *Aeon*, October 9. https://aeon.co/essays/is-the-translator-a-servant-of-the-text-or-an-original-artist

POPKEWITZ, Thomas and Marie BRENNAN (eds). 1998. *Foucault's Challenge: Discourse, Knowledge and Power in Education*. New York: Teacher's College Press.
PYM, Anthony. 1998. *Method in Translation History*. Manchester: St Jerome.
———. (ed). 2001. 'The Return to Ethics' [Special Issue]. *The Translator* 7 (2).
———. 2012. *On Translator Ethics: Principles for Mediation between Cultures*. Translated by Heike Walker. Revised and updated by Anthony PYM. Amsterdam & Philadelphia: Benjamins.
———. 2014. 'Translator Associations – from Gatekeepers to Communities.' *Target* 26 (3): 466–491.
———. 2016. 'A Spirited Defense of a Certain Empiricism in Translation Studies (and in Anything Else Concerning the Study of Cultures).' *Translation Spaces* 5 (2): 289–313.
———. 2023. 'A Naïve Inquiry into Translation between Aboriginal Languages in Pre-Invasion Australia.' In *Translation Flows: Exploring Networks of People, Processes and Products*, edited by Ilse FEINAUER, Amanda MARAIS and Marius SWART, 3–22. Amsterdam & Philadelphia: Benjamins.
PYM, Anthony, François GRIN, Claudio SFREDDO, and Andy L. J. CHAN. 2012. *Studies on Translation and Multilingualism: The Status of the Translation Profession in the European Union*. Luxembourg: Publications Office of the EU.
———. 2013. *The Status of the Translation Profession in the European Union*. London: Anthem.
PYM, Anthony, David ORREGO-CARMONA, and Esther TORRES-SIMÓN. 2016. 'Status and Technology in the Professionalisation of Translators. Market Disorder and the Return of Hierarchy.' *The Journal of Specialised Translation* 25: 33–53.
RAAEN, Finn Daniel. 2011. 'Autonomy, Candour and Professional Teacher Practice: A Discussion Inspired by the Later Works of Michel Foucault.' *Journal of Philosophy of Education* 45 (4): 627–641.
RAFAEL, Vicente. 1993/1988. *Contracting Colonialism: Translation and Christian Conversion in Tagalog Society under Early Spanish Rule*. Durham: Duke University Press.
———. 2010/2007. 'Translation in Wartime.' In *Critical Readings in Translation Studies*, edited by Mona BAKER, 383–390. London & New York: Routledge.
———. 2012. 'Translation and the US Empire: Counterinsurgency and the Resistance of Language.' *The Translator* 18 (1): 1–22.
RAIHANI, Mohamed Said. 2024. 'tārīḫ lfẓī "trǧm" fī al-sīāq al-tqāfī al-'rbī (mn 'ṣr mā qbl al-islām ilā al-'ṣr al-'bāsī) ['The History of the Term "Tarjama" [to Translate] in the Arab Cultural Context (From the Pre-Islamic Period to the Abbasid One)].' *Arab Journal for the Humanities* 165: 93–118.
REN, Wen. 2020. 'The Evolution of Interpreters' Perception and Application of (Codes of) Ethics in China since 1949: A Sociological and Historical Perspective.' *The Translator* 26 (3): 274–296.
RICŒUR, Paul. 1990. *Soi-même comme un autre*. Paris: Éditions du Seuil.
———. 2000. 'De la morale à l'éthique et aux éthiques.' In *Un siècle de philosophie 1900–2000*, 103–120. Paris: Gallimard/Centre Pompidou.

ROBINSON, Bob. 2011. 'Michel Foucault: Ethics.' *Internet Encyclopedia of Philosophy*. www.iep.utm.edu/fouc-eth/ (Accessed on July 20, 2019).
ROBINSON, Douglas. 1997. *Translation and Empire. Postcolonial Translation Theories Explained*. Manchester: St. Jerome.
———. 2003. *Performative Linguistics. Speaking and Translating as Doing Things with Words*. London: Routledge.
ROSEN, Frederick. 2010. 'Utilitarianism to Bentham.' In *The Routledge Companion to Ethics*, edited by J. SKORPUSKI, 144–155. London: Routledge.
ROTTENBURG, Richard. 1996. 'When Organization Travels: On Intercultural Translation.' In *Translating Organizational Change*, edited by Barbara CZARNIAWSKA and Guje SEVON, 191–240. Berlin & New York: Walter de Gruyter.
RUESCHEMEYER, Dietrich. 1964. 'Doctors and Lawyers: A Comment on the Theory of the Professions.' *Canadian Review of Sociology and Anthropology* 1: 17–30.
SADEK, Gaafar. 2018. 'Translation: Rights and Agency. A Public Policy Perspective for Knowledge, Technology and Globalization.' PhD Diss. University of Ottawa. https://ruor.uottawa.ca/handle/10393/37362 (Accessed on February 10, 2020).
SAHLIN-ANDERSSON, Kerstin. 1996. 'Imitating by Editing Success: The Construction of Organization Fields.' In *Translating Organizational Change*, edited by Barbara CZARNIAWSKA and Guje SEVON, 69–92. Berlin & New York: Walter de Gruyter.
SAKS, Mike. 2015. *The Professions, State and the Market: Medicine in Britain, the United States and Russia*. London & New York: Routledge.
———. 2016a. 'Professions and Power: A Review of Theories of Professions and power.' In *The Routledge Companion to the Professions and Professionalism*, edited By Mike DENT, Ivy Lynn BOURGEAULT, Jean-Louis DENIS, and Ellen KUHLMANN, 71–85. London & New York: Routledge.
———. 2016b. 'A Review of Theories of Professions, Organizations and Society: The Case for Neo-Weberianism, Neo-institutionalism and Eclecticism.' *Journal of Professions and Organization* 3 (2): 170–187.
SCHINKEL, Willem and Mirko NOORDEGRAAF. 2011. 'Professionalism as Symbolic Capital: Materials for a Bourdieusian Theory of Professionalism.' *Comparative Sociology* 10: 67–96.
SCHLEIERMACHER, Friedrich. 2012/1813. 'On the Different Methods of Translating.' In *The Translation Studies Reader*, edited by Lawrence Venutis, 43–63. London: Routledge.
SCHWEDA-NICHOLSON, Nancy. 1994. 'Community Interpreter Training in the United States and the United Kingdom: An Overview of Selected Initiatives.' *Hermes* 12, 127–140.
SEARLE, John R. 1976. 'A Classification of Illocutionary Acts.' *Language in Society* 5 (1): 1–23.
———. 1983. *Intentionality: An Essay in the Philosophy of Mind*. Cambridge: Cambridge University Press.
SELA-SHEFFY, Rakefet. 2008. 'The Translators' Personae: Marketing Translatorial Images as Pursuit of Capital.' *Meta* 53 (3): 609–622.

———. 2011. 'Introduction: Identity and Status in the Translational Professions.' In *Identity and Status in the Translational Professions*, edited by SELA-SHEFFY, Rakefet and Miriam SHLESINGER, 1–9. Amsterdam & Philadelphia: Benjamins.

———. 2016. 'Elite and Non-Elite Translator Manpower: The Non-professionalised Culture in the Translation Field in Israel.' *The Journal of Specialised Translation* 25: 54–73.

SELA-SHEFFY, Rakefet and Miriam SHLESINGER (eds). 2011. *Identity and Status in the Translational Professions*. Amsterdam & Philadelphia: Benjamins.

SIMEONI, Daniel. 1998. 'The Pivotal Status of the Translator's Habitus.' *Target* 10 (1): 1–36.

SIMON, Sherry. 1996. *Gender in Translation*. London & New York: Routledge.

SLOTE, Michael. 2010. 'Virtue Ethics.' In *The Routledge Companion to Ethics*, edited by J. SKORPUSKI, 478–489. London: Routledge.

SOMERS, Margaret and Gloria GIBSON. 1994. 'Reclaiming the Epistemological "Other": Narrative and the Social Constitution of Identity.' In *Social Theory and the Politics of Identity*, edited by Craig CALHOUN, 37–99. Oxford and Cambridge, MA: Blackwell.

SPIVAK, Gayatri. 2000. 'The Politics of Translation.' In *The Translation Studies Reader*, edited by Lawrence VENUTI, 397–416. London & New York: Routledge.

———. 2005. 'Translating into English.' In *Nation, Language and the Ethics of Translation*, edited by Sandra BERMANN and Michael WOOD, 93–110. Princeton & Oxford: Princeton University Press.

STATEN, Henry. 2005. 'Tracking the "Native Informant": Cultural Translation as the Horizon of Literary Translation.' In *Nation, Language and the Ethics of Translation*, edited by Sandra BERMANN and Michael WOOD, 111–126. Princeton & Oxford: Princeton University Press.

STEINER, George. 1975. *After Babel. Aspects of Language and Translation*. New York: Oxford University Press.

ST-PIERRE, Paul. 2000. 'Translating (into) the Language of the Colonizer.' In *Changing the Terms: Translating in the Postcolonial Era*, edited by Sherry SIMON and Paul ST-PIERRE, 261–288. Ottawa: University of Ottawa Press.

STURROCK, John. 2010/1990. 'Writing between the Lines: The Language of Translation.' In *Critical Readings in Translation Studies*, edited by Mona BAKER, 49–64. London & New York: Routledge.

SUMMERS, Caroline. 2017. *Examining Text and Authorship in Translation: What Remains of Christa Wolf?* Cham: Palgrave Macmillan.

SUSAM-SARAJEVA, Sebnem. 2002. 'A Multilingual and International Translation Studies?' In *Cross-Cultural Transgressions. Research Models in Translation Studies. Historical and Ideological Issues*, edited by Theo HERMANS, 193–207. Manchester: St Jerome.

TAYLOR, Charles. 1989. *Sources of the Self: The Making of the Modern Identity*. Cambridge: Harvard University Press.

———. 1991. *The Ethics of Authenticity*. Cambridge: Harvard University Press.

TAYLOR, Edward. 2000. 'Analyzing Research on Transformative Learning Theory.' In *Learning as Transformation*, edited by Jack Mezirow and Associates, 285–328. San Francisco: Jossey-Bass.

———. 2008. 'Transformative Learning Theory.' *New Directions for Adult and Continuing Education* 119: 5–15.
———. 2009. 'Fostering Transformative Learning.' In *Transformative Learning in Practice: Insights from Community, Workplace, and Higher Education*, edited by Jack MEZIROW, Edward W. TAYLOR, and Associates, 3–17. San Francisco: Jossey-Bass.
TENNANT, Mark. 1998. 'Adult Education and Technology of the Self.' *International Journal of Lifelong Learning* 16: 364–376.
TOURY, Gideon. 1995. *Descriptive Translation Studies and Beyond*. Amsterdam: Benjamins.
TRIVEDI, Harish. 2006. 'In Our Time, On Our Own Terms.' In *Translating Others*, Vol. 1, edited by Theo HERMANS, 102–119. Manchester: St Jerome.
TYMOCZKO, Maria. 1999. *Translation in a Postcolonial Context: Early Irish Literature in English Translation*. Manchester: St. Jerome.
———. 2000. 'Translation and Political Engagement: Activism, Social Change and the Role of Translation in Geopolitical Shifts.' *The Translator* 6 (1): 23–47.
———. 2005. 'Trajectories of Research in Translation Studies.' *Meta* 50 (4): 1082–1097.
———. 2006. 'Reconceptualizing Translation Theory. Integrating Non-Western Thought about Translation.' In *Translating Others*, Vol. 1, edited by Theo HERMANS, 13–32. Manchester: St Jerome.
———. 2007. *Enlarging Translation, Empowering Translators*. Manchester: St Jerome.
———. 2009. 'Why Translators Should Want to Internationalize Translation Studies.' *The Translator* 15 (2): 401–421.
———. 2010/2003. 'Ideology and the Position of the Translator: In What Sense is a Translator 'In Between'?' In *Critical Readings in Translation Studies*, edited by Mona BAKER, 213–228. London & New York: Routledge.
———. 2010. 'Translation, Resistance, Activism: An Overview.' In *Translation, Resistance, Activism*, edited by Maria TYMOCZKO, 1–22. Amherst & Boston: University of Massachusetts Press.
TYULENEV, Sergey. 2009. 'Why (not) Luhmann? On the Applicability of Social Systems Theory to Translation Studies.' *Translation Studies* 2 (2): 147–162.
———. 2015. 'Towards Theorising Translation as an Occupation.' *Asia Pacific Translation and Intercultural Studies* 2 (1): 15–29.
TYULENEV, Sergey, Bingham ZHENG and Penelope JOHNSON. 2017. 'A Comparative Study of Translation or Interpreting as a Profession in Russia, China and Spain.' *Translating and Interpreting Studies* 12 (2): 332–354.
VALERO-GARCÉS, Carmen. 2017. 'Ethical Codes and their Impact on Prison Communication.' In *Ideology, Ethics and Policy Development in Public Service Interpreting and Translation*, edited by Carmen Valero-Garcés and Rebecca Tipton, 105–130. Bristol & Blue Ridge Summit: Multilingual Matters.
VAN DIJK, Teun. 1993. 'Principles of Critical Discourse Analysis.' *Discourse & Society* 4 (2): 249–283.
VANMASSENHOVE, Eva, Christian HARDMEIER, and Andy WAY. 2018. "Getting Gender Right in Neural Machine Translation." *Proceedings of the*

2018 Conference on Empirical Methods in Natural Language Processing, Brussels, Belgium, October 31–November 4, 3003–8. www.aclweb.org/anthology/D18-1334

VENUTI, Lawrence. 1992. 'Introduction.' In *Rethinking Translation: Discourse, Subjectivity, Ideology*, edited by Lawrence VENUTI, 1–17. London & New York: Routledge.

———. 1995. *The Translator's Invisibility: A History of Translation*. London: Routledge.

———. 1998. *The Scandals of Translation. Towards an Ethics of Difference*. London: Routledge.

———. 2005. 'Translation, History, Narrative.' *META Le prisme de l'Histoire* 50 (3): 800–816.

———. 2010/1993. 'Translation as Cultural Politics: Régimes of Domestication in English.' In *Critical Readings in Translation Studies*, edited by Mona BAKER, 65–79. London & New York: Routledge.

VINTGES, Karen. 2001. '"Must We Burn Foucault?" Ethics as Art of Living: Simone de Beauvoir and Michel Foucault.' *Continental Philosophy Review* 34 (2): 165–181.

WATZLAWICK, Paul. 1987. 'When the Solution is the Problem.' Presented at The Evangelic Mission of the Stuttgart Hospital. Stuttgart. www.youtube.com/watch?v=7etsh4HwG78 (Accessed on June 3, 2018).

WEBER, Max. 1978/1922. *Economy and Society: An Outline of Interpretive Sociology*. Berkeley: University of California Press.

WHITE, Patrick. 1966. *The Solid Mandala*. London: Eyre & Spottiswoode.

WITTER-MERITHEW, Anna, and Leilani JOHNSON. 2004. 'Market Disorder Within the Field of Sign Language Interpreting: Professionalization Implications.' *Distance Opportunities for Interpreter Training Center*: 1–35.

WOLF, Michaela. 2000. 'The Third Space in Postcolonial Representation.' In *Changing the Terms. Translation in the Postcolonial Era*, edited by Sherry SIMON et Paul St. PIERRE, 127–145. Ottawa: University of Ottawa Press.

———. 2002. 'Culture as Translation – and Beyond. Ethnographic Models of Representations in Translation Studies.' In *Crosscultural Transgressions. Research Models in Translation Studies II*, edited by Theo HERMANS, 180–192. Manchester. St. Jerome.

WONG, James. 2013. 'Self and Others: The Work of 'Care' in Foucault's Care of the Self.' *Philosophy Faculty Publications* 6.

ZELLER, Beatriz. 2000. 'On Translation and Authorship.' *Meta* 45 (1): 134–139.

ZIGURAS, Christopher. 2004. *Self-care Embodiment, Personal Autonomy and the Shaping of Health Consciousness*. London & New York: Routledge.

Appendices

Appendix I: Translator Organizations Websites

Asociación de Traductores Profesionales del Perú – ATPP (Peruvian Association of Professional Translators). www.atpp.org.pe/ (Accessed on July 5, 2018).

Association of Translators and Interpreters of Ontario (ATIO). https://atio.on.ca/ (Accessed on July 5, 2018).

Australian Institute of Interpreters and Translators (AUSIT). https://ausit.org/ (Accessed on July 5, 2018).

Fédération Internationale des Traducteurs (FIT). www.fit-ift.org/ (Accessed on March 23, 2018).

Indian Translators Association (ITAINDIA). http://itaindia.org/ (Accessed on July 5, 2018).

International Association for Egyptian Translators (IAFET). https://iafet.org/ (Accessed on September 1, 2018).

Société française des traducteurs (SFT). www.sft.fr/ (Accessed on July 5, 2018).

South African Translators' Institute (SATI). www.translators.org.za/ (Accessed on October 25, 2019).

Appendix II: Codes of Ethics

Asociación de Traductores Profesionales del Perú – ATPP [Peruvian Association of Professional Translators]. *Code of Ethics*. www.atpp.org.pe/code_ethics.pdf (Accessed on July 5, 2018).

Association of Translators and Interpreters of Ontario (ATIO). 2009. *Code of Ethics*. https://atio.on.ca/wp-content/uploads/bsk-pdfmanager/Code_Ethics_EN_(1)_19.pdf (Accessed on July 5, 2018).

Australian Institute of Interpreters and Translators (AUSIT). 2012. *Code of Ethics and Code of Conduct*. https://ausit.org/AUSIT/Documents/Code_Of_Ethics_Full.pdf (Accessed on July 5, 2018).

Indian Translators Association (ITAINDIA). *Membership Information/ Code of Professional Conduct.* http://itaindia.org/wp-content/uploads/ 2017/03/Membership_Information.pdf (Accessed on July 5, 2018).
Société française des traducteurs (SFT). 2009.

- *Code de déontologie général des adhérents de la Société française des traducteurs (SFT).* www.sft.fr/code-de-deontologie-des-traducteurs-et-interpretes.html#.XEcsYlVKjIU; www.sft.fr/clients/sft/telechargements/ file_front/58367_SFTCode_deontologie.pdf.pdf and www.sft.fr/clients/ sft/telechargements/file_front/51907_deontologieanglaisweb.pdf.pdf/ (Accessed on July 5, 2018).
- *Code de déontologie des Interprètes adhérents de la Société française des traducteurs (SFT).* www.sft.fr/code-de-deontologie-des-traducteurs-et-interpretes.html#.XEcsYlVKjIU/ (Accessed on July 5, 2018).

South African Translators' Institute (SATI). 2013.

- *Code of Ethics for Individual Members.* http://translators.org.za/ sati_cms/downloads/dynamic/sati_ethics_individual_english.pdf (Accessed on July 5, 2018).
- *Code of ethics for Language Agency Corporate Members.* http://tran slators.org.za/sati_cms/downloads/dynamic/sati_ethics_corporate_a gencies_english.pdf (Accessed on July 5, 2018).

Code of ethics for Language Agency Corporate Members http://tran slators.org.za/sati_cms/downloads/dynamic/sati_ethics_corporate_offi ces_english.pdf (Accessed on July 5, 2018).
International Association for Egyptian Translators (IAFET). 2017. *Code of Ethics.* https://iafet.cyrillabs.com/wp-content/uploads/2018/09/ Code-of-ethics.pdf (Last accessed August 2019).

Appendix III: FIT Translator's Charter

Fédération Internationale des Traducteurs / International Federation of Translators (FIT). 1994/1963. *Translator's Charter.* Oslo. www.fit-ift.org/ translators-charter/ (Accessed on March 23, 2018).

Appendix IV: UNESCO Nairobi Recommendation

UNESCO Nairobi Recommendation. 1976. *Recommendation on the Legal Protection of Translators and Translations and the Practical Means to improve the Status of Translators.* Nairobi. http://portal.unesco.org/en/ ev.php-URL_ID=13089&URL_DO=DO_TOPIC&URL_SECTION=201. html (Accessed on July 5, 2018).

Appendix V: Berne Convention

World Intellectual Property Organization (WIPO). 1978. *Guide to the Berne Convention for the Protection of Literary and Artistic Works: (Paris Act, 1971)*. Geneva. www.wipo.int/edocs/pubdocs/en/copyright/615/wipo_pub_615.pdf (Accessed on June 13, 2018).

World Intellectual Property Organization (WIPO). *The Berne Convention for the Protection of Literary and Artistic Works*. https://wipolex.wipo.int/en/text/283698 (Accessed on June 13, 2018).

Index

Abdallah, Kristiina 54–5, 103
accountability 8, 16, 74, 99, 201, 208
accuracy 6, 62, 63–4, 66, 67, 68, 69–70, 72–3, 173, 179, 180, 181, 182, 183, 193, 196, 197, 207, 208, 210
Afghanistan 196–7
alienation 48–9, 50, 109, 190, 202, 218, 262, 266, 274, 275
alternative ethics: charter 238–42; translation education 234–6; translation occupation 236–8; translation studies 232–4
ambivalence 1, 2, 3, 45, 75, 97, 163–6, 177, 203–4, 209–10, 212, 214, 218–19, 230, 240, 242, 249, 256, 265, 266, 273
American Translators Association (ATA) 101
aporia 164, 165, 204, 209, 211, 213–14
Appiah, Kwame Anthony 43–4, 56, 184
Arrojo, Rosemary 6, 7, 213
Artificial Intelligence (AI) 52, 216, 241
Asociacion de Traductores Profesionales del Peru (ATPP) 13, 60, 61, 63, 64, 68, 90, 91, 93, 99, 100, 101, 104, 109, 114, 122, 128, 174, 176, 177, 180–1, 183, 185, 186, 192, 203
Association of Translators and Interpreters of Ontario (ATIO) 12, 60, 61, 63, 64, 66, 68, 91, 99–100, 101, 104–5, 106–7, 109, 111–12, 114, 122, 127–8, 136, 147, 173–4, 176, 179–80, 183, 184, 185, 186, 192–3, 194, 201, 203, 206, 207
audiovisual translation (AVT) 261, 262
Australian Institute of Interpreters and Translators (AUSIT) 6, 12, 60, 61, 63–4, 66–7, 68, 69, 90, 91, 94, 99, 100, 101, 104, 105–6, 108, 109, 114, 122, 127, 136, 147, 174–5, 176, 181–2, 183, 184, 185, 186–7, 188, 189, 190, 191, 192–3, 201, 203, 207–9, 210–11, 213, 236

Babel, Tower of 44, 152, 211, 212
Bachmann-Medick, Doris 48
Baixauli-Olmos, Lluís 6, 7–8, 33
Baker, Mona 5, 40–2, 51, 56–7, 68, 152, 179, 196, 232, 234, 235, 262
Bakhtin, Mikhail M. 44, 126
Barthes, Roland 47, 75, 139
Basalamah, Salah 133, 136, 137–8
Baudrillard, Jean 194
Bauman, Zygmunt 163–4, 172, 199, 205, 209, 226, 249; on business 202; challenges of globalization 169–71, 214–15, 217; on moral responsibility 166–7, 193–4, 198; on the moral self 10, 15, 164–6, 171, 203, 204, 212, 213, 221–2, 226, 229, 230; on *Ressentiment* 194–5; on social spaces 168–9, 197
Benjamin, Walter 38, 44, 46, 211, 212
Bentham, Jeremy 139
Berman, Antoine 38–9, 40–1, 56, 68, 69
Berne Convention for the Protection of Literary and Artistic Works (1886)

300 Index

115, 131, 132–3, 135–6, 146–7;
Paris Act 112–13, 115, 138
Bhabha, Homi K. 47
Boulanger, Pier-Pascale 219
Bourdieu, Pierre 9, 14, 33, 34, 51;
on cultural capital 81, 82–3, 89, 90,
92, 93, 94, 96, 126, 153, 156;
on economic capital 81, 82, 94,
103, 113; on *field* 80–1, 86–7, 105,
142–3, 148, 156, 158; on *habitus*
79–80; notion of capital 8, 10,
14, 15, 33, 81–5, 86, 96; on
'profession' 25–6, 119–20; on
social capital 81, 83–5, 97, 99, 100,
101, 102, 104, 106, 109, 110; on
symbolic capital 81, 82, 85–6, 118,
149; on symbolic violence 85–6,
145–6, 147, 155
Bowker, Lynne 31, 52, 97
Brisset, Annie 124, 149, 150
Brookfield, Stephen 246–7
Bush, George W. 196

Calinescu, Matei 70
Canada 192; Translation Bureau 124,
149, 154
Canadian Translators, Terminologists
and Interpreters Council (CTTIC)
66, 101
capital 81–2; *see also* cultural capital;
economic capital; social capital;
symbolic capital
Chamberlain, Lori 49
Chesterman, Andrew 5–6, 38, 55–7,
64, 68, 69, 186, 188, 255–6
Cheyfitz, Eric 48
China 32–4
Clarkeburn, Henriikka 249, 250
Commitment 249–50
completeness 44, 67, 69, 164, 197,
211, 212
Computer-Aided Translation (CAT)
73, 94, 241
confidentiality 63, 91, 128, 129, 155,
173, 174, 175, 184–5, 186, 190,
203, 207, 208, 213, 218
copyright law 91, 114–15, 131–44,
145, 146–7, 156, 265
Costa, Beverley 233, 234
creativity 71, 80, 118–19, 123, 129,
133, 138, 141, 152, 177, 253–4

Critical Discourse Analysis 51
Cronin, Michael 42–3, 50, 52, 56–7,
71, 73, 74, 103, 111, 124, 126, 155,
215–16, 217, 239, 247
Crots, Elizabeth 6, 179, 193
cultural capital 33–4, 81, 82–3, 88,
102–3, 120–6, 146, 149, 153, 240;
codified ethics 89–97, 123, 124,
125–6, 153, 156–8; conversion
into symbolic capital 118–19, 120,
125, 129, 143, 145, 149, 156, 157,
158, 234; copyright law 131, 142;
embodied 82, 89–92, 93–4, 96, 97,
102, 103, 120, 124, 125–6, 143,
149, 150, 156, 157, 234, 256–7;
institutionalized 83, 89, 92–4, 97,
102, 103, 120, 124, 125–6, 157,
158, 256; objectified 82, 89, 94–7;
translation ethics 234, 254,
256–7, 271

Dam, Helle 34–6
Davis, Kathleen 44–5, 52–3, 177–8,
213, 214
deconstruction 44–6, 48, 56–7, 70,
178, 211, 212, 213
deflection 266
dehumanisation 179
Derrida, Jacques 44–5, 137, 139,
197–8, 204–5, 211–12, 213
detachment 54, 63, 64, 68, 72, 155,
190, 259, 266
discriminatory language 175, 191–2,
193, 203, 263
Dolmaya, Julie McDonough 6, 173
Drugan, Joanna 6, 43, 57
dualism 170, 248–9, 255, 260, 266,
270

Eaglestone, Robert 46, 69
ecological dimension 42–3, 52–3,
56–7, 216, 247, 252, 257, 260, 265,
267, 273
economic capital 81, 82, 94, 103, 120,
149; translator's 88, 96, 110–15,
118, 126, 131, 137, 150
Epictetus 225, 227
epimeleia heautou 226, 228, 234
equivalence 40, 50, 56–7, 64, 66,
69–70, 71, 72–3, 75, 123, 182, 197,
251, 254, 260

Eurocentrism 2, 40, 45, 46–7, 72, 143, 177, 178–9, 199, 216, 247
European Union (EU) 73, 112, 123, 124, 149, 154

faithfulness 39, 49, 74–5, 76, 123–4, 133–4, 139, 140, 145, 150, 152–3, 155, 196, 211, 260, 263, 272; in codified ethics 5, 7, 64–6, 67, 68, 69–70, 71, 72–3, 74–5, 125, 129, 133–4, 152, 176–9, 180, 181–2, 183–4, 186, 193, 197, 198, 203, 204, 213, 218
Federation Internationale des Traducteurs (FIT) 14; Translator's Charter 13–14, 61–2, 64–5, 69, 86, 91, 93, 98, 100, 111, 112, 114, 121, 132–3, 134, 135, 136, 157, 182, 207, 217
field 80–1, 86–7, 105, 142–3, 148, 156, 158
Flotow, Luise von 49
Folkart, Barbara 40
Follorou, Jacques 196
foreignization 259
Foucault, Michel: alternative ethics 236, 238, 242; *epimeleia heautou* 226, 228, 234; on self care 223–30, 232, 233, 235–6, 237, 242, 243, 274–5
France 4, 12, 14, 99, 137, 198, 261
Freidson, Eliot 26–7, 28, 32, 130
French Society of Translators *see* Societe francaise des traducteurs
French Society of Translators (SFT) 12–13, 60, 61, 63, 64, 68, 90, 91, 93, 99, 100, 105, 106, 107, 109, 111, 112, 114, 121, 122, 136, 147, 174, 176, 180, 183, 184, 185–6, 192–3, 203
functionalism 3; ethics 53–7, 150–1; professionalization 23, 24–5, 27, 32

Gagnon, Chantal 52–3, 191
Garrison, Randy 249, 250
gender 48, 50, 52, 57, 155, 203, 247, 270
Gibbs, James 252–3
Gill, Rosalind 215, 257–9
Gilligan, Carol 248, 252, 259

globalization 30, 41, 55, 93, 216, 254; ethical challenges 3, 41, 169–71, 194, 214–17, 221; 'quality' 183–4
Godard, Barbara 50, 71
Godbout, Marielle 31–2, 125, 126, 157
Gouadec, Daniel 30–1
Guzmán, María Constanza 215, 257–9

Habermas, Jurgen 244
habitus 79–80
Harding, Sue-Ann 43, 50, 52
Hatim, Basil 51
Heidegger, Martin 268
Hermans, Theo 123, 124, 149, 150, 152
hermeneutics 37, 38–9, 42, 57
Hoggan, Chad 245
Hoggett, Paul 195, 197
Holtzhausen, Derina 238
hospitality 197–8

impartiality 6, 43, 56, 63, 64, 68, 72–3, 129, 175, 179, 187, 190, 191, 197, 198, 203, 204, 207, 208, 213, 217, 218
India 137, 193
Indian Translators Association (ITAINDIA) 12, 60, 61, 63, 64, 68, 90–1, 93, 94, 96, 99, 100, 101, 105, 107–8, 109, 111, 114–15, 122, 127, 128, 136, 174, 176, 177, 181, 183, 185, 187–8, 193, 199, 203
individualism 143, 225, 227
Inghilleri, Moira 8, 16, 43–4, 56–7, 154–5, 197, 198, 217, 270
integrity 127, 173–4, 185–6, 187, 189, 241
International Association for Egyptian Translators (IAFET) 13, 61, 64, 69, 71, 90, 91, 93–4, 99, 100, 105, 106, 109, 111, 114, 121–2, 136, 175, 176, 182, 183, 184, 185, 187, 188, 189, 192, 199, 203
International Federation of Translators *see* Federation Internationale des Traducteurs
intertextuality 139

Jackson, Jen 88, 120
Johnson, Penelope 32–3

302 Index

Johnson, Terence 10, 24, 25, 26, 27–30, 31, 36, 60, 119, 120, 122, 129, 148
Jonas, Hans 215

Kafi, Mohsen 32
Kalantari, Esmaeil 52–3, 191
Kant, Emmanuel 163, 205, 228, 260
Katan, David 31, 153
Kearns, John 149, 150
Kelemen, Mihaela 170, 229–30
Kenny, Dorothy 97
Koskinen, Kaisa 5, 16, 34–6, 37, 54, 55, 71, 73, 74, 103, 123, 128, 149, 150, 172, 190, 202, 235, 236, 270
Kristeva, Julia 139
Kruger, Haidee 6, 179, 193

Lambert, Joseph 7, 233–4
Larkosh, Christopher 46–7
Latin America Regional Center (CRAL) 101
Laygues, Arnaud 46
Lee, Hyang 6
Lefevere, André 122, 130, 140
Lévinas, Emmanuel 46, 55, 166–7, 169–70, 193–4
literary theory 139
Littau, Karin 47, 70
Luhmann, Niklas 172
Luxon, Nancy 227

Machine Translation (MT) 52–3, 73, 240
MacIntyre, Alasdair 15, 55–6, 188, 189, 190, 218
Maier, Carol 232, 234, 235, 262
Martín Ruano, Rosario 5, 8, 16, 251
Mason, Ian 51
McDonough Dolmaya, Julie 6, 173
Meijl, Toon van 238
Merleau-Ponty, Maurice 83
Meschonnic, Henri 39, 56
Mezirow, Jack 243–5, 247, 248, 252, 255, 258, 259, 260, 268, 269
Middle East Media Research Institute (MEMRI) 179, 196
Mill, John Stuart 139
Moorkens, Joss 235
moral self 172–3; ambivalent 164–6; confidentiality 184–5; faithfulness and its associates 176–79; public protection 173–6; quality service 179–84; representation and Otherness 190–9; virtue ethics 185–90
multiplicity 2, 47, 177–8, 211, 249, 255

National Accreditation Authority for Translators and Interpreters (NAATI) 12, 101
National Security Language Initiative 196
neutrality 6, 24, 25, 41, 43, 53, 56–7, 190, 213, 234, 251, 273
New Zealand Society of Translators and Interpreters (NZSTI) 101
Nida, Eugene 64
Niranjana, Tejaswini 48–9
Noordegraaf, Mirko 26, 86–7, 130
Nord, Christiane 56
North Atlantic Treaty Organization (NATO) 196

objectivity 63, 64, 68, 197, 198, 205–6
occupational control 10, 14, 24, 27–30, 35, 119, 272
Ordre des traducteurs, terminologues et interpretes agrees du Quebec (OTTIAQ) 236
Other, the 38, 47–8, 188, 234; moral responsibility 43, 45, 55, 166–7, 232–3; representation 38, 40, 46, 68–9, 179, 190–9, 259; social spaces 168, 169
Ozolins, Uldis 6, 67, 127, 207–8, 210

Parks, Tim 141
Parsons, Talcott 23, 24–5, 32
patronage 28–30, 36, 120, 129, 130, 140, 272
Peltonen, Tuomo 170, 229–30
Perry, William 248, 249–50, 252, 260, 266, 270
Peruvian Association of Professional Translators *see* Asociacion de Traductores Profesionales del Peru
Plutarch 227, 228
Polizzoti, Mark 139, 172
postcolonialism 45–7, 48–9, 56–7, 137, 143

postmodern morality 163–4; ambivalent moral self 164–6; ethical challenges of globalization 169–71; moral responsibility 166–7; social spaces 168–9
postpositivism 2, 53, 72, 207
poststructuralism 3, 44, 46, 48, 49
pragmatic translation 3, 51, 52–3, 72, 191, 212
professionalization: cultural capital 120–6; functionalist model 23, 24–5, 27, 32; power dynamics 30–6, 119–20, 126–31; in the sociology of professions 23–30; 'trait model' 4, 9, 23, 24, 25, 27, 31–2, 33, 34–5, 36, 122
public protection 4, 23, 92, 173–6, 201, 203; confidentiality 184–5; faithfulness and its associates 176–79; quality service 179–84; representation and Otherness 190–9; virtue ethics 185–90
Pym, Anthony 3, 11–12, 34, 35, 39, 53–6, 68, 150–2, 234

quality service 179–84, 201, 218, 241
Quebec Certified Translators, Terminologists and Interpreters Association *see* Ordre des traducteurs, terminologues et interpretes agrees du Quebec

Raaen, Finn Daniel 268–9
race 127, 192, 194, 247, 252, 270
Rafael, Vincente 49, 196
Ralarala, Monwabisi K. 43, 50, 52
reception theory 72, 139
Registry of Interpreter of the Deaf (RID) 208
regression 266
regularization 3, 23, 25, 30, 119, 201, 206, 211, 213, 272
relativism 238, 249, 255
Ren, Wen 9, 33
reserved title 12, 31, 32, 101
Ressentiment 194–5
Ricoeur, Paul 189
Robinson, Bob 223
Robinson, Douglas 40, 44–5, 48, 56–7
Rocchi, Marta 235

Rueschemeyer, Dietrich 25
Russia 32–3, 137

Sadek, Gaafar 132, 136, 137, 146–7
Saks, Mike 25, 26, 119–20
Schinkel, Willem 26, 86–7, 130
Schleiermacher, Friedrich 38, 40
Sela-Sheffy, Rakefet 34, 35
self-care 238–9, 275; Foucault on 223–30, 232, 233, 235–6, 237, 242, 243, 274–5; translation education 234–6, 242, 243, 250–2, 256–60, 267–71; translation occupation 236–8; translation studies 232–4
self-perception 31, 32, 88, 129, 252–6, 257, 259–60, 267, 270
self-transformation 226, 232, 247–8, 249–50, 256, 258, 260–7, 268, 269, 273
Seneca 237
Simon, Sherry 49
Skopos theory 3, 56, 67
social capital 81, 83–5, 97–8, 240; associations 88, 94, 98–110, 144
social spaces 168–9, 197
source text (ST) 2, 56, 67, 69–70, 73–4, 75, 183, 211–12
South Africa 193
Spain 32–3
Spivak, Gayatri 45–6, 143, 197, 205
standardization 3, 183–4, 201, 210, 211
Staten, Henry 45
status quo 8, 103, 129, 131, 151, 152, 157, 158, 270–1
Stecconi, Ubaldo 123, 124, 149, 150
Steiner, George 38, 39, 56
Sturrock, John 44
subservience 123, 126, 129, 138, 145, 158, 253, 257
Summers, Caroline 140
Susam-Sarajeva, Sebnem 143, 177
symbolic capital 26, 34, 81, 82, 85–6, 126, 141, 144, 146, 240, 241, 273; conversion of cultural capital 118–19, 120, 125, 129, 143, 145, 149, 156, 157, 158, 234
symbolic violence 85–6, 88, 144–56, 157, 158, 179, 198

target language 2, 63, 64, 66, 67, 140, 181–2, 183, 191, 210
target text (TT) 3, 56, 67, 70, 71, 73–4, 75
Taylor, Edward 244, 245, 246, 247
Tennant, Mark 255
Thirds 167, 194, 221
Tipton, Rebecca 42–3
Transformative Learning theory 243–50, 255–7, 258, 259–60, 270–1; in the classroom 250–2, 258–9, 260–70, 271
translation, concept of 70–6; in codified ethics 61–70
translation ethics, theoretical approaches to 37–8; culturalist perspective 39–44; deconstruction 44–8; gender-oriented studies 48, 50, 52, 57; hermeneutics 38–9; postcolonialism 45–7, 48–50, 56–7
Translation Memory (TM) 96, 112, 174, 240
translator's charter for ethics 239–42
transparency 44, 71, 211, 212, 241
Trump, Donald 141, 195
Tymoczko, Maria 40–1, 42, 56–7, 70–1, 72, 75, 91, 143, 150, 153, 177, 178–9, 216, 237, 253, 254
Tyulenev, Sergey 32–3

UNESCO 14, 51, 100, 101–2, 110; Nairobi Recommendation 4, 14, 61–2, 64, 68, 90, 91, 92–3, 94, 99, 100, 102, 111, 112–14, 123–4, 125, 135, 136, 146–7, 157–8, 176, 182–3, 184–5
United Nations (UN) 51, 112, 123–4, 157
universalization 166, 177, 211, 213, 254, 264

Venuti, Lawrence 40–1, 56–7, 71, 113, 115, 133, 137, 138, 139–40, 143, 144, 150, 259
virtue ethics 6, 55–6, 128, 185–90, 203–4, 218

Wacquant, Loic 25, 80, 119, 155
Watzlawick, Paul 1, 2
Weber, Max 4, 94, 202
Wolf, Michaela 47
World Intellectual Property Organization (WIPO) 146

Yun, Seong Woo 6

Zeller, Beatriz 142
Zethsen, Karen Korning 35
Ziguras, Christopher 229

Printed in the United States
by Baker & Taylor Publisher Services